T0224028

Computational Music Science

Series Editors

Guerino Mazzola
Moreno Andreatta

For further volumes:
http://www.springer.com/series/8349

Eytan Agmon

The Languages of Western Tonality

 Springer

Eytan Agmon
Department of Music
Bar-Ilan University
Ramat-Gan
Israel

ISSN 1868-0305 ISSN 1868-0313 (electronic)
Computational Music Science
ISBN 978-3-662-51225-8 ISBN 978-3-642-39587-1 (eBook)
DOI 10.1007/978-3-642-39587-1
Springer Heidelberg New York Dordrecht London

Printed on acid-free paper

Springer is part of Springer Science+Business Media (www.springer.com)

Preface

... Each of these four notes governs, as its subjects, a pair of tropes.... Thus every
melody... is necessarily led back to one of these same four [notes]. Therefore they are
called "finals," because anything that is sung finds its ending (*finem*) in [one of] them.
—Hucbald of Saint-Amand, late Ninth Century[1]

As an object of inquiry, "tonal music" is far from homogenous. The music of the
ninth century with which Hucbald was familiar was very different, we may assume,
from (say) the music of the seventeenth century. Nonetheless, there are striking
points of contact. Most notably, a "background system" of exactly seven notes,
orderable within the octave as a cyclic permutation of the sequence T-T-S-T-T-T-S
of tones and semitones (alternatively, as a sequence of perfect fifths—the fifth being
the most privileged interval following the perfect octave), is "governed" by one of
its members—the final (and "co-governed," one might add, by another—the
cofinal, the perfect fifth above the final). How can one account for the remarkable
stability of such basic features of "Tonality," and, at the same time, do justice to the
equally remarkable variety of styles—nay, *languages*—that the history of Western
tonal music has taught us exist? This book is an attempt to answer these questions.

The book is divided into two main parts. Part I, *Proto-tonality*, studies the
background system of notes prior to the selection of a final. The "proto-tonal
system" ultimately posited is *harmonic* and contains a "harmonic message." However, the harmonic message may be empty, in which case the system reduces to its
diatonic component. In other words, a harmonic system is diatonic, but not vice
versa (a diatonic system is oblivious of such constructs as "chord," "chord progression," and "voice leading"). An important component of every diatonic system is its
"core": a length-7 segment of the "line of fifths," for example, F, C,..., B.

After some preliminaries that concern consonance and chromaticism, Part II,
The Languages of Western Tonality (also the title of the book as a whole), begins
with the notion "mode." A mode is assumed to contain a "nucleus." A nucleus is a
subset of the core *that is consonant* while containing a maximal number of

---

[1] Trans. from Cohen (2002), p. 322.

v

elements. The mode's final is the unique nucleus element that is *a root* relative to every other nucleus element. For example, the final would be the lower member (rather than the upper) of a perfect-fifth dyadic subset of the nucleus.

Crucially, the notion of "consonance" is itself dependent on the proto-tonal system's status as diatonic or harmonic. In particular, in the harmonic case the major and minor third and sixth are deemed consonant in addition to the diatonic perfect octave, fifth, and fourth. As a result, the modal nucleus is a perfect-fifth dyad in the diatonic case and a triad (major or minor) in the harmonic case. Early in Part II, in other words, a distinction is established between two types of mode, *dyadic* and *triadic*. Moreover, within each type, the degree to which the nucleus (or a privileged subset thereof) is consonant *in relation to the non-nucleus core elements* defines "semi-key" as a special type of mode and "key" as a special type of semi-key. On the basis of these distinctions, seventeenth-century music (for example) presents itself as a (tonal) language of triadic semi-keys; ninth-century music, by contrast, is a (tonal) language of dyadic modes.

Thus, in a nutshell, the theory accounts for tonal variety. The question of tonal stability is addressed mainly in the proto-tonal Part I, though it continues to inform ideas put forth in Part II as well. In a nutshell again, tonality is seen as a highly successful "communication system." Communication, indeed, is the most important high-level principle that guides the theory offered in this book.

Theory; History; Cognition

From the preceding remarks it is clear that the book draws upon three distinct fields of study, namely music theory, music history, and music cognition. Like the three edges of an equilateral triangle, the contribution of each field to the project as a whole is inconceivable without the other two.

Music theory is the oldest and most established of the three. Music theory has not only handed us, early in the nineteenth century, a valuable though elusive concept—Tonality—but is on record for centuries if not millennia for attempting to demystify that extraordinary gift of mankind to itself: music. The story of music theory is fascinating in its own right, replete as it is with turns and twists, progressions and regressions. Be that as it may, the present project is unthinkable in the absence of the rich and complex heritage of ideas that constitute the music-theoretic endeavor.

It is all too easy to absorb oneself in the familiar and the readily accessible, forgetting not only that the past may have been different from the present, but also that the present may be very different elsewhere. Historical musicology and ethnomusicology have taught us to respect the chronological and cultural Other.

As should be clear from the Preface's opening remarks, this study takes seriously the historical challenge, offering a theory that, while not explicitly diachronic, nonetheless renders conceivable a historical process of the sort that seems to have taken place in Western culture, namely from dyadic to triadic tonality, and more or less concurrently, from modes, through semi-keys, to keys. Self-consciously focusing on the West, the study is obviously less responsive to the cultural challenge. Nonetheless, a reference to the Javanese *pélog* scale may be found in Part I, Sect. 8.1; a reference to north Indian music may be found in Part II, Sect. 14.1.

Finally, music cognition has made us keenly aware that music is a reflection of the human mind. In current music-cognitive discourse much emphasis is placed on *perception*. The present book, by contrast, places equal emphasis on *conception*. The difference reflects the book's communicative bias, coupled with the observation that communication takes place where perception meets conception. In many ways, we shall see, the languages of Western tonality reflect the logical and cognitive constraints that make musical communication possible.

Even for the professional music theorist, the book is no easy reading. This is especially true of Part I, *Proto-tonality*, where abstraction and formal rigor reign supreme. Formal rigor in the book, however, is no ornament. As explained in Chap. 2, the book strives for the highest possible standard of scientific acceptability, namely explanatory adequacy. To this end, it was necessary to strip tonality down to its barest elements, generalizing parameters whenever possible. That this approach pays off becomes apparent already in Chap. 8, where an alternative theory is compared to the proposed theory precisely in terms of explanatory adequacy.

A number of strategies may help the interested reader overcome the difficulties of Part I. The tried-and-true strategy of nonsequential reading may not only help combat fatigue but may offer a larger (if not completely coherent) perspective from which the intricacies of a given phase in the theory may be easier to digest. In particular, Chap. 4, "The Conventional Nomenclatures for Notes and Intervals," is a relatively accessible exercise that may be fruitfully studied before or concurrently with Chap. 3. In general, examples of formal definitions are presented *after* the definitions themselves. Easier access into an abstruse definition may be gained by skipping ahead to an accompanying example.

The reader may feel overwhelmed by the sheer number of definitions and notations introduced. Partial help in this matter is provided by three indices found in the back of the book: a General Index, where formal definitions are easily identified by the corresponding page number's formatting in bold; a List of Definitions; and a List of Notation. Two mathematical appendices provide the basic mathematical background.

The origins of this book go back to my 1986 PhD dissertation, "Diatonicism, Chromaticism, and Enharmonicism: A Study in Cognition and Perception." The book has thus acquired many debts over the years.

Carl Schachter, the dissertation's supervisor, with whom I spent a couple of years as a graduate student at the City University of New York, has had a profound influence on my identity as a music theorist. Schachter's immense knowledge and deep understanding of music and music theory, his astounding eloquence in verbalizing his ideas and insights, his generosity towards students and colleagues alike, and his down-to-earth, unpretentious human warmth have enriched and nourished me for life.

I was very lucky to have had Joel Lester as a reader of my dissertation. Lester showed interest in my work early on and has always been extremely generous in lending support and guidance. Lester provided important feedback on early versions of Chaps. 12 and 13.

John Rink and William Rothstein commented insightfully on an early version of Chap. 15. Section 15.2 in fact developed from a brilliant suggestion of Rothstein's.

A number of individuals provided invaluable help with the mathematical aspects of the book.

I feel very lucky to have two renowned mathematicians in my immediate family: my father, Shmuel Agmon, and my brother, Ehud de-Shalit. Both have been involved in my work since the dissertation. Without their patient guidance over the years, this book could not have come into being.

In 2010–2011 Nori Jacoby and I gave a course at Bar-Ilan University, "Music, Mathematics, and Cognition," based on Part I of the book. Nori contributed numerous improvements to the mathematics, substantive as well as stylistic. Thanks must also go to Thomas Noll, who read Part I and offered valuable insights and suggestions, to Avinoam Braverman for commenting insightfully on Chap. 3, and to Reuven Naveh for commenting on a very early version of Chap. 4.

Although it has become a cliché to thank one's spouse and children, in the present case my wife, Lea, and two wonderful daughters, Einat and Orly, are true partners in the endeavor. My wife, an accomplished musician in her own right, has been part of this project from the very start, lending her ear, heart, and mind with uncompromising patience and devotion at every turn. My daughters have grown accustomed to music-theoretic discussions at family dinners. They have found early on that the best way to get Daddy genuinely upset is to argue with him that there is no difference between G♯ and A♭.

I dedicate this book to Lea, Einat, and Orly, with love.

Reference

Cohen, D. (2002). Notes, scales, and modes in the earlier middle ages. In T. Christensen (Ed.), *The Cambridge history of Western music theory* (pp. 307–363). Cambridge: Cambridge University Press.

Contents

List of Figures

List of Tables

List of Definitions

List of Notation

Chapter 1
Proto-tonal Theory: Tapping into Ninth-Century Insights

Abstract The ninth-century treatise *Scolica enchiriadis* (SE) offers two notions of "interval," namely ratio (proportion) and step distance. The latter notion entails a "generic" distance (cf. "fifth"); however, suggestive diagrams clarify that a "specific" distance is assumed as well (cf. *"perfect* fifth"). SE raises the question, how to pair step distances such as perfect octave (*diapason*), perfect fifth (*diapente*), and perfect fourth (*diatessaron*), with ratios such as 2:1, 3:2, and 4:3, respectively. In answer, SE departs from the Boethian tradition whereby the distinction between say, duple (2:1) and *diapason*, is merely terminological. Moreover, SE points out that multiplication of ratios corresponds to *addition* of step distances, in a manner to which a modern-day mathematician would apply the term *homomorphism*. Even though the "daseian" tone system proposed in SE (and the "sister" treatise *Musica enchiriadis*) was discarded already in the middle ages, the SE insights into "proto-tonal" theory, the background system of tones prior to the selection of a central tone or "final," are still relevant.

Well into the third part of *Scolica enchiriadis*, the second of a well-known pair of Carolingian treatises dated by some scholars as early as 850 CE, the disciple asks the master the following question:

> Although it has been sufficiently shown that the principle of commensurability joins musical pitches (*voces*) to one another, how nevertheless can one know to which proportion any symphony must be assigned? For how is it known that the diapason must be assigned to the duple relationship, the diapente to the sescuple, the diatessaron to the epitritus, the diapente-plus-diapason to the triple, [and] the disdiapason to the quadruple?[1]

---

[1] Erickson (1995), p. 79. All excerpts from *Musica enchiriadis* (ME) and *Scolica enchiriadis* (SE) cited henceforth are in Erickson's translation. Unless otherwise noted, all excerpts from Boethius's *De institutione musica* (IM) are in Bower's translation (Boethius 1989). All excerpts

E. Agmon, *The Languages of Western Tonality*, Computational Music Science,
DOI 10.1007/978-3-642-39587-1_1, © Springer-Verlag Berlin Heidelberg 2013

The question, which appears under the title "How it may be known by what proportion any symphony is formed" and to which I shall refer henceforth as Q, follows a detailed exposé (based on Boethius's *De institutione arithmetica*) of the various types of numerical proportions, including the "commensurable" and "connumerable," that is, the multiple proportion (e.g., 2:1, 3:1) and the superparticular (3:2, 4:3). The purpose of this mathematical discussion is to answer a question concerning the "symphonies," that is, the perfect octave, fifth, and fourth (diapason, diapente, and diatessaron), and their compounds, a question posed about halfway through the second part of the treatise (p. 64): "why at some intervals the voices are consonant, whereas in others they are either discordant or not as agreeable?"[2]

It would seem that by rationalizing the commensurable and connumerable proportions the question of consonance has been settled. As the master notes (p. 68), "... the symphonies at the diapason and disdiapason are more perfect than those at the diatessaron and diapente, because the former are of multiple inequality, the latter of superparticular inequality. For multiple inequality is more perfect than superparticular inequality." However, as Q makes clear, for the disciple in SE this explanation is at best incomplete. This is because the master has given no reason for *pairing* the symphonies with the privileged proportions, in particular, the perfect octave with 2:1 (duple), the perfect fifth with 3:2 (sescuple or sesqualter), and the perfect fourth with 4:3 (epitritus or sesquitertian). Indeed, in answering the question "what is a symphony" at the beginning of the treatise's second part, "Concerning the Symphonies" (p. 53), *the master makes no mention whatsoever of numerical proportions*, a topic introduced later in the second part, but treated in detail only in the third. Rather, a symphony ("an agreeable combination of certain pitches") is characterized by *the number of steps* it contains: the diapason eight, the diapente five, and the diatessaron four (counting both extremes in each case). As the master explains,

> diapason is Greek and in Latin is translated "through all," because the ancient kithara contained only eight strings... *diapente* means "through five," because it comprehends five pitches. *Diatessaron* is translated "through four," because it encloses four pitches.

Henceforth in this chapter the terms "type-1 interval" and "type-2 interval" shall be used, respectively, to refer to these two senses of "musical interval" that SE provides, namely, "step distance between two tones" and numerical proportion. The strictly "generic" characterization of type-1 intervals, to borrow Clough and Myerson's (1985) useful term, is misleading. Certain SE diagrams to be discussed shortly (though some appear early on in the treatise) strongly suggest that a type-1 interval is in fact *a pair* of distances, one generic and the other "semitonal" or,

---

from Ptolemy's *Harmonics* are in Solomon's (2000) translation. Special thanks to Oliver Wiener for granting permission to use his Dasia font.

[2] In the course of the mathematical discussion the author presents a diagram that represents the musically most important proportions in terms of the integers 6, 8, 9, 12, 16, 18, and 24. For an interesting interpretation of this diagram see Carey and Clampitt (1996).

to use Clough and Myerson's terminology again, "specific." Indeed, we have already anticipated this finding (and will continue to do so) by referring to type-1 intervals not only generically (for example, "fifth"), but also specifically (*"perfect* fifth").

We must assume that the psychophysical aspect of type-2 intervals (that is, ratios) was rather well understood by the ninth-century author, for not only does he know that "strings or pipes, if they are of equal width and if the length of the greater is twice the smaller, will sound together the diapason," and similarly for the other symphonies (p. 81),[3] having read Boethius (IM, I.3) he even knows that "... high pitches (*voces*) are incited by more frequent and faster motions, whereas low ones are incited by slower and less frequent motions." However, when pressed by the disciple to specify precisely the relationship that holds between ratios and (what we would call today) "pitch intervals," the master, who lacks like his contemporaries in general the mathematical expertise necessary to make the *logarithmic* connection between frequency and pitch, is rather vague:

D. By what principle do pitches (*voces*), consonant or inconsonant, imitate one ratio or another?
M. Just as different tones agree with each other, so do they differ according to their inequalities.
D. Wherein lies this difference?
M. In highness and lowness, in rising and falling.
D. How do they differ among themselves in relation to the ratios cited earlier, and how do they agree while differing?
M. All phthongi, that is, tones compatible with one another, are distant from one another by duple, triple, or quadruple intervals, which are species of multiple inequality; or by sesquialter, sesquitertian, or sesquioctaval intervals, which are species of superparticular inequality. This interval between phthongi is not one of silence but of the space by which one exceeds the other. (p. 75)

Nonetheless, the dialogue continues as follows, suggesting an awareness of at least the *non-linear* nature of the monotonic relation that holds between ratios and pitch intervals:

D. Which phthongi are separated by the duple [interval]?
M. Always any [that are] eight steps apart; this is called the diapason.[4]
D. Which are separated by the triple?
M. Always those [that are] twelve steps apart; this is called the diapason-plus-diapente.
D. Which are separated by the quadruple?
M. Always all those [that are] fifteen steps apart; this is called the disdiapason.

---

[3] This is in fact "another argument" which, the master believes, "adds credence" to the two answers that he gives to the disciple's question Q. I shall consider the answers presently.

[4] Erickson (1995, footnote on p. 75) notes here that "from this exchange it is clear that the discussion concerns the Greater Perfect System rather than the daseian system described earlier in the treatise, since the latter does not 'always' (*semper*) produce the diapason at the eighth step." An alternative explanation is that the *enchiriadis* theorists are simply unable to reconcile the contradiction, inherent in their tone system, between octave periodicity and fifth periodicity. Concerning the *enchiriadis* tone system, see Fig. 1.1 and its discussion. See also footnote 12.

The distinction between type-1 and type-2 intervals (i.e., step distances vs. ratios) is one of several notable insights that SE offers into what one might term from a modern perspective "proto-tonal theory," that is, a theory of the "background system" of tones prior to the selection of one particular tone as referential (the so-called "final").[5] Consider, for example, what seems to be the master's second answer to Q, which is apparently also his main answer (I shall consider the first answer subsequently). Recall that Q concerns the principle by which certain type-1 intervals (particularly, the symphonies) are paired with certain type-2 intervals (i.e., certain ratios).

The master begins (SE, p. 80) by quoting Boethius:

> Which of all the consonances we have mentioned ought to be thought the better one must be judged both by the ear and by reason. For in the way the ear is affected by tones and the eye by visible form, so the judgment of reason is affected by number or by continuous quantity. Thus, given a number or line, nothing is easier to recognize with the eye or reason than its double [the master interpolates: "as, for example, 12 to 6"]. Likewise, after the judgment of the duple follows that of the half or subduple; after the half, that of the triple; after the triple that of the third part. And because the recognition of the duple is easier,

Boethius continues (IM, I.32): "Nicomachus considers the diapason to be the optimum consonance; after this the diapente, which contains the half; then the diapason-plus-diapente, which contains the triple." However, our master continues instead: "it is justly *assigned* to that consonance which is easier and which our critical faculty (*sensus*) perceives more clearly" (emphasis added). Why does the master depart from Boethius at this point?

Boethius, for all practical purposes, *equates* the symphonies with their corresponding proportions.[6] However, if type-1 intervals are assumed to be distinct from type-2 intervals, such a move is clearly unacceptable. Our ninth-century author realizes, in other words, that in order to answer Q it does not suffice to

---

[5] A summary of the proto-tonal insights closes this chapter. The insights are largely independent of the *enchiriadis* tone system (see Fig. 1.1 and its discussion), where of course the existence of four modal qualities is assumed *a priori* (the *enchiriadis* system, in other words, is *not* a proto-tonal theory in the sense defined). For example, the "C-major scale" of Fig. 1.5 specifically *avoids* the augmented octave that the system occasionally dictates. Moreover, the modality of the scale does not seem to be of any particular concern; rather, the relation "fifth plus fourth *equals* fourth plus fifth," is the focus of attention. See also footnotes 12 and 14.

[6] This is so even though Boethius's intervallic terminology, inherited from the Greeks, is double-sided (for example, diapason/duple). For example, in the statement from IM just quoted "duple" is tacitly exchanged with "diapason" ("because the recognition of *the duple* is easier, Nicomachus considers *the diapason* to be the optimum consonance"). Indeed, in I.7 Boethius poses a question that seems remarkably similar to Q: "Which ratios should be fitted to which musical consonances"? However, unlike SE, the answer that he provides is tautological: "... All musical consonances consist of a duple, triple, quadruple, sesquialter, or sesquitertian ratio. Moreover, that which is sesquitertian in number will be called 'diatessaron' in sounds; that which is sesquialter in number is called 'diapente' in pitches; that which is duple in ratios, 'diapason' among consonances...." Despite an occasional lapse, the rigor with which SE pursues the distinction between symphonies (as type-1 intervals) and proportions (as type-2 intervals) is, to the best of my knowledge, unprecedented.

order the *proportions* from "most privileged" to "least privileged," as Boethius does; *one must also order the symphonies*. As the master explains in the paragraph that follows, ". . . since these two proportions [3:2 and 3:1], although in contrary arrangement, follow next after the duple, these symphonies can be ascribed properly to those which we perceive by ear to be *the next in rank after the diapason*, that is, the diapente and the diapason-plus-diapente" (emphasis added).[7]

Admittedly the master's explanation leaves much to be desired. What is, exactly, this "critical faculty" that perceives the diapason "most clearly"?[8] And why does this faculty rank the symphonies as it does, in particular, diapason first, diapente second? Isn't the master simply *assuming* this type-1 ranking, and therefore his explanation is circular, indeed, vacuous?

This may be so. Nonetheless, it is remarkable that the author of SE finds it at all necessary to rank the symphonies *independently of the proportions*, at least in principle.[9] If he fails to do so convincingly this is only because he has set for himself an exceedingly difficult task, a task well beyond the means, empirical as well as conceptual, available at the time.

From a modern perspective the ordering of the frequency ratios 2:1, 3:1 (or 3:2), and so on, is surely a reflection of some sort of the overtone series, and therefore the medieval explanation of this ordering, namely, that "multiple inequality is more perfect than superparticular inequality," may be discarded. But how, indeed, can we place *the type-1* intervals "perfect octave," "perfect fifth," etc. in the desired order, without falling, like our ninth-century author, into the trap of circular reasoning (that is, explicitly or implicitly equating the intervals with ratios)? One possibility is to generalize the algebraic properties of these entities. By such a generalization the octave would rank first as *the agent of equivalence*, whereas the fifth would rank second as *the generating element*. For example, the familiar perfect fifth generates the set of type-1 intervals consisting of all "perfect," "major," and "minor" intervals, P1, P5/P4, M2/m7, M6/m3, M3/m6, and M7/m2, if multiplied by $0, \pm 1, \ldots, \pm 5$, respectively (reduction modulo the perfect octave is assumed).

Needless to say, the authors of the *enchiriadis* treatises fall short of such abstractions. Nonetheless, they do seem to sense that the perfect octave and fifth,

---

[7] Note that the master inadvertently refers to the proportions 3:2 and 3:1 as "symphonies."

[8] Erickson (1995, footnote on p. 80) follows Bower (Boethius 1989, footnote on p. 73) in translating *sensus* as "critical faculty," since "this word... cannot refer to the senses, regarded as untrustworthy by the Pythagoreans." Note, however, that it is "the ear" that perceives the diapente to be "next in rank" after the diapason.

[9] Ptolemy's *Harmonics*, the basis for Book V of Boethius's IM, sets a notable precedent in this regard. Prior to pairing them with ratios, Ptolemy (pp. 22–23) partitions the intervals into (1) "homophones" (the octave and its compounds), "which make an impact on our hearing in the conjunction of one sound"; (2) "consonances" (fourths and fifths), which "are nearest the homophones"; and (3) "emmelic," "those nearest the consonances, for example, the whole tones and the rest of the intervals of that sort" (I.7, "How the Ratios of the Consonances Could Be More Properly Defined"). For Boethius's rendering of this passage (which he conflates with Ptolemy's I.4), see IM, V.11. Recall that in I.7, Boethius, unlike Ptolemy, for all practical purposes equates consonances with ratios.

as type-1 intervals, are systemically privileged. With regard to the octave, consider, for example, the following dialogue from SE (pp. 53–54):

> D. How is the diapason sung?
> M. When one pitch is changed into another, either descending or ascending, so that the higher and lower [pitches] are not so much consonant as equal-sounding (*aequisoni*).[10]

With regard to the fifth, consider the SE notion of *socialitas*, introduced by the master to clarify his reference to a tone that lies a fifth away from a given tone as "its compeer" (p. 43):

> D. Why do you say they are compeers (*compares*), when they are different in highness and lowness?
> M. Indeed, they are different in highness and lowness. Nevertheless, they are concordant with each other because of a certain natural kinship (*socialitas*).[11]

Interestingly, there exists an implicit connection in the *enchiriadis* treatises between the "natural kinship" that holds between tones that lie a perfect fifth apart, and the sense in which this interval, as generator, is systemically privileged. As is well known, the *enchiriadis* treatises posit a tone system that is periodic at the perfect fifth: a series of disjunct T-S-T tetrachords follow each other at a whole-tone distance.[12] Indeed, it is precisely this assumed periodicity that enables the master, just prior to invoking the notion of *socialitas*, to refer to a given tone's "compeer":

> For just as in colors, if they are ordered in groups of four and put into a series, for example, red, green, yellow, and black, the same color will necessarily be found at every fifth position, with the three other colors in between, so too it happens in tones: while they succeed themselves in every new iteration, [a given tone] is answered by its compeer a fifth away on either side. (p. 42)

Now, using the daseian signs ⋏, ⋏, ⌐, and ⋏ for which the *enchiriadis* treatises are famous (*protus* or *archous*, *deuterus*, *tritus*, and *tetrardus*, respectively), the author of ME provides early on an illustration of the same idea (see Fig. 1.1a). "This little illustration" he comments (pp. 2–3) "shows that you may extend the tones up or down in a series until the voice gives out; the succession of these tetrachords will not cease." In other words, it is merely a technicality that the tetrachords do not perpetuate themselves indefinitely in both directions. But given that the agent of

---

[10] Compare the following statement in ME (p. 15) concerning the diapason: "In this symphony the pitches can be said to be not so much 'sounding well together' (*consonae*) as 'equal-sounding' (*aequisonae*), for in this symphony a pitch is revealed anew." See also Boethius, IM, V.12 (paraphrasing Ptolemy).

[11] The idea that notes a fifth apart are related by a "bond of fellowship" (*socialitas*) is found in Hucbald's treatise, known as *De harmonica institutione*, which may antedate SE. See Cohen (2002, p. 322), and Babb (1978, p. 39).

[12] Note that despite the fifth-periodicity of the tone system, in the *enchiriadis* treatises the agent of equivalence is the perfect octave and no other type-1 interval (the notes of an octave are "equal-sounding," whereas those of a fifth "are different in highness and lowness"). It seems fair to say that, in the final analysis, the *enchiriadis* theorists are unable to reconcile the conflict between octave and fifth periodicity. This failure may have contributed to the system's relatively early demise.

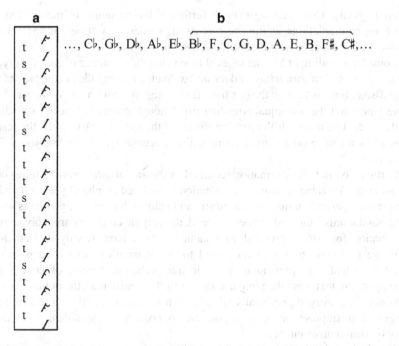

Fig. 1.1 (a) A segment of the conceptually infinite series of disjunct T-S-T tetrachords that forms the *enchiriadis* tone system (*Musica enchiriadis*). Copyright © 1981 Bayerische Akademie der Wissenschaften. Redrawn from H. Schmid, *Musica et scolica enchiriadis*, by permission. (b) The line of fifths. The "note-class content" of the *enchiriadis* tone system is shown in *square brackets*

perpetuation is the perfect fifth (T+S+T+T), the infinite extension of the system would generate, using modern terminology, an infinite number of *note classes*. Implicit in the *enchiriadis* treatises, in other words, is the so-called "line of fifths" (Fig. 1.1b).[13] The length-ten segment of the line of fifths extending from B♭ to C♯ represents the "note-class content" of the *enchiriadis* tone system (see the brackets in Fig. 1.1b).

Thus far we have considered the master's second answer to Q, where he explains that the symphonies are somehow ordered such that the diapason is first and the diapente second, and therefore the diapason naturally pairs with the duple proportion, and the diapente with the superparticular proportion 3:2. Before turning to his first answer it should be useful to consider some highly interesting illustrations found early in SE. Because the interpretation of these illustrations may seem somewhat unconventional, a few introductory remarks are in order.

Reading any text is an act of interpretation, and as such is a reflection of the reader as much as it is of the author. This is particularly so if author and reader are distant one from the other, whether linguistically, culturally, geographically, or

---

[13] "Line of fifths" is Temperley's (2000) term.

chronologically. Complicating matters further is the existence of inconsistencies and even contradictions within the text itself, rendering a "true" or "authentic" reading dubious not only in practice, but also in principle.

Consider a reading of SE that takes at face value the existence of only four types of note, *protus*, *deuterus*, *tritus*, and *tetrardus*. Such a reading flies in the face of the "equal-sounding" octave on the one hand (two notes an octave apart are never of the same type), and the *non* equal-sounding fifth, though otherwise special-sounding, on the other (two notes a fifth apart are always of the same type). Clearly, the reader must make a choice on this matter, one which, necessarily, will be "subjective" to some extent.[14]

Fortunately, not all information recorded in the *enchiriadis* treatises relies on a verbal code. A sizable amount of information is encoded graphically as well and as such at least partially transcends linguistic and cultural barriers ("a picture is worth a thousand words," the saying goes). Indeed, the graphic code may arguably convey information for which a verbal equivalent may not have readily existed. It is therefore important to note with regard to the illustrations discussed next that graphic content was paramount to their interpretation, though of course any accompanying text was taken into account as well. In particular, the notion *discrete increment* is conveyed graphically with the utmost clarity, and therefore with little danger of misrepresentation it is possible to posit a mathematical equivalent, namely, consecutive integers.

The Λ-shaped "block diagrams," as the illustrations in question are sometimes referred to, are introduced in the course of explicating the danger of displacing semitones from their "proper" melodic position.[15] As the master clarifies (p. 37), "We call 'semitones' or 'limmas' those distances between tones that are not of full size." He continues:

> By virtue of their position, they not only impart their properties to the tones but also hold a melody together in sweetness of concord. However, when the semitones are not in their proper place, they make melodies unpleasant. For it is necessary to know that in a series of tones the natural quality exists only when they are a natural distance apart from each other. But if the distance from one tone to another is measured inaccurately, it changes thereupon into another quality and deviates from the original arrangement. This discord results from two errors discussed previously.

Following a somewhat abstract explanation of how such "semitone-displace-ment discords" may come about (pp. 37–38), the master invites his disciple to sing, and/or hear, and/or see a visual representation of a series of pentachords, that is, five-element scale segments, in a pattern that first ascends a perfect fifth and then descends back to the point of origin. Each pentachord comes in two variants, natural

---

[14] The present reader has chosen, of course, *not* to take the existence of only four types of note at face value. Indeed, as discussed in connection with Fig. 1.1a, I believe the *enchiriadis* system allows for an infinite number of note types in principle, though for practical reasons only ten can be used. The *protus*, *deuterus*, *tritus*, and *tetrardus* types, I believe, serve a purely modal purpose.

[15] These diagrams have already received considerable attention in the literature. See, for example, Jacobsthal (1897), Phillips (2000), Cohen (2002).

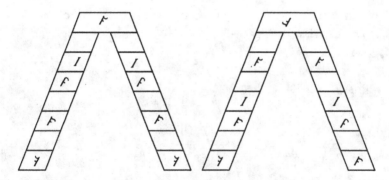

Fig. 1.2 Semitonal displacement (E to E♭) in the C-G-C pentachord (*Scolica enchiriadis*). Copyright © 1981 Bayerische Akademie der Wissenschaften. Redrawn from H. Schmid, *Musica et scolica enchiriadis*, by permission

and "unnatural," the latter containing a semitonal displacement of one tone in either the ascending or descending segment, or both.

Now, the daseian notational system does not naturally lend itself to representing tones displaced from their usual tetrachordal position.[16] Therefore, to forestall any possible misunderstanding, for any pentachord, "natural" as well as "unnatural," the master provides a representation wherein the daseian symbols are positioned on a *semitonal grid*. For example, to show that E is altered to E♭ on both legs of the C-G-C pentachord, the master presents the illustration given as Fig. 1.2.[17]

In studying these remarkable ninth-century depictions of chromatic displacement it is easy to overlook the finding that some of the diagrams come *in triples* rather than just pairs. Figure 1.3, reproduced from a late tenth- or early-eleventh-century copy of SE, is the first such triple; note that the figure includes the pair of Fig. 1.2 as (a) and (b).[18]

Figure 1.3c is in fact the very first block diagram to which the master refers:

---

[16] As several authors have pointed out, at this point the author of SE "bends" the conventions of the daseian notational system such that the symbols relinquish to some extent their "absolute" meaning in favor of a "relative" one. For a particularly insightful account, see Cohen (2002, pp. 328–329).

[17] In another representation of the same type E is altered to E♭ relative to the D-A-D pentachord. Also relative to both the C-G-C and D-A-D pentachords, SE illustrates the alteration of F to F♯. Though the term "semitonal grid" may seem anachronistic, it seems to be the only interpretation of the graphics proposed to date. Phillips, for example (1990, p. 105; 2000, p. 323) states that "there are ... many diagrams in *Scolica enchiriadis* in which series of little blocks represent semitones," noting that the idea of a "semitone-per-block" (*Halbton pro Block*) representation may be traced back to Boethius's "wing" diagram of the modes (IM, IV.16). Erickson (1995, p. 39, footnote) explains that in the block diagrams "... horizontal lines [are] being used to indicate semitone boundaries." As shall be clarified shortly, equal temperament is not necessarily implied.

[18] The next set of diagrams, illustrating the alteration of F to F♯ relative to the D-A-D pentachord, also forms a triple.

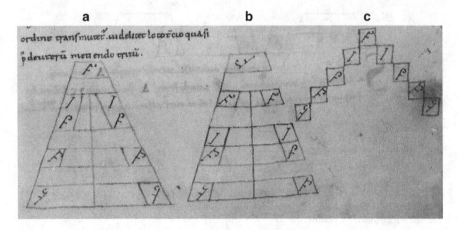

Fig. 1.3 A triple of "block diagrams" from a late tenth- or early-eleventh-century copy of *Scolica enchiriadis*. Stadt Köln, Historisches Archiv. HAStK, Best. 331, fol. 219. Reproduced by permission

> *M.* Sing the pentachord ascending from tetrardus ⅄, calculating so that you will descend by
> the same steps [as in Fig. 1.3c].
> *D.* I have sung it.
> *M.* I, too, shall sing the same [pentachord] [Fig. 1.3a]. Then I shall add another [pentachord]
> [Fig. 1.3b], where something is shifted from the prior order—namely, at the third step,
> by measuring out the tritus as if after the deuterus.[19] Now do you perceive that these two
> pentachords do not agree with one another? (pp. 39–40)

In Erickson (1995), where all block diagrams are rendered in staff notation (only
the first two diagrams of Fig. 1.3 are given, in a footnote, in their original form),
Fig. 1.3c is identical to Fig. 1.3a, and thus seems redundant; indeed, the two
representations display the same sequence of daseian signs. Conceptually, however,
these two representations are very different. For whereas (a) positions the notes
C–G in *specific space*, (c) positions the very same notes in *generic space*; for this
reason (a), but not (c), contains *empty boxes*. As the master explains in comparing
(b) with (a), ". . . the tone tritus / is measured out through a smaller interval in place
of the deuterus. This is signified *by a line rather than a box* (*paginula*) between [⸜
and /]" (p. 40, emphasis added).

Now, it is surely sensible to represent the boxes of Fig. 1.3c as a set of five
consecutive integers.[20] If so, the boxes of Fig. 1.3a may be similarly represented by
eight consecutive integers. Moreover, given the correspondence between boxes in
(a) and boxes in (c) established via the signs ⅄, ⸜, ⸝, /, and ⸝, each of these five signs
is implicitly associated with *a pair of integers*, that is, one integer representing a

---

[19] That is, the semitone follows the second tone rather than the third.

[20] In addition to being *graphically* viable, this interpretation receives at least partial terminological
support, for the daseian signs are identified with the first four ordinal numbers (*protus* is Greek for
"first," *deuterus* is "second," etc.).

Fig. 1.4 Notes as integer pairs. After *Scolica enchiriadis*

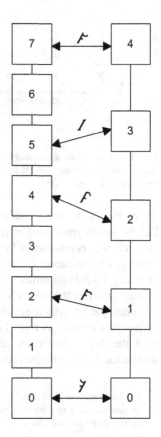

box in (a) and another representing a box in (c). Suppose that we start our numbering, in both cases, from zero.[21] Then $\Upsilon = C = (0, 0)$, $\digamma = D = (2, 1)$, $\digamma = E = (4, 2)$, $\mathit{I} = F = (5, 3)$, and $\digamma = G = (7, 4)$; see Fig. 1.4. Clearly, intervals are also integer pairs under this interpretation. In particular, the perfect fifth (as in C to G) is $(7, 4)$ and the perfect fourth (as in C to F) is $(5, 3)$.[22]

With these ideas in mind we may finally turn to the master's *first* answer to Q (p. 79). In addition to an illustration reproduced here as Fig. 1.5, the answer contains a reference to a slightly earlier discussion (p. 78) explaining how the ratio 2:1 is "completed by" (*completur*) the ratios 3:2 and 4:3: "For when we begin from

---

[21] Since we are interested primarily in intervals, (0, 0) as origin is an arbitrary (though convenient) choice. For present purposes, any two sets of eight and five *consecutive* integers will do.

[22] See Agmon (1990), where "cognitive interval" is given a similar integer-pair interpretation. Needless to say, the author of SE never *explicitly* identifies type-1 intervals with integer pairs (at least in so far as "explicit" refers to verbally, as opposed to graphically, encoded information).

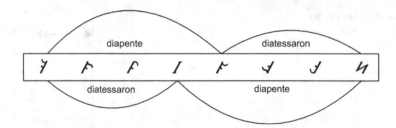

Fig. 1.5 The octave as a combined fifth and fourth (*Scolica enchiriadis*). Copyright © 1981 Bayerische Akademie der Wissenschaften. Redrawn from H. Schmid, *Musica et scolica enchiriadis*, by permission

the number 6, let the sesquialter to 6 increase (*adcrescat*) the number to make 9. Let the sesquitertian to 9 increase the number to make 12. *And thus the duple, the ratio 12 to 6, is completed by the sesquialter and sesquitertian*" (emphasis added). Clearly, the operation by which 3:2 (sesquialter) "increases 6 to make 9" and similarly 4:3 (sesquitertian) "increases 9 to make 12," is multiplication.[23]

Here, then, is the master's first answer to Q. Recall, once again, that Q concerns the principle by which certain symphonies, as type-1 intervals, are paired with certain proportions, as type-2 intervals, in particular, the perfect octave (diapason) with the duple proportion 2:1, the perfect fifth (diapente) with the sesquialter proportion 3:2, and the perfect fourth (diatessaron) with the sesquitertian proportion 4:3.

> The first proof of the matter is that, just as one duple is always made up (*completur*) of a sesquialter and a sesquitertian in the manner described, so do two smaller symphonies, that is, the diapente and the diatessaron, make up a diapason, which contains eight steps (*voculae*).

At first, the answer does not seem to relate to the question, and, indeed, it does not answer Q directly. Nonetheless, the master in effect points out that *if we assume* the pairings octave→2:1, fifth→3:2, and fourth→4:3, we will find that the *operation of multiplication* by which 3:2 and 4:3 combine to form the proportion 2:1, as in $\frac{3}{2} \times \frac{4}{3} = 2$, rhymes, so to speak, with the *operation of addition* by which the five steps of the fifth combine with the four steps of the fourth to form the eight steps of the octave. Note that the mathematical expression in the latter case is $4 + 3 = 7$. In other words, one must subtract 1 from the number of (generic) steps that each interval contains, if both extremes are counted.

There is more than one sense in which the master's observation concerning the "rhyming" operations is most remarkable. First, as any modern-day mathematician will immediately recognize, the mapping from symphonies into ratios that the author of SE describes is an example of a rather sophisticated algebraic structure known as *homomorphism*, that is, a mapping from one group to another that

---

[23] The verbs *intendo* and *remitto* (literally, "to increase" and "to decrease"), used by Boethius in IM III.3, are translated by Bower as "to add" (or "ascend") and "to subtract" (or "descend"). However, multiplication and division are in fact the operations performed in this passage.

"preserves," as the mathematician would say, the operations of the groups.[24] A triangular illustration found earlier in the treatise (see Erickson 1995, p. 71, Fig. 40), where the multiplicative "identity element" (namely 1) is displayed at the apex and the pairs of inversionally related rationals 2 and 1/2, 3 and 1/3, and so forth, are arranged symmetrically on each side, is suggestive of a multiplicative group.[25]

Second, given that, in his block diagrams, the master (under the present interpretation) has implicitly identified the type-1 intervals with integer pairs, in particular, the perfect fifth with $(7, 4)$ and the perfect fourth with $(5, 3)$, on the basis of Fig. 1.5 we can now find *the first* of the two integers that define the perfect octave (the second integer, of course, is 7). Using vector addition we have:

$$(7, \ 4) + (5, \ 3) = (7 + 5, \ 4 + 3) = (12, \ 7).$$

In other words, had the master presented a graphic representation similar to Fig. 1.3a that spans an entire octave (rather than just a fifth), the diagram would have included exactly *thirteen* blocks $(12 + 1 = 13)$.

It is important to realize that such a representation would not have implied 12-tone equal temperament necessarily. Pythagorean intonation is precisely a homomorphism from "type-1 space" into "type-2 space," such that type-1 intervals of the form $k(7, 4) + l(12, 7)$ are mapped into type-2 intervals (frequency ratios) of the form $(3/2)^k \cdot (2)^l$. Indeed, shortly after Q is posed and answered a monochord exercise results in a thoroughly Pythagorean, type-2 image of the "C-major scale" of Fig. 1.5.[26]

---

[24] Once again, Ptolemy (*Harmonics*, I.5) may have paved the way. In the context of "... the Pythagoreans' Positions Concerning the Hypotheses of the Consonances" he states (p. 18) that "... it happens that the diapason is composed from the two, successive first consonances, the diapente and the diatessaron, while the duple ratio is composed of the two, successive first superparticular ratios, the sesquialter (3:2) and the sesquitertion (4:3)." However, only in SE is it explicitly clear, both verbally *and* graphically, that addition of step sizes, as distinct from multiplication of ratios, is the sense in which the diapason is "composed" of the diapente and the diatessaron. The idea that the octave (as the ratio 2:1) is composed of the fourth and fifth (as the ratios 4:3 and 3:2) is stated by the early Pythagorean Philolaus as follows (Barker 1989, p. 37): "The magnitude of *harmonia* is *syllaba* and *di' oxeian*."

[25] Boethius (IM, II.20) presents a similar diagram. It appears after citing in II.19 the early Pythagoreans Eubulides and Hippasus as saying that "... increments of multiplicity correspond to diminution of superparticularity in a fixed order. Accordingly, *there cannot be a duple unless a half occurs nor a triple unless a third part occurs*" (emphasis added).

[26] See Fig. 44 in Erickson (1995). Even though strict equal temperament (ET) may seem incompatible with a ninth-century musical system, it might be worth noting that it shares with Pythagorean intonation (PI) the homomorphism property (in ET intervals (u, v) are mapped, though not one-to-one, into frequency ratios 2 to-the-power-of $u/12$). Indeed, in addition to the perfect octave ET shares with PI the tuning of the crucially important perfect fifth, at least insofar as the difference between the irrational 2 to-the-power-of 7/12 (approximately 1.4983) and the rational 1.5 is, for all practical purposes, negligible. Proving the homomorphism property of both PI and ET as mappings from "type-1" into "type-2" interval space is a relatively straightforward mathematical exercise. In the case of PI it is important to note that for every type-1 interval (u, v) there exist unique integers k and l such that $(u, v) = k(7, 4) + l(12, 7)$.

Let us review the *enchiriadis* insights, implicit as well as explicit, from which proto-tonal theory may benefit.

- A "musical interval" is not just a frequency ratio (see Q); a musical interval is also *a pair* of discretely measured distances, one "specific," and the other "generic." For example, the perfect fifth as a "type-2" interval is the frequency ratio 3:2; as a "type-1" interval, however, it is the integer pair (7, 4) (see the block diagrams).
- The most privileged type-2 interval is 2:1; 3:2 (or 3:1) follows suit. Apparently unaware of the existence of overtones, the *enchiriadis* theorists derive this ordering (following Boethius and ultimately the Pythagoreans) from the theory of proportions.
- Similarly, (12, 7) (perfect octave) is the most privileged *type-1 interval*, and (7, 4) follows suit. Though the *enchiriadis* theorists single out the perfect octave as the agent of equivalence and suggest that the perfect fifth has a special role as generator (see the conceptually infinite series of disjunct T-S-T tetrachords that constitute the *enchiriadis* tone system), a "critical faculty" (*sensus*) is invoked in connection with the type-1 ordering (see the second answer to Q).
- Finally, the relation of the additive, type-1 "interval space" to the multiplicative type-2 space is far from arbitrary; in fact, the mapping of one space to the other is operation-preserving. For example, the type-2 octave $\frac{3}{2} \times \frac{4}{3}$ corresponds to the type-1 octave (7, 4) + (5, 3) (fifth plus fourth; see the first answer to Q).

The disciple in SE seems satisfied with the master's response to Q, for he summarizes the lengthy discussion as follows: "It has been clearly proven through detailed demonstration not only that music is produced from connumerate or commensurate numbers, *but also which symphonies are bound to these species of connumerate numbers*" (p. 81, emphasis added). Indeed, the lessons to be learned from this remarkable discussion, in conjunction with other important ideas introduced in SE or ME, are profound, and are by no means limited to the musical repertoire that these ninth-century treatises address. A solid foundation for proto-tonal theory has been laid. It is up to us, now, with the help of many additional insights gained in the centuries since, to complete the building.

References

Agmon, E. (1990). Music theory as cognitive science: Some conceptual and methodological issues. *Music Perception, 7*(3), 285–308.

Babb, W. (Trans.). (1978). *Hucbald, Guido, and John on music: Three medieval treatises*. New Haven: Yale University Press.

Barker, A. (Ed.). (1989). *Greek musical writings II: Harmonic and acoustic theory*. Cambridge: Cambridge University Press.

Boethius, A. M. S. (1989). *Fundamentals of music* (C. Bower, Trans.). New Haven: Yale University Press.

Carey, N., & Clampitt, D. (1996). Regions: A theory of tonal spaces in early medieval treatises. *Journal of Music Theory, 40*(1), 113–141.

Clough, J., & Myerson, G. (1985). Variety and multiplicity in diatonic systems. *Journal of Music Theory, 29*(2), 249–270.

Cohen, D. (2002). Notes, scales, and modes in the earlier middle ages. In T. Christensen (Ed.), *The Cambridge history of Western music theory* (pp. 307–363). Cambridge: Cambridge University Press.

Erickson, R. (Trans.). (1995). *Musica enchiriadis and Scolica enchiriadis*. New Haven: Yale University Press.

Jacobsthal, G. (1897). *Die chromatische Alteration im liturgischen Gesang der abendländischen Kirche*. Berlin: Springer. 1970. Reprint, Hildesheim: Olms.

Phillips, N. (1990). Classical and late Latin sources for ninth-century treatises on music. In A. Barbera (Ed.), *Music theory and its sources: Antiquity and the Middle Ages* (pp. 100–135). Notre Dame: University of Notre Dame Press.

Phillips, N. (2000). Notationen und Notationslehren von Boethius bis zum 12. Jahrhundert. In T. Ertelt & F. Zaminer (Eds.), *Geschichte der Musiktheorie 4* (pp. 293–623). Darmstadt: Wissenschaftliche Buchgesellschaft.

Schmid, H. (Ed.). (1981). *Musica et scolica enchiriadis una cum aliquibus tractatulis adiunctis*. Munich: Bayerische Akademie der Wissenschaften. Electronic ed. in *Thesaurus Musicarum Latinarum*, G. Di Bacco (Director). http://www.chmtl.indiana.edu. Accessed 10 Jan 2012.

Solomon, J. (2000). *Ptolemy* Harmonics: *Translation and commentary*. Leiden: Brill.

Temperley, D. (2000). The line of fifths. *Music Analysis, 19*(3), 289–319.

Part I
Proto-tonality

Chapter 2
Preliminaries

Abstract Chomsky's distinction between descriptive and explanatory theoretical adequacy is discussed, and his emphasis on "Universal Grammar" as *the* criterion for assessing linguistic explanatory adequacy is criticized (Sect. 2.1). Communication is deemed a primary principle for assessing proto-tonal explanatory adequacy (Sect. 2.2). Additional principles are termed "economical," "categorical," and "maximalist" (Sect. 2.3). Finally, in Sect. 2.4 formalities are established for handling "event sequences" and relationships between different types thereof, for example note sequences and pitch sequences.

The 130-odd pages of Part I of this book, *Proto-tonality*, require explanation. Is there really a need for such a complicated theory, the purpose of which is merely to set the stage for Part II, *The Languages of Western Tonality*, also the title of the book as a whole?

The answer depends on one's expectations from theories in general, and from theories that one might term "proto-tonal," in particular. If one only demands that theories be adequate *descriptively* then the answer to the question above is possibly negative. However, if theories are expected to be adequate *explanatorily* as well then the answer is positive: the theory of proto-tonal systems is a complicated theory, to be sure; and yet, it is no more complicated than necessary to attain explanatory adequacy.

We begin, therefore, with an essential methodological distinction.

2.1 Descriptive and Explanatory Proto-tonal Adequacy: A Lesson from Linguistics

According to Chomsky,

> ... there are two respects in which one can speak of "justifying a generative grammar." On one level (that of descriptive adequacy), the grammar is justified to the extent that it correctly describes its objects, namely the linguistic intuition—the tacit competence—of the native speaker. In this sense, the grammar is justified on *external* grounds, on grounds of correspondence to linguistic fact. (1965, pp. 26–27)

To attain descriptive adequacy, Chomsky explains,

> the structural descriptions assigned to sentences by the grammar, the distinctions that it makes between well-formed and deviant, and so on, must... correspond to the linguistic intuition of the native speaker (whether or not he may be immediately aware of this) in a substantial and significant class of crucial cases. (1965, p. 24)

It would seem that descriptive adequacy represents a rather minimal standard of scientific acceptability, but in fact, as Chomsky points out (*ibid.*), "... even descriptive adequacy on a large scale is by no means easy to approach." This is true of music no less than it is of language.

Consider a hypothetical proto-tonal theory that equates the perfect octave with the pitch interval 1,200 cents (equivalently, the frequency ratio 2). The theory, I submit, is descriptively *in*adequate. Although every musical octave maps psychoacoustically into a pitch interval of ca. 1,200 cents, the reverse relation, as Fig. 2.1 demonstrates, does not hold. Note the asterisked E♭ and D♯ of the celli and second violin, a simultaneity representing the by-product of two note-against-note neighbor-note configurations D-E♭-D and E-D♯-E (the neighbor-note motive is of course central to the movement's design). In performance, the corresponding pitch interval is an approximate whole multiple of 1,200 cents; and yet, the interval from E♭ to D♯ is *not* a compound perfect octave. Indeed, the interval, a compound augmented seventh, *is dissonant* by conventional music theory.

But let us assume that a descriptively adequate proto-tonal theory exists, and indeed, that there are *two* such theories; is there a way to decide in favor of one theory or the other?

According to Chomsky,

> On a much deeper and hence much more rarely attainable level (that of explanatory adequacy), a grammar is justified to the extent that it is a *principled* descriptively adequate system, in that the linguistic theory with which it is associated selects this grammar over others, given primary linguistic data with which all are compatible. In this sense, the grammar is justified on *internal* grounds, on grounds of its relation to a linguistic theory that constitutes an explanatory hypothesis about the form of language as such. The problem of internal justification—of explanatory adequacy—is essentially the problem of constructing a theory of language acquisition, an account of the specific innate abilities that make this achievement possible. (1965, p. 27)

Fig. 2.1 A (compound) augmented seventh in the first movement (m. 116) of J. S. Bach's Brandenburg Concerto No. 3

As Chomsky notes (*ibid.*, p. 26), even though "... it would be utopian to expect to achieve explanatory adequacy on a large scale in the present state of linguistics..., considerations of explanatory adequacy are often critical for advancing linguistic theory." He continues:

> Gross coverage of a large mass of data can often be attained by conflicting theories; for precisely this reason it is not, in itself, an achievement of any particular theoretical interest or importance. As in any other field, the important problem in linguistics is to discover a complex of data that differentiates between conflicting conceptions of linguistic structure in that one of these conflicting theories can describe these data only by *ad hoc* means whereas the other can explain it on the basis of some empirical assumption about the form of language. ... Thus whether we are comparing radically different theories of grammar or trying to determine the correctness of some particular aspect of one such theory, it is questions of explanatory adequacy that must, quite often, bear the burden of justification. This remark is in no way inconsistent with the fact that explanatory adequacy on a large scale is out of reach, for the present. It simply brings out the highly tentative character of any attempt to justify an empirical claim about linguistic structure.

For Chomsky, then, explanatory adequacy is the question of attaining descriptive adequacy *by principled means*. This, for Chomsky, is primarily a matter of construing the grammar of a particular language as a special case of "Universal Grammar" (UG)—a theory of "... the form of language as such."

Chomsky emphasizes UG, as *the* principle in terms of which linguistic explanatory adequacy is to be assessed, even at the expense of what seems to be an equally important principle, namely, the communicative function of language. This imbalance is evident, for example, in the following interview.

> *As I understand, language has an innate biological basis. Its use, however, is social. What do you think of the social functions of language? Is it primarily an instrument of communication?*
>
> I think a very important aspect of language has to do with the establishment of social relations and interactions. Often, this is described as communication. But that is very misleading, I think. There is a narrow class of uses of language where you intend to communicate. Communication refers to an effort to get people to understand what one means. And that, certainly, is one use of language and a social use of it. But I don't think it is the only social use of language. Nor are social uses the only uses of language. For example, language can be used to express or clarify one's thoughts with little regard for the social context, if any.
>
> I think the use of language is a very important means by which this species, because of its biological nature, creates a kind of social space, to place itself in interactions with other people. It doesn't have much to do with communication in a narrow sense; that is, it doesn't involve transmission of information. There is much information transmitted but it is not the content of what is said that is transmitted. There is undoubtedly much to learn about the social uses of language, for communication or for other purposes. But at present there is not much in the way of a theory of sociolinguistics, of social uses of languages, as far as I am aware.
>
> *What, then, in the field of linguistics, are the greatest achievements?*
>
> I think the most important work that is going on has to do with the search for very general and abstract features of what is sometimes called universal grammar: general properties of language that reflect a kind of biological necessity rather than logical necessity; that is, properties of language that are not logically necessary for such a system but which are essential invariant properties of human language and are known without learning. We know these properties but we don't learn them. We simply use our knowledge of these properties as the basis for learning. (Chomsky 2004, pp. 368–369)

Indeed, Chomsky's "overall approach to language" has been roundly criticized by Searle (1972) as "peculiar and eccentric" precisely because "... so much of the theory runs counter to quite ordinary, plausible, and common-sense assumptions about language," namely, that "the purpose of language is communication in much the same sense that the purpose of the heart is to pump blood." Searle continues:

> In both cases it is possible to study the structure independently of function but pointless and perverse to do so, since structure and function so obviously interact. We communicate primarily with other people, but also with ourselves, as when we talk or think in words to ourselves. Human languages are among several systems of human communication (some others are gestures, symbol systems, and representational art) but language has immeasurably greater communicative power than the others.
>
> We don't know how language evolved in human prehistory, but it is quite reasonable to suppose that the needs of communication influenced the structure. For example, transformational rules facilitate economy and so have survival value: we don't have to say, "I like it that she cooks in a certain way," we can say, simply, "I like her cooking." We pay a small

price for such economies in having ambiguities, but it does not hamper *communication* much to have ambiguous sentences because when people actually talk the context usually sorts out the ambiguities.

Transformations also facilitate communication by enabling us to emphasize certain things at the expense of others: we can say not only "Bill loves Sally" but also "It is Bill that loves Sally" and "It is Sally that Bill loves." In general an understanding of syntactical facts requires an understanding of their function in communication since communication is what language is all about.

"The defect of the Chomskyan theory" Searle concludes towards the end of the review "arises from the same weakness we noted earlier, the failure to see the essential connection between language and communication, between meaning and speech acts."

Chomsky (1975, p. 55 ff.) responds to these serious charges at length, while acknowledging (*ibid.*, p. 235), that "the bulk" of Searle's account is "... accurate and compelling, including many of the critical comments"; he even refers (*ibid.*) to Armstrong (1971) as suggesting "... that the theory that communication provides '*the* clue to an analysis of the notion of linguistic meaning' can be traced to Locke."

In his response, Chomsky (1975, p. 59 ff.) isolates the explanatory role of communication *with regard to the theory of meaning* as "... the sole serious point of disagreement."[1] As he notes,

Under innumerable quite normal circumstances—research, casual conversation, and so on—language is used properly, sentences have their strict meaning, people mean what they say or write, but there is no intent to bring the audience (not assumed to exist, or assumed not to exist, in some cases) to have certain beliefs or to undertake certain actions. Such commonplace examples pose a difficulty for an analysis of meaning in terms of speaker's intention with regard to an audience, even if it were possible, for the case where there is intent to communicate, to account for what a sentence means in these terms—and this too I doubt, for reasons to which I will return. (1975, p. 62)

The difficulties that Chomsky notes with regard to a communication-motivated theory of meaning are instructive in the present context because the analogy between language *and music* seems to break precisely at this point: semantics. Though it seems eminently reasonable to speak of "musical syntax," to speak of "musical semantics" is, at best, controversial. Indeed, musical "utterances," even less so than linguistic ones, do not ordinarily carry an "intention with regard to an audience," for example "to have certain beliefs or to undertake certain actions." Moreover, a musical audience is normally not even expected to perform the linguistically commonplace action of *responding* to an utterance in the manner of a conversation, where *semantically related* utterances are tossed back and forth such that the roles of "speaker" and "audience" are constantly interchanged. (A musical audience, in fact,

---

[1] Chomsky (*ibid.*, p. 57) is rather uncomfortable with "... Searle's concept of 'communication' as including communication with oneself, that is, thinking in words." "... I agree with Searle that there is an essential connection between language and communication once we take 'communication' in his broader sense—an unfortunate move, I believe, since the notion 'communication' is now deprived of its essential and interesting character." However, as we shall see in Sect. 6.4, musical self-communication can be a highly interesting form of communication, with far-reaching structural ramifications.

does not seem to object and often even seems to enjoy attending to essentially the same utterance, passively as it were, time and time again.)

In short, if music is a language, and in particular, one that (for all practical purposes) *lacks* a semantic component, then one can hardly object to a Searle-like position that places the idea of communication center-stage. Before proceeding any further, therefore, it is only natural that we state as precisely as possible what such a position entails.

2.2   The Communication Principle

Figure 2.2 reproduces Shannon's (1948, p. 381) schematic diagram of a "general communication system." A "message" conceived at some "information source" is transformed into a "signal" transmitted over some "channel." "The *receiver*" states Shannon "ordinarily performs the inverse operation of that done by the transmitter, reconstructing the message from the signal." Moreover,

> The fundamental problem of communication is that of reproducing at one point exactly or approximately a message selected at another point. ... The significant aspect is that the actual message is one *selected from a set* of possible messages. The system must be designed to operate for each possible selection, not just the one which will actually be chosen since this is unknown at the time of design. (p. 379)

I shall assume henceforth that tonal music is a communication system in the following sense (Fig. 2.3). The message is a sequence of *notes* and the signal is a corresponding sequence of *pitches*. Following Shannon, I shall assume that the received message is as faithful as possible an image of its transmitted counterpart, and shall refer to this assumption as the Communication Principle. Ideally, then, an *identity relationship* should hold between the transmitted message and the received one; however, we shall say that *the Communication Principle is satisfied* if the relationship between the transmitted and received message is one *of transposition*.

In a communicative context it is natural to assume that transmitters and receivers are more than just "neutral" agents for transmitting and receiving messages. Rather, transmitters and receivers are "communication seekers" in the sense of making a *purposeful effort* to engage in fruitful exchange. Transmitters, therefore, will take into account the difficulties that face receivers and will not only transmit messages via a signal deemed optimal, but will also construe their messages in the first place such that they are not cognitively opaque. Conversely, receivers will attempt to decode a less-than-optimal and even corrupted signal; and they will make some effort to cope with a cognitively demanding message.[2]

---

[2] It is difficult to disagree with Molino (1975, p. 47, quoted in translation in Lidov 2005, p. 86), that "nothing guarantees a direct correspondence between the effect produced by a work of art and the intentions of its creator. Every symbolic object presumes an exchange in which producer and consumer, sender and receiver are not interchangeable and have different perspectives on this object which they hardly conceive in the same way." I believe, nonetheless, that despite the lack of guarantee of success, human beings are communication seekers.

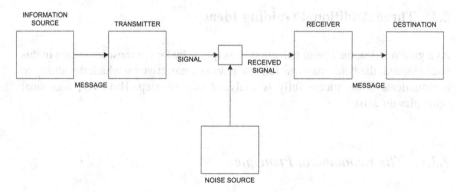

Fig. 2.2 Shannon's General Communication System

Fig. 2.3 The note-communication system

Though we shall usually think of communication as an act in which information passes through an external medium between two distinct persons, we shall also entertain the idea of *reflexive* communication, where information passes *internally* between the transmitting and receiving "faculties" of the same person. There is nothing abnormal or perverse about reflexive communication; indeed, successful "intrapersonal communication" (communication with oneself) is arguably a prerequisite for successful "interpersonal communication" (communication with others).[3] Intrapersonal musical communication, for example, hearing music "in one's head," seems pervasive.

Finally, it is important to note that the note-communication system depicted in Fig. 2.3 falls short of satisfying Shannon's definition of a "communication system" since the "signal" (a sequence of pitches) is not "suitable for transmission over the channel" (Shannon 1948, p. 381). Therefore, in Sect. 3.3, a lower-level system is constructed, a system the message of which—a sequence of pitches—corresponds to the higher-level "signal." A pitch-communication system is a genuine communication system. The message (a sequence of pitches) is transformed into an eminently transmittable signal, namely, a sequence of *sound waves*.

---

[3] The terms "interpersonal communication" and "intrapersonal communication" originate with Ruesch and Bateson (1951, pp. 15–16).

2.3 Three Additional Guiding Ideas

As a guiding idea, the Communication Principle is by far the most important in this book. Indeed, the book may fruitfully be read as a narrative by which the ability to communicate notes successfully is analyzed step by step. However, additional principles do exist.

2.3.1 The Economical Principle

The Economical Principle states that the mental resources available to the listener for decoding a tonal message are not unlimited. In particular, "... the span of absolute judgment and the span of immediate memory impose severe limitations on the amount of information that we are able to receive, process, and remember" (Miller 1956, p. 95). The Economical Principle is not dependent on some specific theory of (short-term) memory. Rather, it states quite generally that the "universal grammar" of tonality is constrained to reduce cognitive load as much as possible.

The Economical Principle is implemented primarily in Sect. 5.2. See also Sects. 14.2 and 15.1.

2.3.2 The Categorical Principle

Consider the phenomenon known as "categorical perception" (CP). According to Harnad (1987, p. 3), an example of CP is

> ... the color spectrum as it is subdivided into color categories, or an acoustic continuum called the "second-formant transition" as it is subdivided into the (synthesized) stop-consonant categories /ba/, /da/, and /ga/. In both cases, equal-sized physical differences between stimuli are perceived as larger or smaller depending on whether the stimuli are in the same category or different ones.

Suppose that perceptions of a certain type (for example, color) are representable as a continuum P analogous to the line of real numbers (Fig. 2.4). Suppose further that there exist points $p_0 < p_1 < \ldots$ on the line that, for some reason or another, are perceptually privileged. Then, if the Categorical Principle applies, for any three privileged points p_{i-1}, p_i, and p_{i+1} the central p_i is *the prototype* of *the category* C_i, a category defined as the continuum of perceptions (real numbers) p_i extending from a "left boundary" $L_i = \frac{p_{i-1}+p_i}{2}$ to a "right boundary" $R_i = \frac{p_i+p_{i+1}}{2}$, exclusive of the boundaries themselves (the category C_i is thus the open interval (L_i, R_i)).

Moreover, if the Categorical Principle applies, then for every category C_i there exists a *categorical-perception function* CP_i from P into some closed interval, say [0, 1], a function with the following properties (see Fig. 2.5). For every $p \in P$ the value $CP_i(p)$, to which we shall refer as *the prototypicality of p relative to C_i,*

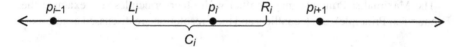

Fig. 2.4 The prototype p_i and the category C_i on the perceptual continuum P. L_i and R_i are the category's left and right boundaries, respectively

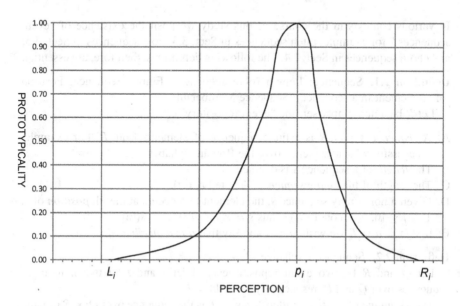

Fig. 2.5 Prototypicality as a function of perception relative to an arbitrary category $C_i = (L_i, R_i)$ with prototype p_i

decreases smoothly, monotonically, and symmetrically with the distance of p from p_i such that $CP_i(p) = 1$ implies that $p = p_i$ and $CP_i(p) = 0$ implies that either $p \le L_i$ or $p \ge R_i$. Note that the symmetry is relative to the ratio $\frac{p_i - L_i}{R_i - p_i}$. That is, for a perception p lying to the left of p_i there exists a perception p' of equal prototypicality lying to the right of p_i such that $\frac{p_i - p}{p' - p_i} = \frac{p_i - L_i}{R_i - p_i}$ (and vice versa, for a perception p' lying to the right of p_i).

The Categorical Principle is applied in Sect. 5.3.

2.3.3 The Maximalist Principle

The Maximalist Principle is rather abstract. It states that in positing the existence of a (non-empty) set S of objects s of a certain type, in the absence of a compelling reason to assume otherwise it is natural to assume that S contains the *maximal* possible number of objects s. The Maximalist Principle is implemented primarily in Sects. 5.1 and 6.4; see also Sect. 10.1.

The Maximalist Principle may conflict with other principles (for example the Economical Principle). Such conflicts and their resolution are discussed as relevant.

2.4   Event Sequences

In various contexts in the course of this study we posit the existence of "event sequences," for example, pitch sequences in Sect. 3.3; note sequences in Sect. 3.5; and chord sequences in Sect. 7.4. The following definitions, therefore, are essential.

Definition 2.1. Sequence; Length (of a sequence); Empty Sequence; Position (of an element in a sequence); Sequence Membership
  Let R be a non-empty set (the "event repository").

A. A *sequence s over R* is a finite sequence of elements from R. For example, "successfully" is a sequence over the Roman alphabet.
B. The *length* of a sequence s is denoted $|s|$.
C. The length of the *empty sequence*, denoted ε, is 0.
D. Given a non-empty sequence s, the element that occurs at the jth *position* of s, $1 \leq j \leq |s|$, is denoted $s(j)$. Thus $s = s(1),\ s(2),\ \ldots,\ s(|s|)$.
E. If $s(j) = a \in R$ we write $a \in s$ and say that a *is a member of s*.

Definition 2.2. Sequence Exchange
  Let Q and R be two event repositories and let s and t be two non-empty sequences over Q and R, respectively, $|s| = |t| = L$.
  The *exchange of s with t*, written $X : s \rightarrow t$, is the sequence over $Q \times R$ of pairs $(s(j),\ t(j)), j = 1,\ 2, \ldots, L.$ [4]

For every pair $(s(j),\ t(j)) \in X$ we write $X(s(j)) = t(j)$. Thus, in the context of an exchange $X : s \rightarrow t$ the notation $X(a) = b$ (often simplified to $Xa = b$), $a \in s$, $b \in t$, is understood to imply that elements a and b occupy the same position relative to their corresponding sequences.

References

Armstrong, D. M. (1971). Meaning and communication. *Philosophical Review, 80*, 427–447.
Chomsky, N. (1965). *Aspects of the theory of syntax*. Cambridge: MIT Press.
Chomsky, N. (1975). *Reflections on language*. New York: Pantheon.
Chomsky, N. (2004). *Language and politics* (2nd ed.). Oakland: AK Press.
Harnad, S. (1987). Psychophysical and cognitive aspects of categorical perception: A critical overview. In S. Harnad (Ed.), *Categorical perception: The groundwork of cognition* (pp. 1–28). Cambridge: Cambridge University Press.

---

[4] Thus X is the order-preserving bijection from the ordered multiset s onto the ordered multiset t.

Lidov, D. (2005). *Is language a music? Writings on musical form and signification.* Bloomington: Indiana University Press.

Miller, G. (1956). The magical number seven, plus or minus two: Some limits on our capacity for processing information. *Psychological Review, 63,* 81–96.

Molino, J. (1975). Fait musical et sémiologie de la musique. *Musique en jeu, 17,* 37–61.

Ruesch, J., & Bateson, G. (1951). *Communication: The social matrix of psychiatry.* New York: Norton.

Searle, J. (1972, June 29). Chomsky's revolution in linguistics. *New York Review of Books, 18*(12).

Shannon, C. (1948). A mathematical theory of communication. *Bell System Technical Journal, 27* (3–4), 379–423, 623–656.

Chapter 3
Communicating Pitches and Transmitting Notes

Abstract Section 3.1 focuses on notes and note intervals, defined as integer pairs, and on the octave relationship, defined in terms of a privileged note interval (a, b), the "cognitive octave." Section 3.2 focuses on pairs of note intervals and a sense in which they may be said to "generate" all note intervals. In Sect. 3.3 "pitch" and "pitch interval" are defined as real numbers. The "signal" by which a pitch is communicated is a periodic wave relative to a frequency f that relates exponentially to the pitch. A theorem is proven, by which a "pitch-communication system" is equivalent to a logarithmic transformation of f. Section 3.4 establishes a hierarchy of privileged pitch intervals, first of which is the psychoacoustical octave $\log 2$. A "*Phi*-centered" pitch-communication system is defined, where a transmitter-privileged pitch φ is assumed privileged for the receiver as well. The system is either "absolute," "relative," or "reflexive," the latter modeling a person engaged in self-communication. Finally, Sect. 3.5 combines the note system of 3.1 with the pitch-communication system of 3.4. "Transmission functions" from notes to pitches and from note intervals to pitch intervals, are posited. It is proven that the transmission function for intervals is a homomorphism from "note-interval space" into "pitch-interval space." It is proven further that a "composite tone system," where the cognitive octave (a, b) is transmitted as the psychoacoustical octave, falls into one of three mutually exclusive types. An example of a "type-1" system is the usual tone system, $(a, b) = (12, 7)$, under 12-tone equal temperament; the usual tone system under Pythagorean intonation is a "type-3" system.

3.1 Octave-Endowed Note Systems

Definition 3.1. Note, Note Interval

Let N and NVL be two copies of the set of all ordered integer pairs $\mathbb{Z} \times \mathbb{Z}$.

We shall refer to N as *the set of notes* and to NVL as *the set of note intervals* (*intervals* for short).

E. Agmon, *The Languages of Western Tonality*, Computational Music Science,
DOI 10.1007/978-3-642-39587-1_3, © Springer-Verlag Berlin Heidelberg 2013

Some motivation for Definition 3.1 is found in Chap. 1. Taking our cue from the medieval treatise *Scolica enchiriadis* we have found that notes such as C, D, E, F, and G may be represented as integer pairs (0, 0), (2, 1), (4, 2), (5, 3), and (7, 4), respectively; similarly, intervals such as perfect octave, fifth, and fourth may be represented as (12, 7), (7, 4), and (5, 3).

Definition 3.1 takes however, a rather bold step beyond such preliminary observations for it identifies the set of all notes (intervals) with the *infinite* set of all integer pairs. In Chap. 4, we shall see that it is indeed possible, under certain conditions, to give meaning to each and every member of N or NVL as a conventional note or interval ("quadruply flatted F," "quintuply augmented ninth," etc.).

N and NVL are distinct copies of $\mathbb{Z} \times \mathbb{Z}$ and therefore a note and an interval are always distinct, even if it happens that, as integer pairs, they are not. For example, $(0, 0) \in N$ is distinct from $(0, 0) \in NVL$ (cf. "middle C" vs. "perfect prime").

Notes and note intervals are mental objects; they are not to be confused, however, with the mental objects subsequently to be defined as "pitches" and "pitch intervals," respectively (Sect. 3.3).

The term "note interval" suggests a connection between the elements of N and the elements of NVL; the following definition renders the connection explicit. Unless otherwise noted, the symbol "$-$" (as in "$-x$") shall be used henceforth to denote the inverse of an element of an additive group; "$+$" will usually denote the usual addition operation on the reals.

Definition 3.2. Note-Interval Function

Let N be the set of notes and let NVL be the set of intervals.

The *note-interval function* $\text{NI} : N \times N \rightarrow NVL$ is defined as follows, for every $((s, t), (s', t')) \in N \times N$:

$$\text{NI}((s, t), \ (s', t')) = (-s + s', \ -t + t').$$

Closely related to the note-interval function is the note-transposition function.

Definition 3.3. Note-Transposition Function

Let N be the set of notes, let NVL be the set of intervals, and let NI be the note-interval function.

The *note-transposition function* $\text{NT} : N \times NVL \rightarrow N$ is defined as follows, for every $((s, t), (u, v)) \in N \times NVL$:

$$\text{NI}((s, t), \text{NT}((s, t), (u, v))) = (u, v).$$

*Proposition 3.4.[1]

$$NT((s, t), (u, v)) = (s + u, t + v).$$

To simplify notation we shall write henceforth

$$NI\big((s, t), (s', t')\big) = (s', t') - (s, t),$$
$$NT\big((s, t), (u, v)\big) = (s, t) + (u, v).$$

Note the specialized use of the symbols "$-$" and "$+$" in these expressions. Abusing notation we shall also write $(s, t) = (u, v)$, $(s, t) \in N$ $(u, v) \in NVL$, in the sense of $(s, t) + (-(u, v)) = (0, 0)$, that is, $NT((s, t), - (u, v)) = (0, 0)$.

The following definition expresses algebraically some basic intuitions concerning intervals, namely, that subject to certain rules, two intervals, or an interval and an integer, may be combined to form an interval. To indicate usual multiplication on the reals, factors will often be juxtaposed, as in xy.

Definition 3.5. Interval Space

The *interval space NVL* is the set *NVL* endowed with functions $\oplus$ and $\bullet$ from $NVL \times NVL$ and $\mathbb{Z} \times NVL$, respectively, into *NVL*, defined as follows:

$$(u, v) \oplus (u', v') = (u + u', v + v') \text{ for every } ((u, v), (u', v')) \in NVL \times NVL;$$
$$i \bullet (u, v) = i(u, v) = (iu, iv) = (i \cdot u, i \cdot v) \text{ for every } (i, (u, v)) \in \mathbb{Z} \times NVL.$$

The interval space *NVL* is a $\mathbb{Z}$-module. See Appendix B for further discussion.

As will happen time and again in the course of this study, in the following definition a higher-level object is formed by combining existing objects.

Definition 3.6. Note System

Let N be the set of notes, let *NVL* be the interval space, and let NI be the note-interval function.

We shall refer to the set $NS = (N, NVL, \text{NI})$ as *the note system*.

Definition 3.7. Cognitive Octave; Octave Relation

Let $NS = (N, NVL, \text{NI})$ be the note-system. Fix an interval $(a, b) \neq (0, 0)$ and let (u, v) and (u', v') be two intervals.

A. We shall refer to (a, b) as *the cognitive octave*.
B. We shall write $(u, v) \equiv_{(a, b)} (u', v')$ and shall say that (u, v) and (u', v') *are octave related* if there exists an integer l such that $(u', v') = (u, v) \oplus l(a, b)$.
C. If (u, v) and (u', v') are not octave related we shall write $(u, v) \not\equiv_{(a, b)} (u', v')$.

The cognitive octave is not to be confused with the *pitch interval* subsequently to be defined as "psychoacoustical octave" (Sect. 3.4).

---

[1] An asterisked theorem, proposition, or lemma is stated without proof, and may be proven by the interested reader as an exercise.

Proposition 3.8. The octave relation is an equivalence relation.

Proof. Every interval (u, v) satisfies $(u, v) = (u, v) \oplus 0(a, b)$ and therefore the relation is reflexive. If $(u', v') = (u, v) \oplus l(a, b)$ then $(u, v) = (u', v') \oplus - l(a, b)$, and the relation is symmetric. Finally, if $(u', v') = (u, v) \oplus l(a, b)$ and $(u'', v'') = (u', v') \oplus l'(a, b)$ then $(u'', v'') = (u, v) \oplus (l + l') \cdot (a, b)$, and therefore the octave relation is transitive. Q.E.D.

Example 3.9. Set $(a, b) = (12, 7)$. Then:

A. $(0, 0) \equiv_{(a, b)} (12, 7)$.
B. $(14, -3) \equiv_{(a, b)} - (10, 17)$.
C. $(0, 0) \not\equiv_{(a, b)} (12, 0)$.

Example 3.9C illustrates the finding that $u' \equiv u \pmod{|a|}$ and $v' \equiv v \pmod{|b|}$ do *not* jointly imply that (u, v) and (u', v') are octave related.[2]

The octave relation is in *NVL*. It should be useful to have a similar relation in *N*. The "abuse of notation" $(s, t) = (u, v)$ introduced earlier shall prove useful for this purpose.

Definition 3.10. Octave-Related Notes

Let (s, t), (s', t') be a pair of notes. Set $(u, v) = (s, t)$, $(u', v') = (s', t')$, (u, v), (u', v') is a pair of intervals.

We shall write $(s, t) \equiv_{(a, b)} (s', t')$ and shall refer to (s, t) and (s', t') as *octave related* if (u, v) and (u', v') are octave related. If (s, t) and (s', t') are not octave related we shall write $(s, t) \not\equiv_{(a, b)} (s', t')$.

Strictly speaking, the octave relation on notes is distinct from the octave relation on note intervals. Therefore, using the same symbol (namely $\equiv_{(a, b)}$) for both relations is an abuse of notation.

Finally, we have the following definition.

Definition 3.11. Octave-Endowed Note System; Usual Note System

Let $NS = (N, NVL, NI)$ be the note system. Fix a cognitive octave (a, b) and let $\equiv_{(a, b)}$ be the octave relation.

We shall refer to the pair $\overset{(a, b)}{ONS} = \left(NS, \equiv_{(a, b)} \right)$ as *an octave-endowed note system*.

We shall refer to the octave-endowed note system $\overset{(12, 7)}{ONS}$ as *usual*, and shall write $\overset{(12, 7)}{ONS} = ONS = (NS, \equiv)$.

An octave-endowed note system $\overset{(a, b)}{ONS}$ is the note system *NS together with* the octave relation $\equiv_{(a, b)}$; by abuse of notation $\equiv_{(a, b)}$ actually stands for *two* relations, one on *N* and the other on *NVL*.

---

[2] Hence, the octave relation is distinct from Agmon's (1989, p. 11) "Octave Equivalence." Note also that unlike Agmon (1989), we do *not* assume that *a* and *b* are coprime (that is, we do not assume that the *greatest common divisor* of *a* and *b* is 1).

In Sects. 3.3 and 3.4 we shall study pitch communication. First, however, we shall consider the notion of a basis of the interval space. Bases of the interval space shall play an important role beginning in Sect. 3.5.

3.2 Bases of the Interval Space

Definition 3.12. Basis of the Interval Space

Let *NVL* be the interval space and let $((g_1, h_1), (g_2, h_2))$ be a pair of intervals.

We shall refer to $((g_1, h_1), (g_2, h_2))$ as *a basis of NVL* if there exists a function $f : NVL \to \mathbb{Z} \times \mathbb{Z}$ such that $f(u, v) = (i, j)$ implies that

$$(u, v) = i(g_1, h_1) \oplus j(g_2, h_2). \tag{3.1}$$

Example 3.13. $((1, 0), (0, 1))$ is a basis of *NVL*. For every $(u, v) \in NVL$ we have

$$(u, v) = u(1, 0) \oplus v(0, 1),$$

that is, $f(u, v) = (u, v)$.

Similarly, $((0, 1), (1, 0))$ is a basis of *NVL*. For every $(u, v) \in NVL$ we have

$$(u, v) = v(0, 1) \oplus u(1, 0),$$

that is, $f(u, v) = (v, u)$.

Theorem 3.14.[3]

Let $((g_1, h_1), (g_2, h_2))$ be a pair of intervals. Set $g_1 h_2 - g_2 h_1 = \Delta$.

Then $((g_1, h_1), (g_2, h_2))$ is a basis of *NVL* if, and only if, $\Delta = \pm 1$. Moreover, if $((g_1, h_1), (g_2, h_2))$ is a basis of *NVL* the function $f : NVL \to \mathbb{Z} \times \mathbb{Z}$ (Definition 3.12) is a bijection satisfying the following condition A.

A. $f(u, v) = (i, j) = (\pm(h_2 u - g_2 v), \mp(h_1 u - g_1 v))$.

To prove the theorem we shall first prove the following lemma.

Lemma 3.15. Let $((g_1, h_1), (g_2, h_2))$ be a basis of *NVL*. Set $g_1 h_2 - g_2 h_1 = \Delta$.

Then $\Delta \neq 0$.

Proof. If $((g_1, h_1), (g_2, h_2))$ is a basis of *NVL* then for every $(u, v) \in NVL$ there exist integers i and j such that

$$u = ig_1 + jg_2, \quad v = ih_1 + jh_2. \tag{3.2}$$

Letting $u = 1 = v$ one sees that $\gcd(g_1, g_2) = 1 = \gcd(h_1, h_2)$; letting $u \neq v$ one sees that $(g_1, g_2) \neq (h_1, h_2)$. The lemma follows easily.

---

[3] See Hardy and Wright (1938, p. 28), Theorem 32.

Proof of the theorem. Using $(i, j) = (\pm(h_2 u - g_2 v), \mp(h_1 u - g_1 v))$, it can easily be checked that $\Delta = \pm 1$ implies that $((g_1, h_1), (g_2, h_2))$ is a basis of *NVL*. Suppose that $((g_1, h_1), (g_2, h_2))$ is a basis of *NVL*. Using Lemma 3.15, Eqs. (3.2) may be solved for i and j, as follows:

$$i = \frac{h_2 u - g_2 v}{\Delta}, \quad j = -\frac{h_1 u - g_1 v}{\Delta}. \tag{3.3}$$

Let $(u, v) = (1, 0)$. Then Δ divides h_1 and h_2. Similarly, $(u, v) = (0, 1)$ implies that Δ divides g_1 and g_2. It follows that Δ^2 divides $g_1 h_2 - g_2 h_1$, that is, Δ^2 divides Δ, or equivalently, $1/\Delta$ is an integer, that is $|\Delta| = 1$.

It is easily seen that the function $f : NVL \to \mathbb{Z} \times \mathbb{Z}$ is surjective. Suppose that $|\Delta| = 1$ and suppose by contradiction that f is not one-to-one. From Eqs. (3.3) it follows that there exist distinct intervals (u, v) and (u', v') satisfying

$$\begin{aligned} h_2(u - u') &= g_2(v - v'), \\ h_1(u - u') &= g_1(v - v'). \end{aligned} \tag{3.4}$$

Set $u - u' = k$, $v - v' = l$. If $k = 0$ from Eq. (3.4) we have $g_2 = 0 = g_1$, implying that $\Delta = 0$, contrary to our assumption. Similarly, $l = 0$ is impossible. Multiplying the two equations of (3.4) diagonally and collecting it follows that there exist non-zero integers k and l satisfying $kl\Delta = 0$, again contradicting our assumption, $|\Delta| = 1$. Thus f is one-to-one. Q.E.D.

3.3 Pitch-Communication Systems

By the Communication Principle tonality is a communication system such that the message is a sequence of notes and the signal is a corresponding sequence of pitches. The *received* message is an image of the message, as faithful as possible to its source (Fig. 2.3).

As already noted, a sequence of pitches is not truly a signal, because it is not "suitable for transmission over the channel" (Shannon 1948, p. 381). We must therefore construct a *lower-level* communication system such that the higher-level "signal" (a sequence of pitches) is the message, and the signal is a corresponding sequence of waves. Such a "pitch-communication system" is depicted schematically in Fig. 3.1.

In studying pitch communication we must enter the highly controversial and problematic fields of psychoacoustics and "pitch perception" (see for example de Cheveigné 2005; Schnupp et al. 2011, Chap. 3, for convenient summaries); in particular, we must specify how pitches are converted into waves, and even more problematically, how waves are converted back into pitches. One may therefore wonder whether we could not have rather *assumed* the existence of pitch-communication systems as depicted schematically in Fig. 3.1, bypassing the details

Fig. 3.1   A pitch-communication system

of pitch encoding and decoding. However, it would have surely seemed odd that a study in musical communication avoids the interface between the mental and the physical that goes to the heart of communicative acts. Moreover, as shall be noted in Sect. 3.4 in connection with the "psychoacoustical octave," the actual signal by which pitch intervals *are physically* encoded can have crucial communicative ramifications, and therefore it must be explicitly addressed.

The American National Standards Institute (ANSI S1.1 1994) defines pitch as "that attribute of auditory sensation in terms of which sounds may be ordered on a scale extending from low to high." An earlier American Standards Association definition states that pitch is "that attribute of auditory sensation in terms of which sounds may be ordered on a musical scale" (ASA 1960). Both definitions fall short of identifying the "scale" with the continuum of real numbers, though the suggestion seems clear. The following definition takes the crucial step. Since pitch *intervals* are assumed as well, the definition is analogous to Definition 3.1.[4]

Definition 3.16.   Pitch; Pitch Interval
   Let P and PVL be two copies of the reals.
   We shall refer to P as *the set of pitches* and to PVL as *the set of pitch intervals*.

By identifying the pitches (pitch intervals) with the set of all real numbers we are making two implicit idealizations. First, the pitch continuum extends indefinitely in both directions; second, there is no limit to the human pitch-discriminatory ability. These idealizations, however, are temporary. Definition 3.25 subsequently in this section sets upper and lower boundaries to pitch; at a later point in this study (Sect. 5.1) the occasion will seem appropriate to consider an obvious constraint on "just-noticeable" pitch distances.

The following definition is analogous to Definitions 3.2 and 3.3.

Definition 3.17.   Pitch-Interval Function; Pitch-Transposition Function
   The *pitch-interval function* PI : $P \times P \rightarrow PVL$ is defined as follows, for every $(p, p') \in P \times P$:

---

[4] Pitch is not the only "... attribute of auditory sensation in terms of which sounds may be ordered on a scale extending from low to high"; loudness, the scale of which extends from "quiet" to "loud," is another. However, unlike pitch, loudness does not seem to form *a system* analogous to the "pitch system" of Definition 3.19 ahead. In particular, we seem to possess a limited ability, if at all, to measure *intervals* along the loudness scale. See also footnote 6.

$$\mathrm{PI}(p, p') = -p + p'.$$

The *pitch-transposition function* $\mathrm{PT} : P \times PVL \to P$ is defined as follows, for every $(p, q) \in P \times PVL$:

$$\mathrm{PI}(p, \mathrm{PT}(p, q)) = q.$$

To simplify notation we shall write henceforth $\mathrm{PI}(p, p') = p' - p$, $\mathrm{PT}(p, q) = p + q$. Moreover, by abuse of notation we shall occasionally write $p = q$, $p \in P$, $q \in PVL$, in the sense of $p + (-q) = 0$.

Intuitively, one may combine one pitch interval with another to obtain a third pitch interval; one may also "scale" a pitch interval to any size. The following definition, therefore, is analogous to Definition 3.5.

Definition 3.18. Pitch-Interval Space

The *pitch-interval space PVL* is the set *PVL* of pitch intervals endowed with usual addition from $PVL \times PVL$ into *PVL* and usual (scalar) multiplication from $\mathbb{R} \times PVL$ into *PVL*.

The pitch-interval space is a vector space. It is easily seen that if scalar multiplication is restricted to $\mathbb{Z} \times PVL$ then the pitch-interval space is a $\mathbb{Z}$-module.

The following definition is analogous to Definition 3.6.

Definition 3.19. Pitch System

Let P be the set of pitches, let *PVL* be the pitch-interval space, and let PI be the pitch-interval function.

We shall refer to the set $PS = (P, PVL, \mathrm{PI})$ as *the pitch system*.

Note that there is no need for an external stimulus in order for someone to have a "pitch sensation" (indeed, no stimulus has been assumed thus far). Human beings can and often do hear pitches purely "in their heads"; some very famous individuals have even managed to engage in astounding acts of musical creativity while completely deaf.

Suppose that a transmitter is interested in communicating to a receiver other than himself a sequence of internally represented pitches. In the absence of telepathy the transmitter has no choice but to transform the sequence into some sort of signal that can be transmitted along some physical channel for the receiver to receive and decode. Normally the signal will be acoustical in nature, though trained musicians are capable of decoding a pitch message from a *visual* signal as well, for example, a musical score. Be that as it may, it should be useful to ignore for a moment the psychophysical process of pitch encoding and decoding and concentrate instead on the strictly initial and terminal stages of the communicative process. What can one assume the relationship between these stages to be?[5]

---

[5] Note that from the present, music-communicative perspective, pitch is not so much "a percept that is evoked by sounds" (Schnupp et al. 2011, p. 93), as it is a *concept* that is *usually conveyed by* sounds. The differences are subtle yet important. Pitch can exist in the human mind independently

Assuming that acts of pitch communication are successful, if p is a "transmitted pitch" and p' is its received counterpart, then one might reasonably expect that the relation $p' = p$ be satisfied. Generally speaking, however, this expectation is unrealistic, most notably for the reason that so-called "absolute pitch" is a relatively rare ability, even among musicians. Definition 3.20 next, therefore, proposes a weaker relation.

Definition 3.20. Pitch-Communication System (PC system)

Let $PS = (P, PVL, PI)$ be the pitch system, let $\alpha \neq 0$ and β be two real numbers, and let $M_\beta^\alpha : P \rightarrow P$ be a function.

We shall refer to a pair p, $M_\beta^\alpha(p)$ of pitches as *transmitted* and *received*, respectively, and to $PCS_\beta^\alpha = (PS, M_\beta^\alpha)$ as *a pitch-communication system (PC system)* if the following condition A is satisfied for every $p \in P$.

A. $M_\beta^\alpha(p) = \alpha p + \beta$.

Received pitch, in other words, is a linear function of transmitted pitch.[6]

The following easily proven proposition concerns the reception-transmission relation of pitch *intervals*.

*Proposition 3.21. Let PCS_β^α be a PC system. Let $p, p' \in P$ such that $p' - p = q$, and set $M_\beta^\alpha(p') - M_\beta^\alpha(p) = r$.

Then $r = \alpha q$.

Definition 3.22. Standard; Anti-standard; Faithful PC System

Let $PCS_\beta^\alpha = (PS, M_\beta^\alpha)$ be a PC system.

A. We shall refer to the system as *standard* if $\alpha = 1$.
B. We shall refer to the system as *anti-standard* if $\alpha = -1$.
C. We shall refer to a standard system as *faithful* if $\beta = 0$.

By Proposition 3.21 a standard pitch-communication system satisfies $r = q$, where q (r) is a transmitted (received) pitch interval; an anti-standard system satisfies $r = -q$. A faithful system satisfies $M_\beta^\alpha(p) = p$, thus representing the consummation of the Communication Principle at the pitch level.

---

of sound, and can be conveyed from one human mind to another by means other than sound. At least in a music-communicative setting, therefore, pitch is more than a "sensation" correlated with some physical attribute of the environment. *Pitch is a message, conceived in the mind of one human being and conveyed by physical (usually, acoustical) means to the mind of another.* See also Definition 3.33 ahead, and Sect. 3.4.1.2.

[6] One may question the necessity of assuming a linear function from transmitted to received pitch, proposing instead, say, a mere monotonic function (ascending or descending). However, although a monotonic function may suffice for communicating, say, speech intonation, it surely does not suffice for musical purposes, where information resides not only in the relative "height" of transmitted pitches but also in the relative directed size of transmitted pitch *intervals*; see Proposition 3.21. In other words, the existence of a linear function is a *musical* assumption consistent with the existence of pitch intervals (Definition 3.16), which is also music-specific.

Thus far we have bypassed the crucial psychophysical process by which a transmitted pitch p is encoded by the transmitter as a physical *signal*, which latter is decoded by the receiver as a received pitch p'. The American National Standards Institute definition of pitch cited earlier goes on to state that "pitch depends primarily on the frequency content of the sound stimulus, but it also depends on the sound pressure and the waveform of the stimulus."

The reference to "frequency content," however, is far more problematic than may initially seem. A pitch-evoking signal may consist of more than one "frequency" of a given type (cf. the sinusoidal components of a complex sound). Moreover, there may be more than one level at which an acoustical signal may be described in terms of "frequency" (cf. a carrier sinusoidal wave, amplitude modulated). Indeed, regardless of its low-level structure, if an acoustical signal possesses a *high-level frequency* or "periodicity," it will often elicit a pitch sensation correlated with that "frequency."

These difficulties, however, are largely irrelevant to the *transmission* of pitches.

Consider the traditional musical "pitch transmitters," namely, the standard musical instruments of Western music (the human voice included). Whether based on string vibration, air-column vibration, or membrane vibration, these devices are *known* to produce for every pitch an (approximate) periodic wave the spectrum of which includes a sinusoidal, "fundamental" frequency that corresponds to the period (though the fundamental may be relatively weak). Moreover, an exponential relation is *known* to hold between a transmitted pitch and its corresponding fundamental frequency.[7] Therefore, if PCS_β^α is a pitch-communication system and p is a transmitted pitch, one may safely assume not only that the signal associated with p is a periodic wave relative to some fundamental frequency f (Definition 3.24), but also that f relates exponentially to p (Definition 3.25).

We begin, however, with the following crucial definition.

Definition 3.23. Frequency

By "frequency" we shall mean henceforth a sinusoidal wave. We shall represent a frequency by a strictly positive number f that corresponds to the frequency of the

---

[7] There should be nothing controversial about these statements. It is hardly a secret that musical instruments and the human voice produce for every transmitted pitch a periodic sound wave *the spectrum of which contains a fundamental frequency corresponding to the period* (that is, the fundamental frequency is expressed in the spectrum with non-zero amplitude). Indeed, precisely for this reason there exists an obvious correlation between the "range" of musical instruments in a given family and their relative physical size. Similarly, it is hardly a secret that musically transmitted pitches map *exponentially* into fundamental frequencies. Unlike the inverse, logarithmic relation, that is often assumed to hold between fundamental frequencies and *received* pitches (cf. the so-called Weber-Fechner Law), there is no need to tap the minds of listeners by all sorts of circuitous means to obtain this relationship. It suffices, for example, to study the relation of musical scores (conceived as notated pitch messages) to their recorded performances (conceived as the corresponding signals), a matter of public record in both cases.

wave, that is, the number of wave cycles as counted relative to an agreed upon time unit.

Note that the definition leaves open the ontological status of frequencies as physical, mental, or purely mathematical objects.

Definition 3.24. Periodic Wave Class (relative to a fundamental frequency)

Let f be a frequency.

Henceforth we shall write $\omega(f)$ to refer to the set of all periodic waves the spectrum of which contains a frequency f that corresponds to the period; that is, f is expressed in the spectrum with non-zero amplitude. We shall refer to $\omega(f)$ as *a periodic wave class relative to f*, and to any member of $\omega(f)$ as *a periodic wave relative to f*, the wave's *fundamental frequency*.

We shall usually think of a periodic wave as a physical object, i.e., a *sound* wave. However, in the special case of a *sinusoidal* wave the wave/frequency can be physical, mental, or purely mathematical.

In the following definition "τ" is the Greek letter *Tau*.

Definition 3.25. Pitch-Transmission Function; Transmittable Pitch Range

Let Ω be the set of all periodic wave classes $\omega(f)$ such that f lies within the range of ca. 30 Hz to ca. 5 kHz. Let $PS = (P, PVL, \text{PI})$ be the pitch system, and let $P(\Omega)$ be a non-empty subset of P. Finally, let $\tau \neq 1$ be a strictly positive real number and let T^{τ} be a surjection from $P(\Omega)$ onto Ω.

We shall refer to $P(\Omega)$ as *the transmittable pitch range* and to T^{τ} as *a pitch-transmission function* if the following condition A is satisfied, under the condition that frequency is measured in units of 261.63 s^{-1}.

A. $T^{\tau}(p) = \omega(f) = \omega(\exp(\tau, p))$ for every $p \in P(\Omega)$.[8]

Since the range Ω of the surjective pitch-transmission function excludes periodic wave classes with fundamental frequency below ca. 30 Hz and above ca. 5 kHz, the function's domain $P(\Omega)$ is *a segment* of the real number line, not the entire line. Also, since the time unit by which frequency is measured is 261.63 s^{-1}, $T^{\tau}(0) = \omega(1)$ is a periodic wave relative to the fundamental frequency 261.63 Hz, the frequency usually associated with the pitch of the note C_0, or "middle C." *Note that this latter convention applies only to the transmitter* (who, one may readily assume, calibrates a transmission to some internal or external standard, for example, a tuning fork). The receiver may not have "absolute pitch," and therefore may use a different unit of measurement (Sect. 3.4).

The following proposition may be thought of as a modern-day formulation of Pythagoras's famous alleged discovery, seen from the transmitter's point of view. The proposition is suggestive of an "interval-transmission function" $I^{\tau}(q) = \exp(\tau, q)$,

---

[8] Although the pitch-transmission function maps pitches into periodic wave *classes*, it shall be assumed that in practice an arbitrary *member* of that class is transmitted, not the entire class. In other words, the distinction between a periodic wave class and an arbitrary member thereof shall be (harmlessly) blurred; indeed, by abuse of notation $\omega(f)$ shall be written for both.

clearly a homomorphism from the additive pitch-interval group into a multiplicative group, the group of ratios of fundamental frequencies.[9]

*Proposition 3.26. Let $PS = (P, PVL, \text{PI})$ be the pitch system. Let $\tau \neq 1$ be a strictly positive real number, let T^τ be the pitch-transmission function, and let $P(\Omega)$ be the transmittable pitch range. Fix a pitch interval q and let $p, p' \in P(\Omega)$ be two pitches satisfying $p' - p = q$. Finally, set $T^\tau(p) = \omega(f)$, $T^\tau(p') = \omega(f')$.

Then $f'/f = \exp(\tau, q)$.

Thus far we have considered the function by which *the transmitter* converts pitches into periodic waves. Consider a pitch-communication system (Definition 3.20) such that a sequence of transmitted pitches, all within the transmittable pitch range, is converted in order into a sequence of periodic waves using the pitch-transmission function. How does *the receiver* extract from the acoustical sequence as faithful as possible an image of the original pitch sequence?

If the acoustical sequence, from the point of view of the receiver, is assumed to preserve its *mathematical* structure as *a sequence*, in particular, a sequence of periodic waves each relative to some fundamental frequency, we have a theorem (3.27, below). The mathematical assumption is of course counter to *physical* fact. However, as shall be clarified subsequently, there is good reason to proceed as if it were true.

In studying Theorem 3.27 it should be convenient to consult Fig. 3.2, depicting the main objects and relations to which the theorem refers. In particular, a pitch-*reception* function R that completes the *lower* path from transmitted to received pitch, the path that passes through the acoustical level of periodic waves—a function the properties of which are as yet unknown—is the main focus of the theorem. In the theorem, "ρ" is the Greek letter *Rho* ("τ" is the Greek letter *Tau*).

Theorem 3.27. Let $PS = (P, PVL, \text{PI})$ be the pitch system and let $T^\tau : P(\Omega) \to \Omega$ be the pitch-transmission function. Let $\text{M} : P(\Omega) \to P$ be a function.

Then (PS, M) is a pitch-communication system if, and only if, there exists a logarithmic function $R_\sigma^\rho : \Omega \to P$ satisfying the following condition A for some pair of strictly positive real numbers $\rho \neq 1$ and σ, and $M = R_\sigma^\rho \circ T^\tau$ such that the following condition B is satisfied.

A. $R_\sigma^\rho(\omega(f)) = \log(\rho, \sigma f)$.
B. $M(p) = \alpha p + \beta$ for every $p \in P(\Omega)$, $\alpha = \frac{\ln \tau}{\ln \rho}$, $\beta = \frac{\ln \sigma}{\ln \rho}$.

Proof. If a function R_σ^ρ satisfying Condition A exists, then (PS, M) is a pitch-communication system PCS_β^α such that $M = M_\beta^\alpha = R_\sigma^\rho \circ T^\tau$, $\alpha = \frac{\ln \tau}{\ln \rho}$, $\beta = \frac{\ln \sigma}{\ln \rho}$.

Suppose that (PS, M) is a PC system PCS_β^α, $T^\tau : P(\Omega) \to \Omega$ is the pitch-transmission function. Let $p \in P(\Omega)$ and set $T^\tau(p) = \omega(f)$. Then there exists a function $R : \Omega \to P$ such that $R(\omega(f)) = \alpha p + \beta$.

---

[9] On group homomorphism, see Appendix A. See also Chap. 1.

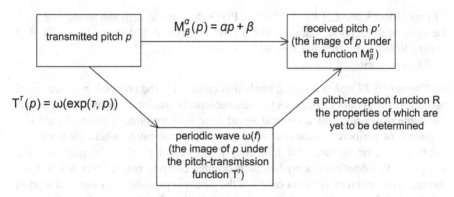

Fig. 3.2 The main objects and relationships studied in Theorem 3.27

Set $\sigma \in \mathbb{R}$ such that $\ln\sigma = \frac{\beta\ln\tau}{\alpha}$. Then $\sigma > 0$ satisfies $\sigma = 1$ if, and only if, $\beta = 0$. If $\sigma = 1$ set $\rho \in \mathbb{R}$ such that $\ln\rho = \frac{\ln\tau}{\alpha}$. Then $\rho > 0$ $\rho \neq 1$, and we have

$$R(\omega(f)) = \alpha p = p \cdot \log(\rho, \ \tau) = \log(\rho, \ \exp(\tau, \ p)) = \log(\rho, \ \sigma f).$$

If $\sigma \neq 1$ set $\rho \in \mathbb{R}$ such that $\ln\rho = \frac{\ln\tau}{\alpha} = \frac{\ln\sigma}{\beta}$. We have:

$$R(\omega(f)) = \alpha p + \beta = p \cdot \log(\rho, \ \tau) + \log(\rho, \ \sigma) = \log(\rho, \ \sigma f).$$

Q.E.D.

By Theorem 3.27 a pitch-communication system PCS_β^α is equivalent to the pitch system together with an exponential pitch-transmission function T^τ from pitches to fundamental frequencies *and a logarithmic "pitch-reception function"* R_σ^ρ *from fundamental frequencies to pitches such that* $\frac{\ln\tau}{\ln\rho} = \alpha$ *and* $\frac{\ln\sigma}{\ln\rho} = \beta$. The two functions fall short of being inverses one of the other because the receiver does not necessarily use the same base, namely τ, used by the transmitter for converting pitches into fundamental frequencies, nor does the receiver necessarily use the same time unit, namely 261.63 s^{-1}, for measuring frequency. If the receiver's base ρ equals the transmitter's τ (equivalently, if $\alpha = 1$) the system is proportional (cf. Definition 3.22); if, in addition, $\sigma = 1$ (equivalently, $\beta = 0$) the system is faithful, and the two functions are exact inverses one of the other.

The following proposition, based on Theorem 3.27, may be viewed as yet another modern-day formulation of Pythagoras's famous alleged discovery (cf. Proposition 3.26), this time from the receiver's point of view.[10] Cf. also the so-called "Weber-Fechner Law."

---

[10] Pythagoras focused on such "privileged" pitch intervals as log2, log3, etc.; see Definition 3.30.

*Proposition 3.28. Let $PS = (P, PVL, \text{PI})$ be the pitch system and let $\text{R}_\sigma^\rho : \Omega \to P$ be the pitch-reception function. Fix a pitch interval q and let $\omega(f)$, $\omega(f') \in \Omega$ satisfy $\text{R}_\sigma^\rho(\omega(f')) - \text{R}_\sigma^\rho(\omega(f)) = q$.

Then $q = \log(\rho, f'/f)$.

Theorem 3.27 makes a strong prediction concerning the processing of acoustical signals by the auditory system as pitches, but strictly speaking it rests on a fallacious assumption. For although a musical signal from the transmitter's point of view is *a sequence* of periodic waves, one wave per transmitted pitch, where each wave is relative to some fundamental frequency f, the signal reaches the receiver as *a composite* that does not readily betray its original components. In other words, from the receiver's point of view not only is it the case that periodic waves are not a priori labeled by their fundamental frequencies, but *the signal as a whole*, from the receiver's point of view, is a physical composite of its separate elements.[11] In addition, noise may contaminate the signal, such that, even if the receiver is able to separate the composite wave into its sinusoidal components, the fundamental frequency f of a periodic wave $\omega(f) = \text{T}^\tau(p)$ may be masked. How can the receiver tell which frequency of the spectrum is a fundamental frequency, and which is an overtone of some (possibly masked) fundamental?

There seems to be no consensus regarding these questions. The two major contending theories are currently pattern matching, by which the receiver compares the spectrum of the wave to an internally stored overtone-series-like or "harmonic" template, and autocorrelation, a process by which periodicities (that is, fundamental-frequency equivalents) are detected within the wave-form itself.[12]

Note that by either theory, from the perspective of musical communication the auditory system is assumed to be reconstructing as best as possible the information that was lost in the transmission process.[13] Therefore, regardless of *how* this reconstruction is accomplished, in the final analysis Theorem 3.27 may be held as true. This means that one may essentially ignore the psychoacoustical process of pitch encoding and decoding and simply assume the existence of pitch-communication systems as per Definition 3.20, that is, systems oblivious of a physical signal that passes from transmitter to receiver.[14]

---

[11] The mathematical notion of *a sequence* of periodic waves is indifferent to *how* this sequence is transmitted over time, for example, one element at a time or all at once. We must assume, however, that any two elements of the sequence may be transmitted simultaneously.

[12] In general, these approaches have been developed on the assumption that no more than one pitch is transmitted at a given moment. "How often do you hear a single sound by itself?" asks Darwin (2005, p. 278), and answers: "Only when doing psychoacoustic experiments in a soundproof booth!"

[13] Thus, at least in the context of *musical* communication a "missing fundamental" is indeed missing. Recall that the conventional musical instruments produce for every transmitted pitch a periodic wave *the spectrum of which contains a fundamental frequency* (i.e., a sinusoidal frequency corresponding to the period).

[14] On the basis of Theorem 3.27 one may nonetheless conjecture that processing an acoustical signal as a sequence of pitches is a matter of finding an optimal match between *tentative* fundamental frequencies, on the one hand, and *tentative* periodicities, on the other. This suggests

The qualification "essentially" in the last sentence, however, is important. As shall become clear in the following section, the actual signal by which pitch intervals are *physically* encoded can have crucial communicative ramifications.

3.4 Absolute, Relative, and Reflexive Pitch Communication

Definition 3.29. Overtone Pair (of order n)
Let f be a frequency and set $(f, 2f, \ldots) = (f_0, f_1, \ldots)$.
We shall refer to the pair (f_0, f_n), $n \geq 1$, as *an overtone pair of order n.*

In connection with the following definition, review Definition 3.25 and Theorem 3.27.

Definition 3.30. Privileged Pitch Interval; Psychoacoustical Octave
Let (f_0, f_n) and (f'_0, f'_m) be overtone pairs such that a periodic wave class $\omega(f_0)$, $\omega(f_n)$, $\omega(f'_0)$, and $\omega(f'_m)$ is a member of Ω. Set

$$q_n = \log(\tau, f_n/f_0) = \log(\tau, n+1),$$
$$q_m = \log(\tau, f'_m/f'_0) = \log(\tau, m+1);$$
$$r_n = \log(\rho, f_n/f_0) = \log(\rho, n+1),$$
$$r_m = \log(\rho, f'_m/f'_0) = \log(\rho, m+1).$$

A. We shall refer to q_n, q_m (respectively, r_n, r_m) as *transmitter-privileged (receiver-privileged) pitch intervals.*
B. If $n < m$ we shall say that q_n (r_n) is *more privileged than* q_m (r_m).
C. We shall refer to $q_1 = \log(\tau, 2)$ ($r_1 = \log(\rho, 2)$), the most privileged pitch interval, as *the transmitter's (receiver's) psychoacoustical octave.*

In connection with the following definition, review Definition 3.22.

Definition 3.31. ψ-Standard PC System
Consider a PC system $PCS_\beta^\alpha = (PS, M_\beta^\alpha)$ together with the pitch-transmission and pitch-reception functions $T^\tau : P(\Omega) \to \Omega$ and $R_\sigma^\rho : \Omega \to P$.
We shall refer to PCS_β^α as *ψ-standard* if $\log(\rho, 2) = \psi = \log(\tau, 2)$. That is, $\alpha = 1$ such that for some real number $\psi \neq 0$, $\tau = \rho = \sqrt[\psi]{2}$.

Henceforth we shall assume that a PC system (together with the pitch-transmission and pitch-reception functions) is ψ-standard. *This assumption is justified, observing*

---

that the auditory system separates the signal into its sinusoidal components to obtain all *potential* fundamental frequencies (assuming, also tentatively, that none is masked). Simultaneously, it groups together harmonically related subsets of the spectrum to find all potential periodicities. Finally, it finds a match between tentative fundamental frequencies (including possibly masked ones) and tentative periodicities that best accounts for the signal as a whole.

that the highly privileged psychoacoustical octave is associated for both transmitter and receiver with the same physical object, the frequency ratio 2.

Note that the psychoacoustical octave ψ does not imply an equivalence relationship *on pitches* (cf. the equivalence relationship on notes, Definition 3.7). As de Cheveigné (2005, p. 213) notes, "octave equivalence is not an obvious emergent property of pitch models."

Definition 3.32. Pitch Height; Pitch-Interval Direction; Pitch Register

Let $PCS_\beta^\alpha = (PS, M_\beta^\alpha)$ be a ψ-standard PC system, and assume that ψ is positive (negative). Let p, p' be two transmitted pitches, and set $q = p' - p$. Let r be an integer.

A. If $p > p'$ ($p < p'$) we shall refer to p as *higher than p'*; conversely, if $p < p'$ ($p > p'$) we shall refer to p as *lower than p'*.
B. If q is strictly positive (negative) we shall refer to q as *ascending*; conversely, if q is strictly negative (positive) we shall refer to q as *descending*.
C. We shall write $\mathrm{REG}(p) = r$ and shall say that p *lies in the rth register* if $r = \lfloor p/\psi \rfloor$.[15]

Note that although the expression "p is higher than p'" may be represented mathematically as either $p > p'$ or $p < p'$ (depending on whether ψ is positive or negative, respectively), assuming $p = \log\left(\sqrt[\psi]{2},\ f\right)$ for some fundamental frequency f, in both cases the frequencies of the corresponding periodic waves, f and f', satisfy $f > f'$. In other words, *the intuition* "higher than" corresponds to *the physical relation* "faster than," and is independent of any *convention* by which "higher than" is represented mathematically by "larger than" or "smaller than." Similarly, although the expression "q is an ascending pitch interval" may be represented mathematically by either a positive or negative q (again depending on whether ψ is positive or negative, respectively), in both cases the ratio of the corresponding fundamental frequencies, f and f', is larger than 1.

Definition 3.33. Reflexive PC System

Let $PCS_\beta^\alpha = (PS, M_\beta^\alpha)$ be a ψ-standard PC system.

We shall refer to the system as *reflexive* if transmitter and receiver share an identity as the same person.

A reflexive pitch-communication system models a human being engaged in self-communication. A reflexive pitch-communication system is faithful, since the receiver is also the transmitter, and therefore only one time unit for measuring frequency exists. In a reflexive system the distinction between "pitch" and "frequency" is arguably merely notational, since both objects are mental; review Definitions 3.23, 3.24, and discussion.

---

[15] For a real number x the notation $\lfloor x \rfloor$ signifies *the integral part of x*, the largest integer smaller than or equal to x.

Definition 3.34. Absolute PC System

Let $PCS_\beta^\alpha = (PS, M_\beta^\alpha)$ be a ψ-standard PC system.

We shall refer to the system as *absolute* if the receiver has "absolute pitch," that is, the receiver has in store a (mental) frequency f_{AP} that serves as a unit for measuring frequency in general.

With no loss of generality we shall assume that a non-reflexive absolute PC system satisfies $f_{AP} = 261.63$Hz. Thus an absolute PC system, like a reflexive one, is faithful.

Definition 3.35. φ-Centered PC System; Relative φ-Centered PC System

Let $PCS_\beta^\alpha = (PS, M_\beta^\alpha)$ be a ψ-standard PC system. Assume there exists a transmitter-privileged pitch φ, $REG(\varphi) = 0$, such that the following two conditions, A and B, are satisfied.

A. $M_\beta^\alpha(\varphi)$ is privileged by the receiver.
B. If the system is not absolute or reflexive, $M_\beta^\alpha(\varphi) = 0$.

We shall refer to the system as φ-*centered*. We shall refer to a φ-centered pitch-communication system satisfying Condition B as *relative*.

Since an absolute or reflexive φ-centered PC system satisfies $M_\beta^\alpha(p) = p$ (equivalently, $\beta = 0$) and a relative φ-centered PC system satisfies $M_\beta^\alpha(p) = p - \varphi$ (equivalently, $\beta = -\varphi$), with no ambiguity we may discard henceforth the function M_β^α, writing PCS_φ^ψ for a φ-centered PC system, known to be absolute, relative, or reflexive.

We shall refer to Condition 3.35A as "*Phi*-image centricity." *Phi*-image centricity is of course a problematic assumption (3.35B, by comparison, is merely conventional). How can the receiver *know* that $M_\beta^\alpha(\varphi)$ is the image of a pitch privileged by the transmitter?[16]

At this stage we can only offer our pledge to set well-motivated conditions subsequently in this study that render the assumption of *Phi*-image centricity superfluous. We ask the reader's indulgence in this regard, for we will not be able to keep our pledge right away. "Contextual" conditions for *Phi*-image centricity (indeed, *final*-image centricity) will be suggested, informally, in Sect. 10.2; a "context-free" theory of *Phi*/final-image centricity (indeed, *tonic*-image centricity) will not be offered, however, until Chap. 14 (see Sect. 14.2). As we shall see in Sect. 15.1, under certain conditions, even a *hypothetical* received image of a transmitter-privileged tonic may be deemed privileged by the receiver.

---

[16] Unlike the psychoacoustical octave ψ, the privileged status of which for both transmitter and receiver is a reflection of the signal by which it is transmitted, there is nothing *a priori* special about the signal by which φ is transmitted.

3.4.1 Two Postscripts

3.4.1.1 A Possible Biology for Harmonic Templates

The ordered set q_1, q_2 ... of privileged pitch intervals (Definition 3.30) is a "harmonic template" as posited by the theory of pattern matching. "In the perception of pitch" writes Darwin (2005, p. 301), "some grouping together of the harmonics of a particular sound source by principles of harmonicity and onset time (but not location) seems to be required as a precursor to existing models of pitch perception."

In their 2000 study "The Case of the Missing Pitch Templates: How Harmonic Templates Emerge in the Early Auditory System," Shamma and Klein "... illustrate how biologically plausible processes, response patterns, and connectivity in the early auditory nuclei can give rise to ordered harmonic templates without the need for any specially tailored inputs (such as clean harmonic complex tones), or supervised constraints (such as labeled and ordered inputs and outputs)" (p. 2632). The model consists of two main stages. "An analysis stage consists of filter bank followed by temporal and spectral sharpening analogous to the processing seen in the cochlea and cochlear nucleus. The second stage is a matrix of coincidence detectors that computes the pairwise instantaneous correlation among all filter outputs." "The coincidence network" they subsequently note (p. 2634) "... is capable of producing the harmonic templates as its final averaged output regardless of the exact nature of its input signal, provided it is broadband conveying energy at all frequencies <3 kHz."

Figure 3.3 (Shamma and Klein's Fig. 3) illustrates harmonic templates generated by (a) a broadband noise stimulus and (b) a random click train with random widths. "Three templates are shown individually by the cross sections (fundamentals at 175, 315, 560 Hz)" Shamma and Klein note regarding (a). "For each, the pattern shows prominent peaks at harmonically related CFs [center frequencies, EA], *that gradually decrease in amplitude for higher order harmonics*" (emphasis added). As de Cheveigné (2005, p. 185) notes, Shamma and Klein's model "is a significant step in the development of pattern matching models."

3.4.1.2 Pitch as a High-Level Mental Construct

In their 2006 study "High-level and Low-level Processing in the Auditory System: The Role of Primary Auditory Cortex," Nelken and Ahissar suggest that the study of auditory perception in general and pitch perception in particular may benefit from an approach known as the "reverse hierarchy theory," originally applied to visual perception. "The main aspect of the Reverse Hierarchy Theory is the separation between the bottom-up processing hierarchy on the one hand, and conscious perception, which follows along the reverse direction, on the other hand. ... Conscious [visual] perception does not follow this [bottom-up] processing

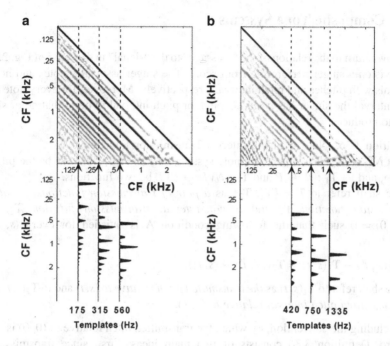

Fig. 3.3 Harmonic templates generated by (**a**) a broadband noise stimulus and (**b**) a random click train with random widths. Reprinted with permission from Shamma and Klein, *Journal of the Acoustical Society of America 107*(5), p. 2635, (2000). Copyright © 2000, Acoustical Society of America

scheme. On the contrary—initial conscious perception reflects higher-level representations" (p. 349). Concerning pitch, "the Reverse Hierarchy theory suggests that, because of its global temporal and spectral aspects, pitch is a high-level construct, resulting in its being perceived globally and holistically, late in the bottom-up processing hierarchy." In particular,

> The primary auditory cortex is. . . at an intermediate stage in the processing hierarchy—whereas it is already sensitive to spectro-temporal context, this sensitivity is related to the creation of auditory objects rather than with the computations of their properties. In this respect, we hypothesize that pitch, space and speech perception are related to higher processing stages. (p. 350).

From the present perspective, the idea that pitches are high-level mental constructs, higher, indeed, than the mental objects posited to exist in A1, is consistent with the idea that musical pitch may exist in the mind as a potential *message* independently of any physical stimulus. See also Sect. 3.3, footnote 5, as well as Definition 3.33.

3.5 Composite Tone Systems

We now return to the relation of the "message" to the "signal" in the sense of Fig. 2.3.

Envision a singer performing from score. The singer associates notes and note intervals with pitches and pitch intervals, respectively. Moreover, for every note or note interval the singer has *a unique* pitch or pitch interval in mind that he or she aims to produce.

Definition 3.36. Note and Note-Interval Transmission Functions

Let $NS = (N, NVL, NI)$ be the note system, let $PS = (P, PVL, PI)$ be the pitch system, and let $T_1 : N \to P$ and $T_2 : NVL \to PVL$ be two functions.

We shall refer to $T = \{T_1, T_2\}$ as *a pair of transmission functions, a note-transmission function* T_1 and *a note-interval transmission function* T_2, if $T_1(0, 0) = 0$ such that the following condition A is satisfied for every (s, t), $(s', t') \in N$.

A. $T_1(s', t') - T_1(s, t) = T_2((s', t') - (s, t))$.

We shall refer to $T_1(s, t)$ as *the transmitted pitch relative to* (s, t) and to $T_2(s, t)$ as *the transmitted pitch interval relative to* (u, v).

Excluding the convention, by which the transmitted pitch relative to $(0, 0)$ is set to zero, Definition 3.36 consists of two main ideas. First, since transmission *functions* are assumed, for *every* note or note interval—of which there is a countable infinity—there exists *exactly one* transmitted pitch or pitch interval, respectively. Second, every pair of notes satisfies Condition A.

If one accepts the first idea (the *existence* of note and note-interval transmission functions), accepting the second should pose little difficulty. Condition 3.36A is the common-sense expectation that if p and p' are the transmitted pitches relative to the notes (s, t) and (s', t'), respectively, then, if q is the pitch interval from p to p' and (u, v) is the note interval from (s, t) to (s', t'), q is the transmitted pitch *interval* relative to the note *interval* (u, v).

There are two possible objections, however, to the idea of having a unique transmitted pitch (pitch interval) in the first place. First, even if the idea is valid in principle, it is invalid in practice. A singer, after all, is rarely perfectly "on pitch." Second, certain note intervals, notably the perfect fifth and major (or minor) third, seem to be associated with more than one transmitted pitch interval in the first place. In particular, a third can be pure as well as "Pythagorean."

In response to the first objection we refer the reader to Sect. 5.3, where the unrealistic constraint of absolutely accurate note transmission is indeed relaxed.[17]

---

[17] To this end it is first necessary to rule out "dense" systems (see ahead, Theorem 3.46 and discussion), which are special types of "type-3" systems (see Theorem 3.44 and Definition 3.45). In Sect. 5.1 it is proven that "efficient" tone systems are not type-3 systems.

In response to the second objection, at this stage we can only assure the reader that so-called "just intonation" in the sense of Counterexample 3.41 ahead is not only ad hoc vis-à-vis the transmission functions, but for all *practical* purposes, is indistinguishable from categorical (12-tone) equal temperament. For further discussion see Sect. 8.2.

*Proposition 3.37. Let $T = \{T_1, T_2\}$ be a pair of transmission functions.
   If $(s, t) = (u, v)$ then $T_1(s, t) = T_2(u, v)$.[18]

Theorem 3.38.[19] Let $NS = (N, NVL, NI)$ be the note system and let $PS = (P, PVL, PI)$ be the pitch system. Let $T_1 : N \to P$, $T_2 : NVL \to PVL$ be a pair of functions and assume that $T_1(0, 0) = 0$.
   Then $T = \{T_1, T_2\}$ is a pair of transmission functions if, and only if, T_2 is a module homomorphism from note-interval space NVL into pitch-interval space PVL. In other words, the following two conditions, A and B, are equivalent for every (s, t), $(s', t') \in N$, (u, v), $(u', v') \in NVL$, and i, $j \in \mathbb{Z}$.[20]

A. $T_1(s', t') - T_1(s, t) = T_2((s', t') - (s, t))$.
B. $T_2(i \bullet (u, v) \oplus j \bullet (u', v')) = i \cdot T_2(u, v) + j \cdot T^2(u', v')$.

   To prove the theorem we shall first state the following lemma, by which the note and pitch systems are "generalized interval systems" in the sense of Lewin (1987) or "homogeneous principal sets" in the sense of Bourbaki (1980).

*Lemma 3.39. Let $NS = (N, NVL, NI)$ be the note system and let $PS = (P, PVL, PI)$ be the pitch system. Let (s, t), (s', t') and (s'', t'') be three notes and let p, p', and p'' be three pitches. Set

$$
\begin{aligned}
(u, v) &= (s', t') - (s, t), \\
(u', v') &= (s'', t'') - (s', t'); \\
q &= p' - p, \\
q' &= p'' - p'.
\end{aligned}
$$

Then $(u, v) \oplus (u', v') = (s'', t'') - (s, t)$, and similarly, $q + q' = p'' - p$.

---

[18] Recall that we write $(s, t) = (u, v)$ for $(s, t) + (-(u, v)) = (0, 0)$ and similarly, $p = q$ for $p + (-q) = 0$ (abuses of notation).

[19] The algebraic structure described in Theorem 3.38 is an example of "GIS homomorphism" as studied more generally in Kolman (2004, pp. 158–159) and Hook (2007, pp. 8–12). GIS homomorphism may also be used to describe *pitch* transmission; review Definition 3.25, Proposition 3.26, and discussion.

[20] On group and module homomorphisms, see Appendices A and B. See also Chap. 1.

Proof of the theorem. Let (s, t), (s', t'), and (s'', t'') be three notes and set $(u, v) = (s', t') - (s, t)$, $(u', v') = (s'', t'') - (s', t')$. Assume that Condition 3.38A is satisfied. Using Lemma 3.39 we have

$$T_2\big((u, v) \oplus (u', v')\big) =$$
$$T_2\big((s'', t'') - (s, t)\big) =$$
$$T_1(s'', t'') - T_1(s, t) =$$
$$T_2(u, v) + T_2(u', v'),$$

and therefore T_2 is a group homomorphism of *NVL* into *PVL*. It is easily seen that T_2 is also a module homomorphism.[21]

Assume that Condition 3.38B is satisfied. Again using Lemma 3.39 we have

$$T_2\big((s'', t'') - (s, t)\big) =$$
$$T_2\big((u, v) \oplus (u', v')\big) =$$
$$T_2(u, v) + T_2(u', v') =$$
$$T_1(s'', t'') - T_1(s, t).$$

Q.E.D.

Example 3.40. Let $ONS = (NS, \equiv)$ be the usual octave-endowed note system (Definition 3.11) and let PCS_φ^ψ be a φ-centered PC system (Definition 3.35). Let $T_1 : N \to P$, $T_2 : NVL \to PVL$ be a pair of functions and assume that $T_1(0, 0) = 0$, $T_2(12, 7) = 12 = \psi$. Assume also that $(s, t) \equiv (u, v)$ implies that $T_1(s, t) = T_2(u, v)$.

Then, if one of the following two conditions, A or B, holds for every note interval (u, v), $T = \{T_1, T_2\}$ is a pair of transmission functions.

A. $T_2(u, v) = u$.
B. $T_2(u, v) = u \cdot T_2(1, 0) + v \cdot T_2(0, 1)$, where $T_2(1, 0) = \log(3^7/2^{11})$ is the so-called "apotome," and $T_2(0, 1) = \log(2^{19}/3^{12})$ is the "Pythagorean comma."[22]

The transmission functions defined by Example 3.40A are familiar as 12-tone equal temperament. The transmission functions defined by 3.40B are familiar as Pythagorean intonation.[23]

---

[21] See Appendix B, Theorem B6.

[22] Since the psychoacoustical octave ψ is set to twelve the logarithm base is the twelfth root of 2. See Definition 3.31.

[23] Pythagorean intonation may alternatively be defined in terms of the octave and fifth; see Counterexample 5.7.

Counterexample 3.41. Let $ONS = (NS, \equiv)$ be the usual octave-endowed note system, let PCS_φ^{12} be a φ-centered PC system, and let R_1, R_2 be two *relations*, from N into P and from NVL into PVL, respectively, where $((u, v), q) \in R_2$ and $((s, t), p) = ((u, v), q)$ jointly imply that $((s, t), p) \in R_1$. Assume further that for every interval (u, v) and every triple of integers k, l, and m satisfying

$$k(7, 4) \oplus l(12, 7) \oplus m(4, 2) = (u, v),$$

$((u, v), q) \in R_2$ if

$$q = k\log(3/2) + l12 + m\log(5/4).$$

Then $\{R_1, R_2\}$ is *not* a pair of transmission functions; R_1, R_2, indeed, are not functions. For example, we have both

$$\begin{aligned}((4, 2), \log(5/4)) &\in R_2 \text{ and}\\ ((4, 2), \log(81/64)) &\in R_2,\end{aligned}$$

where $\log(81/64) - \log(5/4) = \log(81/80)$ is the so-called "syntonic comma."

R_2 may be envisioned geometrically as a three-dimensional lattice every point (k, l, m) of which represents the pair $((u, v), q)$, where (u, v) is the sum of k perfect fifths $(7, 4)$, l perfect octaves $(12, 7)$, and m major thirds $(4, 2)$, and q is the sum of k *psychoacoustical* fifths $\log(3/2)$, l psychoacoustical octaves 12, and m psychoacoustical thirds $\log(5/4)$.

R_1 is the so-called *Tonnetz*, a structure apparently first conceived by the eighteenth-century mathematician Leonard Euler.[24] Figure 3.4a is Euler's original diagram (1739, p. 147); Fig. 3.4b is by Alexander J. Ellis.[25] In both figures R_1 is collapsed into two dimensions modulo the cognitive/psychoacoustical octave. In Ellis's diagram pitches are given as transpositions of the pitch associated with middle C in cents (large figures). Note that we have, for example, an E of ca. 386 cents as well as an E of ca. 408 cents.[26]

Although the "Euler relations" are rejected as transmission functions, one need not reject what is *traditionally* referred to as "just intonation," for example, a compact, finite area of R_1 such as the inner rectangle of Ellis's diagram. See Sects. 5.3 and 8.2, for further discussion.

We are quite ready now for the following important definition; review Sect. 2.4, as well as Definitions 3.20 and 3.35.

---

[24] See Cohn (1997, pp. 62–63) for some possible precursors of Euler's idea.

[25] See Helmholtz (1885, p. 463). The diagram is identified by Ellis as "The Duodenarium" with reference only to Gottfried Weber's *Tabelle der Tonartenverwandtschaften* (see Fig. 13.3).

[26] There is also an E of ca. 364 cents positioned near the lower right-hand corner of the figure. Indeed, an imaginary diagonal representing multiples of the syntonic comma (ca. 22 cents) connects infinity of notes E, such that a parallel diagonal exists for every note.

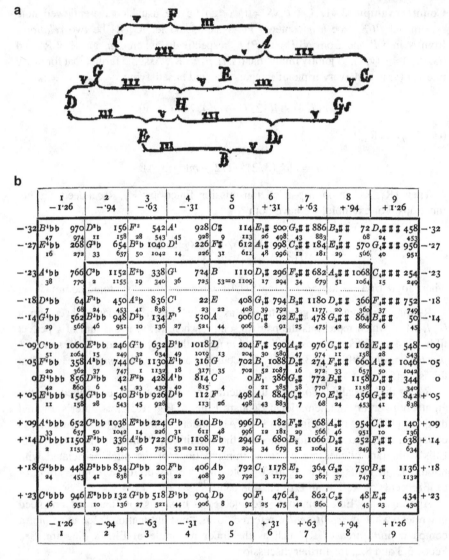

Fig. 3.4　(a) *Tonnetz* by Euler (1739). (b) *Tonnetz* by Ellis. Copyright © 1954 Dover Publications. Reproduced from H. Helmholtz, *On the sensations of tone*, by permission

Definition 3.42. Composite Tone System (with message *MSG*)

Let $\overset{(a,\,b)}{ONS} = \left(NS, \equiv_{(a,\,b)}\right)$ be an octave-endowed note system, let PCS_φ^ψ be a φ-centered PC system, and let $T = \{T_1, T_2\}$ be a pair of transmission functions.

Let *MSG* be a non-empty note sequence. Assume there exists a note $(\underline{s}, \underline{t})$ privileged by the transmitter.

We shall refer to $\overset{(a,b)}{CTS_\varphi^\psi} = \left(\overset{(a,b)}{ONS}, PCS_\varphi^\psi, T, MSG \right)$ as *a composite tone system*

with message MSG, relative, absolute, or *reflexive* (depending on PCS_φ^ψ), if $T_1(\underline{s}, \underline{t}) = \varphi$, $T_2(a, b) = \psi$, and the following condition A is satisfied.

A. Every note $(s, t) \in MSG$ is transmitted as the pitch $T_1(s, t)$.

The condition $T_2(a, b) = \psi$ sets the psychoacoustical octave ψ as the transmitted pitch interval relative to the *cognitive* octave (a, b); the condition $T_1(\underline{s}, \underline{t}) = \varphi$ similarly sets φ as the transmitted *pitch* relative to a transmitter-privileged note $(\underline{s}, \underline{t})$.[27] Condition A requires no special comment.

In connection with the following definition, review Definition 3.32.

Definition 3.43. Note Height; Note-Interval Direction; Note Register

Let $\overset{(a,b)}{CTS_\varphi^\psi} = \left(\overset{(a,b)}{ONS}, PCS_\varphi^\psi, T, MSG \right)$ be a composite tone system. Let (s, t),

$(s', t') \in MSG$ be two notes, and set $(u, v) = (s', t') - (s, t)$.

A. We shall say that (s, t) *is higher* (*lower*) *than* (s', t') if $T_1(s, t)$ is higher (lower) than $T_1(s', t')$.
B. We shall refer to (u, v) as *ascending* (*descending*) if $T_2(u, v)$ is ascending (descending).
C. We shall write $\mathrm{REG}(s, t) = r$ if $\mathrm{REG}(T_1(s, t)) = r$ and shall say that (s, t) *lies in the rth register*.

By Definition 3.42 a transmitted note (s, t) is *exactly* tuned to $T_1(s, t)$. In other words, our "transmission device" is not of any known type, since it is *absolutely accurate*. In Sect. 5.3, we shall be able to relax this intimidating constraint, making pitch transmission more human-friendly.

In connection with the following theorem it should be useful to review Sect. 3.2.

Theorem 3.44. Let $\overset{(a,b)}{CTS_\varphi^\psi} = \left(\overset{(a,b)}{ONS}, PCS_\varphi^\psi, T, MSG \right)$ be a composite tone

system, let $((g_1, h_1), (g_2, h_2))$ be a basis of *NVL*, and set $g_1 h_2 - g_2 h_1 = \pm 1$. Let (u, v) be an interval and set $i_{(u, v)} = \pm(h_2 u - g_2 v)$, $j_{(u, v)} = \mp(h_1 u - g_1 v)$. Finally, set

$$T_2(g_1, h_1) = q_1, \quad T_2(g_2, h_2) = q_2.$$

Then exactly one of the following three mutually exclusive conditions, A, B, or C, holds.

---

[27] $(\underline{s}, \underline{t})$ as a transmitter-privileged *note* is analogous to φ as a transmitter-privileged *pitch*. See Definition 3.35 and discussion.

A. $q_2 = 0$, and $T_2(u, v) = \frac{\psi}{i_{(a, b)}} \cdot i_{(u, v)}$.

B. $q_1 = 0$, and $T_2(u, v) = \frac{\psi}{j_{(a, b)}} \cdot j_{(u, v)}$.

C. $q_1 \neq 0 \neq q_2$, and $T_2(u, v) = i_{(u, v)} \cdot q_1 + j_{(u, v)} \cdot q_2$.

Proof. By Theorems 3.14 and 3.38 we have

$$T_2(u, v) = i_{(u, v)} \cdot q_1 + j_{(u, v)} \cdot q_2.$$

In particular,

$$T_2(a, b) = i_{(a, b)} \cdot q_1 + j_{(a, b)} \cdot q_2 = \psi \neq 0,$$

implying that if $q_2 = 0$ then $i_{(a, b)}, q_1 \neq 0$ and Condition A holds; vice versa, if $q_1 = 0$ then $j_{(a, b)}, q_2 \neq 0$ and Condition B holds. Otherwise, Condition C holds. Q.E.D.

Definition 3.45. Oriented Type-*t* System; Naturally Oriented System; Usual Composite Tone System

Let $\overset{(a, b)}{CTS_\varphi^\psi}$ be a composite tone system, and let $((g_1, h_1), (g_2, h_2))$ be a basis of *NVL*.

A. We shall refer to $\overset{(a, b)}{CTS_\varphi^\psi}$ as *a type-t system oriented to* $(g_1, h_1; g_2, h_2)$, $t = 1, 2, 3$, if Condition 3.44 A, B, C, respectively holds.

B. We shall refer to a type-*t* system as *naturally oriented* if $(g_1, h_1; g_2, h_2) = (1, 0; 0, 1)$.

C. We shall refer to a naturally oriented type-1 system satisfying $(a, b) = (12, 7)$, $\psi = 12$, as *usual* and shall write $\overset{(12, 7)}{CTS_\varphi^{12}} = CTS_\varphi$.

Note in connection with the following important theorem that a note-interval transmission function cannot be surjective since the infinity of note intervals is countable, whereas the infinity of pitch intervals is uncountable. Also, a subset $\mathbb{R}'$ of $\mathbb{R}$ is said to be "dense" if for every $x, y \in \mathbb{R}'$, $x < y$, there exists a $z \in \mathbb{R}'$ such that $x < z < y$. For example, the set $\mathbb{Q}$ of rationals is a dense subset of $\mathbb{R}$.

Theorem 3.46. Let $\overset{(a, b)}{CTS_\varphi^\psi} = \left(\overset{(a, b)}{ONS}, PCS_\varphi^\psi, T, MSG \right)$ be a type-3 system oriented to $(g_1, h_1; g_2, h_2)$. Set $q_1 = T_2(g_1, h_1)$, $q_2 = T_2(g_2, h_2)$, $x = q_1/q_2$.

Then the following three conditions, A, B, and C, are all equivalent.

A. x is irrational.
B. The range of T_2 is a dense subset of $\mathbb{R}$.
C. T_2 is injective.

Proof. Set $g_1 h_2 - g_2 h_1 = \pm 1$. By Theorem 3.44 we can write

$$T_2(u, v)/q_2 = ix + j,$$

where $i = i_{(u,\ v)} = \pm(h_2 u - g_2 v)$, $j = j_{(u,\ v)} = \mp(h_1 u - g_1 v)$. If x is irrational together with Theorem 3.14 it easily follows that T_2 is injective. Conversely, if by contradiction x is rational there exist integers $i, j \neq 0$ satisfying $ix + j = 0$; together with Theorem 3.14 it follows that T_2 is not injective. Thus Conditions A and C are equivalent. We will now show that Conditions A and B are also equivalent.

It easily follows that if the range of T_2 is a dense subset of $\mathbb{R}$ then x is irrational, for if by contradiction $x = p/q$ is rational, $\gcd(p, q) = 1$, $ix + j > 0$ can be no smaller than $|1/q|$. Suppose that x is irrational, fix a natural n, and consider the $n + 1$ strictly positive irrationals $x_m = m|x| - \lfloor m|x| \rfloor$,[28] all distinct, $m = 1, 2, \ldots, n + 1$. Every x_m lies strictly between 0 and 1. But since the number of intervals $(0, 1/n)$, $(1/n, 2/n)$, $\ldots$, $((n - 1)/n, 1)$ is exactly n, it follows from the so-called Pigeonhole Principle that two distinct irrationals x_m lie within one and the same of these n intervals. Equivalently, there exist non-zero integers i and j such that $ix + j > 0$ is smaller than $1/n$. Since n can be as large as one may wish $ix + j > 0$ can be as small as one may wish. Q.E.D.

We shall refer henceforth to a type-3 system satisfying one of the three equivalent conditions of Theorem 3.46 as *dense*. A Pythagorean system (Example 3.40B) is dense, as is the system known as "quarter-comma meantone temperament" (see Counterexample 5.7).

References

Agmon, E. (1989). A mathematical model of the diatonic system. *Journal of Music Theory, 33*(1), 1–25.

ANSI S1.1. (1994). *American National Standard Acoustical Terminology*. New York: American National Standards Institute.

ASA. (1960). *Acoustical terminology SI, 1–1960*. New York: American Standards Association.

Bourbaki, N. (1980). *Elements of mathematics: Algebra I*. Berlin: Springer.

Cohn, R. (1997). Neo-Riemannian operations, parsimonious trichords, and their *Tonnetz* representations. *Journal of Music Theory, 41*(1), 1–66.

Darwin, C. J. (2005). Pitch and auditory grouping. In C. J. Plack et al. (Eds.), *Pitch: Neural coding and perception* (pp. 278–305). New York: Springer.

de Cheveigné, A. (2005). Pitch perception models. In C. J. Plack et al. (Eds.), *Pitch: Neural coding and perception* (pp. 169–233). New York: Springer.

Euler, L. (1739). *Tentamen novae theoriae musicae*. St. Petersburg Academy. 1926. Reprint in *Leonhardi Euleri opera omniae* (series 3, Vol. 1). Leipzig: Teubner.

Hardy, G., & Wright, E. (1938). *An introduction to the theory of numbers*. Oxford: Clarendon Press.

---

[28] For a real number x the notation $\lfloor x \rfloor$ signifies *the integral part of x*, the largest integer smaller than or equal to x.

Helmholtz, H. (1885). *On the sensations of tone* (A. J. Ellis, Trans. & Rev.). 1954. Reprint, New York: Dover.

Hook, J. (2007). Cross-type transformations and the path consistency condition. *Music Theory Spectrum, 29*(1), 1–39. 2007. Reprint, *MTS 29*(2).

Kolman, O. (2004). Transfer principles for generalized interval systems. *Perspectives of New Music, 42*(1), 150–189.

Lewin, D. (1987). *Generalized musical intervals and transformations.* New Haven: Yale University Press. 2007. Reprint, Oxford: Oxford University Press.

Nelken, I., & Ahissar, M. (2006). High-level and low-level processing in the auditory system: The role of primary auditory cortex. In P. Divenyi et al. (Eds.), *Dynamics of speech production and perception* (pp. 343–354). Amsterdam: IOS Press.

Schnupp, J., Nelken, I., & King, A. (2011). *Auditory neuroscience: Making sense of sound.* Cambridge: MIT Press.

Shamma, S., & Klein, D. (2000). The case of the missing pitch templates: How harmonic templates emerge in the early auditory system. *Journal of the Acoustical Society of America, 107*(5), 2631–2644.

Shannon, C. (1948). A mathematical theory of communication. *Bell System Technical Journal, 27* (3–4), 379–423, 623–656.

Chapter 4
The Conventional Nomenclatures for Notes and Intervals

Abstract If the cognitive octave (a, b) is set to $(12, 7)$ and privileged status is bestowed upon the "natural core"—the set of seven notes $(0, 0)$, $(2, 1)$, $(4, 2)$, $(5, 3)$, $(7, 4)$, $(9, 5)$, and $(11, 6)$—then the conventional nomenclature for notes (for example, "E double-flat") may be accounted for. Similarly, if privileged status is bestowed upon the "usual primary intervals"—the set of eleven note intervals $(0, 0)$, $(1, 1)$, $(2, 1)$, $(3, 2)$, $(4, 2)$, $(5, 3)$, $(7, 4)$, $(8, 5)$, $(9, 5)$, $(10, 6)$, and $(11, 6)$—then the conventional nomenclature for note intervals (for example, "descending triply-augmented fifth"), may be accounted for (Sect. 4.1). Staff-notational idiosyncrasies with regard to relative note height, interval direction, and register, are noted (Sect. 4.2).

We have barely begun our journey and have already posited a fairly complex object consisting of a note system, a pitch-communication system, a pair of transmission functions, and a message of notes. Are we on the right track? And if so, what should be our next move?

In the present chapter we test the theory thus far under certain tentative assumptions. In particular, we show that if certain sets of notes and intervals are privileged, then the theory of *usual* composite tone systems (Definition 3.45) successfully accounts for the conventional nomenclatures for notes and intervals. However tentative, this is an encouraging result; moreover, a property of the privileged notes and intervals posited, namely, that they may be arranged as a connected segment of the "line of fifths," shall be suggestive of our next move. Since a usual composite tone system is essentially the usual note system (Definition 3.11) under 12-tone ET, to simplify discussion and notation only the note-systemic component of a usual composite tone system shall be explicitly posited throughout this chapter.

To avoid misunderstanding, the present chapter is essentially an out-of-sequence exercise. A number of apparently *ad hoc* assumptions are introduced; these, and in particular $(a, b) = (12, 7)$, shall be obtained as results by the end of Part I.

4.1   The Conventional Nomenclatures for Notes and Intervals

Our goal in the present section is to show that given a usual octave-endowed note system, under certain conditions a note (s, t) or interval (u, v) may be uniquely paired with a conceivable, conventional note or interval, for example, $\flat(E_{-2})$ (E in register minus 2, once flatted), descending augmented sixth, and so forth[1]; vice versa, a conceivable conventional note or interval may be uniquely paired with a note (s, t) or interval (u, v).

To achieve our goal it should be necessary to stretch the meaning of "*conceivable* conventional note" to include notes "chromatically altered" by any number of sharps or flats, and placed in any register, contrary to auditory limitations. We shall similarly stretch the meaning of "conceivable conventional note interval."

Definition 4.1. Natural Core

Let $ONS = \overset{(12,\,7)}{ONS} = (NS, \equiv)$ be the usual octave-endowed note system, $NS = (N, NVL, \text{NI})$.

We shall refer to a set *CORE* of notes (w, x) as *the natural core* if

$$CORE = \{(0,0), (2,1), (4,2), (5,3), (7,4), (9,5), (11,6)\}.$$

The natural core may readily be interpreted as the set of conventional notes C, D,..., B. The natural core is central to conventional note nomenclature for the following reason. A note (s, t) may be represented as a *natural* note (w, x), "chromatically altered" by a number i of "sharps" $(1, 0)$ and transposed by a number j of octaves $(12, 7)$. Moreover, the representation of (s, t) as $((w, x), i, j)$, is unique.

Proposition 4.2. Let *ONS* be the usual octave-endowed note system and let *CORE* be the natural core. Let (s, t) be a note.

Then there exists a unique core element (w, x) and unique integers i and j such that

$$(s, t) = (w, x) + ((i, 0) \oplus j(12, 7)). \tag{4.1}$$

Proof. Since for every $x = 0, 1, \ldots, 6$ there exists a unique w such that $(w, x) \in CORE$, for every note (s, t) there exists a unique $(w, x) \in CORE$ and a unique integer j such that $t = x + 7j$.

Set $s = w + i + 12j$ for some integer i; then i is unique. Moreover, $(s, t) = (w, x) + ((i, 0) \oplus j(12, 7))$. Q.E.D.

---

[1] Henceforth it should be convenient to modify conventional letter notation by writing an accidental *before* a register-modified letter name, the latter expression sometimes set in parentheses. Moreover, for multiple sharps and flats we shall use an exponent-like notation. See Table 4.1 and discussion. The 0th register is the register of (0, 0) or "middle C."

By Proposition 4.2 Eq. (4.1) defines a function from N into $CORE \times \mathbb{Z} \times \mathbb{Z}$.

Proposition 4.3. Let ONS be the usual octave-endowed note system and let $CORE$ be the natural core. Let NAME be the function from N into $CORE \times \mathbb{Z} \times \mathbb{Z}$ defined by Eq. (4.1).

Then NAME is a bijection.

Proof. It is easily seen that for every triple $((w, x), i, j)$ there exists a note (s, t) satisfying Eq. (4.1) and therefore NAME is surjective.

Let (s, t), (s', t') be a pair of notes satisfying

$$\text{NAME}(s', t') = ((w, x), i, j) \doteq \text{NAME}(s, t).$$

Then $(s', t') = (w, x) + ((i, 0) \oplus j(12, 7)) = (s, t)$ and therefore NAME is injective. Q.E.D.

Examples of the bijection NAME are given in Table 4.1 (first two columns). The third column provides the conventional equivalent, under the convention that the 0th register is the "one-line" register (often counted as 4th). Note that we follow a letter-name convention by which notes are assumed by default to satisfy $i = j = 0$, that is, to be "natural" (unaltered chromatically) and to lie in the 0th register; for example, $C = \natural(C_0)$

The translation of $\text{NAME}(s, t)$ into a conventional note name is straightforward. Clearly, $(w, x) = (0, 0), (2, 1), \ldots, (11, 6)$ is equivalent to a letter name $C, D, \ldots, B$, and i is the number of sharps (if strictly positive) or flats (if strictly negative). The register of a note (s, t) is *the integral part* of $s/12$, that is:

$$\text{REG}(s, t) = \lfloor s/12 \rfloor.$$

We now turn to conventional interval nomenclature. Compare the following definition with Definition 4.1.

Definition 4.4. Usual Primary Intervals

Let ONS be the usual octave-endowed note system.

We shall refer to a set $RVL = P \cup M \cup m$ of intervals as *the usual primary intervals* if

$$P = \{(0,0), (5,3), (7,4)\},$$
$$M = \{(2,1), (4,2), (9,5), (11,6)\},$$
$$m = \{(1,1), (3,2), (8,5), (10,6)\}.$$

P may readily be interpreted as the set of "perfect" note intervals P1, P4, and P5; similarly, M is the set of "major" intervals M2, M3, M6, and M7, and m is the set of "minor" intervals m2, m3, m6, and m7. The usual set of primary intervals $RVL = P \cup M \cup m$ is central to conventional interval nomenclature for the following reason. An interval (u, v) may be represented as a usual primary interval (y, z), "chromatically altered" by a number i of "augmented primes" $(1, 0)$ and

.

Table 4.1 Examples of the bijection NAME (first two columns); the third column provides the conventional equivalent

(s, t)	NAME(s, t)	Conventional equivalent
$(0, 0)$	$((0, 0), 0, 0)$	$\natural(C_0) = C$ ("middle C")
$(3, 1)$	$((2, 1), 1, 0)$	$\sharp(D_0) = D\sharp$
$(3, 2)$	$((4, 2), -1, 0)$	$\flat(E_0) = E\flat$
$(17, 10)$	$((5, 3), 0, 1)$	$\natural(F_1) = F_1$
$(-5, -3)$	$((7, 4), 0, -1)$	$\natural(G_{-1}) = G_{-1}$
$(19, 12)$	$((9, 5), -2, 1)$	$\flat^2(A_1) = \flat\flat(A_1) = (A_1)\flat\flat$
$(-10, -8)$	$((11, 6), 3, -2)$	$\sharp^3(B_{-1})$

"compounded" by a number j of octaves $(12, 7)$. Moreover, subject to certain constraints on the pair $((y, z), i)$ the representation $((y, z), i, j)$ is unique.

In what follows it should be useful to partition NVL into two subsets: the set of all intervals (u, v) satisfying $v \geq 0$ and the set of all intervals (u, v) satisfying $v \leq -1$.

Theorem 4.5. Let ONS be the usual octave-endowed note system and let RVL be the usual set of primary intervals. Let NVL^+ (NVL^-) be the set of all intervals (u, v) satisfying $v \geq 0$ ($v \leq -1$) and let $\mathbb{Z}^+$ ($\mathbb{Z}^-$) be the set of all non-negative (strictly negative) integers.

Then there exist bijections NAME$^{\pm} : NVL^{\pm} \to RVL \times \mathbb{Z} \times \mathbb{Z}^{\pm}$, where NAME$^+$ is defined by the relation

$$(u, v) = (y, z) \oplus (i, 0) \oplus j(12, 7), \tag{4.2}$$

subject to the condition that $(y, z) \in m$ implies that $i \leq 0$ and $(y, z) \in M$ implies that $i \geq 0$, and NAME$^-$ is defined by the relation

$$\text{NAME}^-(u, v) = -\text{NAME}^+(-u, -v).$$

To prove the theorem we shall first prove one lemma and state another. Compare the following lemma with Proposition 4.2.

Lemma 4.6. Let ONS be the usual octave-endowed note system and let RVL be the usual set of primary intervals. Let (u, v) be an interval satisfying $v \geq 0$.

Subject to the condition that $(y, z) \in m$ implies that $i \leq 0$ and $(y, z) \in M$ implies that $i \geq 0$, there exists a unique $(y, z) \in RVL$ and unique integers i and $j \geq 0$ such that Eq. (4.2) is satisfied.

Proof. For every $z = 0, 1, \ldots, 6$ there exists a y such that $(y, z) \in RVL$. Therefore, for every note interval (u, v) there exists a $(y, z) \in RVL$ and a unique integer $j \geq 0$ such that $v = z + 7j$.

If $z = 0, 3, 4$ $(y, z) \in P$ is unique, and there exists a unique i satisfying the equation $u = y + i + 12j$.

If $z = 1, 2, 5, 6$ there exists a pair $(y^-, z) \in m$, $(y^+, z) \in M$, $y^+ = y^- + 1$. Set $u = y^{\pm} + i^{\pm} + 12j$ for some integer $i^{\pm}$, $i^- \leq 0$, $i^+ \geq 0$. If $i^{\pm} = 0$ then either $u = y^+ + 12j$ and $u \neq y^- + 12j$, or $u = y^- + 12j$ and $u \neq y^+ + 12j$. Otherwise, it can easily be seen that either $u = y^+ + i^+ + 12j$ such that there exists no i^- satisfying $u = y^- + i^- + 12j$, or $u = y^- + i^- + 12j$ such that there exists no i^+ satisfying $u = y^+ + i^+ + 12j$. Q.E.D.

*Lemma 4.7. Let *ONS* be the usual octave-endowed note system and let *RVL* be the usual set of primary intervals. Let $(y, z) \neq (0, 0)$ be a member of *RVL*.
   Then $(12 - y, 7 - z) \in RVL$.

Proof of the theorem. By Lemma 4.6 there exists a function $\text{NAME}^+ : NVL^+ \rightarrow RVL \times \mathbb{Z} \times \mathbb{Z}^+$ defined by Eq. (4.2) and subject to the condition that $(y, z) \in m$ implies that $i \leq 0$ and $(y, z) \in M$ implies that $i \geq 0$.
   Let (u, v) be an interval satisfying $v \leq -1$, and write

$$\text{NAME}^+(-u, \ -v) = ((y, z), i, j).$$

   Then $(u, v) = (-y, \ -z) \oplus (-i, 0) \oplus - j(12, 7)$.
   If $(y, z) = (0, 0)$ we have $- j \leq -1$. Otherwise, we have

$$(u, v) = (12 - y, 7 - z) \oplus (-i, 0) \oplus -(j + 1)(12, 7),$$

where $(12 - y, 7 - z) \in RVL$ (Lemma 4.7), and $-(j + 1) \leq -1$. Thus, for every $(u, v) \in NVL^-$ we can write $\text{NAME}^-(u, v) = -\text{NAME}^+(-u, -v)$, where NAME^- is a function $NVL^- \rightarrow RVL \times \mathbb{Z} \times \mathbb{Z}^-$. It can easily be seen that $\text{NAME}^\pm$ are bijections. Q.E.D.

   Examples of the bijections $\text{NAME}^\pm$ are given in Table 4.2 (first two columns), using the relation $\text{NAME}^-(u, v) = -\text{NAME}^+(-u, -v)$. The third column provides the conventional equivalent.
   The translation of $\text{NAME}^+(u, v)$ (if v is non-negative) or $- \text{NAME}^+(-u, -v)$ (if v is strictly negative) into a conventional interval name is straightforward. Clearly, i is the number of times an interval is "augmented" (if strictly positive) or "diminished" (if strictly negative). Since, if $(y, z) \notin P$, $i \leq 0$ implies that $(y, z) \in m$ and $i \geq 0$ implies that $(y, z) \in M$, if $i \neq 0$ it suffices to refer to an interval "generically" as $(|v| + 1)$th, for example, "doubly augmented *tenth*" (rather than "doubly augmented *major* tenth"). Finally, an interval is "ascending" or "descending" if u is strictly positive or negative.
   The theory of conventional nomenclature just completed makes it possible to translate basic intuitions concerning notes and intervals into algebraic relations as defined in Sect. 3.1, and vice versa. Table 4.3 illustrates.

4.2   Staff Notation and Its Idiosyncrasies

The idiosyncrasies of staff notation may best be appreciated by comparing the following definition with Definition 3.43.

Table 4.2 Examples of the bijections NAME$^{\pm}$ (first two columns); the third column provides the conventional equivalent

(u, v)	$\pm$NAME$^{+}(\pm u, \pm v)$	Conventional equivalent
$(-11, -7)$	$-((0, 0), -1, 1)$	Diminished descending octave
$(21, 11)$	$((7, 4), 2, 1)$	Doubly augmented ascending 12th
$(-1, -2)$	$-((3, 2), -2, 0)$	Doubly diminished descending 3rd
$(0, -1)$	$-((1, 1), -1, 0)$	Diminished 2nd
$(1, 0)$	$((0, 0), 1, 0)$	Augmented prime (ascending)
$(-1, 0)$	$((0, 0), -1, 0)$	Diminished prime (descending)
$(-1, 2)$	$((3, 2), -4, 0)$	Quadruply diminished descending 3rd
$(1, -3)$	$-((5, 3), -6, 0)$	Sextuply diminished ascending 4th

Table 4.3 Musical intuitions as algebraic expressions

Intuition	Equivalent algebraic expression
M3 combined with m3 yields P5	$(4, 2) \oplus (3, 2) = (7, 4)$
Two M3s yield A5	$2 \cdot (4, 2) = (8, 4)$
The octave complement of A5 is d4	$(12, 7) \oplus - (8, 4) = (4, 3)$
M3, combined with a descending octave, is a descending m6	$(4, 2) \oplus (-12, -7) = (-8, -5)$
$\flat(E_1)$ and $\flat\flat(E_{-1})$ are octave related	$(14, 9) \equiv (-10, -5)$
The interval from ♯B to $\flat(F_{-1})$ is a triply-augmented descending eleventh	$(-8, -4) - (12, 6) = (-20, -10)$
$\flat(D_{-1})$ transposed up A13 yields B	$(-11, -6) + (22, 12) = (11, 6)$

Definition 4.8. Staff-Note Height; Staff Note-Interval Direction; Staff-Note Register

Let *ONS* be the usual octave-endowed note system. Let (s, t), (s', t') be two notes, and set $(u, v) = (s', t') - (s, t)$.

A. We shall say that (s, t) *is staff higher (lower) than* (s', t') if $t > t'$ $(t < t')$.
B. We shall refer to (u, v) as *staff ascending (descending)* if v is strictly positive (negative).
C. We shall write *REG/STAFF*$(s, t) = r$ if $r = \lfloor t/7 \rfloor$ (the *integral part* of t divided by 7) and shall say that (s, t) *lies in the rth staff register*.

Concerning A, note that the staff *position* of a note (s, t) is dependent only on t, such that for every $s, s', t > t'$ implies that (s, t) lies "higher" on the staff than (s', t'). It follows that in conjunction with chromatic alteration a higher note in the sense of Definition 3.43 may not be "higher" in terms of staff position, and vice versa. For example, $(0, -1)$ is higher than $(-1, 0)$ by Definition 3.43; yet on the staff, it is the latter note that is higher (Fig. 4.1).

Concerning B, note that by Definition 3.43 the interval from $(0, -1)$ to $(-1, 0)$ is descending, whereas in terms of staff position the interval is ascending (Fig. 4.1). Similarly, the two intervals depicted in Fig. 4.2 are ascending and descending,

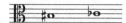

Fig. 4.1 The notes (0, −1) and (−1, 0) in conventional staff notation

Fig. 4.2 A quadruply diminished ascending third and a sextuply diminished descending fourth in conventional staff notation

respectively, in terms of staff position; yet by Definition 3.43 they are descending and ascending (cf. the last two rows of Table 4.2). Thus 4.8B is consistent with 4.8A.

Finally, Condition 4.8C is also consistent with 4.8A. For example, the staff-notational registers of the notes (0, −1) and (−1, 0) (cf. Fig. 4.1) are −1 and 0, respectively. This is unlike Definition 3.43, according to which the registers are 0 and −1, respectively.

In addition to assuming the usual composite tone system, $(a, b) = (12, 7)$, the results obtained in this chapter (in particular Proposition 4.3 and Theorem 4.5), are heavily dependent on privileging a set of notes and a set of intervals, namely, the natural core and the usual set of primary intervals. It is not difficult to see that both sets have the property that they may be ordered "by fifth." We have:

$$CORE = F, \ C, \ G, \ D, \ A, \ E, \ B,$$
$$RVL = m2, \ m6, \ m3, \ m7, \ P4, \ P1, \ P5, \ M2, \ M6, \ M3, \ M7.$$

This strongly suggests that our system should include a fifth-like element.

Chapter 5
Communicating the Primary Intervals

Abstract A "semi-efficient" tone system consists of a composite tone system and a set of "primary" intervals generated by a privileged note interval (c, d), the "quintic element" (Sect. 5.1). In such a system, the note-interval transmission function, restricted to the primary intervals, is assumed to be one-to-one. A semi-efficient system is *efficient* if, in addition, the difference between the pitch images of two primary intervals (under the transmission function) is not arbitrarily small. It is proven that efficient tone systems are not type-3 systems (of which the complete "Pythagorean" system is a familiar example); on the other hand, equal-tempered systems, which are special types of naturally oriented type-1 or 2 tone systems, are efficient. An efficient tone system is "coherent" if a certain algorithm, by which a primary interval may easily be computed from its transmitted image, exists (Sect. 5.2). It is proven that coherent tone systems satisfy $cb - ad = \pm 1$, where (a, b) is the cognitive octave and (c, d) is the quintic element. Finally (Sect. 5.3), since efficient tone systems are equal tempered and not dense, one may relax the unrealistic assumption of absolutely accurate note transmission. By the theory of *categorical* equal temperament deviations from strict ET of up to one-half of one equal-tempered increment are allowed, in either direction.

In Chap. 3 we have studied pitch communication and note transmission. In particular, we have constructed a "φ-centered" pitch-communication system where pitches p are received as transmitted (if the system is reflexive or absolute) or translated by $-\varphi$ (if the system is relative), and have arrived at certain important conclusions concerning the relation of the *message* (a sequence of notes), to the sequence of pitches by which it is transmitted. In terms of satisfying the Communication Principle, however, we are still in the dark. *For the transmission functions from notes (note intervals) to pitches (pitch intervals) are not one-to-one.* Under such conditions, how can the receiver correctly map a received pitch into a message element?

A partial answer is given over the course of two consecutive chapters (the answer is completed in Part II). In the present chapter a privileged set of note *intervals*, the set of so-called "primary intervals," is assumed to have the property that the transmission function for intervals, restricted to this set, *is* one-to-one. In other words, the primary intervals are communicable. The communicability of the primary intervals will play an important role in Chap. 6, where the problem of note *reception* is first addressed.

5.1 Efficient Tone Systems

Definition 5.1. Primary Intervals; Quintic Element

Let $\overset{(a,\,b)}{ONS}$ be an octave-endowed note system, and let $(c,\,d)$ be an interval. Let $K = \{0, \pm 1, \ldots, \pm m\}$ for some non-negative m, or $K = \mathbb{Z}$.

We shall refer to $(c,\,d)$ as *a quintic element* and to a set of intervals

$$\overset{(c,\,d)}{RVL} = \{(y_k, z_k) = (y, z)_k \equiv_{(a,\,b)} k(c,\,d) \,|\, k \in K\}$$

as *a set of primary intervals*, if $(c,\,d) \in \overset{(c,\,d)}{RVL}$ such that the following condition A is satisfied for all $k, k' \in K$.

A. $k \neq k'$ implies that $(y, z)_k \not\equiv_{(a,\,b)} (y, z)_{k'}$.

*Proposition 5.2. Let $\overset{(c,\,d)}{RVL}$ be a set of primary intervals $(y, z)_k$ of cardinality M, $k \in K$.

If $K = \mathbb{Z}$ then $M = \infty$; otherwise $M = 2m + 1$ such that $M = 1$ if, and only if, $(c,\,d) \equiv_{(a,\,b)} (0,\ 0)$.

Example 5.3. Let ONS be the usual octave-endowed note system.

Then, for $K = \{0, \pm 1, \ldots, \pm m\}$ or $K = \mathbb{Z}$, $\overset{(7,\,4)}{RVL}$ is a set of primary intervals $(y, z)_k$, if $(7, 4) \in \overset{(7,\,4)}{RVL}$. In particular, if $m = 5$ and $0 \leq y_k \leq 11$, $\overset{(7,\,4)}{RVL} = RVL$ is the usual set of eleven primary intervals P1, m2, M2, m3, M3, P4, P5, m6, M6, m7, and M7 (Definition 4.4). We have $(y, z)_0 = (0, 0) = P1$; moreover,

$$\begin{aligned}
(y, z)_1 &= (7, 4) = P5, & (y, z)_{-1} &= (5, 3) = P4; \\
(y, z)_2 &= (2, 1) = M2, & (y, z)_{-2} &= (10, 6) = m7; \\
(y, z)_3 &= (9, 5) = M6, & (y, z)_{-3} &= (3, 2) = m3; \\
(y, z)_4 &= (4, 2) = M3, & (y, z)_{-4} &= (8, 5) = m6; \\
(y, z)_5 &= (11, 6) = M7, & (y, z)_{-5} &= (1, 1) = m2.
\end{aligned}$$

In connection with the following definition, review Definition 3.45. Note the use of the Maximalist Principle. We write $\overset{(c,\,d)}{RVL}/oct$ for the set of all intervals octave equivalent to a member of $\overset{(c,\,d)}{RVL}$, that is, the set of all intervals $(u, v) \equiv_{(a,\,b)} (y, z)$, $(y, z) \in \overset{(c,\,d)}{RVL}$.

Definition 5.4. Semi-efficient Tone System (of order M)

Let $\overset{(a,\,b)}{CTS^{\psi}_{\varphi}}$ be a type-t system oriented to $(g_1, h_1; g_2, h_2)$, $t = 1$, 2, 3, and let $\overset{(c,\,d)}{RVL}$

be a set of primary intervals of cardinality $M \geq 3$. Let (u, v), $(u', v') \in \overset{(c,\,d)}{RVL}/oct$
and set

$$\delta = |T_2(u, v) - T_2(u', v')|.$$

We shall refer to $\overset{(a,\,b;\,c,\,d)}{FTS^{\psi}_{\varphi}} = \left(\overset{(a,\,b)}{CTS^{\psi}_{\varphi}}, \overset{(c,\,d)}{RVL} \right)$ as *a semi-efficient tone system (of*

type t and order M, oriented to $(g_1, h_1; g_2, h_2)$) if subject to the following condition
A M is as large as possible.

A. $\delta = 0$ implies that $(u, v) = (u', v')$.

Depending on the composite tone system $\overset{(a,\,b)}{CTS^{\psi}_{\varphi}}$ (Definition 3.42), we shall refer
to a semi-efficient tone system $\overset{(a,\,b;\,c,\,d)}{FTS^{\psi}_{\varphi}}$ as *relative, absolute,* or *reflexive*.

Example 5.5. Consider a usual composite tone system CTS_{φ} (Definition 3.45)
together with the usual set RVL of primary intervals P1, m2,..., M7.
   Then $(CTS_{\varphi},\ RVL)$ is a naturally oriented semi-efficient tone system of type 1 and
order 11. Condition 5.4A is satisfied because every two distinct members (y, z) and
(y', z') of RVL satisfy $y' \not\equiv y \pmod{12}$. Moreover, $M = 11$ is maximal since, if
$M > 11$, $(y, z)_6$ and $(y, z)_{-6}$ satisfy $y_6 = y_{-6} = 6$, contradicting 5.4A.

   Condition 5.4A is a constraint on the set of primary intervals such that, for every
pair (u, v) and (u', v') of intervals octave equivalent to some primary intervals (y, z)
and (y', z'), respectively, if the transmitted pitch interval relative to (u, v) is identical
to the transmitted pitch interval relative to (u', v'), (u, v) and (u', v') are themselves
identical.
   The significance of Condition 5.4A for the successful communication of
intervals is transparent. Since the note-interval transmission function T_2 is not
one-to-one the receiver cannot associate $T_2(u, v)$, the transmitted pitch interval
relative to (u, v), uniquely, with (u, v). This is not the case, however, if (u, v) is
assumed to be octave related to some *primary* interval (y, z). In other words,
although T_2 is not one-to-one, its *restriction* to the set $\overset{(c,\,d)}{RVL}/oct$ *is* one-to-one.
Condition 5.4A is thus an (indirect) expression of the Communication Principle.[1]

---

[1] "Indirect," because it concerns an *auxiliary* communication system for (privileged) intervals. The
present theory of "efficient primary intervals" is not unrelated to Agmon's (1986, 1989) theory of
"efficient diatonic intervals." A comparison of the two theories would be a valuable study in
descriptive and, particularly, explanatory adequacy.

We are finally ready for the following definition. Note that the Maximalist Principle is used once again. Recall that $\overset{(c,\,d)}{RVL}/oct$ is the set of all intervals octave equivalent to a member of $\overset{(c,\,d)}{RVL}$, that is, the set of all intervals $(u, v) \equiv_{(a,\,b)}(y, z)$, $(y, z) \in \overset{(c,\,d)}{RVL}$.

Definition 5.6.   Efficient Tone System

Let $\overset{(a,\,b;\,c,\,d)}{FTS_{\varphi}^{\psi}}/t = \left(\overset{(a,\,b)}{CTS_{\varphi}^{\psi}}, \overset{(c,\,d)}{RVL} \right)$ be a semi-efficient tone system of type t and

order M_t, oriented to $(g_1, h_1; g_2, h_2)$. Let $(u, v), (u', v') \in \overset{(c,\,d)}{RVL}/oct$ and set

$$\delta = |T_2(u, v) - T_2(u', v')|.$$

We shall refer to $\overset{(a,\,b;\,c,\,d)}{FTS_{\varphi}^{\psi}}/t$ as *efficient* if subject to the following condition A a semi-efficient tone system $\overset{(a,\,b;\,c,\,d)}{FTS_{\varphi}^{\psi}}/t'$ of type t' and order $M_{t'} > M_t$, also oriented to $(g_1, h_1; g_2, h_2)$, does not exist.

A. $\delta \neq 0$ is not arbitrarily small.

Counterexample 5.7.   Consider the two semi-efficient tone systems $\overset{(12,\,7;\,7,\,4)}{FTS_{\varphi}^{12}}$ of type 3 and order infinity, both oriented to $(12, 7; 7, 4)$, respectively defined by the following two relations A and B, systems familiar as Pythagorean intonation and "quarter-comma meantone temperament."[2]

A. $T_2(7, 4) = \log(3/2)$.
B. $T_2(7, 4) = \log\left(\sqrt[4]{80}/2\right)$.

Although $\overset{(7,\,4)}{RVL}$ contains an infinite number of elements (and thus M is as large as possible), these systems are dense such that $\overset{(7,\,4)}{RVL}/oct = NVL$, and therefore they are not efficient (Condition 5.6A is contradicted).

Condition 5.6A states that *even if there exist devices capable of transmitting notes with absolute accuracy* (as we have assumed thus far—cf. Definition 3.42 and discussion), and even if the transmitted signal accrues no distortions by the time it reaches the receiver, the JND ("just-noticeable difference") for the primary

---

[2] Cf. Example 3.40B. Since the psychoacoustical octave ψ is set to twelve the logarithm base is the twelfth root of 2.

intervals cannot be arbitrarily small.[3] Condition 5.6A is thus another expression of the Communication Principle.

In connection with the following theorem recall that $\lfloor x \rfloor$ signifies *the integral part of* x (a real number), the largest integer smaller than or equal to x.

Theorem 5.8. Let $FTS_\varphi^\psi \overset{(a,\, b;\, c,\, d)}{=} \left(CTS_\varphi^\psi, \overset{(c,\, d)}{RVL} \right)$ be a semi-efficient tone system of

order M oriented to $(g_1, h_1; g_2, h_2)$, $g_1 h_2 - g_2 h_1 = \pm 1$, $\overset{(c,\, d)}{RVL}$ is a set $(y, z)_k$ of primary intervals. Set $ah_2 - bg_2 = \pm A$, $bg_1 - ah_1 = \pm B$, $ch_2 - dg_2 = \pm C$, $dg_1 - ch_1 = \pm D$.

If $\overset{(a,\, b;\, c,\, d)}{FTS_\varphi^\psi}$ is efficient, it is a type-1 (type-2) system satisfying $|A| \geq 3$, $\gcd(A, C) = 1$ ($|B| \geq 3$, $\gcd(B, D) = 1$), such that $M = 2m + 1$ satisfies

$$m = \left\lfloor \frac{|A| - 1}{2} \right\rfloor \geq \left\lfloor \frac{|B| - 1}{2} \right\rfloor \quad \left(m = \left\lfloor \frac{|B| - 1}{2} \right\rfloor \geq \left\lfloor \frac{|A| - 1}{2} \right\rfloor \right).$$

Moreover, if $\overset{(a,\, b)}{CTS_\varphi^\psi}$ is a naturally oriented composite tone system of type 1 (type 2) and $\overset{(c,\, d)}{RVL}$ is a set of intervals $(y, z)_k \equiv_{(a,\, b)} k(c, d)$, $k = 0, \pm 1, \ldots, \pm m$, then, if $(c, d) \in \overset{(c,\, d)}{RVL}$ the conditions $|a| \geq 3$, $\gcd(a, c) = 1$, and $m = \left\lfloor \frac{|a|-1}{2} \right\rfloor \geq \left\lfloor \frac{|b|-1}{2} \right\rfloor$ ($|b| \geq 3$, $\gcd(b, d) = 1$, and $m = \left\lfloor \frac{|b|-1}{2} \right\rfloor \geq \left\lfloor \frac{|a|-1}{2} \right\rfloor$) are both necessary and sufficient for $\overset{(a,\, b;\, c,\, d)}{FTS_\varphi^\psi} = \left(\overset{(a,\, b)}{CTS_\varphi^\psi}, \overset{(c,\, d)}{RVL} \right)$ to be efficient.

To prove the theorem we shall first prove two lemmas.

Lemma 5.9. In a semi-efficient tone system $\overset{(a,\, b;\, c,\, d)}{FTS_\varphi^\psi}$ of type 3, the range of T_2 restricted to the set $\overset{(c,\, d)}{RVL}/oct$ is a dense subset of $\mathbb{R}$.

Proof. Set $T_2(c, d) = \chi$. By Theorem 3.14, if $\overset{(a,\, b;\, c,\, d)}{FTS_\varphi^\psi}$ is oriented to $(a, b; c, d)$ there exists no $(k, l) \neq (0, 0)$ such that $k(c, d) \oplus l(a, b) = (0, 0)$, thereby contradicting Condition 5.1A. Similarly, if χ/ψ is irrational there exists no $(k, l) \neq (0, 0)$ such that $k\chi + l\psi = 0$, thereby contradicting Condition 5.4A. In other

---

[3] Although a device capable of transmitting notes with absolute accuracy cannot be constructed in principle, neither can one restrict *a priori* the degree of precision such a device is hypothetically capable of attaining. On the other hand, one cannot assume as much concerning *reception* since in general, reception parameters are not under one's control in the same strong sense as are transmission parameters.

words, $\overset{(a,\,b;\,c,\,d)}{FTS^{\psi}_{\varphi}}$ is oriented to $(a,\,b;\,c,\,d)$ and χ/ψ is irrational are sufficient conditions for m to have no upper limit such that $\{(y,\,z)_k\}$ is a set of primary intervals, $k = 0,\,\pm1,\,\ldots,\,\pm m$. It is easily seen that these conditions are also necessary. Since M is maximal, the two conditions hold, such that $\overset{(c,\,d)}{RVL}/oct = NVL$. Moreover, by Theorem 3.46 the system is dense. Q.E.D.

Lemma 5.10. Let $\overset{(a,\,b;\,c,\,d)}{FTS^{\psi}_{\varphi}} = \left(\overset{(a,\,b)}{CTS^{\psi}_{\varphi}}, \overset{(c,\,d)}{RVL} \right)$ be a semi-efficient tone system of

type 1 (type 2) and order M oriented to $(g_1,\,h_1;\,g_2,\,h_2)$, $g_1 h_2 - g_2 h_1 = \pm1$, $\overset{(c,\,d)}{RVL} = \{(y,z)_k\}$. Set $ah_2 - bg_2 = \pm A$, $bg_1 - ah_1 = \pm B$, $ch_2 - dg_2 = \pm C$, $dg_1 - ch_1 = \pm D$.
   Then $|A| \geq 3$, $\gcd(A,\,C) = 1$ ($|B| \geq 3$, $\gcd(B,\,D) = 1$), such that $M = 2m + 1$ satisfies

$$ m = \left\lfloor \frac{|A| - 1}{2} \right\rfloor \quad \left(m = \left\lfloor \frac{|B| - 1}{2} \right\rfloor \right). $$

Proof. Suppose that $\overset{(a,\,b;\,c,\,d)}{FTS^{\psi}_{\varphi}}$ is a type-1 (type-2) system. By Theorem 3.44 a primary interval $(y,\,z)_k \equiv_{(a,\,b)} k(c,\,d)$ satisfies $T_2(y,\,z)_k \equiv \psi \cdot \frac{kC}{A} (\psi \cdot \frac{kD}{B})$ mod $|\psi|$. To satisfy Definition 5.4, the lemma follows. In particular, $|A| < 3$ ($|B| < 3$) is impossible, since by assumption $M \geq 3$ (Definition 5.4), equivalently, $(c,\,d) \neq_{(a,\,b)} (0,\,0)$ (Proposition 5.2). Q.E.D.

Proof of the theorem. Suppose that $\overset{(a,\,b;\,c,\,d)}{FTS^{\psi}_{\varphi}}$ is efficient and suppose by contradiction that the system is of type 3. By Lemma 5.9 the range of T_2 restricted to the set $\overset{(c,\,d)}{RVL}/oct$ is a dense subset of $\mathbb{R}$, and therefore Condition 5.6A is not satisfied. Thus the system is of type 1 (type 2). By Lemma 5.10 and Definition 5.6 we have $|A| \geq 3$, $\gcd(A,\,C) = 1$, and $m = \left\lfloor \frac{|A|-1}{2} \right\rfloor \geq \left\lfloor \frac{|B|-1}{2} \right\rfloor$ ($|B| \geq 3$, $\gcd(B,\,D) = 1$, and $m = \left\lfloor \frac{|B|-1}{2} \right\rfloor \geq \left\lfloor \frac{|A|-1}{2} \right\rfloor$).
   Let $\overset{(a,\,b)}{CTS^{\psi}_{\varphi}}$ be a naturally oriented composite tone system of type 1 (type 2), and let $\overset{(c,\,d)}{RVL}$ be a set of intervals $(y,\,z)_k \equiv_{(a,\,b)} k(c,\,d)$, $k = 0,\,\pm1,\,\ldots,\,\pm m$. If $\overset{(a,\,b;\,c,\,d)}{FTS^{\psi}_{\varphi}} = \left(\overset{(a,\,b)}{CTS^{\psi}_{\varphi}}, \overset{(c,\,d)}{RVL} \right)$ is efficient then by Lemma 5.10 and Definition

5.6 the conditions $|a| \geq 3$, $\gcd(a,\,c) = 1$, and $m = \left\lfloor \frac{|a|-1}{2} \right\rfloor \geq \left\lfloor \frac{|b|-1}{2} \right\rfloor$ ($|b| \geq 3$, $\gcd(b,\,d) = 1$, and $m = \left\lfloor \frac{|b|-1}{2} \right\rfloor \geq \left\lfloor \frac{|a|-1}{2} \right\rfloor$), are necessary. Suppose these conditions hold. Then, if $(c, d) \in \overset{(c, d)}{RVL}$ $\overset{(c, d)}{RVL}$ is a set of primary intervals satisfying Condition 5.1A. Moreover, Conditions 5.4A and 5.6A are satisfied. Thus the conditions are also sufficient. Q.E.D.

Although type-3 systems are rejected by Theorem 5.8, one need not reject the systems that are *ordinarily* referred to as "Pythagorean intonation" or "meantone temperament," i.e., a *finite* segment of the "line of fifths" (see Definition 5.19 ahead) such that every fifth is tuned pure or slightly narrower than equal tempered. See Sects. 5.3 and 8.2, for further discussion.[4]

Note that the following definition is purely conventional, except for the assumption of natural orientation.

Definition 5.11.   Standard Efficient Tone System

Let $\overset{(a, b; c, d)}{FTS_\varphi^\psi} = \left(\overset{(a, b)}{CTS_\varphi^\psi}, \overset{(c, d)}{RVL} \right)$ be a naturally oriented type-1 (type-2) efficient

system.

We shall refer to the system as *standard* if $\psi = a \geq |b|$ ($|a| \geq \psi = b > 0$) such that the following condition A holds for every primary interval (y, z).

A. $0 \leq T_2(y, z) = y \leq a - 1$ $(0 \leq T_2(y, z) = z \leq b - 1)$.

Henceforth we shall write, for a standard efficient tone system,

$$\overset{(a, b; c, d)}{FTS_\varphi^\psi} = \overset{(a, b; c, d)}{FTS_\varphi} = \left(\overset{(a, b)}{CTS_\varphi}, \overset{(c, d)}{RVL} \right).$$

Proposition 5.12.   Let $\overset{(a, b; c, d)}{FTS_\varphi} = \left(\overset{(a, b)}{CTS_\varphi}, \overset{(c, d)}{RVL} \right)$ be a standard type-1 (type-2)

efficient tone system, and let $(y, z)_k = (y_k, z_k)$ be a primary interval, $k \neq 0$.

Then $(y, z)_{-k} = (a - y_k, b - z_k)$. Moreover, a type-2 system satisfies $b = |a| - 1$ is odd.

---

[4] One may object to Theorem 5.8 on the grounds that it strongly depends on Definition 5.4 ("semi-efficiency"), where the Maximalist Principle is applied in a weak sense (i.e., systems of *the same type t* are compared; cf. Definition 5.6, "efficiency," where systems of type t are compared to systems of type t'). However, one cannot simultaneously apply the Maximalist Principle in a *strong* sense (comparing two systems, not necessarily of the same type) and ask for non-density, since by Lemmas 5.9 and 5.10 these two conditions are mutually exclusive (i.e., strong maximality is equivalent to dense systems). Suppose that instead of requiring efficiency, one simply rules out type-3 systems *a priori*. One saves nothing in terms of the Maximalist Principle, since systems of type 1 and 2 still have to satisfy this principle. Since the non-density requirement comes at no extra cost, the choice is therefore between (a) ruling out type-3 systems *a priori*, and (b) applying the Maximalist Principle, albeit in a weak sense. Between these two choices, (a) is unquestionably *ad hoc*. I am indebted to Nori Jacoby for helping clarify these and other important considerations relating to Theorem 5.8.

Proof. Write $(y, z)_k = k(c, d) \oplus l_k(a, b)$, for some l_k. From 5.11A we have $l_k = -\lfloor kc/a \rfloor$ $(l_k = -\lfloor kd/b \rfloor)$.

By Theorem 5.8 we have $a \geq 3$, $\gcd(a, c) = 1$ $(b \geq 3, \gcd(b, d) = 1)$ implying that $c \not\equiv 0 \bmod a$ $(d \not\equiv 0 \bmod b)$. Together with $|k| < a$ $(|k| < b)$ it follows that kc/a (kd/b) is not an integer. Therefore, $l_{-k} = -l_k + 1$, and we have:

$$(y, z)_{-k} =$$
$$-k(c, d) \oplus l_{-k}(a, b) =$$
$$(a, b) - (k(c, d) \oplus l_k(a, b)) =$$
$$(a - y_k, b - z_k).$$

Moreover, a type-2 system satisfies $|a| > b \geq 1$, $\lfloor \frac{b-1}{2} \rfloor \geq \lfloor \frac{|a|-1}{2} \rfloor$, implying that $b = |a| - 1$ is odd. Q.E.D.

Finally, we have the following definition.

Definition 5.13. Usual/Anti-usual Efficient Tone System

We shall refer to an efficient tone system $FTS_\varphi^{12}\,^{(12,\ 7;\ c,\ d)} = FTS_\varphi = (CTS_\varphi, RVL)$, CTS_φ is a usual composite tone system (Definition 3.45) and RVL is the usual set of primary intervals, as *usual* (*anti-usual*), if $(c, d) = (7, 4)$ $((c, d) = (5, 3))$.

5.2   Coherent Tone Systems

Let $FTS_\varphi^{(a,\ b;\ c,\ d)} = \left(CTS_\varphi^{(a,\ b)}, RVL^{(c,\ d)} \right)$ be a standard, type-1 efficient tone system, and let $(u, v) \in RVL^{(c,\ d)}/oct$. Given $T_2(u, v) = u$, how can the receiver, *in practice*, find v? The receiver can of course start by memorizing, for every $0 \leq y \leq a - 1$ except $a/2$ (if a is even), the unique z such that $(y, z) \in RVL^{(c,\ d)}$. However, committing such a map to memory is cognitively costly, counter to the Economical Principle. Is there *an algorithm* the receiver can use instead?

Indeed there is. Consider the algorithm defined by the five steps enumerated below. The algorithm assumes a prior computation giving the unique integer m, $1 \leq m \leq a - 1$, satisfying $mc \equiv 1 \pmod a$.[5]

1. Compute $n = m \cdot T_2(u, v) = mu$.
2. Compute $k' = n - a\lfloor n/a \rfloor$.
3. If $k' < a/2$ set $k = k'$; otherwise set $k = k' - a$.

---

[5] Since a and c are coprime the existence of m is assured. The so-called "Extended Euclidean Algorithm" will find the desired m.

4. Compute $l = \frac{u-kc}{a}$.

5. Compute $v = kd + lb$.

Although our algorithm generates the desired result, it is no less "counter-economical" than committing a map to memory. The rationale for a "coherent" tone system, defined next, is precisely the existence of an *economical* algorithm for finding (u, v) given $T_2(u, v)$, $(u, v) \in \overset{(c,\,d)}{RVL}/oct$.

Note, in connection with Definition 5.14 below, that by Definition 5.11 a standard type-1 (type-2) efficient tone system satisfies $T_2(u, v) = u$ ($T_2(u, v) = v$) for every note interval $(u, \ v) \in \overset{(c,\,d)}{RVL}/oct$. For an integer *nearest to* a real number x we write $[x]$. It is easy to see that the value of $[x]$ is unique, unless x lies exactly halfway between two consecutive integers.

Definition 5.14.   Coherent Tone System

Let $\overset{(a,\,b;\,c,\,d)}{FTS_\varphi} = \left(\overset{(a,\,b)}{CTS_\varphi}, \overset{(c,\,d)}{RVL} \right)$ be a standard, type-1 (type-2) efficient tone

system. Let $\overset{(c,\,d)}{RVL}/oct = \left\{ (u, v) \equiv_{(a,\,b)} (y, z) \,\middle|\, (y, z) \in \overset{(c,\,d)}{RVL} \right\}$.

We shall refer to $\overset{(a,\,b;\,c,\,d)}{FTS_\varphi}$ as *coherent* if for every interval $(u, v) \in \overset{(c,\,d)}{RVL}/oct$ $T_2(u, v) = u$ ($T_2(u, v) = v$) is a unique integer such that the following condition A is satisfied.

A. $v = \left[\frac{b}{a} \cdot u \right] \left(u = \left[\frac{a}{b} \cdot v \right] \right)$.

Example 5.15.   Consider a usual (or anti-usual) efficient tone system $FTS_\varphi = (CTS_\varphi, RVL)$ (Definition 5.13). Since

$$\left[\frac{7}{12} \cdot 1 \right] = \left[\frac{7}{12} \cdot 2 \right] = 1,$$

$$\left[\frac{7}{12} \cdot 3 \right] = \left[\frac{7}{12} \cdot 4 \right] = 2,$$

$$\left[\frac{7}{12} \cdot 5 \right] = 3, \quad \left[\frac{7}{12} \cdot 7 \right] = 4,$$

Fig. 5.1 A usual or anti-usual efficient tone system is coherent

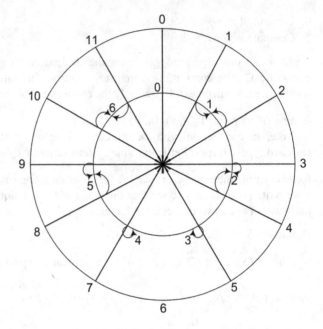

$$\left[\frac{7}{12} \cdot 8\right] = \left[\frac{7}{12} \cdot 9\right] = 5,$$

$$\left[\frac{7}{12} \cdot 10\right] = \left[\frac{7}{12} \cdot 11\right] = 6,$$

FTS_φ is coherent.

Consider Fig. 5.1. Two concentric circles, an outer circle with a circumference of length 12 and an inner circle with a circumference of length 7, are drawn such that two points 0, one on each circumference, and the common center, fall on a straight line. Since the ratio of the inner-circle's circumference to that of the outer circle is 7/12, the straight arrows connecting points 1, 2,..., 5, 7,..., 11 on the outer circle with the common center intersect the inner circle at points 7/12, 14/12,..., 35/12, 49/12,..., 77/12, respectively. These points are then "shifted," so to speak, to the nearest integral point (see the curved arrows). For example, points 7/12 and 14/12 on the inner circle are both shifted to 1, points 21/12 and 28/12 are shifted to 2, and so forth. Thus, a usual or anti-usual efficient tone system is coherent.[6]

---

[6] Douthett (2008) uses similar diagrams to illustrate the "maximal evenness" algorithm. In Douthett's diagrams the arrows point outwards, such that points 12x/7 on the *outer* circle are shifted to points representing the *integral part* of this value. See also Sect. 8.3.

Although the need for an economical algorithm generating (u, v) given $T_2(u, v)$, $(u, v) \in \overset{(c,\,d)}{RVL}/oct$, is clear, to assume *the coherence* algorithm 5.14A, which depends on natural orientation as a property of standard efficient systems (Definition 5.11), is to assume much.[7] However, in Part II of this study the payoff from these assumptions will prove sufficiently abundant to offset their cost here. See also Sect. 8.3.

Unless otherwise noted (see for example the proof of Lemma 5.17), henceforth we shall assume with no loss of generality that an efficient tone system is of type 1.

Theorem 5.16. Let $\overset{(a,\,b;\,c,\,d)}{FTS_\varphi}$ be a standard efficient tone system. Set $cb - ad = \Delta$. Then $\overset{(a,\,b;\,c,\,d)}{FTS_\varphi}$ is coherent if, and only if, $|\Delta| = 1$.

To prove the theorem we shall first prove the following lemma.

Lemma 5.17. Let $\overset{(a,\,b;\,c,\,d)}{FTS_\varphi} = \left(\overset{(a,\,b)}{CTS_\varphi}, \overset{(c,\,d)}{RVL} \right)$ be a standard efficient tone system. Then $cb - ad \neq 0$.

Proof. Suppose by contradiction that $cb - ad = 0$, that is, $\frac{c}{a} = \frac{d}{b}$. This is impossible, since a type-1 system satisfies $\gcd(a, c) = 1$, $a > |b|$, and a type-2 system satisfies $\gcd(b, d) = 1$, $|a| - 1 = b \geq 3$. Q.E.D.

Proof of the theorem. Suppose the system is coherent. Then every primary interval $(y, z)_k = (y_k, z_k)$ satisfies

$$z_k = \left[\frac{b}{a} \cdot y_k \right] \text{ is unique.} \tag{5.1}$$

Equation (5.1) is equivalent to

$$-\frac{1}{2} < z_k - \frac{by_k}{a} < \frac{1}{2}. \tag{5.2}$$

Since $z_k = kd + lb$ and $y_k = kc + la$, Eq. (5.2) is equivalent to

---

[7] Since the coherence algorithm assumes, via Definition 5.11, a naturally oriented system, one may wonder why natural orientation was not assumed in the first place, say, as part of semi-efficiency (Definition 5.4). However, from Lemma 5.9 it is clear that such an assumption would have amounted to ruling out type-3 systems *a priori*. By Theorem 5.8, on the other hand, the ruling out of type-3 systems is *not* orientation-dependent.

$$-\frac{1}{2} < kd - \frac{bkc}{a} < \frac{1}{2}.$$

Using Theorem 5.8, set $k = \lfloor \frac{a-1}{2} \rfloor \geq 1$. We have

$$-\frac{a}{2k} < \Delta < \frac{a}{2k}.$$

which is equivalent to $|\Delta| \leq 1$. By Lemma 5.17 $\Delta = 0$ is impossible. Q.E.D.

Proposition 5.18. Let $FTS_\varphi^{(a,\,b;\,c,\,d)}$ be a coherent tone system, and let $(y, z)_k = (y_k, z_k)$ be a primary interval, $k \neq 0$.
   Then $1 \leq z_k \leq b - 1$ if b is positive, $b + 1 \leq z_k \leq -1$ if b is negative.

Proof. Suppose that b is positive. By Definition 5.11 a and y_k are both positive, and therefore by 5.14A z_k is positive. Suppose by contradiction that $z_k > b$. This is impossible, since by Proposition 5.12 we have $z_{-k} < 0$. Suppose by contradiction $z_k = b$. This is also impossible since $z_k \equiv kd \pmod{b}$, where $|k| < b$, and from Theorem 5.16 $\gcd(b, d) = 1$. Therefore, $z_k \equiv 0 \pmod{b}$ only if $z_k = 0 = k$. Thus $1 \leq z_k \leq b - 1$. Similarly, if b is negative $b + 1 \leq z_k \leq -1$. Q.E.D.

   Since a coherent system $FTS_\varphi^{(a,\,b;\,c,\,d)}$ satisfies $|cb - ad| = 1$, by Theorem 3.14 $((a, b), (c, d))$ is a basis of NVL such that for every interval (u, v) there exists a unique integer j such that $(u, v) \equiv_{(a,\,b)} j(c, d)$. We therefore have the following definition. Recall that unless otherwise noted, a type-1 tone system is assumed.

Definition 5.19. Quintic Line; Quintic Segment; Line of Fifths
   Let $FTS_\varphi^{(a,\,b;\,c,\,d)}$ be a coherent tone system. Write Q_j for the note $(s, t) \equiv_{(a,\,b)} (0, 0) + j(c, d), 0 \leq s \leq a - 1$.

A. We shall refer to the infinite ordered set (Q_j), where j runs over all integers, as *the quintic line*.
B. We shall write $Q_j^i, i \geq 1$, to denote the i-element connected segment Q_j, Q_{j+1}, ..., Q_{j+i-1}, of the quintic line.
C. If $FTS_\varphi = (CTS_\varphi, RVL)$ is usual (anti-usual) we shall refer to the quintic line as *the line of fifths* (*line of fourths*).[8]

   By Proposition 5.12, for type-2 systems a proposition analogous to the following does not exist.

Proposition 5.20. Let $FTS_\varphi^{(a,\,b;\,c,\,d)}$ be a type-1 coherent tone system, where a is even. Set $\Delta = cb - ad = \pm 1$, and let (u, v) be an interval satisfying $0 \leq u \leq a - 1$.
   Then the following two conditions, A and B, are equivalent.

---

[8] The line of fifths is central to Handschin (1948); see Clampitt and Noll (2011). "Line of fifths" is Temperley's (2000) term; Regener (1973) refers to essentially the same construct as "quint group."

A. $(u, v) \equiv_{(a, b)} \frac{a}{2}(c, d)$.

B. $(u, v) = \left(\frac{a}{2}, \frac{b \mp 1}{2}\right)$.

Proof. Since $\gcd(a, c) = 1$, a is even implies that c is odd. Therefore, the following three conditions are all equivalent.

1. $u = a/2$.
2. $u \equiv ac/2 \pmod{a}, 0 \le u \le a - 1$.
3. $u = \frac{ac}{2} + la, l = -\frac{c-1}{2}$.

Set $v = \frac{ad}{2} + lb$. Using Theorem 5.16 we have $v = \frac{b - \Delta}{2} = \frac{b \mp 1}{2}$. Q.E.D.

5.3 Categorical Equal Temperament

Since a coherent tone system is naturally oriented, it is strictly equal tempered in the sense that every note interval (u, v) satisfies $T_2(u, v) = u$ (assuming a type-1 system). Applying the Categorical Principle we shall now relax somewhat the unrealistic condition of absolutely accurate note transmission, offering a theory of "categorical" equal temperament. In particular, Definition 5.21 next applies the Categorical Principle to Definition 3.36, with the hindsight that $T_2(u, v) = u$. Review Sect. 2.3.2.

Definition 5.21. Categorical ET Functions; Prototypicality

Let $\overset{(a, b)}{ONS}$ be an octave-endowed note system and let PCS_φ^ψ be a φ-centered pitch-communication system satisfying $\psi = a$. Let I be the closed real interval $[0, 1]$ and let $CET_1 : N \times P \to I$ and $CET_2 : NVL \times PVL \to I$ be two functions.

We shall refer to $CET = \{CET_1, \ CET_2\}$ as *a pair of categorical equal temperament (ET) functions* if $CET_1((s, \ t), \ p)$ decreases monotonically, smoothly, and symmetrically with $|s - p|$, such that $CET_1((s, \ t), \ p) = 1$ implies that $p = s$ and $CET_1((s, t), \ p) = 0$ implies that $|s - p| \ge 1/2$. Moreover, if $((u, v), \ q) = ((s, t), \ p)$ then $CET_2((u, v), \ q) = CET_1((s, t), \ p)$.

We shall refer to $CET_1((s, t), \ p)$ as *the prototypicality of p relative to* (s, t). See Fig. 5.2 for a graphic representation of pitch-interval prototypicality relative to three arbitrary note intervals $(u - 1, v'')$, (u, v), and $(u + 1, v')$.

Although Definition 5.21 seems to introduce a host of new assumptions, this is in fact not the case; the definition merely applies the Categorical Principle to the strict-ET result.

The theory of categorical ET relaxes the unrealistic assumption of absolutely accurate note transmission. In so doing the theory transforms the transmitter into *a performer*: someone whose choices within the limits allowed by the system may serve to clarify or enhance the composer's message. In particular, the limited freedom awarded to the performer in mapping notes into pitches may be used for "expressive" purposes, for example, enhancing the sense of "tension" and

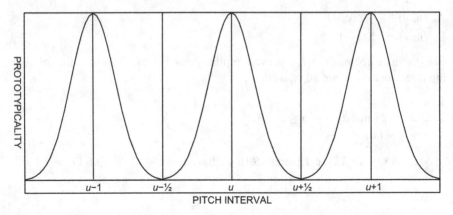

Fig. 5.2 Pitch-interval prototypicality relative to three arbitrary note intervals $(u-1, v'')$, (u, v), and $(u+1, v')$

"resolution" that may inhere in certain "event sequences" of tonal music.[9] Though we touch briefly on such expressive issues in Sect. 8.2, strictly speaking they lie beyond the scope of the present study.

The following definition is an updated version of Definition 3.42, assuming a type-1 system. Note that the assumption $\text{CET}_1\left((\underline{s}, \underline{t}), \varphi\right) = 1$ now implies that $\varphi = \underline{s}$ is an integer.

Definition 5.22 (Updating Definition 3.42). Composite Tone System

Let $\overset{(a,\,b)}{ONS}$ be an octave-endowed note system, let $PCS_\varphi^a = PCS_\varphi$ be a φ-centered pitch-communication system, and let $CET = \{\text{CET}_1,\ \text{CET}_2\}$ be a pair of categorical equal-temperament functions. Let MSG be a non-empty note sequence. Assume there exists a note $(\underline{s}, \underline{t})$ privileged by the transmitter.

We shall refer to $\overset{(a,\,b)}{CTS}_\varphi = \left(\overset{(a,\,b)}{ONS}, PCS_\varphi, CET, MSG \right)$ as *a composite tone system*

with message MSG, relative, absolute, or reflexive, depending on PCS_φ, if CET_1 $\left((\underline{s},\underline{t}),\varphi\right) = 1$ such that the following two conditions, A and B, are satisfied.

A. Every note $(s, t) \in MSG$ is transmitted as a pitch p that satisfies $\text{CET}_1((s, t), p) > 0$.
B. Every note interval $(u, v) = (s, t) - (s', t')$, (s, t), $(s', t') \in MSG$, is transmitted as a pitch interval q that satisfies $\text{CET}_2((u, v), q) > 0$.

We shall proceed henceforth as if Definition 3.42 has been replaced by Definition 5.22, and all subsequent definitions have been adjusted accordingly. Unless otherwise noted, we assume with no loss of generality that a composite tone system is of type 1.

---

[9] An instrument capable of producing a continuum of pitches (violin, the human voice) is assumed. However, depending on one's personal taste, even such a "discrete" instrument as the modern piano may be purposefully "mistuned" such that strict equal temperament is only approximated.

References

Agmon, E. (1986). *Diatonicism, chromaticism, and enharmonicism: A study in cognition and perception*. PhD diss., City University of New York.

Agmon, E. (1989). A mathematical model of the diatonic system. *Journal of Music Theory, 33*(1), 1–25.

Clampitt, D., & Noll, T. (2011). Modes, the height-width duality, and Handschin's tone character. *Music Theory Online 17*(1). http://www.mtosmt.org/issues/mto.11.17.1/toc.17.1.html. Accessed 10 Jan 2012.

Douthett, J. (2008). Filtered point-symmetry and dynamic voice-leading. In J. Douthett et al. (Eds.), *Music theory and mathematics: Chords, collections, and transformations* (pp. 72–106). Rochester: University of Rochester Press.

Handschin, J. (1948). *Der Toncharakter: Eine Einführung in die Tonpsychologie*. Zürich: Atlantis.

Regener, E. (1973). *Pitch notation and equal temperament: A formal study*. Berkeley: University of California Press.

Temperley, D. (2000). The line of fifths. *Music Analysis, 19*(3), 289–319.

Chapter 6
Receiving Notes

Abstract Following a lead found in Bartók's *Music for String Instruments, Percussion, and Celesta* (Sect. 6.1), a "note-reception system" is constructed in Sect. 6.2, as follows. Relative to a referential note selected from a set of notes termed "core," a received pitch is paired with the note a *primary* interval away. Section 6.3 then explores the idea of self-communicating the core in a potentially endless feedback cycle, such that the "received message" of one cycle becomes the "transmitted message" of the next. "Stability" is reached if at some iteration and onwards the received message always equals the original transmitted message, namely the core. It is proven that if stability is reached at all, it is reached at the very first iteration. In Sect. 6.4 "diatonic note" is defined as a transmitted note the reflexive image of which (at some iteration) is constant relative to *every* core element. It is shown that *every* note (at some iteration) is diatonic if and only if the system is stable, and thus the core itself is a set of diatonic notes. It is shown further that a diatonic core consists of exactly $\lfloor a/2 \rfloor + 1$ elements that may be ordered quintically. Finally, Sect. 6.5 revisits interesting properties of diatonic systems as previously studied by Balzano, Agmon, Clough and Douthett, and Carey and Clampitt.

At this point it should be useful to recall the Communication Principle (Fig. 2.3). A message (a sequence of notes) is transformed into a signal (a corresponding sequence of categorically equal-tempered pitches), which in turn is transformed into an image of the message, as faithful as possible to its source (at least, a transposition of the message).

In the previous chapter we have focused on a privileged set of intervals, the "primary" intervals. By virtue of the properties of efficiency and coherence the primary intervals (and their octave compounds) may be readily communicated. But how is this finding relevant to the main task of communicating *notes*? An early twentieth-century musical masterpiece suggests an answer.

6.1   Note Reception: A Lesson by Bartók

The first movement of Bartók's *Music for String Instruments, Percussion, and Celesta* (Budapest, 1936) is not tonal in a conventional sense; indeed, the movement is not even diatonic, let alone chordal or harmonic. And yet, the movement seems to have been conceived in certain terms that are "tonal" nonetheless.

As Bartók himself discloses in a well-known analysis prefacing the first published pocket score of the work, the fugue-like movement is "in A," the "key" from which the music departs and to which it ultimately returns.[1] The "A-centric" qualities of the movement's beginning and end are fairly obvious. A_{-1} is the movement's very first note as well as the note on which the initial statement of the subject cadences (Fig. 6.1a). The movement ends with a phrase that consists of a two-voice, note-against-note setting of the subject's second phrase against its own A-centered inversion (Fig. 6.1b). Thus, in the final cadence a combined upper and lower "leading-tone" motion converges on A.

Much easier to miss is the sense in which Bartók's choice of notes is *a priori* A-centric.

Together with its inversion, the subject is a set S of notes such that for every integer-class s' (mod 12) there exists a note $(s,\ t) \in S$ satisfying $s \equiv s'$ (mod 12). Yet unlike, say, Schoenberg or Webern, for whom the choice of t given s is essentially arbitrary, Bartók chooses his ts with great care. In fact, if exactly one integer class s', namely 3, is excluded, for every $s \equiv s'$ (mod 12) Bartók chooses *a unique t* such that $(s,\ t) \in S$. Table 6.1 depicts Bartók's choices (using conventional notation) in the opening and closing measures, $s' = 0,\ 1, \ldots,\ 11$, $(s',\ t') \equiv_{(12,\ 7)}(s,\ t) \in S$. It may readily be checked that almost every transposed appearance S' of the subject preserves this notational idiosyncrasy.[2] In particular, if $\left(\underline{s},\ \underline{t}\right)$ is the central note in S for example $\left(\underline{s},\ \underline{t}\right) = $ A in the movement's opening and closing measures), then the unique s for which there exists *a pair* $t, t', t' \neq t$, such that $(s,\ t), (s,\ t') \in S$, satisfies $s - \underline{s} \equiv 6$ (mod 12).[3]

A moment's reflection will reveal that Bartók's choice of ts is far from arbitrary. *With the exception of D♯/E♭ every note in the subject or its inversion lies a usual primary interval away from the central A*, give or take some whole multiple of the

---

[1] Bartók's self-analysis may still be found in Boosey and Hawkes's study score. See Hunkemöller (1983) for an interesting perspective on Bartók's analysis, including its comparison to two other analyses of the work, also by the composer.

[2] Exceptions do occur in the fragmentary C♯ and G♯ entries of mm. 34–37, and, most notably, the movement's climax, mm. 45–56, supposedly "in D♯."

[3] On Bartók's notational practices see Gillies (1982, 1983, 1989, and 1993); see also Leichtentritt (1929), von der Null (1930), and Brukman (2008). Gillies cites Bartók's ethnomusicological activities as possible influences on his notation. For relevant passages in Bartók's "Harvard Lectures," see Gillies (1989, pp. 288–290). Gillies (1989, pp. 26, 133–138) specifically addresses the "enharmonically consistent" notation of the fugue subject of *Music for String Instruments*, evoking the idea of "modulation" to account for the single D♯/E♭ inconsistency. See footnote 5.

Fig. 6.1 Bartók, *Music for String Instruments, Percussion, and Celesta*, I, beginning (**a**) and end (**b**). Copyright © 1937 Universal Edition A.G., Wien/UE34129

Table 6.1 The A-centric note collection of Bartók's fugue subject	s'	(s', t')
	9	A♮
	10	B♭
	11	B♮
	0	C♮
	1	C♯
	2	D♮
	3	D♯/E♭
	4	E♮
	5	F♮
	6	F♯
	7	G♮
	8	G♯

perfect octave. Thus, ♭(B₋₁) = −(2, 1) lies a *descending major seventh* from A = (9, 5), (not, say, a *descending diminished octave*, like ♯(A₋₁)). Similarly, C♯ = (1, 0) lies a *descending minor sixth* from A (not, say, a *descending augmented fifth*, like D♭), and so forth. The music is thus A-centric not only by virtue of its beginning and end, but also by virtue of the primary intervallic relation that holds between every note except D♯/E♭ and the note A.[4]

---

[4] The large-scale structure of Bartók's movement, where the subject is successively transposed by ±1,..., ±6 perfect fifths relative to the first entry, reflects the finding that the usual primary intervals together with the non-primary A4/d5 form a mirror-symmetrical connected segment of an intervallic "line of fifths." Interestingly, Hindemith's (1937) "Series 1" consists of the same set of thirteen intervals relative to the "scalar root." See for example his Fig. 65 (p. 96).

Consider next a usual coherent tone system the message of which is the fugue subject of Bartók's *Music*, reduced to a sequence of notes. Quoting Shannon (1948, p. 381), how can the receiver perform "... the inverse operation of that done by the transmitter, reconstructing the message from the signal"? Suppose the system is faithful such that for every message element (s, t) and transmitted pitch p, $[p] = s$, the corresponding received pitch p' satisfies $p' = p$. Still, from the point of view of the receiver the number of notes (s', t') satisfying $s' = [p']$ is infinite. For example, $\flat(B_{-1})$, $\sharp(A_{-1})$, $\flat\flat(C)$, and $\sharp\sharp\sharp\sharp(G_{-1})$ all satisfy $s' = -2$.

Suppose, however, that the receiver fixes some A (say, A_0), mentally, as referential. Suppose, further, that the receiver processes every received pitch p', $[p'] \not\equiv 3$ (mod 12), as the note (s', t'), $s' = [p']$, *such that the interval from the referential A to (s', t') is primary*. As may easily be verified, except for D♯/E♭ the receiver will recover Bartók's message correctly.[5]

We have just received an invaluable lesson in note reception from an important twentieth-century musician. We shall put this lesson to good use in the following section.

6.2   Note-Reception Systems

Recall in connection with the following proposition that Definition 3.42 has been replaced by Definition 5.22 (in particular, the pair T of transmission functions have been replaced by a pair CET of categorical equal-temperament functions). Review also Definition 3.35, and recall that we write $[x]$ for an integer *nearest to x*.

Proposition 6.1. Let $CTS_\varphi = (\overset{(a,\ b)}{ONS}, PCS_\varphi, CET, MSG)$ be a composite tone system, where PCS_φ is a φ-centered pitch-communication system. Let (s, t) be a message element and let p be the corresponding transmitted pitch, $|s - p| < 1/2$. Let p' be the corresponding received pitch and set $s' = [p']$.
Then $s' - p' = s - p$.

Proof. It is easily seen that the proposition holds if $\overset{(a,\ b)}{CTS_\varphi}$ is absolute or reflexive.

Suppose $\overset{(a,\ b)}{CTS_\varphi}$ is relative. Then $p' = p - \varphi$. Moreover, from Definition 5.22 $\varphi = \underline{s}$ for some privileged $(\underline{s}, \underline{t})$. It follows that

---

[5] In choosing between D♯ and E♭ Bartók seems to be guided by *local* primary-intervallic relations. Thus, Bartók writes E♭ in the context of D and C, whereas in the context of C♯ and E he writes D♯. For Gillies (1989, p. 135), "the change to a D♯ notation in the third phrase is the sign that a modulation has taken place to an in-filled fourth B–E..."

$$s' - p' =$$
$$[p - \varphi] - (p - \varphi) =$$
$$[p] - \varphi - (p - \varphi) =$$
$$s - p.$$

Q.E.D.

By Proposition 6.1, the act of transmitting notes by categorical rather than *exact* equal temperament is of no communicational concern even in the relative case, assuming a receiver that performs the "inverse" operation of rounding received pitches to the nearest integer. The following definition makes use of this important finding.

Definition 6.2. Image (of a message element); Empty Image

Let $\overset{(a,\,b;c,\,d)}{FTS_\varphi} = \left(\overset{(a,\,b)}{CTS_\varphi}, \overset{(c,\,d)}{RVL} \right)$ be a coherent tone system, where $\overset{(a,\,b)}{CTS_\varphi}$ is a

composite tone system $\left(\overset{(a,\,b)}{ONS}, PCS_\varphi, CET, MSG \right)$, and $\overset{(c,\,d)}{RVL}$ is a set of primary

intervals. Let (s, t) be a message element, let p' be the corresponding received pitch, and let (s', t') be a note satisfying $s' = [p']$. Let (w, x) be a note.

We shall refer to (s', t') as *the image of (s, t) relative to (w, x)*, and shall write

$$\overset{(w,\,x)}{IMG} (s,\ t) = (s',\ t'),$$

if there exists a $(y,\ z) \in \overset{(c,\,d)}{RVL}$ such that the following condition A is satisfied.

A. $(s',\ t') \equiv_{(a,\ b)} (w,\ x) + (y,\ z).$

If a primary interval (y, z) satisfying Condition A does not exist we shall say that

the image of (s, t) relative to (w, x) is empty, writing $\overset{(w,\,x)}{IMG} (s,\ t) = \varnothing$.

Example 6.3. Let $FTS_\varphi = (CTS_\varphi,\ RVL)$ be a usual coherent tone system such that CTS_φ is absolute. Set $(w,\ x) = A$.

Then $\overset{(w,x)}{IMG\flat}(B_{-1}) = \overset{(w,x)}{IMG}(-2, -1) = \flat(B_{-1})$, since the received pitch p' corresponding to $\flat(B_{-1})$ satisfies $[p'] = -2$, and $\flat(B_{-1}) \equiv A + m2$ satisfies $m2 = (1,\ 1) \in \overset{(7,\,4)}{RVL}$. By contrast, since there exists no primary interval $(y,\ z)$ satisfying $y = 6$, $\overset{(w,x)}{IMG\flat}(E_{-1}) = \varnothing$.

It easily follows from Definition 6.2 that $\overset{(w,\,x)}{IMG} (s,\ t) = \varnothing$ if, and only if, a is even and (w, x) is such that the received pitch p' satisfies $[p'] \equiv w + a/2 \pmod{a}$. Moreover, since for every $y \neq a/2$, $0 \leq y \leq a - 1$, there exists exactly one z such that (y, z) is a primary interval, we have the following proposition.

*Proposition 6.4. Let $\overset{(a,\,b;c,\,d)}{FTS_\varphi} = \left(\overset{(a,\,b)}{CTS_\varphi}, \ \overset{(c,\,d)}{RVL} \right)$ be a coherent tone system. Fix

a note (w, x) and let (s, t) be a message element.

Then, unless $\overset{(w,\,x)}{IMG}(s, t) = \varnothing$, there exists a unique (s', t') satisfying

$(s', t') = \overset{(w,\,x)}{IMG}(s, t)$.

We are now ready for the following definition.

Definition 6.5. Note-Reception System (with message *MSG*); Core; Received Message; Usual/Anti-usual Note-Reception System

Let $\overset{(a,\,b;c,\,d)}{FTS_\varphi} = \left(\overset{(a,\,b)}{CTS_\varphi}, \ \overset{(c,\,d)}{RVL} \right)$ be a coherent tone system, where $\overset{(a,\,b)}{CTS_\varphi}$ is a

composite tone system $\left(\overset{(a,\,b)}{ONS}, \ PCS_\varphi, \ CET, \ MSG \right)$. Fix a non-empty set *CORE*

of notes (w, x) satisfying $0 \le w \le a - 1$, and let *MSG/R* be a sequence of notes, $|MSG/R| = |MSG|$.

We shall refer to *CORE* as *a core*, to *MSG/R* as *a received message*, and to
$\overset{(a,\,b;c,\,d)}{NRS_\varphi} = \left(\overset{(a,\,b;c,\,d)}{FTS_\varphi}, CORE, \ MSG/R \right)$ as *a note-reception system* (*with message*

MSG), if the following condition A is satisfied.

A. For every $(s, t) \in MSG$ there exists a $(w, x) \in CORE$ such that the exchange
$$X : MSG \rightarrow MSG/R \text{ satisfies } X(s, t) = \overset{(w,\,x)}{IMG}(s, t).$$

Depending on $\overset{(a,\,b;c,\,d)}{FTS_\varphi}$ (Definition 5.4) we shall refer to a note-reception system
$\overset{(a,\,b;c,\,d)}{NRS_\varphi}$ as *relative*, *absolute*, or *reflexive*. Moreover, if $\overset{(a,\,b;c,\,d)}{FTS_\varphi} = FTS_\varphi$ is usual or
anti-usual (Definition 5.13) we shall refer to $\overset{(a,\,b;c,\,d)}{NRS_\varphi} = NRS_\varphi$ as *usual* or *anti-usual*,
respectively.

In other words, in a note-reception system the exchange of every element in the message with an element in the received message is the image of that message element relative to *some* core element, in the sense of Definition 6.2. Note that nothing is said concerning the extent to which the Communication Principle is satisfied, that is, the extent to which the received message is a transposition of the transmitted one. A reflexive note-reception system, like a reflexive pitch-communication system, models a person engaged in self-communication. Review Definition 3.33 and discussion.

Example 6.6. Let $FTS_\varphi = (CTS_\varphi, RVL)$ be a usual, absolute coherent tone system such that $MSG =$

$$A, A; G\sharp, B\flat; F, \sharp(C_1); E, D_1; F\sharp, C_1; G, B; G\sharp, B\flat; A, A.$$

That is, the message corresponds to the final phrase of the first movement of Bartók's *Music for String Instruments, Percussion, and Celesta* (Fig. 6.1b), such that (1) the order of the dyadic simultaneities is preserved; (2) the elements of every dyad are ordered from low to high; (3) the fifth dyad, the octave E♭, is omitted. Set $CORE = \{A\}$.

Then, as we have seen in Sect. 6.1, for every message element (s, t) there exists a unique received image $\overset{A}{\text{IMG}}(s, \ t) = (s, \ t)$ such that $(FTS_\varphi, \ CORE, \ MSG/R)$ is a usual, absolute note-reception system that satisfies the Communication Principle.

Recall from Sect. 6.1 that for Bartók the note A is privileged. Since the phrase begins with the dyad A, and moreover, it ends with the "double leading-tone" dyadic progression $(G\sharp, B\flat) \rightarrow (A, A)$, Bartók sets the conditions by which the image of the transmitted A is privileged also *for the receiver*. However, even if the system is absolute the received message may be a transposition of the transmitted one. For a faithful pitch-communication system does not prevent the message from being processed in terms of an "enharmonically related" core such as B♭♭ or G𝄪, yielding a received message such as the following:

B♭♭, B♭♭; A♭, C♭♭; G♭♭, ♭(D_1); F♭, ♭♭(E_1); G♭, ♭♭(D_1); A♭♭, C♭; A♭, C♭♭; B♭♭, B♭♭.

Finally, note the following important definition.

Definition 6.7. Cluster (of a note-reception system)

Let $\overset{(a,\,b;c,\,d)}{NRS_\varphi} = \left(\overset{(a,\,b;c,\,d)}{FTS_\varphi}, \ CORE, \ MSG/R \right)$ be a note-reception system, relative, absolute, or reflexive.

We shall refer to the set *CLUST* of all notes (s, t), $0 \leq s \leq a - 1$, as *the cluster of* $\overset{(a,\,b;c,\,d)}{NRS_\varphi}$, if there exists a note-reception system $\left(\overset{(a,\,b;c,\,d)}{FTS'_\varphi}, CORE, MSG/R' \right) = \overset{(a,\,b;c,\,d)}{NRS'_\varphi}$, relative, absolute, or reflexive, respectively, such that $(s, \ t) \in MSG/R'$.

The cluster of a note-reception system, in other words, is the set of received images, represented by their register-zero equivalents, of all *hypothetically* transmittable notes (the received images of all transmittable notes *relative to the same core*). Thus the *actual* received message *MSG/R*, represented as a set of register-zero equivalents, is a subset of the cluster.

Example 6.8. Let $NRS_\varphi = (FTS_\varphi, \ CORE, \ MSG/R)$ be an absolute, usual (or anti-usual) note-reception system, $CORE = \{A\}$.

Then the cluster *CLUST* of NRS_φ is the set of 11 notes A, B♭, B, C, C♯, D, E, F, F♯, G, G♯.

*Proposition 6.9. Let $\overset{(a,\,b;c,\,d)}{NRS_\varphi} = \left(\overset{(a,\,b;c,\,d)}{FTS_\varphi}, \ CORE, \ MSG/R \right)$ be a note-reception system with cluster *CLUST*.

Then $CORE \subset CLUST$.

6.3   Proto-diatonic Systems

We shall now develop a structure that consists of a note-reception system together with a series of *reflexive* note-reception systems, all with the same core. The ultimate purpose of this development is to define "diatonic system" in terms that reflect the Communication Principle, in particular the idea that a "diatonic" core may successfully be *self-communicated* (Definition 6.21, ahead). We begin with the following definition, the relevance of which to our purpose will become apparent in connection with Theorem 6.15 ahead.

Definition 6.10. Enharmonic Notes

We shall refer to two notes (s, t), (s', t') as *enharmonic* if $s \equiv s'$ (mod a).

Definition 6.11. Proto-diatonic System

Let $\overset{(a,\ b;\ c,\ d)}{NRS_\varphi} = \left(\overset{(a,\ b;\ c,\ d)}{FTS_\varphi}, CORE, MSG/R \right)$ be a note-reception system with

message *MSG* and cluster *CLUST*, and let $\overset{(a,\ b;\ c,\ d)}{NRSi_\varphi} = \left(\overset{(a,\ b;\ c,\ d)}{FTSi_\varphi}, CORE, MSG/Ri \right)$

be a series $i = 1, 2, \ldots$ of reflexive note-reception systems with message *MSGi*.

We shall refer to $\overset{(a,\ b;c,\ d)}{DTS_\varphi} = \left(\overset{(a,\ b;c,\ d)}{NRS_\varphi}, \overset{(a,\ b;c,\ d)}{NRSi_\varphi} \right)$ as *a proto-diatonic system*

(with core CORE, cluster CLUST, message MSG, and received message MSG/R), if *MSG*1 is an ordering of *CORE* such that the following condition A is satisfied.

A. $MSG/Ri = MSG(i + 1)$.

Depending on $\overset{(a,\ b;c,\ d)}{NRS_\varphi}$ (Definition 6.5) we shall refer to a proto-diatonic tone

system $\overset{(a,\ b;c,\ d)}{DTS_\varphi} = \left(\overset{(a,\ b;c,\ d)}{NRS_\varphi}, \overset{(a,\ b;c,\ d)}{NRSi_\varphi} \right)$ as *absolute*, *relative*, or *reflexive*.

A proto-diatonic system models a person that does not merely retain a core of notes mentally for the purpose of note reception, whether absolute, relative, or reflexive; the person also *transmits* these notes, reflexively, in an act of self-communication (hence, *MSG*1 is an ordering of the core). Moreover, there exists a potentially endless cycle whereby the received message at iteration i is fed back into the reflexive system to become the transmitted message at iteration $i + 1$ (Condition A of the definition). Note that the core is unchanged throughout the entire process.

Since (1) *MSG*1 is an ordering of *CORE*; (2) a reflexive note-reception system is a faithful pitch-communication system; and (3) $MSG/Ri = MSG(i + 1)$, we have the following proposition.

*Proposition 6.12. Let $\overset{(a,\,b;c,\,d)}{NRSi_\varphi} = \left(\overset{((a,\,b;c,\,d)}{FTSi_\varphi},\ CORE,\ MSG/Ri\right)$ be a series
$i = 1,\ 2,\ \ldots$ of reflexive note-reception systems with message $MSGi$. Let w be
an integer, $0 \le w \le a - 1$, and let Xi be the exchange $MSGi \to MSG/Ri$.

If $(w,\ x) \in CORE$ for some x, then for some $t_i,\ r_i$ there exist $(w,\ t_i) \in MSGi$,
$(w,\ r_i) \in MSG/Ri$, such that X$i(w,\ t_i) = (w,\ r_i)$. Conversely, if for some $t_i,\ r_i$
there exist $(w,\ t_i) \in MSGi$ and $(w,\ r_i) \in MSG/Ri$ such that X$i(w,\ t_i) = (w,\ r_i)$,
then $(w,\ x) \in CORE$ for some x.

Definition 6.13. Stable Proto-diatonic System

Let $\overset{(a,\,b;c,\,d)}{DTS_\varphi} = \left(\overset{(a,\,b;c,\,d)}{NRS_\varphi},\ \overset{(a,\,b;c,\,d)}{NRSi_\varphi}\right)$ be a proto-diatonic system, where

$\overset{(a,\,b;c,\,d)}{NRSi_\varphi} = \left(\overset{((a,\,b;c,\,d)}{FTSi_\varphi},\ CORE,\ MSG/Ri\right)$ is a series $i = 1,\ 2,\ \ldots$ of reflexive

note-reception systems with message $MSGi$.

We shall refer to the system as *stable at i* if for every $j \ge i$ $MSG/Rj = MSG1$.

By reaching a state where the reflexively received message always equals $MSG1$
(an ordering of the core), a stable proto-diatonic system consummates the Communication Principle in the sense of self-communicating the core.

Proposition 6.14. Let $\overset{(a,\,b;c,\,d)}{DTS_\varphi} = \left(\overset{(a,\,b;c,\,d)}{NRS_\varphi},\ \overset{(a,\,b;c,\,d)}{NRSi_\varphi}\right)$ be a proto-diatonic

system, where $\overset{(a,\,b;c,\,d)}{NRSi_\varphi} = \left(\overset{((a,\,b;c,\,d)}{FTSi_\varphi},\ CORE, MSG/Ri\right)$ is a series $i = 1,\ 2,\ \ldots$

of reflexive note-reception systems with message $MSGi$.

If $CORE$ is a singleton then the system is stable at $i = 1$.

Proof. Set $CORE = \{(w,\ x)\}$. By Proposition 6.12 for some $t_i,\ r_i$ there exist
$(w,\ t_i) \in MSGi$, $(w,\ r_i) \in MSG/Ri$ such that X$i(w,\ t_i) = (w,\ r_i)$, where Xi is
the exchange $MSGi \to MSG/Ri$. By Definitions 6.5 and 6.2

$$(w,\ r_i) \equiv_{(a,\ b)} (w,\ x) + (y,\ z)$$

for some $(y,\ z) \in \overset{(c,\ d)}{RVL}$, implying that $y = 0 = z$. Thus $r_i = x$, and $MSG/Ri = MSG1 = \{(w,\ x)\}$ for every i. Thus the series is stable at $i = 1$. Q.E.D.

Theorem 6.15. Let $\overset{(a,\,b;c,\,d)}{DTS_\varphi} = \left(\overset{(a,\,b;c,\,d)}{NRS_\varphi},\ \overset{(a,\,b;c,\,d)}{NRSi_\varphi}\right)$ be a proto-diatonic system

with a core $CORE$ of at least two elements.

If the system is stable at some i then $i = 1$.

To prove the theorem we shall first prove the following lemma; review
Definition 6.10.

Lemma 6.16. Let $DTS_\varphi^{(a,\,b;c,\,d)} = \left(NRS_\varphi^{(a,\,b;c,\,d)} , \; NRSi_\varphi^{(a,\,b;c,\,d)} \right)$ be a proto-diatonic system

with a core $CORE$ of at least two elements.

If the system is stable at some i then no two distinct core elements are enharmonic.

Proof. Suppose the system is stable at i and suppose by contradiction that (w, x), (w, x') is a pair of distinct core elements. Using Proposition 6.12, the following two conditions hold for some t_i, t'_i:

$$Xi(w, \; t_i) = (w, \; x),$$
$$Xi(w, \; t'_i) = (w, \; x').$$

From Definitions 6.5 and 6.2 it follows that for every $(w'', \; x'') \in CORE$ for which there exists a (unique) $(y, \; z) \in RVL^{(c,\,d)}$ satisfying $w'' + y \equiv w \pmod{a}$, we have

$$(w, \; x) \equiv_{(a,\,b)} (w'', \; x'') \oplus (y, \; z) \equiv_{(a,\,b)} (w, \; x'),$$

implying that $(w, \; x) = (w, \; x')$, contrary to our assumption. In particular, if $(w'', \; x'') = (w, \; x)$, $(w, \; x')$, then $(y, \; z) = (0, \; 0)$. Q.E.D.

Proof of the theorem. Using Proposition 6.12 set $Xi(w, \; t_i) = (w, \; r_i)$, where Xi is the exchange $MSGi \to MSG/Ri$, and suppose by contradiction that the system is stable at $i \geq 2$. Using Lemma 6.16, by Definition 6.13 there exists a unique x such that $(w, \; x) \in CORE$ satisfies the following two conditions (1) and (2):

1. $X1(w, \; x) = (w, \; r_1) \neq (w, \; x)$.
2. $Xi(w, \; t_i) = (w, \; x)$.

By Definitions 6.5 and 6.2 the following two conditions (3) and (4) respectively follow:

3. For some $(w', \; x') \in CORE$, where $w' \not\equiv w + a/2 \pmod{a}$, there exists a $(y, \; z) \in RVL^{(c,\,d)}$ such that $(w, \; r_1) \equiv_{(a,\,b)} (w', \; x') + (y, \; z)$.
4. For every $(w'', \; x'') \in CORE$, where $w'' \not\equiv w + a/2 \pmod{a}$, there exists a $(y', \; z') \in RVL^{(c,\,d)}$ such that $(w, \; x) \equiv_{(a,\,b)} (w'', \; x'') + (y', \; z')$.

Set $(w'', \; x'') = (w', \; x')$. Then $(y', \; z') = (y, \; z)$, implying that $r_1 = x$, contradicting (1). Thus $i = 1$. Q.E.D.

Fig. 6.2 Schubert, String Quintet in C major, D. 956, mm. 1–6

6.4   Diatonic Systems

Consider a note-reception system (Definition 6.5) from the point of view of the receiver. If the core consists of exactly one element (as in the Bartók, Example 6.6) a message element may be processed as a received element in exactly one way. If, however, the core consists of more than one element, the result may depend on the choice of referential core element. For example, if $CORE = \{A, B\flat\flat\}$, assuming an absolute or reflexive usual (or anti-usual) system we have
$$\overset{A}{IMG}(A) = A \neq B\flat\flat = \overset{B\flat\flat}{IMG}(A).$$
A more familiar example follows.

Example 6.17. If NRS_φ is an absolute, usual note-reception system, and $CORE$ is the natural core C, D,..., B, then $\overset{C}{IMG}(E\flat) = E\flat \neq D\sharp = \overset{E}{IMG}(E\flat)$.

The opening of Schubert's C major Quintet, D. 956 (Vienna, 1828), illustrates precisely such a case (Fig. 6.2). Consider the viola's E♭, mm. 3–4, along with the core elements with which, contextually, it is most strongly associated, namely C (harmonically) and E (melodically). Relative to C one hears E♭, yet relative to E—D♯.

The viola's E♭ is of course "non-diatonic." As may easily be verified, inconsistencies of the type just illustrated do not occur in the case of "diatonic" notes. For example, $\overset{C}{IMG}(C) = C = \overset{E}{IMG}(C)$. In particular, although $\overset{B}{IMG}(F) = \overset{F}{IMG}(B) = \varnothing$, we have $\overset{N}{IMG}(F) = F$ for every core element N other than B, and similarly, $\overset{M}{IMG}(B) = B$ for every core element M other than F.

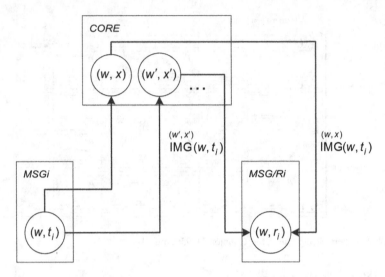

Fig. 6.3 A proto-diatonic system with a diatonic note (w, t_i)

The crucial notion, "diatonic note," is defined next; review Definitions 6.5 and 6.11, and Proposition 6.12. Recall that $MSG1$ is an ordering of the core.

Definition 6.18. Diatonic Note

Let $\overset{(a,\,b;c,\,d)}{DTS_\varphi} = \left(\overset{(a,\,b;c,\,d)}{NRS_\varphi}, \overset{(a,\,b;c,\,d)}{NRSi_\varphi} \right)$ be a proto-diatonic system with core

$CORE$, where $\overset{(a,\,b;c,\,d)}{NRSi_\varphi} = \left(\overset{(a,\,b;c,\,d)}{FTSi_\varphi}, CORE, MSG/Ri \right)$ is a series $i = 1, 2, \ldots$
of reflexive note-reception systems with message $MSGi$. Let $(w, t_i) \in MSGi$, for some t_i.

We shall refer to (w, t_i) as *diatonic (at i)* if for some r_i the following condition A is satisfied for every $(w', x') \in CORE$.

A. Unless $\overset{(w',\,x')}{IMG}(w, t_i) = \varnothing$, $\overset{(w',\,x')}{IMG}(w, t_i) = (w, r_i)$.

Consider a proto-diatonic system and particularly the series of reflexive note-reception systems $\overset{(a,\,b;c,\,d)}{NRSi_\varphi}$ that it contains. By Definition 6.18 a transmitted note (w, t_i) is diatonic at i if, for some r_i, the image of (w, t_i) relative to *every* core element, unless it is empty, is (w, r_i).

Figure 6.3 clarifies; recall that $MSG1$ is an ordering of the core.

By the following theorem, the property that *every* transmitted note at iteration i is diatonic is equivalent to stability. Since this implies that $i = 1$ (Theorem 6.15), it follows that the core itself is a set of diatonic notes.

Theorem 6.19. (Diatonic Stability)

Let $DTS_\varphi^{(a,\,b;\,c,\,d)} = \left(NRS_\varphi^{(a,\,b;\,c,\,d)}, \; NRSi_\varphi^{(a,\,b;\,c,\,d)} \right)$ be a proto-diatonic system.

Then the following two conditions, A and B, are equivalent.

A. For some i, every $(w, \; t_i) \in MSGi$ is diatonic at i.

B. $DTS_\varphi^{(a,\,b;\,c,\,d)}$ is stable.

To prove the theorem we shall first prove the following lemma.

Lemma 6.20. Let $DTS_\varphi^{(a,\,b;\,c,\,d)} = \left(NRS_\varphi^{(a,\,b;\,c,\,d)}, \; NRSi_\varphi^{(a,\,b;\,c,\,d)} \right)$ be a proto-diatonic system.

If, for some i, every $(w, \; t_i) \in MSGi$ is diatonic at i, then no two distinct core elements are enharmonic.

Proof. Suppose that every $(w, \; t_i) \in MSGi$ is diatonic at i, and suppose by contradiction that (w, x), (w, x') is a pair of distinct core elements. By Definition 6.18 the following two conditions hold for some r_i:

$$\overset{(w,\;x)}{IMG} (w, \; t_i) = (w, \; r_i),$$

$$\overset{(w,\;x')}{IMG} (w, \; t_i) = (w, \; r_i).$$

From Definitions 6.5 and 6.2 it follows that there exist $(y, \; z)$, $(y', \; z') \in \overset{(c,\;d)}{RVL}$ satisfying

$$(w, \; x) \oplus (y, \; z) \equiv_{(a,\;b)} (w, \; r_i) \equiv_{(a,\;b)} (w, \; x') \oplus (y', \; z'),$$

implying that $(y, \; z) = (0, \; 0) = (y', \; z')$. Thus $(w, \; x) = (w, \; x')$, contrary to our assumption. Q.E.D.

Proof of the theorem. Suppose that Condition A holds. By Definition 6.18 there exists a $(w, \; r_i) \in MSG/Ri$ such that, unless $\overset{(w',\;x')}{IMG} (w, \; t_i) = \varnothing$, $\overset{(w',\;x')}{IMG} (w, \; t_i) = (w, \; r_i)$ for every $(w', \; x') \in CORE$. By Lemma 6.20 there exists a unique x such that $(w, \; x) \in CORE$.

Set $(w', \; x') = (w, \; x)$. By Definitions 6.5 and 6.2 $(w, \; r_i) \equiv_{(a,\;b)} (w, \; x) \oplus (y, \; z)$ for some $(y, \; z) \in \overset{(c,\;d)}{RVL}$. Thus $y = 0 = z$, and $r_i = x$. Thus the system is stable, and Condition B holds.

Suppose that Condition B holds. By Definition 6.13 and Theorem 6.15 $MSG/R1 = MSG1$, an ordering of the core. By Definition 6.5, for every $(w', x') \in CORE$, unless $\overset{(w',\ x')}{\text{IMG}}(w, x) = \varnothing$, $\overset{(w',\ x')}{\text{IMG}}(w, x) = (w, x)$, and therefore Condition A holds. Q.E.D.

Definition 6.21. Diatonic System

Let $\overset{(a,\ b;c,\ d)}{DTS_\varphi} = \left(\overset{(a,\ b;c,\ d)}{NRS_\varphi}, \overset{(a,\ b;c,\ d)}{NRSi_\varphi} \right)$ be a proto-diatonic system with

core $CORE$.

We shall refer to the system as *diatonic* if $CORE$ contains a maximal number of elements every one of which is diatonic (Definition 6.18).

A diatonic system in the sense of Definition 6.21 consummates the Communication Principle *in the sense of self-communicating the core* (Theorem 6.19). As we shall see, this is also the *only* sense in which the Communication Principle can be guaranteed to be consummated, for the "real" message MSG is at best received transposed (Sect. 10.4). By confirming one's ability to successfully communicate *at least* the core and *at least* with oneself, a diatonic system renders tolerable, from the point of view of the communication-thirsty self, the imperfections that necessarily infest communication under any other set of conditions.

The condition that diatonic cores contain a maximal number of elements is an expression of the Maximalist Principle. The Maximalist Principle here conflicts with the Economical Principle, by which cores should preferably contain *a minimal* number of elements, so as to reduce cognitive load on the receiver as much as possible. We defer resolution of this conflict to Part II of the book, where a coherence-like algorithm will replace the need to memorize the entire core (Sect. 10.4).

Finally, note that by Lemma 6.20 "diatonic" and "enharmonic" are mutually exclusive concepts. However, as we shall see in Sect. 9.2, the notion "chromatic" mediates between the two.

In the following theorem "κ" is the Greek letter *Kappa*; review Definition 5.19.

Theorem 6.22. Let $\overset{(a,\ b;c,\ d)}{DTS_\varphi} = \left(\overset{(a,\ b;c,\ d)}{NRS_\varphi}, \overset{(a,\ b;c,\ d)}{NRSi_\varphi} \right)$ be a proto-diatonic system

with core $CORE$.

Then $\overset{(a,\ b;c,\ d)}{DTS_\varphi}$ is diatonic if, and only if, for some κ, $CORE$ may be written as the quintic segment Q_κ^n, where $n = \lfloor a/2 \rfloor + 1$.

To prove the theorem we shall first state one lemma and prove another.

*Lemma 6.23. Let $\overset{(a,\ b;c,\ d)}{DTS_\varphi} = \left(\overset{(a,\ b;c,\ d)}{NRS_\varphi}, \overset{(a,\ b;c,\ d)}{NRSi_\varphi} \right)$ be a diatonic system with

core $CORE$. Let (w, x), $(w', x') \in CORE$, where $w' \not\equiv w + a/2 \pmod a$.

Then $(w, x) - (w', x') \equiv_{(a, b)} (y, z) \in \overset{(c, d)}{RVL}$.

Lemma 6.24. Let $\overset{(a, b; c, d)}{DTS_\varphi} = \left(\overset{(a, b; c, d)}{NRS_\varphi}, \overset{(a, b; c, d)}{NRSi_\varphi} \right)$ be a diatonic system such that a is even, and $CORE$ contains at least three elements (w_i, x_i), $i = 1, 2, 3$, satisfying $w_2 \equiv w_1 + a/2 \pmod{a}$. Set $(u, v) = (w_2, x_2) - (w_1, x_1)$.

Then $(u, v) \equiv_{(a, b)} \pm \frac{a}{2}(c, d)$.

Proof. By Lemma 6.20 $w_3 \not\equiv w_2, w_1$. Therefore, by Lemma 6.23 we have for some k, k',

$$(w_3, x_3) - (w_1, x_1) \equiv_{(a, b)} (y, z)_k \in \overset{(c, d)}{RVL},$$
$$(w_2, x_2) - (w_3, x_3) \equiv_{(a, b)} (y, z)_{k'} \in \overset{(c, d)}{RVL}.$$

It follows that

$$(u, v) \equiv_{(a, b)} (y, z)_k \oplus (y, z)_{k'} \equiv_{(a, b)} (k + k') \cdot (c, d).$$

Set $k + k' = m$. Since $|k|, |k'| \leq \frac{a}{2} - 1$, we have

$$|m| \leq a - 2. \tag{6.1}$$

Suppose by contradiction that $|m| \neq a/2$. Since a is even and $\gcd(a, c) = 1$ we have $u \equiv mc \equiv a/2 \pmod{a}$, implying that $|m| \geq 3a/2$, contrary to Condition 6.1. Thus $|m| = a/2$. Q.E.D.

Proof of the theorem. Let $\overset{(a, b; c, d)}{DTS_\varphi} = \left(\overset{(a, b; c, d)}{NRS_\varphi}, \overset{(a, b; c, d)}{NRSi_\varphi} \right)$ be a diatonic system with core $CORE$. Let (w, x), (w', x') be two core elements, and set $(u, v) = (w', x') - (w, x)$. Since $CORE$ contains a maximal number of elements, $a \geq 3$, we may assume that $w' \not\equiv w \pmod{a}$.

Suppose that $w' \not\equiv w + a/2 \pmod{a}$. Then by Lemma 6.23 $(u, v) \equiv_{(a, b)} (y, z) \in \overset{(c, d)}{RVL}$. Suppose a is even, and $w' \equiv w + a/2 \pmod{a}$. If $CORE \neq \{(w, x), (w', x')\}$ then by Lemma 6.24 $(u, v) \equiv_{(a, b)} \pm \frac{a}{2}(c, d)$. It follows that one of the following two conditions, 1 or 2, holds.

1. a is even, and $CORE = \{(w, x), (w', x')\}$ satisfies $w' \equiv w + a/2 \pmod{a}$.
2. $(u, v) \equiv_{(a, b)} k(c, d), |k| \leq \lfloor a/2 \rfloor$.

Suppose that a is even. If Condition 1 holds the core contains exactly two elements; if Condition 2 holds the core contains a maximum of exactly $\lfloor a/2 \rfloor + 1 \geq 3$ elements. Since the core contains a maximal number of elements it follows that it contains exactly $\lfloor a/2 \rfloor + 1$ elements which may be written as a quintic segment. This proves that for $DTS_\varphi^{(a,\,b;c,\,d)}$ to be diatonic, it is necessary for $CORE$ to be a quintic segment Q_κ^n, $n = \lfloor a/2 \rfloor + 1$; it may be easily seen that these conditions are also sufficient. Q.E.D.

In connection with the following definition, recall that a type-2 system satisfies $b = |a| - 1$ is odd (Proposition 5.12).

Definition 6.25. Standard Diatonic System

Let $DTS_\varphi^{(a,\,b;c,\,d)} = \left(NRS_\varphi^{(a,\,b;c,\,d)}, \; NRSi_\varphi^{(a,\,b;c,\,d)} \right)$ be a type-1 diatonic system with core $CORE$.

We shall refer to the system as *standard* if b equals the number of core elements, that is, $b = \lfloor a/2 \rfloor + 1$.

We shall assume henceforth that a diatonic system is standard. Since, for some integer κ, the core of a standard diatonic system may be written as the quintic segment Q_κ^b, we shall write henceforth $CORE = CORE^\kappa$. Moreover, we shall write

$$DTS_\varphi^{(a,\,b;c,\,d)} = DTS_\varphi^\kappa = \left(NRS_\varphi^{\kappa\,(a,\,b;c,\,d)}, \; NRSi_\varphi^{\kappa\,(a,\,b;c,\,d)} \right).$$

In contrast to the primary intervals, which are associated (in a type-1 system) with the integer a (in particular, the number of primary intervals is either a or $a - 1$), the core and its elements are now associated with the integer b (the number of core elements is exactly b). Note that the number b is now assumed with no loss of generality to be positive (as we have assumed previously with regard to a, assuming a type-1 system; see Definition 5.11). Note also that the status of Q_κ as the *first* element of the core in quintic order does not lend it any particular privilege.

Definition 6.26. Usual/Anti-usual Diatonic System

We shall refer to a diatonic system $DTS_\varphi^{\kappa\,(12,\,7;c,\,d)}$ as *usual (anti-usual)* and shall write

$$DTS_\varphi^{\kappa\,(12,\,7;c,\,d)} = DTS_\varphi^\kappa = \left(NRS_\varphi^\kappa, \; NRSi_\varphi^\kappa \right), \text{ if } (c,\,d) = (7,\,4)\,((c,\,d) = (5,\,3)).$$

Example 6.27. The core $CORE^{-1}$ of a usual diatonic system DTS_φ^{-1} is the natural core $(0, 0), (2, 1), (4, 2), (5, 3), (7, 4), (9, 5), (11, 6)$.

Starting with $Q_{-1} = (5,\;3) = F$ the natural core may be written as the connected segment of the usual line of fifths, F, C,..., B.

6.5 Properties of Diatonic Systems

Proposition 6.28. Let $DTS_\varphi^{\kappa\,(a,\,b;c,\,d)}$ be a diatonic system.

Then one of the following two conditions, A or B, holds.

A. a is odd, and $(c,\ d) = (2,\ 1),\ (a-2,\ b-1)$.

B. $a \equiv 0 \pmod 4$, and $(c,\ d) = \left(\dfrac{a}{2} \pm 1,\ \dfrac{b \pm 1}{2}\right)$.

Proof. From Theorem 5.16 $cb \equiv \pm 1 \pmod a$, $d = \frac{cb \mp 1}{a}$; by Definition 6.25 $b = \lfloor a/2 \rfloor + 1$. Since $0 \le c \le a - 1$ Condition A or B follows. In particular, if a is even we have

$$cb = \left(\frac{a}{2} \pm 1\right)\left(\frac{a}{2} + 1\right) = \frac{a^2}{4} + a + 1,\ \frac{a^2}{4} - 1,$$

and therefore $d = \frac{cb \mp 1}{a}$ satisfies $d = \frac{a}{4} + 1$, $\frac{a}{4}$, implying that $a \equiv 0 \pmod 4$. Q.E.D.

Definition 6.29. Interval Content of the Core

Let $DTS_\varphi^\kappa{}^{(a,\ b;c,\ d)}$ be a diatonic system. Set $(u,\ v) \equiv_{(a,\ b)} (w',\ x') - (w,\ x)$, where $(w,\ x), (w',\ x') \in CORE^\kappa$.

We shall refer to the set $I/CORE^\kappa$ of all intervals $(u,\ v), 0 \le u \le a - 1$, as *the interval content of the core*.

Propositions 5.12 and 5.20 are useful in proving the following proposition.

*Proposition 6.30. Let $DTS_\varphi^\kappa{}^{(a,\ b;c,\ d)}$ be a diatonic system. Set $v^\pm = \frac{b \pm 1}{2} \equiv \mp \frac{ad}{2} \pmod b$ if a is even.
   Then

$$I/CORE^\kappa = RVL^{(c,\ d)}\ \text{if}\ a\ \text{is odd},$$
$$I/CORE^\kappa = RVL^{(c,\ d)} \cup \{(a/2,\ v^+),\ (a/2,\ v^-)\}\ \text{if}\ a\ \text{is even}.$$

Moreover, $I/CORE^\kappa$ may be written as the following set A or B, respectively.

A. $(0,\ 0),\ (1,\ 1),\ (2,\ 1),\ (3,\ 2),\ (4,\ 2), \ldots,$
     $(a-4,\ b-2),\ (a-3,\ b-2),\ (a-2,\ b-1),\ (a-1,\ b-1)$.

B.
$(0,\ 0),\ (1,\ 1),\ (2,\ 1),\ (3,\ 2),\ (4,\ 2), \ldots,$

$$\left(\frac{a}{2} - 1,\ \frac{b-1}{2}\right),\ \left(\frac{a}{2},\ \frac{b-1}{2}\right),\ \left(\frac{a}{2},\ \frac{b+1}{2}\right),\ \left(\frac{a}{2} + 1,\ \frac{b+1}{2}\right),$$

$$\left(\frac{a}{2} + 2,\ \frac{b+3}{2}\right),\ \left(\frac{a}{2} + 3,\ \frac{b+3}{2}\right), \ldots,$$

$(a-4,\ b-2),\ (a-3,\ b-2),\ (a-2,\ b-1),\ (a-1,\ b-1)$.

Fig. 6.4 The scalar
ordering of the core relative
to its quintic ordering. (**a**)
$(a, b) = (13, 7)$, $(c, d) =$
$(2, 1)$; (**b**) $(a, b) = (12, 7)$,
$(c, d) = (7, 4)$

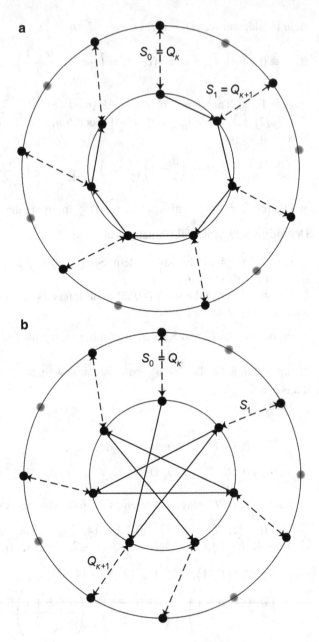

By Proposition 6.30 the core of a diatonic system is a "maximally even set" in the sense of Clough and Douthett (1991).[6] Moreover, the system is "coherent" in Agmon's (1986, 1989, 1996) earlier sense, borrowed, together with the term "coherence," from Balzano (1982).

In connection with the following proposition, recall that every core element (w, x) satisfies $0 \leq w \leq a - 1$.

*Proposition 6.31. Let DTS_φ^{κ} $\overset{(a,\,b;\,c,\,d)}{}$ be a diatonic system, and assume that $d = 1$ if a is odd, $d = \frac{b+1}{2}$ if a is even. Set $Q_\kappa = (w_\sigma, \ x_\sigma)$, write

$$CORE^\kappa = (w_\sigma, \ x_\sigma), \ (w_{\sigma+1}, \ x_{\sigma+1}), \ \ldots, \ (w_{\sigma+b-1}, \ x_{\sigma+b-1})$$

such that $x_{\sigma + i} \equiv x_\sigma + i \,(\text{mod } b)$, $i = 0, \ 1, \ \ldots, \ b - 1$, and refer to this ordering of the core as "scalar." Finally, set

$w_{\sigma+i} \equiv w_\sigma + o_i \,(\text{mod } a)$ if a is odd, $i = 0, \ 1, \ \ldots, \ a - 2, \ a - 1,$

$w_{\sigma+i} \equiv w_\sigma + e_i \,(\text{mod } a)$ if a is even, $i = 0, \ 1, \ \ldots, \ d - 1, \ d, \ d + 1, \ \ldots,$
$a - 2, \ a - 1.$

Then, respectively,

$$o_i = 0, \ 2, \ \ldots, \ a - 3, \ a - 1,$$

$$e_i = 0, \ 2, \ \ldots, \ \frac{a}{2}, \ \frac{a}{2} + 1, \ \frac{a}{2} + 3, \ \ldots, \ a - 3, \ a - 1.$$

Moreover, $w_{\sigma + i} > w_{\sigma + j}$ if, and only if, $x_{\sigma + i} > x_{\sigma + j}$, $0 \leq i, \ j \leq b - 1$.

Finally, we have the following proposition.

*Proposition 6.32. Let DTS_φ^{κ} $\overset{(a,\,b;\,c,\,d)}{}$ be a diatonic system, and assume that $d = 1$ if a is odd, $d = \frac{b+1}{2}$ if a is even. Write S_i for the ith element of the core in scalar order, $i = 0, \ 1, \ \ldots, b - 1$.

---

[6] Cf. Clough and Douthett's (1991, p. 100) Definition 1.7: "A set of pcs is *maximally even*... if it has the following property: the spectrum of each dlen is either a single integer or two consecutive integers." Clough and Douthett's Definition 1.7 is closely related to "Myhill's Property," according to which "every generic interval appears in exactly two specific sizes" (Clough and Myerson 1985, p. 250). For further discussion see Sect. 8.3.

Then

$$S_i = Q_{\kappa+i} \text{ if } a \text{ is odd,}$$
$$S_i = Q_{\kappa+(2i)_b} \text{ if } a \text{ is even,}$$

where $(2i)_b$ is the reduction modulo b of $2i$ to an integer between 0 and $b - 1$.

By Proposition 6.32 a diatonic system is a "well-formed scale" in the sense of Carey and Clampitt (1989).[7]

Figure 6.4 illustrates Proposition 6.31 for $(a, \ b) = (13, \ 7)$, $(c, \ d) = (2, \ 1)$, and $(a, \ b) = (12, \ 7)$, $(c, \ d) = (7, \ 4)$. Points w on the outer circles are paired via the dashed double arrows with points x on the inner circles, such that (w, x) is a core element. The quintic ordering is given by the inner-circle solid arrows.

References

Agmon, E. (1986). *Diatonicism, chromaticism, and enharmonicism: A study in cognition and perception*. PhD diss., City University of New York.

Agmon, E. (1989). A mathematical model of the diatonic system. *Journal of Music Theory, 33*(1), 1–25.

Agmon, E. (1996). Coherent tone-systems: A study in the theory of diatonicism. *Journal of Music Theory, 40*(1), 39–59.

Balzano, G. (1982). The pitch set as a level of description for studying musical pitch perception. In M. Clynes (Ed.), *Music, mind, and brain: The neuropsychology of music* (pp. 321–351). New York: Plenum.

Brukman, J. (2008). The relevance of Friedrich Hartmann's fully-chromaticised scales with regard to Bartók's *Fourteen Bagatelles*, Op. 6. *Theoria, 15*, 31–62.

Carey, N., & Clampitt, D. (1989). Aspects of well-formed scales. *Music Theory Spectrum, 11*(2), 187–206.

Clough, J., & Douthett, J. (1991). Maximally even sets. *Journal of Music Theory, 35*(1–2), 93–173.

Clough, J., & Myerson, G. (1985). Variety and multiplicity in diatonic systems. *Journal of Music Theory, 29*(2), 249–270.

Gillies, M. (1982). Bartók's last works: A theory of tonality and modality. *Musicology, 7*, 120–130.

Gillies, M. (1983). Bartók's notation: Tonality and modality. *Tempo, 145*, 4–9.

Gillies, M. (1989). *Notation and tonal structure in Bartók's later works*. New York: Garland.

Gillies, M. (1993). Pitch notations and tonality: Bartók. In J. Dunsby (Ed.), *Models of musical analysis: Early twentieth-century music* (pp. 42–55). Oxford: Blackwell.

Hindemith, P. (1937). *The craft of music composition: Book I* (A. Mendel, Trans. & Rev.). 1945. New York: Associated Music Publishers.

Hunkemöller, J. (1983). Bartók analysiert seine "Musik für Saiteninstrumente, Schlagzeug und Celesta". *Archiv für Musikwissenschaft, 40*(2), 147–163.

Leichtentritt, H. (1929). On the art of Béla Bartók. *Modern Music, 6*(3), 3–11.

Shannon, C. (1948). A mathematical theory of communication. *Bell System Technical Journal, 27* (3–4), 379–423, 623–656.

von der Nüll, E. (1930). *Béla Bartók: Ein Betrag zur Morphologie der neuen Musik*. Halle: Mitteldeutsche Verlags A. G.

---

[7] See Carey and Clampitt (1989), p. 196.

Chapter 7
Harmonic Systems

Abstract Harmonic communication is fundamentally different from melodic communication in the sense that the "harmonic message" (a sequence of chords), unlike
the "melodic message" (a sequence of notes), is generally not stated explicitly in the
score (Sect. 7.1). Nonetheless, on the basis of *harmonic grammar* the analyst is able
to infer a harmonic message from a given score, and the receiver a corresponding
received harmonic message from the received score. Sections 7.2, 7.3, and 7.4
respectively focus on an aspect of harmonic grammar usually associated with one of
the three great luminaries of harmonic theory, Rameau, Riemann, and Schenker.
Associated with Rameau is the idea that the vast variety of note sequences describable as "chords" reduce to constructs forming a "stack of thirds from a root," in
particular, "triads" and "seventh chords." Associated with Riemann is the idea that,
relative to a referential triad, triads group into categories or "functions," based on
common elements (similarly for seventh chords). Associated with Schenker is the
idea that harmony has an irreducible melodic component in the form of "voice
leading," that is, the manner in which the elements of a given chord are paired with
the elements of its successor. Stepwise motion plays an important role in such
pairings. The harmonic ideas associated with all three theorists are combined in
Sect. 7.5, leading to a theorem concerning the necessary and sufficient conditions
for the existence of triad-like and seventh-chord-like harmonic objects.

7.1 The Grammatical Basis of Harmonic Communication

"The 'Alpha and Omega' of musical artistry" writes Hugo Riemann (1914/15,
tr. Wason and Marvin 1992, pp. 82–83, original emphasis),

> *is not found in the actual, sounding music, but rather exists in the mental image of musical
> relationships that occurs in the creative artist's imagination—a mental image that lives
> before it is transformed into notation and re-emerges in the imagination of the hearer. The
> process of notating an artistic creation as well as the sounding performance of the work are
> merely expedients to transplant musical experiences from the composer's imagination
> into the imagination of the musical listener.... In other words: neither acoustics, nor*

E. Agmon, *The Languages of Western Tonality*, Computational Music Science,
DOI 10.1007/978-3-642-39587-1_7, © Springer-Verlag Berlin Heidelberg 2013

*tone-physiology nor tone-psychology can give the key to the innermost essence of music,
but rather only a "Theory of Tonal Imagination"—a theory which, to be sure, has yet to be
postulated, much less developed and completed.*

Riemann's language is remarkably suggestive of a communicative act, and thus
his "tonal imagination" resonates strongly with the central theme of the present
book, in particular the process by which a musical message is "transplanted," using
Riemann's vivid imagery, "from the composer's imagination into the imagination
of the musical listener."

Riemann's (1914/15) main concern is harmony, a topic we have so far neglected
to address. It is therefore necessary to ask: Is harmonic communication analogous
to "melodic" communication, the sole difference being that a "harmonic message"
is a sequence *of sequences* of notes, namely "chords," rather than a sequence of
notes? If the answer is positive, then harmonic considerations should have little or
no bearing on our study, certainly at its present, proto-tonal stage. That is to say,
nothing would fundamentally change in our argument thus far if a "melodic"
message is replaced with a "harmonic" one, that is, a sequence of notes with a
sequence of chords.

A moment's reflection, however, will reveal that the notion of a harmonic
message, epistemologically speaking, is very different from a melodic one.

Consider a musical score as a record of its composer's "musical imagination,"
that is, as a representation of a musical message. Reduced to its *note content under
temporal order* (that is, the "left-to-right" order in which notes are displayed on the
page), the score is essentially a sequence *of sequences* S_t of notes, as follows. A
sequence of notes S_t is a "simultaneity" corresponding to all the notes displayed at
given "time point" t (a point on the score's left-to-right, "horizontal" axis);
a simultaneity is ordered, say, from low to high.[1] Moreover, if two simultaneities
S_t and $S_{t'}$ satisfy $t > t'$, then $S_t > S_{t'}$. Thus conceived, a score may be uniquely
represented as a sequence of notes n, using the following simple algorithm:

1. If n is attacked before n', then $n < n'$.
2. Otherwise, if n is lower than n', then $n < n'$.

Consider Fig. 7.1a, the score of the opening phrase of the third movement of
Beethoven's "Serioso" String Quartet in F minor, Op. 95 (Vienna, 1810). By the
algorithm above the bracketed segment uniquely reduces to the sequence of notes
7.1b. In other words, the sense in which the segment constitutes a *melodic* message,
that is, a sequence of notes, is well defined. We thus have an epistemologically
sound point of departure for the study of melodic communication.[2]

---

[1] For present purposes, dynamics, timbre, etc., are ignored (also ignored is the extent to which a
note is sustained beyond its attack). If a simultaneity contains a pair of distinct, enharmonic notes,
these may be ordered by "staff height," for example, C♯ before D♭.

[2] "Melodic" is taken here in the broad sense of "being representable as a sequence of notes." A
"melody" in the usual sense consists of exactly one note per attack, thus rendering rule 2 of our
algorithm superfluous. The question may be raised whether "melodies" consist not only of notes

Fig. 7.1 Beethoven, String Quartet in F minor, Op. 95, III. (**a**) Score of first phrase; (**b**) melodic content of bracketed segment; (**c**) harmonic content of bracketed segment

When it comes to harmonic messages, however, the situation is radically different. Consider again the Beethoven excerpt. An algorithm by which the bracketed segment may be reduced to the chord progression of Fig. 7.1c, a progression one is likely to concur captures the "harmonic content" of the segment, is hard to come by. In particular, an algorithm based on *simultaneity* would fail miserably, for example, at the points in (a) marked with an asterisk. At the first asterisk, for example (m. 6), D_1 in the first violin is a non-chord tone; at the second asterisk (m. 8) not only is the chord incomplete, but a non-chord tone, B♭, is present *in the bass* (the status of the bass A♭ that follows is debatable, not only as a genuine bass tone but also as a chord tone). Clearly, in comparison to the melodic content of the bracketed segment, its harmonic content is rather elusive.

Does this mean that Riemann's bold vision of a "Theory of (Harmonic) Tonal Imagination" will remain forever unrealized? Not necessarily.

Note first that Fig. 7.1c closely resembles what in the Baroque period might have been a continuo accompaniment to the passage. Indeed, the figured-bass notations found in most Baroque scores are tangible evidence for the existence of harmonic messages. Moreover, "harmonic reductions" such as Fig. 7.1c have been

---

but also *of rests* (cf. in the Beethoven the *rest events* of mm. 2 and 4). This interesting question has little bearing on the present discussion.

conceptually linked to the figured-bass practice, most notably by William Rothstein (1991) who refers to them as "imaginary continuo."[3] "... The imaginary continuo" Rothstein writes

> is a feature of all tonal music—and, to be sure, of some pre-tonal music as well. It might even be regarded as one of the defining characteristics of tonality itself. In other words, the possibility of abstracting an imaginary continuo part—one that follows the rules of chord construction and voice leading typical of thoroughbass—may be considered a necessary, though not a sufficient, condition for describing a piece of music as tonal. (p. 297)

How is one able to abstract an imaginary continuo part from a harmonically conceived score? I propose that the answer (or at least an important part thereof) lies in the existence of "harmonic grammar" which consists, I propose, of three main ideas, associated each with one of the three great luminaries of harmonic theory: Rameau, Riemann, and Schenker. (Rameau arguably anticipated ideas more typically associated with Riemann and Schenker.)

Associated with Rameau is the idea that the vast variety of note sequences describable as "chords" reduce to constructs forming a "stack of thirds from a root," in particular, "triads" and "seventh chords." Thus, formations such as those asterisked in the Beethoven excerpt may be understood as *standing for* a triad or a seventh chord, even if "incomplete" or containing foreign elements.

Associated with Riemann is the idea that, relative to a referential triad, triads group into categories or "functions," based on common elements (similarly for seventh chords). Thus, the sense in which the downbeat of m. 8 of the Beethoven excerpt represents a "tonic function" (relative to C minor) allows its peculiar note content to be disambiguated.

Finally, associated with Schenker is the idea that harmony has an irreducible melodic component in the form of "voice leading," that is, the manner in which the elements of a given chord are paired with the elements of its successor. Stepwise motion plays an important role in such pairings. In the Beethoven excerpt, for example, the cello's G in m. 7 is understood to "move" to the A♭ of m. 8 despite the intervening B♭.

Harmonic grammar, then, allows *the analyst* to infer a harmonic message from a (harmonically conceived) score with a fair amount of confidence. It follows that in conjunction with a theory of melodic communication harmonic grammar also allows *the receiver* to infer a harmonic message from the received score. To be sure, the criteria by which the composer's "harmonic imagination" may be said to have been successfully "transplanted" into the listener's mind, that is, that harmonic communication has taken place, can hardly be set as high as in the melodic case. Nonetheless, so long as the discrepancy between the harmonic message and its received image (assuming, say, a receiver with absolute pitch) is roughly equivalent to the discrepancy one expects to find between two different realizations of the

---

[3] Rothstein (*ibid.*, p. 297) credits Kirnberger and his followers in the late eighteenth century for using the imaginary continuo as an analytical tool, and Schenker for mentioning the concept.

same figured bass, harmonic communication may indeed be said to have taken place.

Since harmonic grammar as sketched above lends itself readily to generalization of the sort pursued thus far, it makes much sense to incorporate harmonic grammar in the definition of "proto-tonal system." The work that follows in this chapter is aimed precisely towards this goal. The reader will easily recognize the influence of Rameau in Sect. 7.2; the influence of Riemann in Sect. 7.3; and the influence of Schenker in Sect. 7.4. The harmonic ideas associated with all three theorists are combined in Sect. 7.5, leading to a theorem concerning the necessary and sufficient conditions for the existence of triad-like and seventh-chord-like harmonic objects.

7.2 Generic Klang Systems

Consider Fig. 7.2, a small sample of the vast variety of musical objects one would refer to as "C-major triads." What do these objects have in common? Indeed, what does a *major* triad have in common with another *triad*, say, "minor," "augmented," or "diminished"? To answer these questions it should be useful to posit an abstract object termed "klang." To anticipate, a klang is a partially ordered set of sets; in particular, it is a finite partially ordered set *of infinite unordered sets*, to which latter I shall refer as "generic note classes."

We begin with a series of definitions the general format of which should be familiar by now; cf. Sects. 3.1 and 3.3.

Definition 7.1. Generic Note Class; Generic Note-Class Interval

Fix an integer $\beta \geq 2$ and let N_β and NVL_β be two copies of the set $\mathbb{Z}_\beta$ of integer classes mod β.

We shall refer to N_β as *the set of generic note classes* (*generic notes* for short) and to NVL_β as *the set of generic note-class intervals* (*generic intervals* for short). We shall write g and l, $0 \leq g, l \leq \beta - 1$, to represent, respectively, a generic note class g (mod β) and a generic note-class interval l (mod β).

The sense in which note classes and note-class intervals are "generic" (cf. Clough and Myerson 1985) will become clear in Sect. 7.4, where the β of N_β and NVL_β is identified with the b of a diatonic system $DTS_\varphi^{\kappa}{}^{(a,b;c,d)}$.

Definition 7.2. Generic Interval Function; Generic Note-Transposition Function

The *generic interval function* $GI : N_\beta \times N_\beta \to NVL_\beta$ is defined as follows, for every $(g, g') \in N_\beta \times N_\beta$:

$$GI(g, \ g') \equiv -g + g' \pmod{\beta}.$$

The *generic note-transposition function* $GT : N_\beta \times NVL_\beta \to N_\beta$ is defined as follows, for every $(g, l) \in N_\beta \times NVL_\beta$:

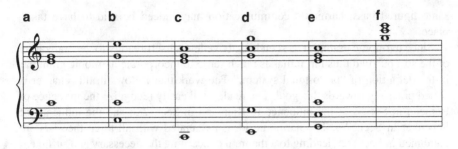

Fig. 7.2 Six different "C-major triads"

$$\mathrm{GI}(g, \mathrm{GT}(g, l)) \equiv l \pmod{\beta}.$$

It is easily seen that for every $(g, l) \in N_\beta \times NVL_\beta$, $\mathrm{GT}(g, l) = g + l \pmod{\beta}$.

Definition 7.3. Generic Note System

Let N_β be the set of generic notes, let GI be the generic interval function, and let NVL_β be the *generic interval space*, that is, the set NVL_β of generic intervals endowed with usual mod-β addition from $NVL_\beta \times NVL_\beta$ into NVL_β and usual (scalar) mod-β multiplication from $\mathbb{Z} \times NVL_\beta$ into NVL_β.

We shall refer to the set $GNS_\beta = (N_\beta, NVL_\beta, \mathrm{GI})$ as the *generic note system*.

We are now ready for the following definition.

Definition 7.4. Klang (m-ad) with Root r

Let $GNS_\beta = (N_\beta, NVL_\beta, \mathrm{GI})$ be the generic note system. Fix a generic interval $e \neq 0$ and set $\gcd(\beta, e) = \delta$. Let r be a generic note, and let m be an integer satisfying $1 \leq m \leq \frac{\beta}{\delta} - 1$.

We shall refer to the m-element set

$$K(r, m) = \left\{ g_i \equiv r + ie \pmod{\beta} \,\middle|\, 0 \leq i \leq m - 1 \right\},$$

as *a klang* or *m-ad (relative to e) with root r.*

We shall think of a klang $K(r, m)$ with root r as partially ordered: $r = g_0$ precedes every other klang element. It is easily seen that given β and e, $K(r', m') = K(r, m)$ if, and only if, $(r', m') = (r, m)$.

Example 7.5. Let $(\beta, e) = (12, 2)$.

Then $K(10, 1) = \{10\}$ is a monad and $K(0, 5) = \{0; 2, 4, 6, 8\}$ is a quintad, one with root 10 and the other with root 0.

Let $(\beta, e) = (7, 2)$.

Then $K(0, 3) = \{0; 2, 4\}$ is a triad and $K(6, 4) = \{6; 1, 3, 5\}$ is a tetrad, one with root 0 and the other with root 6; see Fig. 7.3.

In connection with the following proposition note in Fig. 7.3 the two alternative ways in which the solids dots may be viewed as a triad in (a) or a tetrad in (b).

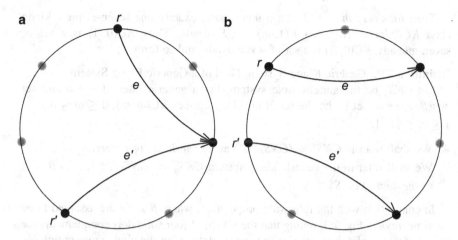

Fig. 7.3 The seven-dot circles (**a**) and (**b**) represent N_7. The *solid dots* may be seen as a triad (**a**) and a tetrad (**b**) with root $r = 0$ and $r = 6$, respectively, relative to $e = 2$. (The *solid dots* may also be seen as a triad and a tetrad with root $r' = 4$ and $r' = 5$, respectively, relative to $e' = 5$)

*Proposition 7.6. Let $GNS_\beta = (N_\beta, NVL_\beta, \text{GI})$ be the generic note system. Let $K(r, m), K(r', m)$ be two klangs, relative to e and $e' = \beta - e$, respectively.

Then the following two conditions, A and B, are equivalent.

A. $r' \equiv r + (m - 1)e \pmod{\beta}$.

B. As unordered sets, $K(r', m) = K(r, m)$.

Definition 7.7. Klang Class (of order ω)

Let GNS_β be the generic note system. Fix a generic interval $e \neq 0$ and set $\gcd(\beta, e) = \delta$. Fix two integers m and ω, $1 \leq m \leq \frac{\beta}{\delta} - 1$, $0 \leq \omega \leq \delta - 1$.

We shall refer to a set $KC(\omega, m)$ of exactly $\frac{\beta}{\delta}$ klangs $K(r, m)$,

$$KC(\omega, m) = \left\{ K(r, m) \middle| r \equiv \omega + je \pmod{\beta}, \ j = 0, 1, \ldots, \frac{\beta}{\delta} - 1 \right\},$$

as *a klang class of order ω.*

Example 7.8. Set $(\beta, e) = (12, 2)$.

Then for every $m = 1, 2, \ldots, 5$ there exist exactly two klang classes $KC(0, m) = \{K(0, m), K(2, m), \ldots, K(10, m)\}$ and $KC(1, m) = \{K(1, m), K(3, m), \ldots, K(11, m)\}$ each consisting of exactly six elements. For example, $KC(0, 5)$ is the set of six quintads $K(0, 5) = \{0; 2, 4, 6, 8\}$, $K(2, 5) = \{2; 4, 6, 8, 10\}$, and so forth, whereas $KC(1, 5)$ is the set of six quintads $K(1, 5) = \{1; 3, 5, 7, 9\}$, $K(3, 5) = \{3; 5, 7, 9, 11\}$, and so forth.

Set $(\beta, e) = (7, 2)$.

Then for every $m = 1, 2, \ldots, 6$ there exists exactly one seven-element klang class $KC(0, m) = \{K(0, m), K(1, m), \ldots, K(6, m)\}$. Thus, $KC(0, 1)$ is a set of seven monads, $KC(0, 2)$ is a set of seven dyads, and so forth.

Definition 7.9. Generic Klang System; Dual of a Generic Klang System

Let GNS_β be the generic note system. Fix a generic interval $e \neq 0$ and set $\gcd(\beta, e) = \delta$. Let U^e be the set of all klang classes $KC(\omega, m)$, $0 \leq \omega \leq \delta - 1$, $1 \leq m \leq \frac{\beta}{\delta} - 1$.

A. We shall refer to $GKS_\beta^e = (GNS_\beta, U^e)$ as *a generic klang system*.
B. We shall refer to the generic klang system $GKS_\beta^{e'} = (GNS_\beta, U^{e'})$, $e' = \beta - e$, as *the dual of GKS_β^e*.

In connection with the following proposition, where β and e are assumed to be coprime, review Fig. 7.3, noting that the set (b) of four solid dots complements the set (a) of three solid dots, relative to the complete seven-dot circle representing N_7. Moreover, if (a) is conceived as the r-rooted triad relative to e, and (b) is conceived as the r'-rooted tetrad relative to e', we have $r' \equiv r - e \pmod{\beta}$.

*Proposition 7.10. Let $GKS_\beta^e = (GNS_\beta, U^e)$ be a generic klang system and let $GKS_\beta^{e'} = (GNS_\beta, U^{e'})$ be its dual, $\gcd(\beta, e) = 1$. Let $b: U^e \rightarrow U^{e'}$ be the bijection such that $b(KC(0, m)) = KC(0, m')$ satisfies $m' = \beta - m$.

Then there exists a bijection $b_0 : KC(0, m) \rightarrow b(KC(0, m))$ such that for every $K(r, m) \in KC(0, m) \in U^e$, $b_0(K(r, m)) = K(r', m') \in KC(0, m') \in U^{e'}$ satisfies the following two equivalent conditions A and B.

A. $r' \equiv r - e \pmod{\beta}$.
B. As unordered sets $K(r', m') = N_\beta \backslash K(r, m)$, that is, $K(r', m')$ is the complement of $K(r, m)$ relative to N^β.

Finally, we have the following definition.

Definition 7.11. Usual/Anti-usual Generic Klang System

We shall refer to the generic klang system $GKS_7^2 = (GNS_7, U^2) = GKS$ as *usual*, and to its dual $GKS_7^5 = (GNS_7, U^5) = GKS'$ as *anti-usual*.

7.3 Functional Klangs and Klang Classes

The chords displayed in Fig. 7.4 using standard musical notation represent usual (or anti-usual) klangs. The leftmost chord in each of the two staves, representing a 0-rooted usual triad and tetrad, respectively (or a 4-rooted anti-usual triad and a 6-rooted anti-usual tetrad), is referential; the remaining six chords on each staff are grouped in pairs according to the number of elements (open note heads) that they do

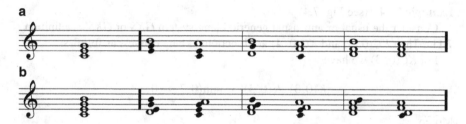

Fig. 7.4 Relative to the usual or anti-usual generic klang system the number of notes (*open note heads*) that a triad (**a**) or a tetrad (**b**) does *not* share with a referential triad and tetrad, respectively, increases with the distance between the roots, measured in multiples of thirds (or sixths)

not share with the referential chord. As may be seen, the number of open note heads monotonically increases with the distance between the roots of the respective chords, measured in multiples of thirds (or sixths).

Definition 7.12 generalizes this idea, upon which the existence of "harmonic functionality" in the familiar sense crucially depends (Agmon 1995).

Definition 7.12. Functional Klang; Functional Klang Class

Let $GKS_\beta^e = (GNS_\beta, U^e)$ be a generic klang system, $\gcd(\beta, e) = \delta$. Set $\beta' = \frac{\beta}{\delta}$ and let $K = K(r, m)$ and $K' = K(r', m)$ be two members of the same klang class $KC(\omega, m) \in U^e$ such that $r' = r + ke \pmod{\beta}$ for some k, $0 \le k \le \beta' - 1$. Finally, let f be the number of generic notes that are members of one of the two klangs but not the other, that is,

$$|K \setminus K'| = f = |K' \setminus K|.$$

We shall refer to $KC(\omega, m)$ and to its members as *functional* if the following condition A is satisfied.

A. $f = \min(k, \beta' - k)$.

Example 7.13. Consider the generic klang system GKS_{12}^2 or its dual GKS_{12}^{10}. Then $KC(0, 3)$ and $KC(1, 3)$ are functional klang classes, as follows.

Consider the klang class $KC(0, 3)$. We have

$$|K(0,3) \setminus K(0,3)| = \min(0,6) = 0, \quad |K(0,3) \setminus K(6,3)| = \min(3,3) = 3.$$

Moreover,

$$|K(0,3) \setminus K(2,3)| = \min(1,5) = |K(0,3) \setminus K(10,3)| = 1;$$
$$|K(0,3) \setminus K(4,3)| = \min(2,4) = |K(0,3) \setminus K(8,3)| = 2.$$

Similarly, for $KC(1, 3)$ we have $|K(1, 3) \setminus K(1, 3)| = \min(0, 6) = 0$, and so forth.

Example 7.14. (see Fig. 7.4)

Consider the usual or anti-usual generic klang system GKS or GKS' (Definition 7.11). Then $KC(0, 3)$ and $KC(0, 4)$ are functional klang classes, as follows.

For $KC(0, 3)$ we have

$$|K(0,3) \setminus K(0,3)| = \min(0,7) = 0.$$

Moreover,

$$|K(0,3) \setminus K(2,3)| = \min(1,6) = |K(0,3) \setminus K(5,3)| = 1;$$
$$|K(0,3) \setminus K(4,3)| = \min(2,5) = |K(0,3) \setminus K(3,3)| = 2;$$
$$|K(0,3) \setminus K(6,3)| = \min(3,4) = |K(0,3) \setminus K(1,3)| = 3.$$

Similarly, for $KC(0, 4)$ we have $|K(0, 4) \setminus K(0, 4)| = \min(0, 7) = 0$, and

$$|K(0,4) \setminus K(2,4)| = \min(1,6) = |K(0,4) \setminus K(5,4)| = 1;$$
$$|K(0,4) \setminus K(4,4)| = \min(2,5) = |K(0,4) \setminus K(3,4)| = 2;$$
$$|K(0,4) \setminus K(6,4)| = \min(3,4) = |K(0,4) \setminus K(1,4)| = 3.$$

Theorem 7.15. Let $GKS^e_\beta = (GNS_\beta, U^e)$ be a generic klang system. Set $\beta' = \frac{\beta}{\delta}$, $\delta = \gcd(\beta, e)$, and let $KC(\omega, m)$ be a klang class.

Then $KC(\omega, m)$ is functional if, and only if, the following condition A is satisfied.

A. $m = \left[\frac{\beta'}{2}\right]$; that is, $m = \frac{\beta'}{2}$ if β' is even, $m = \frac{\beta' \pm 1}{2}$ if β' is odd.

To prove the theorem we shall first state one lemma and prove another.

*Lemma 7.16. Let $GKS^e_\beta = (GNS_\beta, U^e)$ and $GKS^{e'}_{\beta'} = (GNS_{\beta'}, U^{e'})$ be two generic klang systems, $\beta' = \frac{\beta}{\delta}$, $e' = \frac{e}{\delta}$, $\delta = \gcd(\beta, e)$. Let $s : U^e \to U^{e'}$ be the surjection satisfying $s(KC(\omega, m)) = KC(0, m)$ for every $KC(\omega, m) \in U^e$, $0 \le \omega \le \delta - 1$, $1 \le m \le \beta' - 1$.

Then there exists a bijection $b_\omega : KC(\omega, m) \to s(KC(\omega, m))$ such that for every $K(r, m) \in KC(\omega, m) \in U^e$, if $r \equiv \omega + je \pmod{\beta}$ for some j, then $b_\omega(K(r, m)) = K(r', m) \in KC(0, m) \in U^{e'}$ satisfies $r' \equiv je' \pmod{\beta'}$.

Lemma 7.17. Let $GKS^e_\beta = (GNS_\beta, U^e)$ be a generic klang system. Set $\beta' = \frac{\beta}{\delta}$, $\delta = \gcd(\beta, e)$, and let $K(r, m)$ and $K(q, m)$ be two distinct members of some klang class $KC(\omega, m)$, $0 \le \omega \le \delta - 1$, $1 \le m \le \beta' - 1$, $r \equiv \omega + je \pmod{\beta}$, $q \equiv r + ke \pmod{\beta}$, $0 \le j, k \le \beta' - 1$. Set $D = K(r, m) \setminus K(q, m)$, the set subtraction of $K(q, m)$ from $K(r, m)$. Finally, set $\bar{r} \equiv r + (m + k)e \pmod{\beta}$.

Then D may be written as a klang $K(s, n)$ such that one of the following four conditions, A–D, holds.

A. If $m \le k \le \beta' - m$ then $(s, n) = (r, m)$.
B. If $k \le m \le \beta' - k$ then $(s, n) = (r, k)$.

C. If $\beta' - m \leq k \leq m$ then $(s, n) = (\bar{r}, \beta' - m)$.
D. If $\beta' - k \leq m \leq k$ then $(s, n) = (\bar{r}, \beta' - k)$.

Proof. If $m \leq k \leq \beta' - m$ we have $K(r, m) \cap K(q, m) = \varnothing$, and Condition A holds. Suppose that $k \leq m \leq \beta' - k$. We have $k + m - 1 < \beta'$, implying that Condition B holds.

Consider the generic klang system $GKS_{\beta'}^{e'}$, $e' = \frac{e}{\delta}$. Using Lemma 7.16 write $b_\omega(K(r, m)) = K(r', m)$, $b_\omega(K(q, m)) = K(q', m)$. Then

$$r' \equiv je', \quad q' \equiv r' + ke' \pmod{\beta'}.$$

Using Proposition 7.6, set $r'' \equiv r' + (m - 1)e'$, $q'' \equiv q' + (m - 1)e' \pmod{\beta'}$, and consider the dual $GKS_{\beta'}^{e''}$ of $GKS_{\beta'}^{e'}$, $e'' = \beta' - e'$.

Set $k' = \beta' - k$, and assume that $k' \leq m \leq \beta' - k'$. Then $k' + m - 1 < \beta'$, and $D' = K(r'', m) \setminus K(q'', m)$ may be written dually (that is, in terms of $GKS_{\beta'}^{e''}$) as the klang $K(r'', k')$. By rewriting D' non-dually (that is, in terms of $GKS_{\beta'}^{e'}$), Condition D follows.

Set $m' = \beta' - m$, and consider again the dual $GKS_{\beta'}^{e''}$ of $GKS_{\beta'}^{e'}$, $e'' = \beta' - e'$.

Using Proposition 7.10 write $b_0(K(r', m)) = K(r''', m')$, $b_0(K(q', m)) = K(q''', m')$, and set

$$D' = K(q''', m') \setminus K(r''', m').$$

The condition $m' \leq k \leq \beta' - m'$ implies that $K(q''', m') \cap K(r''', m') = \varnothing$, and D' may be written dually (that is, in terms of $GKS_{\beta'}^{e''}$) as the klang $K(q''', m')$. Since

$$D' = K(q''', m') \setminus K(r''', m') = K(r', m) \setminus K(q', m),$$

and moreover, by Proposition 7.10

$$q''' \equiv q' - e' \pmod{\beta'},$$

by rewriting D' non-dually (that is, in terms of $GKS_{\beta'}^{e'}$) Condition C follows. Q.E.D.

Proof of the theorem. Let $KC(\omega, m)$ be a functional klang class and let $K = K(r, m)$ and $K' = K(q, m)$ be two members of $KC(\omega, m)$, $q \equiv r + ke \pmod{\beta}$ for some $k, 0 \leq k \leq \beta' - 1, \beta' = \frac{\beta}{\delta}$. Set

$$D = K \setminus K',$$
$$f = |K \setminus K'|.$$

It is easily seen that $f = |D| = 0$ if, and only if, $k = 0$.

If $\beta' \leq 3$ we have $m = \left\lceil \frac{\beta'}{2} \right\rceil$. Suppose that $\beta' \geq 4$, and suppose by contradiction that $m < \left\lceil \frac{\beta'}{2} \right\rceil$. Then, if $k = m + 1$, by Lemma 7.17 we have $f = m$ (see Condition

A). However, by the functional condition $f = \min(k, \beta' - k)$, and therefore, since $k \leq \beta' - k, f = k \neq m$. A similar contradiction of the functional condition (involving Condition C of the Lemma) results if $m > \left\lceil \frac{\beta'}{2} \right\rceil$. Thus $m = \left\lceil \frac{\beta'}{2} \right\rceil$ is necessary for $KC(\omega, m)$ to be a functional klang class. It may easily be checked that if $m = \left\lceil \frac{\beta'}{2} \right\rceil$, Lemma 7.17 is compatible with the functional condition $f = \min(k, \beta' - k)$. Thus $m = \left\lceil \frac{\beta'}{2} \right\rceil$ is also sufficient. Q.E.D.

The following proposition should prove useful subsequently.

Proposition 7.18. Let GKS_β^e be a generic klang system satisfying $\gcd(\beta, e) = 1$, where β is odd, and let $K(r, m)$ and $K(q, m)$ be two distinct functional m-ads, $q \equiv r + ke \pmod{\beta}$ for some k. Set

$$K(r', m') = K(r, m) \setminus K(q, m), \text{ and}$$
$$K(q', m') = K(q, m) \setminus K(r, m).$$

Then one of the following two conditions, A or B, holds.

A. $1 \leq k \leq \frac{\beta - 1}{2}$ and $q' - r' \equiv me \pmod{\beta}$.
B. $\frac{\beta + 1}{2} \leq k \leq \beta - 1$ and $q' - r' \equiv -me \pmod{\beta}$.

Proof. Since $\gcd(\beta, e) = 1$, β is odd, so by Theorem 7.15 $m = \frac{\beta + 1}{2}$.

If $1 \leq k \leq \frac{\beta - 1}{2} (\frac{\beta + 1}{2} \leq k \leq \beta - 1)$ we have $k \leq m \leq \beta - k$ $(\beta - k \leq m \leq k)$ and by Lemma 7.17 $r' = r$ $(r' \equiv r + (m + k)e \bmod \beta)$, $q' \equiv q + (m - k)e \pmod{\beta}$ $(q' = q)$. Since $q \equiv r + ke \pmod{\beta}$, the proposition follows. Q.E.D.

7.4 Harmonic Systems, Voice-Leading Enabled

A chord "expressing" a klang is a sequence of notes, every one of which is *generically* equivalent to an element of the klang; moreover, for *every* klang element there exists a chord element such that the two are generically equivalent.

Definition 7.19. Chord (expressing a klang); Functional Chord

(a, b)
Let ONS be an octave-endowed note system, let S be a non-empty set of notes, and let GKS_β^e be a generic klang system satisfying $\beta = b$. Let K be a klang and let $C(K)$ be a non-empty sequence of notes $(s, t) \in S$.

We shall refer to $C(K)$ as *a chord* (over S) *expressing the klang* K if the following three conditions, A, B, and C, are satisfied.

A. If $(s, t) \in C(K)$, there exists a $g \in K$ satisfying $g \equiv t \pmod{b}$.
B. If $g \in K$, there exists an $(s, t) \in C(K)$ satisfying $g \equiv t \pmod{b}$.

C. If $(s, t), (s', t') \in C(K)$ satisfy $s \equiv s'$ (mod a) or $t \equiv t'$ (mod b), then $(s, t) \equiv_{(a, b)} (s', t')$. [4]

If $C(K)$ is a chord expressing a functional klang K (Definition 7.12), we shall refer to $C(K)$ as *functional*.

Example 7.20. Consider the objects (a)–(f) in Fig. 7.2 as sequences of usual notes, ordered, say, from low to high.

Then every sequence is a (functional) chord $C(K)$ over N expressing the usual triad $K = K(0, 3)$. Moreover, *any* musical object conventionally describable as "a triad with root C#," where # is a number representing sharps (if positive) or flats (if negative), and "triad" refers to *any* triad, not necessarily major, is a chord $C(K)$ over N.

Definition 7.21. Congruent Chords
    Let $C(K)$ and $C'(K)$ be chords expressing the same klang K. Let $(s, t) \in C(K)$ and $(s', t') \in C'(K)$ satisfy $t' \equiv t$ (mod b).
    We shall refer to $C(K)$ and $C'(K)$ as *congruent* if $(s', t') \equiv_{(a, b)} (s, t)$.

Example 7.22. Every two chords in Fig. 7.2 are congruent.
    By contrast, a "C-major triad" is *not* congruent to either a "C-minor triad" or a "C#-major triad."

In connection with the following definition it should be useful to review Sect. 2.4.

Definition 7.23. Chord Progression (expressing a klang progression)
    Let S be a non-empty set of notes and let GKS_β^e be a generic klang system satisfying $\beta = b$. Let $KP = K(r_1, m_1), K(r_2, m_2), \ldots, K(r_n, m_n)$ be a sequence of klangs and let $CP = C(K_1), C(K_2), \ldots, C(K_n)$ be a sequence of chords over S, $|CP| = |KP|$.
    We shall refer to CP as *a progression of chords* (over S) *expressing KP* if one of the following two conditions, A or B, is satisfied.

A. $CP = \varnothing = KP$, in which case we shall refer to the progression as *empty*.
B. $CP \neq \varnothing$, and the exchange $X : CP \rightarrow KP$ satisfies $K_i = K(r_i, m_i)$ for every $i = 1, 2, \ldots, n$.

Example 7.24. Let S be the set of all notes octave equivalent to C, D, E♭, F, G, A♭, and B and let $KP = K_1, K_2, \ldots, K_7$ be a usual klang progression, $KP =$

$$K(0,3), K(0,3), K(3,3), K(3,3), K(4,3), K(5,3), K(0,3).$$

---

[4] Two chromatic variants of the "same" note (for example, in the usual case, D♭ and D♯) are excluded *a priori* as chord members both, even though one may think of a handful of counter-examples. See for example Piston (1978), p. 438 ff. It is difficult to think of a counter-example to the condition that no two chord members are enharmonically distinct (for example, E♭ and D♯).

Then the sequence of chords of Fig. 7.1c, the (assumed) harmonic message of the Beethoven passage bracketed in Fig. 7.1a, is a progression of chords over S expressing KP.

We are now ready for the following definition. Review Definitions 6.7, 6.11, 6.21, and 6.25.

Definition 7.25. Harmonic System; Empty Harmonic System

Let $\overset{(a,\,b;c,\,d)}{DTS_\varphi^\kappa} = \left(\overset{(a,b;c,d)}{NRS_\varphi^\kappa} , \overset{(a,b;c,d)}{NRSi_\varphi^\kappa} \right)$ be a diatonic system with cluster $CLUST$,

where $\overset{(a,\,b;c,\,d)}{NRS_\varphi^\kappa} = \left(\overset{(a,\,b;c,\,d)}{FTS_\varphi} , CORE^\kappa, MSG/R \right)$ is a note-reception system with

message MSG, and let GKS_β^e be a generic klang system satisfying $\beta = b$. Let KP be a klang progression and let CP be a progression of chords over S expressing KP, where S is the set of all notes $(s', t') \equiv_{(a,\,b)}(s, t)$, $(s, t) \in CLUST$, such that $-4 \leq$ REG$(s', t') \leq 3$.

We shall refer to $\overset{(a,\,b;c,\,d;e)}{HS_\varphi^\kappa} = \left(\overset{(a,\,b;c,\,d)}{DTS_\varphi^\kappa} , GKS_b^e, CP \right)$ as *a harmonic system*;

if CP is empty (Definition 7.23), we shall refer to the system as *empty*.

The relation between MSG and a non-empty CP, though unspecified, is assumed to correspond to the relation between a score, conceived "melodically," and its harmonic message (review Sect. 7.1).

Definition 7.26. Usual/Anti-usual Harmonic System

If $\overset{(a,\,b;c,\,d)}{DTS_\varphi^\kappa} = DTS_\varphi^\kappa$ is (anti-)usual (Definition 6.26), $GKS_\beta^e = GKS$ is (anti-)usual (Definition 7.11), and CP is not empty, we shall refer to a harmonic system $HS_\varphi^\kappa = (DTS_\varphi^\kappa, GKS, CP)$ as *(anti-)usual*.

Example 7.27. If MSG is the note sequence of Fig. 7.1b and CP is the chord sequence of Fig. 7.1c, and if $(c, d) = (7, 4)$ and $e = 2$, then $HS_0^{-4} = (DTS_0^{-4}, GKS, CP)$ is a usual harmonic system the melodic and harmonic message of which correspond to those of mm. 6–9 of the third movement of Beethoven's String Quartet in F minor, Op. 95, bracketed in Fig. 7.1a.[5]

In connection with the following definition, review Definition 7.21.

---

[5] φ equals zero in this example if we assume (informally at this stage) that C is privileged as the local "tonic." Review Definition 5.22 and see ahead, Definition 10.14 (Part II).

Fig. 7.5 Two congruent
chord progressions

Definition 7.28. Congruent Chord Progressions; Congruent Harmonic Systems

$$\text{Let} \quad HS_{\varphi}^{\kappa}{}^{(a,\,b;c,\,d;e)} = \left(DTS_{\varphi}^{\kappa}{}^{(a,\,b;c,\,d)}, GKS_{b}^{e}, CP \right) \text{ and } HS'_{\varphi}^{\kappa}{}^{(a,\,b;c,\,d;e)} = \left(DTS_{\varphi}^{\kappa}{}^{(a,\,b;c,\,d)}, GKS_{b}^{e}, CP' \right) \text{ be}$$

two harmonic systems with the same message MSG, $|CP| = |CP'| \geq 1$.

We shall refer to CP and CP' as *congruent chord progressions* and to $HS_{\varphi}^{\kappa}{}^{(a,\,b;c,\,d;e)}$

and $HS'_{\varphi}^{\kappa}{}^{(a,\,b;c,\,d;e)}$ as *congruent harmonic systems* if $C(K)$ and $X(C(K))$ are congruent,
where X is the exchange $CP \rightarrow CP'$.

Figure 7.5 presents two congruent chord progressions (the first of which is
familiar as Fig. 7.1c), representing what for many musicians would count as "the
same" imaginary continuo to the Beethoven passage, bracketed in Fig. 7.1a.[6]

Finally, we have the following definition.

Definition 7.29. Voice Leading; Voice-Leading Enabled Harmonic System

$$\text{Let} \quad HS_{\varphi}^{\kappa}{}^{(a,\,b;c,\,d;e)} = \left(DTS_{\varphi}^{\kappa}{}^{(a,\,b;c,\,d)}, GKS_{b}^{e}, CP \right) \text{ be a harmonic system, } |CP| \geq 2. \text{ Let}$$

$C(K), C(K')$ be two consecutive chords in CP, and let VL be a relation from $C(K)$ to
$C(K')$.

We shall refer to VL as *a voice leading* and to a pair $LP = ((s, t), (s', t')) \in$ VL
as *a linear pair* if the following two conditions, A and B, are satisfied.

A. For every $(s, t) \in C(K)$ there exists an $(s', t') \in C(K')$ such that
$((s, t), (s', t')) \in$ VL.

---

[6] There are aspects to the relation between the two congruent chord progressions displayed in
Fig. 7.5, particularly with regard to the "lowest voice," that are not captured by Definition 7.28.
These aspects, though important otherwise, are irrelevant to the present discussion.

Fig. 7.6 *Lines* connecting elements of the fifth chord with elements of the sixth chord represent a voice leading between them

B. For every $(s', t') \in C(K')$ there exists an $(s, t) \in C(K)$ such that $((s, t), (s', t')) \in$ VL.

We shall assume henceforth that a harmonic system such that *CP* is of length 2 or more is *voice-leading enabled* in the sense that for every pair $C(K)$, $C(K')$ of consecutive chords in *CP* there exists a voice leading VL : $C(K) \to C(K')$.

Example 7.30. Figure 7.6 reproduces Fig. 7.1c, the (assumed) harmonic content of a passage from the third movement of Beethoven's String Quartet in F minor, Op. 95, bracketed in 7.1a. Lines connecting elements of the fifth chord with elements of the sixth chord represent linear pairs that form the following voice leading:

$$((G_{-2}, C_{-2}), (G_{-2}, {}^\flat A_{-2}), (G_{-1}, {}^\flat E_{-1}), (B_{-1}, C), (D, C)).$$

In the following section we shall establish a connection between *functional* chords (Definition 7.19) and a special type of voice leading which we shall call "efficient."

7.5   Efficient Harmonic Systems

Definition 7.29 offers a very broad notion of "voice leading." For example, Fig. 7.7 below is a voice leading between two congruent chords expressing a usual triad.

The following definition, therefore, introduces certain parameters by which the notion may be usefully constrained; review Definition 7.29.

Definition 7.31. Density (of VL); Span (of *LP*); Activity (of VL)

Let $\overset{(a,\,b;c,\,d;e)}{HS_\varphi^\kappa} = \left(\overset{(a,\,b;c,\,d)}{DTS_\varphi^\kappa}, \ GKS_b^e, CP \right)$ be a harmonic system, $|CP| \geq 2$, and

let VL be a voice leading between two consecutive chords in *CP*. Let $LP = ((s, t), (s', t'))$ be a linear pair in VL.

Fig. 7.7 A voice leading
between two congruent
chords expressing a triad. A
pair of notes connected by a
straight line is a linear pair

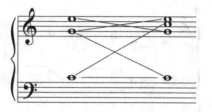

A. We shall refer to the number of linear pairs *LP* as *the density of VL*.

B. We shall refer to the distance $|t' - t|$ as *the span of LP*.

C. We shall refer to *LP* as *stationary* if its span is zero.

D. We shall refer to *LP* as *active* if its span is non-zero.

E. We shall refer to the number of active pairs in VL as *the activity of VL*.

Example 7.32. The density of the voice leading VL of Fig. 7.7 is 5; its activity is
4 (since the linear pair C–C is stationary). The span of the four active linear pairs
$(C, C_1), (G, C), (G, E_1)$, and (E_1, G), is 7, 4, 5, and 5, respectively.

In what follows we shall be interested in voice leadings VL of a very special type
which we shall call *efficient*.[7] Three senses of "efficiency" are involved. One
concerns density; another concerns the span of an active linear pair; and yet another
concerns activity. Review Definition 7.28.

Definition 7.33. Efficient Voice Leading

Let $HS_\varphi^{\kappa}{}^{(a,\,b;c,\,d;e)} = \left(DTS_\varphi^{\kappa}{}^{(a,\,b;c,\,d)}, \; GKS_b^e, CP \right)$ be a harmonic system, $|CP| \geq 2$, and

let VL be a voice leading between two consecutive chords $C(K)$ and $C(K')$ in CP,
$K = K(r, m)$, and $K' = K(r', m')$.

We shall refer to VL as *efficient* if its density is minimal, namely $\max(m, m')$,
and the span of every active linear pair is also minimal, namely 1. Moreover, a

congruent harmonic system $\left(DTS_\varphi^{\kappa}{}^{(a,\,b;c,\,d)}, \; GKS_b^e, CP' \right)$ satisfying the following con-

dition A does not exist.

A. $VL' : X(C(K)) \rightarrow X(C(K'))$ is less active than $VL : C(K) \rightarrow C(K')$, where X is
the exchange $CP \rightarrow CP'$.

Example 7.34. Let HS_φ^{-1} be a usual harmonic system (see Definition 7.26), and
consider the voice leadings displayed in Fig. 7.8.

---

[7] For a closely related notion of "efficient" voice leading see Agmon (1991). "Efficiency" was used
in an entirely different sense in Chap. 5.

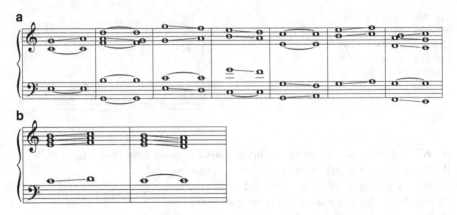

Fig. 7.8 All voice leadings in (**a**) are efficient; in (**b**) only the second is efficient

Then all seven voice leadings in (a) are efficient. By contrast, of the two voice leadings in (b) only the second is efficient, since the first is a more active congruent progression. In all cases slurs represent stationary linear pairs whereas lines represent active linear pairs.

The three senses of efficiency, namely, that the density of a voice leading is minimal; that the span of an active linear pair is 1; and that activity is minimal relative to a congruent harmonic system, may be readily rationalized if one thinks of efficiency metaphorically in terms of minimizing the amount of "work" that a voice leading involves. According to Schoenberg (1954, p. 4), Anton Bruckner taught his class at the Vienna University that the four "voices" generally used in harmonic progressions "...obey the *law* of the shortest way" ("sie gehorchen dem *Gesetz* des nächsten Weges"). By Schoenberg's formulation (*ibid.*), the law states that "when connecting chords it is advisable that each of the four voices... should move no more than necessary."

The second sense of efficiency may be dubbed "the rule of stepwise motion." As Aldwell and Schachter (2003, pp. 60–61) note, "just as the basis of harmonic progression is motion by 5th, so the basis of melodic progression is motion by step. In successions of chords controlled by voice leading (*contrapuntal progressions*), stepwise motion predominates." The rule is implicit, for example, in the fourth of Tinctoris's (1477) eight contrapuntal rules: "The fourth rule is that counterpoint ought to be made as near and as orderly as can be, particularly if the tenor has been conversely formed by the conjunction of distant intervals, as is seen here."[8]

---

[8] Tinctoris (1961), pp. 134–135. "Quarta regula est quod quam proximus et quam ordinatissimus poterit contrapunctus fieri debebit, etiam licet coniunctionibus longorum intervallorum tenor sic e converso formatus, ut hic patet." Tinctoris (1961, p. 135) continues, however, by noting that "... those who seek a sweeter and more delightful counterpoint than one based on neighboring notes are freed from this rule."

The following proposition states *sufficient* conditions for the existence of efficient voice leading between two chords; cf. Fig. 7.8.

Proposition 7.35. Let GKS_b^e be a generic klang system and let KP be a sequence of at least two klangs. Let K and K' be two consecutive klangs in KP and let GVL be a relation from K to K' of exactly max(m, m') elements such that for every $g \in K$ there exists a $g' \in K'$ such that $(g, g') \in$ GVL, and for every $g' \in K'$ there exists a $g \in K$ such that $(g, g') \in$ GVL.

If the following two conditions, A and B, hold, there exists a harmonic system

$$HS_\varphi^\kappa{}^{(a,\,b;c,\,d;e)} = \left(DTS_\varphi^\kappa{}^{(a,\,b;c,\,d)}, GKS_b^e, CP \right) \text{ such that VL}: C(K) \to C(K') \text{ is efficient.}$$

A. If $(g, g') \in$ GVL, then $g' - g \equiv 0, \pm 1 \pmod{b}$.
B. If $g' = g, (g', g) \in K' \times K$, then $(g, g') \in$ GVL.

Proof. The proposition follows from the observation that under the conditions stated, it is a simple matter to express K and K' with chords such that Definition 7.33 is satisfied. Q.E.D.

We are finally ready for the following definition. Note the crucial reference to *functional* chords (Definition 7.19).

Definition 7.36. Efficient Harmonic Systems

$$\text{Let} \quad HS_\varphi^\kappa{}^{(a,\,b;c,\,d;e)} = \left(DTS_\varphi^\kappa{}^{(a,\,b;c,\,d)}, GKS_b^e, CP \right) \text{ be a harmonic system. Assume that } CP$$

contains a pair of consecutive functional chords.

We shall refer to $HS_\varphi^\kappa{}^{(a,\,b;\,c,\,d;\,e)}$ as *efficient* if there exists a congruent harmonic system $\left(DTS_\varphi^\kappa{}^{(a,\,b;c,\,d)}, GKS_b^e, CP' \right)$ such that for every pair $C(K)$ and $C(K')$ of consecutive functional chords in CP there exists an efficient voice leading VL': $X(C(K)) \to X(C(K'))$, where X is the exchange $CP \to CP'$.

As Fig. 7.9 illustrates using HS_φ^{-1}, a usual harmonic system (see Definition 7.26) is efficient, if CP contains a pair of consecutive functional chords. For every pair of functional klangs there exist chords expressing these klangs such that the voice leading between them is efficient.

Note that Definition 7.36 only requires that for every pair of consecutive functional chords in a given harmonic system there *exists* a harmonic system congruent to the given system, such that the voice leading between the chords in the congruent system, corresponding to the given chords, is efficient. This may be interpreted to mean that it is *normative* (but not mandatory) to have for every pair of consecutive functional klangs expressive chords such that the voice leading between them is efficient. For example, assuming a usual system, progression

Fig. 7.9 A usual harmonic system is efficient. There exist efficient voice leadings between chords expressing every pair of functional klangs. (**a**) Triad to triad; (**b**) tetrad to tetrad; (**c**) triad to tetrad; (**d**) tetrad to triad. After Agmon (1991), Figs. 2 and 6. Copyright © 1991 Universitätsverlag Brockmeyer, redrawn from *Musikometrika 3*, by permission

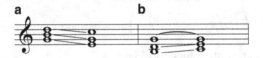

Fig. 7.10 (**b**) is an efficient realization of the congruent progression (**a**)

(b) of Fig. 7.10 is more normative than (a), relative to the klang progression $K(4, 3)$, $K(0, 3)$.[9]

Finally, we have the following theorem.

Theorem 7.37. Let $\overset{(a,\,b;c,\,d;e)}{HS^{\kappa}_{\varphi}} = \left(\overset{(a,\,b;c,\,d)}{DTS^{\kappa}_{\varphi}} , GKS^{e}_{b}, CP \right)$ be a harmonic system,

where CP contains a pair of consecutive functional chords.

---

[9] Cf. Cohn (1997, p. 62): "Beginning with (at latest) the eighteenth century, the normative status of common-tone retention and stepwise motion is not only statistical but cognitive: one conceives of them as occurring even when the actual leading of the 'voices' violates them, e.g. when instantiations of the common or step-related pitch-classes are realized in different registers." The present conception, by which a chord progression is the "imaginary continuo" of a (harmonically conceived) score, fully endorses the "cognitive" sense of normative voice leading to which Cohn refers.

Then the system is efficient if, and only if, one of the following two conditions, A or B, holds.

A. $b = 2, e = 1$.

B. b is odd, $e \equiv \pm 2 \pmod{b}$.

To prove the theorem we shall first prove two lemmas. Review Proposition 7.35.

Lemma 7.38. Let GKS_b^e be a generic klang system, where b is odd, $e \equiv \pm 2 \pmod{b}$. Let $K(r, m)$ and $K(q, m)$ be a pair of distinct functional m-ads. Set

$$K(r, m) \setminus K(q, m) = K(r', m');$$
$$K(q, m) \setminus K(r, m) = K(q', m').$$

Then there exists an m'-element relation GVL : $K(r', m') \to K(q', m')$ satisfying the conditions of Proposition 7.35.

Proof. By Theorem 7.15 $m = \frac{b \pm 1}{2}$. Using Proposition 7.18 we have

$$q' - r' \equiv \pm 1 \pmod{b}.$$

It is easily seen that $\mathrm{GVL}(r' + k'e) = q' + k'e \pmod{b}$, $k' = 0, 1, \ldots, m' - 1$, satisfies the conditions of Proposition 7.35. Q.E.D.

Lemma 7.39. Let GKS_b^e be a generic klang system, where b is odd, $e \equiv \pm 2 \pmod{b}$, and assume that for every pair $K(r, m)$ and $K(q, m)$ of functional m-ads, $q \equiv r + ke \pmod{b}$, $0 \le k \le b - 1$, there exists an m-element relation GVL : $K(r, m) \to K(q, m)$ satisfying the conditions of Proposition 7.35. Let $K(q, m')$ be a functional m'-ad, $m' \neq m$.

Then there exists a relation GVL : $K(r, m) \to K(q, m')$ satisfying the conditions of Proposition 7.35.

Proof. With no loss of generality we may assume (using Theorem 7.15) that $e = 2$, $m = \frac{b-1}{2}$, $m' = \frac{b+1}{2}$.

Since there exists an m-element relation GVL : $K(r, m) \to K(q, m)$ satisfying the conditions of Proposition 7.35, to prove the lemma it suffices to show that there exists an element $g_i \in K(r, m)$, $g_i \equiv r + ie \pmod{b}$, $0 \le i \le m - 1$, satisfying

$$h_{m-1} - g_i \equiv 0, \pm 1 \pmod{b},$$

where $h_{m-1} \in K(q, m')$ satisfies $h_{m-1} \equiv q + me \equiv q - 1 \pmod{b}$. In other words, one must show that there exists an i satisfying

$$h_{m-1} - g_i \equiv 2(k - i) - 1 \equiv 0, \pm 1 \pmod{b}.$$

It is easily seen that if $k < \frac{b-1}{2}$, $i = k$; if $k = \frac{b-1}{2}$, $i = k - 1$; if $k = \frac{b+1}{2}$, $i = 0$; and if $k > \frac{b+1}{2}$, $i = -\frac{b+1}{2} + k$. Q.E.D.

Proof of the theorem. From Lemmas 7.38–7.39 it follows that b is odd, $e \equiv \pm 2$ (mod b), are sufficient conditions for $HS_\varphi^{\kappa}{}^{(a,\,b;\,c,\,d;\,e)}$ to be efficient. It is easily seen that $b = 2$, $e = 1$, are also sufficient conditions.

Let $HS_\varphi^{\kappa}{}^{(a,\,b;\,c,\,d;\,e)}$ be an efficient harmonic system, and let $C(K)$ and $C(K')$ be a pair of consecutive functional chords in CP, where $K = K(r, m)$, $K' = K(q, m')$. Assume that $m = m'$ and that $K(r, m)$, $K(q, m')$ are members of the same klang class.

Set $h_{m-1} \in K(q, m)$, $h_{m-1} \equiv q + me$ (mod b), and suppose that $r \equiv q + e$ (mod b). Then

$$q - h_{m-1} \equiv -me \equiv \pm 1 \quad (\mathrm{mod}\, b). \tag{7.1}$$

By Theorem 7.15 $m = \frac{b}{2}$ if b is even, $m = \frac{b \pm 1}{2}$ if b is odd. If $b \geq 4$ is even, Equation 7.1 cannot be satisfied. It follows that $b = 2$, $e = 1$, or b is odd, $e \equiv \pm 2$ (mod b) are necessary conditions for $HS_\varphi^{\kappa}{}^{(a,\,b;\,c,\,d;\,e)}$ to be an efficient harmonic system. Q.E.D.

Efficient harmonic systems have two interesting properties.

First, since $\gcd(b, e) = 1$, the functional condition $f = \min(k, b - k)$ (Definition 7.12) defines *a metric* on a set consisting of all functional m-ads, for some m.[10] The metric is based on the number of generic notes that are members of one of two functional m-ads but not the other, a number which (by definition) equals the minimal positive integer that, multiplied (mod b) by ± 2, transposes the root of one klang to equal that of the other. Cf. Fig. 7.4 for the usual case. The existence of so-called "harmonic functionality" in the familiar sense is crucially dependent on this property (Agmon 1995).

Moreover, since a functional m-ad satisfies $me \equiv \pm 1$ (mod b), the *activity* of an efficient voice leading between two functional m-ads equals *their distance*. In other words, a functional distance of 0 implies activity 0 (no stepwise motion) and vice versa; a distance of 1 implies activity 1 (one stepwise motion), and so forth. Cf. Fig. 7.9 for the usual case. Thus, functionality and efficient voice leading are interconnected.

---

[10] A set S together with a function d from $S \times S$ into the non-negative real numbers is *a metric space* if d satisfies the following three conditions, A, B, and C, for every x, y, and z in S. A. $d(x, y) = 0$ if, and only if, $x = y$; B. $d(x, y) = d(y, x)$ (symmetry); C. $d(x, z) \leq d(x, y) + d(y, z)$ (triangle inequality).

References

Agmon, E. (1991). Linear transformations between cyclically generated chords. *Musikometrika, 3*, 15–40.

Agmon, E. (1995). Functional harmony revisited: A prototype-theoretic approach. *Music Theory Spectrum, 17*(2), 196–214.

Aldwell, E., & Schachter, C. (2003). *Harmony and voice leading* (3rd ed.). Belmont: Wadsworth Group.

Clough, J., & Myerson, G. (1985). Variety and multiplicity in diatonic systems. *Journal of Music Theory, 29*(2), 249–270.

Cohn, R. (1997). Neo-Riemannian operations, parsimonious trichords, and their *Tonnetz* representations. *Journal of Music Theory, 41*(1), 1–66.

Piston, W. (1978). *Harmony* (4th ed., M. DeVoto, Rev.). New York: Norton.

Riemann, H. (1914/15). Ideen zu einer 'Lehre von den Tonvorstellungen'. *Jahrbuch der Musikbibliothek Peters, 21/22*, 1–26. Reprint 1965.

Rothstein, W. (1991). On implied tones. *Music Analysis, 10*(3), 289–328.

Schoenberg, A. (1954). *Structural functions of harmony* (H. Searle, Ed., Rev. 1969). New York: Norton.

Tinctoris, J. (1477). *Liber de arte contrapuncti*. 1975. Reprint in *Corpus Scriptorum de Musica 22* (2), A. Seay (Ed.). Rome: American Institute of Musicology.

Tinctoris, J. (1961). *The art of counterpoint* (A. Seay, Trans. & Ed.). *Musicological Studies and Documents 5*. Rome: American Institute of Musicology.

Wason, R., & Marvin, E. W. (1992). Riemann's *Ideen zu einer 'Lehre von den Tonvorstellungen'*: An annotated translation. *Journal of Music Theory, 36*(1), 69–117.

Chapter 8
Proto-tonality

Abstract A "tertial element" is a primary interval (y, z) such that z is a generic "klang generator" e of a non-empty harmonic tone system (Sect. 8.1). A "proto-tonal system" is a harmonic tone system such that the quintic element (c, d) satisfies c is as close as possible to $a\log_2(3/2)$; moreover, assuming a non-empty system, there exists a tertial element (y, z) such that y is as close as possible to $a\log_2(5/4)$. It is proven that a proto-tonal system satisfies $a = 12, b = 7 = c, d = 4$, and (if the system is not empty) $e = 2$. Section 8.2 revisits the theory of categorical equal temperament from a historical and historical-theoretical perspective, now that $a = 12$ has been established. Finally, Sect. 8.3 considers an alternative to the theory of proto-tonality, based on Clough and Douthett's (1991) theory of "maximally even sets." It is shown that the alternative theory is weaker than the proposed theory in terms of explanatory power.

8.1 Proto-tonal Systems

In connection with the following definition, review Definition 7.25.

Definition 8.1. Tertial Element

Let $\overset{(a,\,b;c,\,d;e)}{HS^{\kappa}_{\varphi}}$ be a non-empty harmonic system $\left(\overset{(a,\,b;c,\,d)}{DTS^{\kappa}_{\varphi}}, GKS^{e}_{b}, CP \right)$, where

$\overset{(a,\,b;c,\,d)}{DTS^{\kappa}_{\varphi}}$ is a diatonic system $\left(\overset{(a,\,b;c,\,d)}{NRS^{\kappa}_{\varphi}}, \overset{(a,\,b;c,\,d)}{NRSi^{\kappa}_{\varphi}} \right)$, $\overset{(a,\,b;c,\,d)}{NRS^{\kappa}_{\varphi}}$ is a note-reception

system $\left(\overset{(a,\,b;\,c,\,d)}{FTS_{\varphi}}, CORE^{\kappa}, MSG/R \right)$, and $\overset{(a,\,b;\,c,\,d)}{FTS_{\varphi}} = \left(\overset{(a,\,b)}{CTS_{\varphi}}, \overset{(c,\,d)}{RVL} \right)$ is a coherent

tone system.

We shall refer to a primary interval $(y,\ z) \in \overset{(c,\,d)}{RVL}$ as *a tertial element* if $z = e$.

E. Agmon, *The Languages of Western Tonality*, Computational Music Science,
DOI 10.1007/978-3-642-39587-1_8, © Springer-Verlag Berlin Heidelberg 2013

By Definition 3.30 the privileged pitch intervals log2, log3, etc. are ordered, starting with the psychoacoustical octave log2. The privileged *note* intervals, namely the cognitive octave (a, b), the quintic element (c, d), and a tertial element (y, z), are also ordered (by virtue of their tone-systemic roles), starting with the cognitive octave (a, b). In Definition 3.42 (updated as Definition 5.22) the cognitive octave is paired with the psychoacoustical octave. The following crucial definition pairs, in order, the remaining note intervals of privilege with privileged pitch intervals. Since a privileged interval $\log 2^n$ is paired with a compound cognitive octave, a tertial element is paired with log5, not log4. Since $\psi = a$, the logarithm base is $\sqrt[a]{2}$.

In connection with the following definition, review Definitions 7.25 and 7.36.

Definition 8.2. Proto-tonal System

$$\text{Let} \quad HS_\varphi^{\kappa}{}^{(a,\,b;\,c,\,d;\,e)} = \left(DTS_\varphi^{\kappa}{}^{(a,\,b;\,c,\,d)}, \ GKS_b^e, \ CP \right) \text{ be a harmonic system, and assume}$$

that if CP contains a pair of consecutive functional chords, the system is efficient. Let $q_n = \log(n + 1)$ be a privileged pitch interval.

We shall refer to $HS_\varphi^{\kappa}{}^{(a,\,b;\,c,\,d;\,e)}$ as *a proto-tonal system* if it satisfies the following condition A, such that a non-empty system satisfies the following condition B as well, for some tertial element (y, z).

A. c is as close as possible to $q_2 - q_1 = a\log_2(3/2)$.
B. y is as close as possible to $q_4 - 2q_1 = a\log_2(5/4)$.

Theorem 8.3. Let $HS_\varphi^{\kappa}{}^{(a,\,b;\,c,\,d;\,e)}$ be a proto-tonal system.

Then one of the following two conditions, A or B, holds.

A. $HS_\varphi^{\kappa}{}^{(a,\,b;\,c,\,d;\,e)}$ is not empty, and is a usual harmonic system HS_φ^{κ} (Definition 7.26).

B. $HS_\varphi^{\kappa}{}^{(a,\,b;\,c,\,d;\,e)}$ is empty, and is a usual diatonic system DTS_φ^{κ} (Definition 6.26).

To prove the theorem we shall first prove three lemmas.

Lemma 8.4. Let $HS_\varphi^{\kappa}{}^{(a,\,b;\,c,\,d;\,e)}$ be a proto-tonal system.

Then $(a, \ b; \ c, \ d) = (12, \ 7; \ 7, \ 4)$.

Proof. By Condition 8.2A c/a is as close as possible to $\log_2(3/2) \approx 0.584962$. Using Proposition 6.28, if a is odd $c/a = 3/5 = 0.6$. If a is even $c/a = 7/12 = 0.5833$, which is closer to $\log_2(3/2)$ than 0.6. Q.E.D.

Lemma 8.5. Let $HS_\varphi^{\kappa}{}^{(a,\,b;\,c,\,d;\,e)} = \left(DTS_\varphi^{\kappa}{}^{(a,\,b;\,c,\,d)}, \ GKS_b^e, \ CP \right)$ be a proto-tonal system,

where CP is not empty.

Then $(a, \ b; \ c, \ d; \ e) = (12, \ 7; \ 7, \ 4; \ 2)$.

Proof. By Lemma 8.4 $(a, \ b; \ c, \ d) = (12, \ 7; \ 7, \ 4)$. By Condition 8.2B $y/12$ is as close as possible to $\log_2(5/4) \approx 0.321928$. Thus $y/12 = 4/12 = 0.3333$, implying that $z = 2 = e$. Q.E.D.

Lemma 8.6. Let $\overset{(a, \, b; c, \, d; e)}{HS^{\kappa}_{\varphi}} = \left(\overset{(a, \, b; c, \, d)}{DTS^{\kappa}_{\varphi}}, \ GKS^{e}_{b}, \ CP \right)$ be a proto-tonal system, where CP contains a pair of consecutive functional chords.

Then $(a, \ b; \ c, \ d; \ e) = (12, \ 7; \ 7, \ 4; \ 2)$.

Proof. By assumption $\overset{(a, \, b; c, \, d; e)}{HS^{\kappa}_{\varphi}}$ is efficient, and therefore by Theorem 7.37 either $b = 2, \ e = 1$, or b is odd, $e = 2, \ b - 2$.

By Condition 8.2B y/a is as close as possible to $\log_2(5/4) \approx 0.321928$. If $b = 2$ then $y/a = 1/3$. Suppose that b is odd. Together with Propositions 6.28 and 6.30 if a is odd then $y/a = 3/9$. If a is even, $y/a = 4/12$. Together with Lemma 8.4, the lemma follows. Q.E.D.

Proof of the theorem. By Lemma 8.4 a proto-tonal system $\overset{(a, \, b; c, \, d; e)}{HS^{\kappa}_{\varphi}}$ satisfies $(a, \ b; \ c, \ d) = (12, \ 7; \ 7, \ 4)$.

Consider the following three conditions 1, 2, or 3.

1. CP is empty.
2. CP is not empty.
3. CP contains a pair of consecutive functional chords.

Suppose that Condition 1 holds. Then $\overset{(a, \, b; c, \, d; e)}{HS^{\kappa}_{\varphi}}$ reduces to a usual diatonic system DTS^{κ}_{φ}, such that e is an irrelevant parameter. Suppose that Condition 2 holds. Then $\overset{(a, \, b; c, \, d; e)}{HS^{\kappa}_{\varphi}} = HS^{\kappa}_{\varphi}$ is usual, by Lemma 8.5. Finally, suppose that Condition 3 holds. Then $\overset{(a, \, b; c, \, d; e)}{HS^{\kappa}_{\varphi}} = HS^{\kappa}_{\varphi}$ is usual by Lemma 8.6, which happily is compatible with Lemma 8.5. Q.E.D.

Note from the proof of Lemma 8.6 that if Condition 8.2A is dropped a nine-tone categorically equal-tempered pentatonic tone system is proto-tonal. Interestingly, some scholars of Javanese music have suggested that the pentatonic *pélog* scale is (ideally) nine-tone equal tempered. See Rahn (1978); see also Kunst (1973), vol. 1, pp. 52–53.

Note also that had it not been for Definition 3.30, where the privileged pitch intervals are defined in terms of overtones rather than overtones *or "undertones"* (equivalently, privileged pitch intervals are measured *from* a fundamental to an overtone, not vice versa as well), a proto-tonal system would have been anti-usual as well as usual, that is, the perfect fourth and the minor/major sixth would have been privileged as quintic and tertial, respectively, as an alternative to the perfect fifth and the major/minor third. In other words, our system is not "dualistic" because, unlike Riemann (1875), we reject "the objective existence of undertones in the sound wave."

As we shall see in Part II, our "monistic" result is nevertheless perfectly compatible with the duality of "major" vs. "minor."

8.2 Categorical ET: Theory Lagging (Far) Behind Practice?

The story of Western intonation, we are told, is fairly straightforward. Reflecting the privileged status of the perfect octave and fifth, in medieval times the preferred tuning system was Pythagorean (PI). During the Renaissance, after the major and minor thirds gradually gained a place within the privileged set, various forms of "meantone" temperament (MT) came to the fore, reflecting a "just" ideal. Finally, with the advent of major/minor tonality in the Baroque era 12-tone equal tempera-ment gradually took over, supplanting various forms of "well temperament" along the way. ET, however, is a compromise. It allows for worry-free modulation at the price of the mistuning to some degree or another of all intervals, except the perfect octave.

This narrative (or some variant thereof) is so well rehearsed that its truth seems never to have been seriously called into question. And yet, the present study does exactly that. A proto-tonal system is *categorically* 12-tone equal tempered in the sense of Definition 5.21. Can such a view, so blatantly contrary to received wisdom (or so it seems), be true?

Before addressing this question it should be useful to retrace the path that has led us to the categorical ET result, or at least to revisit the important milestones along the way. To simplify discussion we shall assume a naturally oriented type-1 system satisfying $a > b > 0$, where (a, b) is the cognitive octave, and the psychoacoustical octave ψ satisfies $\psi = a$.

In Sect. 3.5 we find that a composite tone system is either *strictly* equal tempered in the sense that a note interval (u, v) satisfies $T_2(u, v) = u$, or is a "type-3" system (Theorem 3.44).[1] This result follows from our assumption (Definition 3.36) that there exists a pair of transmission functions, from notes (note intervals) to pitches (pitch intervals), satisfying the property that if p and p' are the transmitted pitches relative to the notes (s, t) and (s', t'), respectively, then, if q is the pitch interval from p to p' and (u, v) is the note interval from (s, t) to (s', t'), q is the transmitted pitch *interval* relative to the note *interval* (u, v). From this property it follows that the transmission function for intervals is a homomorphism (Theorem 3.38).

---

[1] In type-3 systems pitch intervals are of the form $u \cdot T_2(1, 0) + v \cdot T_2(0, 1)$ for some non-zero pitch intervals $T_2(1, 0)$ and $T_2(0, 1)$, for every note interval (u, v) (natural orientation is assumed). PI and MT are of this type.

In Sect. 5.1 we find that an efficient tone system is *not* a type-3 system (Theorem 5.8). This is because "semi-efficient" type-3 systems are dense (Lemma 5.9), contradicting the efficiency condition (5.6A) by which the JND for "primary" pitch intervals (that is, pitch intervals that transmit primary intervals or their octave compounds) is not arbitrarily small. Having ruled out type-3 tone systems (particularly dense ones), we are able in Sect. 5.3 to relax the condition of absolutely accurate note transmission. The theory of categorical equal temperament applies the Categorical Principle (Sect. 2.3.2) to the strict ET result. By this theory deviations from strict ET of up to one-half of one equal-tempered increment in either direction, are possible.[2] Thus, for every note interval (u, v) there exists a *category* of corresponding pitch intervals q extending from $u - 0.5$ to $u + 0.5$ (exclusive). A pitch interval q is rated in terms of its *prototypicality* relative to the category. In particular, prototypicality is maximal if $q = u$; otherwise, prototypicality decreases smoothly, monotonically, and symmetrically with the distance $|q - u|$; review Fig. 5.2.

In an important sense the difference between the traditional narrative and the present one is academic. This is because, in a sufficiently short segment of the line of fifths, certainly a segment of, say, just seven or even twelve elements, if all fifths are pure (cf. PI) or slightly narrower than tempered (cf. MT), deviations from strict ET are relatively small. Thus, PI and MT, and indeed, practically all systems of intonation that have been proposed over the course of the history of the theory of intonation, may readily be viewed as varieties of (categorical) equal temperament. In other words, prototypicality is always non-zero; yet it is often less (usually, slightly less) than maximal.

How can one possibly establish that the theory of categorical ET is true?

It so happens that theories can only be proven false. Therefore, neither the theory of categorical ET nor any alternative can have the stamp of truth, in any absolute sense. At the same time, to prove a theory *false* and, in particular, to decide between two competing theories, empirical data are needed. Such data might include, in the present case, measurements of pitch intervals transmitted in acts of musical communication as note-interval *signals*. A large number of such transmissions (musical performances) should be sampled, representing a wide variety of transmitting devices (musical instruments), including strings, winds, and the human voice. From the distributions of values relative to a given note interval one might be able to infer a central tendency, in terms of which a theoretical prediction, be it PI, MT, or ET (to name the most likely candidates), may conceivably be falsified.

The earliest reliable pitch measurements, however, date from ca. 1826.[3] We seem, therefore, to have reached a dead end. Like scientific theories in general, the

---

[2] A pitch deviation in one direction constrains the maximal possible deviation in the opposite direction. See Condition 5.22B.

[3] See Shackford (1962b, pp. 296–298) for a historical survey. As important a tool as the monochord was in earlier eras, it was useful only for mapping the physical into the audible, not the other way around.

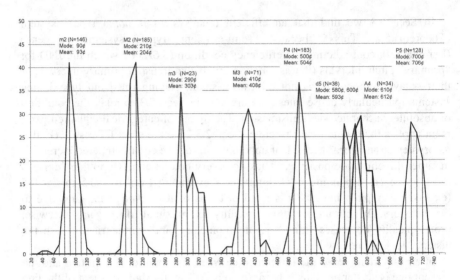

Fig. 8.1 String-trio intonation of selected intervals. Data from Shackford (1961, 1962a). For each interval, pitch-interval size in cents (*horizontal axis*) is plotted against percentage of occurrences (*vertical axis*). Also given are the sample size (N), as well as its mode and mean

theory of categorical ET cannot be proven true. Its historical claims could *conceivably* have been proven false, had relevant data existed and survived (which is not the case). Nonetheless, it should be useful briefly to consider data of the sort that is historically lacking. This should at least provide a sense of the difficulties involved in attempting to draw conclusions from intonation data in general.

Figure 8.1 displays the distributions of pitch intervals relative to selected transmitted intervals (m2, M2, m3, M3, P4, A4, d5, and P5), as measured by Shackford (1961, 1962a).[4] The data relate to performances by three different professional string trios of four short tonal pieces composed by Shackford himself (different settings of the same melody, one being rather dissonant, in the style of Hindemith).[5] Open strings were avoided.

Judging by their mean values, major seconds, minor thirds, and perfect fourths are roughly equal tempered. Perfect fifths are on average slightly wide (706 cents), though most fifths are, indeed, approximately equal tempered. On the other hand, minor seconds are on the average somewhat narrower (93 cents) than strict ET, whereas major thirds, to the contrary, are wider (408 cents).

---

[4] See Shackford's (1961, 1962a), Examples 17, 18, 20, 23, 25, 28, and 31–35. Figure 8.1 makes no distinction between melodic and harmonic intervals, as well as between simple and compound ones. For example, "P5" in the figure refers to harmonic perfect fifths (Shackford's Example 17), harmonic twelfths (Example 18), as well as melodic fifths (second part of Example 35). The distributions were obtained by counting occurrences within 10-cent "windows." For example, 700 on the horizontal axis represents the pitch-interval range of 695–704 cents. Ward (1970) summarizes Shackford's data, as well as data from similar studies.

[5] Shackford (1961), Examples 4–7.

One might be tempted to conclude from these findings that string players in the 1960s preferred PI, in particular, "Pythagorean" minor seconds and major thirds (approximately 90 and 408 cents, respectively). However, such a conclusion would seem to overlook "expressive" issues. In Shackford's compositions many (melodic) minor seconds correspond to "leading tones" followed by their "resolutions"; similarly, many (harmonic) major thirds have a leading tone as the upper note. For expressive purposes, it is natural for a performer to "stretch," if the instrument allows, a leading tone in the direction of its resolution, resulting in a somewhat narrow (melodic) minor second and a correspondingly wide (harmonic) major third, both relative to strict ET (for the same reason diminished fifths tend to be narrower than augmented fourths; cf. Fig. 8.1). Indeed, the theory of categorical ET makes such expressive uses of intonation possible in the first place; by contrast, if accuracy is an overriding concern expressivity in intonation simply cannot exist.

Considered in context, then, Shackford's data do *not* falsify the categorical ET prediction as far as the contemporary scene is concerned. Moreover, the exercise suggests that had similar *historical* data been available, the possible existence of expressive factors would have complicated their analysis. For example, a hypothetical preference for wide major sixths (relative to strict ET) could have been the expressive result of "stretching" the sixth towards its octave resolution, rather than some *a priori* preference for PI.

Shackford's study concerns note transmission. Vos (1986) studied note *reception* on an assumption contrary to categorical ET, namely, that the most prototypical perfect fifths and major thirds are "pure" (ca. 702 and 386 cents, respectively). It is therefore instructive that despite this bias, Vos's results seem to suggest prototypes that are in fact closer to ET. This effect is particularly prominent in settings that use sinusoidal rather than complex tones (see Fig. 8.2), presumably because subjects, in the case of complex tones, associate "purity" with "lack of beating." Especially with respect to the major third, where the difference between the pure and equal-tempered "prototypes" is not insignificant, it is not at all clear from the data that 386 cents was indeed judged "purest," rather than a value much closer to 400 cents.

In Sect. 5.1 we have noted that there is no real alternative to assuming "semi-efficient" tone systems, an assumption on the basis of which type-3 systems are excluded (see footnote 4, following the proof of Theorem 5.8). We now see, in addition, that restricting "Pythagorean" or "meantone" intonation to a line-of-fifths *segment* is fully consistent with categorical equal temperament. In other words, in practice nothing was lost by having ruled out type-3 systems early on.

It is equally clear that there is no real alternative to the assumption of a unique transmitted pitch (see Definition 3.36 and discussion), that is, a unique, *maximally prototypical* pitch for every transmitted note. To assume the *Tonnetz* of "just intonation," by comparison, is not only blatantly *ad hoc* (see Counterexample 3.41, where a, b, c, d, and e are in effect set to 12, 7, 7, 4, and 2, respectively), but again, a small, connected area of the *Tonnetz* (which is what one usually means

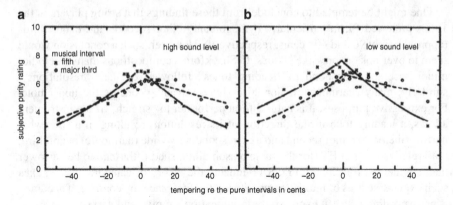

Fig. 8.2 Mean subjective purity ratings for intervals that comprised two simultaneous sinusoidal tones. From Vos (1986). Copyright © 1986 Regents of the University of California. Reproduced from *Music Perception 3*(3), by permission

by "just intonation") is consistent with categorical ET. All this, of course, is no accident. In Sect. 8.1 we have assumed that the quintic and tertial elements are *as pure as possible*.

Is it not possible that the shift towards ET in the history of intonation theory was not so much a reflection of changing musical styles, as is commonly assumed to be the case, as it was a reflection of the *mathematical* advents, in the sixteenth and seventeenth centuries, of root and logarithm extraction? Certainly the evidence is consistent with such a view.[6] If so, we have a rather extreme case of theory lagging behind practice. Indeed, one can think of only one other area in tonal theory, namely modality, where theory lagged so far behind musical practice, though for a very different reason.[7]

A hypothetical alternative to the theory of proto-tonality is considered next. As we shall see, the alternative theory, based on Clough and Douthett's (1991) theory of "maximally even sets," simply *assumes* type-1 equal temperament.

8.3 A Possible Alternative to the Theory of Proto-tonal Systems

In Sect. 8.1 we have established that proto-tonal systems $HS_\varphi^{\kappa}{}^{(a,\,b;\,c,\,d;\,e)}$ satisfy $(a,\,b;\,c,\,d) = (12,\,7;\,7,\,4)$. In other words, the "cognitive octave" is the perfect octave $(12, 7)$ and the "quintic element" is the perfect fifth $(7, 4)$. Moreover, assuming a proto-tonal system that is not empty harmonically, a "tertial element" is a "third," whether major $(4, 2)$ or minor $(3, 2)$.

---

[6] See Rasch (2002), pp. 204–214.

[7] See Sect. 12.1.

It should be obvious by now that proto-tonal systems, that is, usual diatonic or harmonic systems (Theorem 8.3), are much more than four or five parameters set to certain familiar values. Nonetheless, it should be useful at this juncture to review the properties of these systems.

A usual diatonic system DTS_φ^κ (Definition 6.26) consists of a usual note-reception system NRS_φ^κ and a series $NRSi_\varphi^\kappa$ of usual reflexive note-reception systems all with the same "core" (a seven-element line-of-fifths segment). In terms of self-communicating the core, *diatonic systems satisfy the Communication Principle* (Theorem 6.19).

A usual note-reception system NRS_φ^κ consists of a usual coherent tone system FTS_φ (Definitions 5.13 and 5.14), a core, and a sequence of notes representing the received message. A usual coherent tone system FTS_φ consists of a usual composite tone system CTS_φ (Definitions 3.45 and 5.22) and the usual set of eleven primary intervals P1, m2, M2,..., M7. In terms of communicating the primary intervals, *coherent tone systems satisfy the Communication Principle as well as the Economical Principle.*

Finally, a usual composite tone system consists of a usual, octave-endowed note system (Definition 3.11), a φ-centered, a-standard pitch-communication system PCS_φ (Definition 3.31, 3.35), a message of notes, and an exchange of the message with a sequence of categorically equal-tempered pitches (Definition 5.21). In terms of communicating pitches and pitch intervals, *standard pitch-communication systems satisfy the Communication Principle.*

A usual harmonic system HS_φ^κ (Definition 7.26) consists of a usual diatonic system, a usual generic klang system (Definition 7.11), and a chord progression relative to a klang progression (Definition 7.23; a "klang," in the usual case, is a set of mod-7 note classes that can be "stacked tertially" relative to a "root"). Between every pair of consecutive *functional* chords (Definition 7.19), that is, chords that express triads or tetrads, there exists an efficient voice leading (Definition 7.33). *A usual harmonic system represents the "grammar" that allows the analyst, on the one hand, to infer a harmonic message from a given score, and the listener, on the other, to infer a corresponding message from the received score.*

Granted that the properties enumerated above of usual diatonic and harmonic systems seem important; is there nonetheless an alternative, possibly simpler theory by which the systems in question may be accounted for?

In what follows we consider a proto-tonal theory based on Clough and Douthett's (1991) notion of "maximally even" sets (henceforth, "ME proto-tonality"), an intriguing alternative to the proposed theory of proto-tonal systems (henceforth, "proposed proto-tonality"). We show that ME proto-tonality indeed accounts for the same constructs, namely usual diatonic and harmonic systems, using fewer assumptions than proposed proto-tonality. However, as noted in Sect. 2.1, two theories of equal (or near-equal) descriptive power may not be equal in terms of *explanatory* power, since one theory's dependency on *ad hoc* assumptions

Table 8.1 The main assumptions of proposed proto-tonality (left-hand column, with definition number in parentheses) and the principles that they express (top row). A *parenthesized check* indicates that the principle accounts for the assumption only in part

		Communication	Economical	Categorical	Maximalist
Composite tone systems	(5.22)	($\sqrt{}$)	–	($\sqrt{}$)	–
Primary intervals	(5.1)	–	–	–	–
Efficient tone systems	(5.6)	$\sqrt{}$	–	–	$\sqrt{}$
Coherent tone systems	(5.14)	–	($\sqrt{}$)	–	–
Diatonic systems	(6.21)	$\sqrt{}$	–	$\sqrt{}$	$\sqrt{}$
Efficient harmonic systems	(7.36)	($\sqrt{}$)	–	–	–
Proto-tonal systems	(8.2)	–	–	–	–

may be greater than that of the other. For example, a proto-tonal theory that simply assumes, say, $a = 12$, can be incomparably simpler than proposed proto-tonality or any alternative. The hypothetical theory, however, though conceivably descriptively adequate, will have little or no explanatory power, since $a = 12$ is a blatantly *ad hoc* assumption.

We begin, therefore, by listing the main assumptions of proposed proto-tonality together with the guiding principles, if any, that they express. We then show that an alternative theory, namely ME proto-tonality, exists. After cancelling pairs of *equivalent* assumptions, one from each theory, we consider whether a remaining assumption may be reduced to one or more high-level principles. Finally, we consider whether any assumption that still remains has explanatory value, *beyond* the proto-tonal level.

Table 8.1 lists the main assumptions of proposed proto-tonality (some seven in number). To the extent that an assumption may be accounted for in terms of one or more of the four guiding ideas noted in Chap. 2, the appropriate column of the corresponding row is checked. Parenthesized checks indicate that an assumption is only partially accounted for by the indicated principle(s). For example, "coherence" (Definition 5.14) expresses the Economical Principle. However, the principle only accounts for the *existence* of a simple algorithm by which an interval (u, v) octave equivalent to a primary interval may be computed from $T_2(u, v)$. The *specific* algorithm assumed is not implied.

We shall now show that an alternative proto-tonal theory based on Clough and Douthett's (1991) notion of ME sets, namely ME proto-tonality, indeed exists. As our points of departure we take on the one hand a composite tone system $CTS_\varphi^{(a,\ b)} = \left(ONS^{(a,\ b)}, PCS_\varphi, CET, MSG \right)$ (Definition 5.22), and on the other a generic note system $GNS_b = (N_b, NVL_b, GI)$ (Definition 7.3, with $\beta = b$). To simplify discussion and notation we assume that $\varphi = 0$ (that is, pitch communication is faithful). We also assume that $a \geq b \geq 1$ such that $CTS_0^{(a,\ b)} = CTS^{(a,\ b)}$ is a type-1 system. Relative to both $\overset{(a,\ b)}{CTS}$ and GNS_b we define a "maximally even set" in a sense derived from Clough and Douthett's (1991, p. 100) Definition 1.9, a definition that expresses the intuitive sense of "maximal evenness," namely, "a set whose elements are distributed as evenly as possible around the chromatic circle" (*ibid.*, p. 96). Finally, the relation between the two types of ME sets and, respectively, diatonic and harmonic systems, is studied via two theorems, 8.11 and 8.12.

Definition 8.7. Composite Maximally Even Set

Let $\overset{(a,\ b)}{CTS}$ be a composite tone system, $\gcd(a,\ b) = \delta$. Fix two integers i and j, $0 \leq j \leq \frac{b}{\delta} - 1$, and let $\overset{(a,\ b;i,j)}{CME}$ be a set of exactly b notes $(s,\ t)$, $t = 0$, $1, \ldots,\ b - 1$.

We shall refer to $\overset{(a,\ b;i,j)}{CME}$ as *a composite maximally even set* if the following condition A is satisfied.

A. $s = i + \left\lfloor \dfrac{a}{b} \cdot (t + j) \right\rfloor$.

Example 8.8.

$\overset{(12,\ 6;0,\ 0)}{CME} = \{(0,0),\ (2,1),\ (4,2),\ (6,3),\ (8,4),\ (10,5)\}.$

$\overset{(12,\ 8;0,\ 0)}{CME} = \{(0,0),\ (1,1),\ (3,2),\ (4,3),\ (6,4),\ (7,5),\ (9,6),\ (10,7)\}.$

$\overset{(12,\ 7;0,\ 0)}{CME} = \{(0,0),\ (1,1),\ (3,2),\ (5,3),\ (6,4),\ (8,5),\ (10,6)\}.$

$\overset{(12,\ 7;1,\ 0)}{CME} = \{(1,0),\ (2,1),\ (4,2),\ (6,3),\ (7,4),\ (9,5),\ (11,6)\}.$

$\overset{(12,\ 7;0,\ 1)}{CME} = \{(1,0),\ (3,1),\ (5,2),\ (6,3),\ (8,4),\ (10,5),\ (12,6)\}.$

$\overset{(12,\ 7;-1,\ 1)}{CME} = \{(0,0),\ (2,1),\ (4,2),\ (5,3),\ (7,4),\ (9,5),\ (11,6)\}.$

$\overset{(12,\ 7;-5,\ 3)}{CME} = \{(0,0),\ (1,1),\ (3,2),\ (5,3),\ (7,4),\ (8,5),\ (10,6)\}.$

Definition 8.9. Generic Maximally Even Set

Let $GNS_b = (N_b,\ NVL_b,\ GI)$ be the generic note system. Fix two integers k and m, $0 \leq k \leq b - 1$, $1 \leq m \leq b$, and let $\overset{(b,\ m;k)}{GME}$ be a set $\{g_0,\ g_1,\ \ldots,\ g_{m-1}\}$ of exactly m generic notes.

We shall refer to $\overset{(b,\ m;k)}{GME}$ as *a generic maximally even set* if the following condition A is satisfied for every $n = 0,\ 1,\ \ldots,\ m - 1$.

A. $g_n = k + \left\lfloor \dfrac{b}{m} \cdot n \right\rfloor \pmod{b}$.

Example 8.10.

$$\begin{array}{ll}
\overset{(12,\,6;0)}{GME} = \{0, \ 2, \ 4, \ 6, \ 8, \ 10\}. \\[4pt]
\overset{(12,\,8;0)}{GME} = \{0, \ 1, \ 3, \ 4, \ 6, \ 7, \ 9, \ 10\}. \\[4pt]
\overset{(12,\,7;0)}{GME} = \{0, \ 1, \ 3, \ 5, \ 6, \ 8, \ 10\}. \\[4pt]
\overset{(7,\,7;0)}{GME} = \{0, \ 1, \ldots, 6\}. \\[4pt]
\overset{(7,\,3;0)}{GME} = \{0, \ 2, \ 4\}. \\[4pt]
\overset{(7,\,3;6)}{GME} = \{6, \ 1, \ 3\}. \\[4pt]
\overset{(7,\,4;0)}{GME} = \{0, \ 1, \ 3, \ 5\}. \\[4pt]
\overset{(7,\,4;6)}{GME} = \{6, \ 0, \ 2, \ 4\}.
\end{array}$$

Theorem 8.11. Let $\overset{(a,\,b)}{CTS}$ be a composite tone system, $a \geq 3$, $b = \lfloor a/2 \rfloor + 1$. Let (c, d) be a note interval, let (i, j) be a pair of integers, $0 \leq j \leq b - 1$, and let κ be an integer. Finally, assume that either a is odd and $(c, \ d) = (a - 2, \ b - 1)$ $((c, \ d) = (2, \ 1))$, or $a \equiv 0 \pmod{4}$ and $(c, \ d) = \left(\frac{a}{2} - 1, \ \frac{b-1}{2}\right)$ $((c, \ d) = \left(\frac{a}{2} + 1, \ \frac{b+1}{2}\right))$.

Then the following two conditions, A and B, are equivalent.

A. The composite maximally even set $\overset{(a,\,b;i,\,j)}{CME}$ may be written as the quintic segment Q_κ^b, where (c, d) is the quintic element.[8]

B. $(i, \ -j) \equiv_{(a,\ b)} \kappa(c, \ d)$ (respectively, $(i, \ -j) \equiv_{(a,\ b)} (\kappa + b - 1)(c, \ d)$).

Proof. If a is odd and $(c, \ d) = (a - 2, \ b - 1)$ or $a \equiv 0 \pmod{4}$ and $(c, \ d) = \left(\frac{a}{2} - 1, \ \frac{b-1}{2}\right)$, write

$$(s_n, \ t_n) \equiv_{(a,\ b)} (i, \ -j) \oplus n(c, \ d), \ 1 \leq n \leq b - 1. \tag{8.1}$$

If a is odd and $(c, \ d) = (2, \ 1)$ or $a \equiv 0 \pmod{4}$ and $(c, \ d) = \left(\frac{a}{2} + 1, \ \frac{b+1}{2}\right)$, write

$$(s_n, \ t_n) \equiv_{(a,\ b)} (i, \ -j) \oplus n'(c, \ d), \ 1 \leq n \leq b - 1, \ n' = n - (b - 1). \tag{8.2}$$

We want to show that Eqs. (8.1) and (8.2) are each equivalent to

$$\left\lfloor \frac{a}{b} \cdot (t_n + j) \right\rfloor + i = s_n, \ 0 \leq t_n \leq b - 1, \ t_n \neq b - j. \tag{8.3}$$

---

[8] "Register" is disregarded. Recall that the elements of a quintic segment, unlike those of a composite ME set, are all in the "one-line" register.

It is easy to see that under 8.1, 8.3 is equivalent to $\lfloor n \cdot \frac{ad}{b} \rfloor = nc,\ 1 \le n \le b - 1$. Indeed, if a is odd we find that

$$\left\lfloor n \cdot \frac{ad}{b} \right\rfloor = \left\lfloor n \cdot \left(2b - 3 + \frac{1}{b} \right) \right\rfloor = n \cdot (2b - 3) + \left\lfloor \frac{n}{b} \right\rfloor = nc,$$

and if $a \equiv 0 \pmod{4}$ we find that

$$\left\lfloor n \cdot \frac{ad}{b} \right\rfloor = \left\lfloor n \cdot \left(b - 2 + \frac{1}{b} \right) \right\rfloor = n \cdot (b - 2) + \left\lfloor \frac{n}{b} \right\rfloor = nc.$$

Similarly, under 8.2, 8.3 is equivalent to $\lfloor n' \cdot \frac{ad}{b} \rfloor = n'c,\ 1 \le n \le b - 1$, $n' = n - (b - 1)$. Indeed, if a is odd we find that

$$\left\lfloor n' \cdot \frac{ad}{b} \right\rfloor = \left\lfloor n' \cdot \frac{2b - 1}{b} \right\rfloor = \left\lfloor n' \cdot 2 - \frac{n'}{b} \right\rfloor = n'c,$$

and if $a \equiv 0 \pmod{4}$ we find that

$$\left\lfloor n' \cdot \frac{ad}{b} \right\rfloor = \left\lfloor n' \cdot \left(2d - \frac{2d}{b} \right) \right\rfloor = \left\lfloor n' \cdot \left(2d - \frac{b + 1}{b} \right) \right\rfloor = \left\lfloor n' \cdot (2d - 1) - \frac{n'}{b} \right\rfloor = n'c.$$

Q.E.D.

Theorem 8.12. Let $GNS_b = (N_b,\ NVL_b,\ \text{GI})$ be the generic note system. Let K, K' be two sets of generic notes.

Then the following two conditions, A and B, are equivalent.

A. K and K' may be written as two functional klangs $K(r,\ m)$ and $K(r',\ m')$, respectively, for some r, r'. Moreover, there exists a relation GVL: $K \to K'$ satisfying the conditions of Proposition 7.35.

B. K and K' may be written as two generic maximally even sets $\overset{(b,\,m;k)}{GME}$ and $\overset{(b,\,m';k')}{GME}$, for some k, k'. Moreover, b is odd, and $m,\ m' = \dfrac{b \pm 1}{2}$.

To prove the theorem we shall first prove the following lemma.

Lemma 8.13. Let $GNS_b = (N_b,\ NVL_b,\ \text{GI})$ be the generic note system, where $b \ge 3$ is odd. Set $m = \dfrac{b \pm 1}{2}$, $m' = b - m$, and let G be a set of generic notes. Set $G' = N_b \backslash G$, the complement of G relative to N_b.

Then the following two conditions, A and B (C and D) are equivalent, and imply the other two conditions C and D (A and B).

A. G may be written as a generic maximally even set $GME^{(b,\,m;k)}$, for some k.

B. G may be written as a klang $K(r,\ m)$ relative to $e \equiv \pm 2 \pmod{b}$, for some r.

C. G' may be written as a generic maximally even set $GME^{(b,\,m';k')}$, for some k'.

D. G' may be written as a klang $K(r',\ m')$ relative to $e \equiv \mp 2 \pmod{b}$, for some r'.

Proof. If $m = \frac{b-1}{2}$ for $0 \leq n \leq m - 1$ we have

$$\left\lfloor \frac{b}{m} \cdot n \right\rfloor = \left\lfloor \frac{2m+1}{m} \cdot n \right\rfloor = \left\lfloor 2n + \frac{n}{m} \right\rfloor = 2n + \left\lfloor \frac{n}{m} \right\rfloor = 2n < b,$$

and if $m = \frac{b+1}{2}$ for $1 \leq n \leq m - 1$ we have

$$\left\lfloor \frac{b}{m} \cdot n \right\rfloor = \left\lfloor \frac{2m-1}{m} \cdot n \right\rfloor = \left\lfloor 2n - \frac{n}{m} \right\rfloor = 2n - 1 < b.$$

Thus, conditions A and B (C and D) are equivalent.

If Condition B (D) holds by Proposition 7.10 G' (G) may be written as the klang $K(r',\ m')$ ($K(r,\ m)$) relative to $b - e,\ r' \equiv r - e \pmod{b}$. Thus Condition D (B) holds, which is equivalent to C (A). Q.E.D.

Proof of the theorem. Suppose that Condition A of the theorem holds, and assume that $m' = m, r = r' + e$. Since K and K' are functional by Theorem 7.15 $m = [b/2]$. Since there exists a relation GVL : $K \to K'$ satisfying the conditions of Proposition 7.35, it follows that $g_{m-1} \in K$ satisfies

$$r' - g_{m-1} \equiv -me \equiv \pm 1 \pmod{b}. \tag{8.4}$$

If $b = 2$ we have $m = e = 1$, and K, K' are (trivially) maximally even. Suppose that $b \geq 3$. If $m = b/2$ Equation (8.4) cannot be satisfied. It follows that b is odd, $e = \pm 2 \pmod{b}$. Set $m = \frac{b \pm 1}{2}$. From Lemma 8.13 Condition B of the theorem follows.

Suppose that Condition B holds. Then by Lemma 8.13 $K = K(r,\ m)$, $K' = K(r',\ m')$ are two functional klangs relative to $e \equiv \pm 2 \pmod{b}$, respectively. From Lemmas 7.38 and 7.39 it follows that there exists a relation GVL : $K \to K'$ satisfying the conditions of Proposition 7.35. Thus Condition B of the theorem implies Condition A. Q.E.D.[9]

---

[9] Tymoczko (2006b, p. 13) claims that a corollary to "one of the central conclusions" of his 2006a theory of "chord geometry," namely "...that 'nearly even' chords can be linked to their transpositions by efficient voice leading" (Callender et al. 2008b, p. 10) "generalizes" Agmon's (1991) result, concerning "the special voice-leading properties of diatonic tertian triads and seventh chords." (Similar sentiments are expressed in Tymoczko 2011, footnotes on pp. 14 and 64.) However, although Tymoczko's theory relates in obvious ways to Agmon's 1991 study, the latter being the basis for the theory of efficient harmonic systems presented in Chap. 7, the

From Theorems 8.11 and 8.12 we have the following proposition.

*Proposition 8.14. Under the following six conditions A–F, $(a, b; c, d; e) = (12, 7; 7, 4; 2)$.

A. $b = \lfloor a/2 \rfloor + 1$ (see Theorem 8.11).

B. Type-1 composite systems $\overset{(a,\ b)}{CTS}$.

C. Composite maximally even sets $\overset{(a,\ b;\ i,\ j)}{CME}$.

D. Generic maximally even sets $\overset{(b,\ m;\ k)}{GME}$.

E. $b = 2m \pm 1$ (see Theorem 8.12).

F. For some c as in Theorem 8.11 and some $e = 2$, $b - 2$, c/a is as close as possible to $\log_2(3/2)$, and e/a is as close as possible to $\log_2(5/4)$ (cf. Definition 8.2).

We shall refer henceforth to the theory defined by conditions A–F of Proposition 8.14 as *ME proto-tonality*.

Since certain pairs of assumptions, one of proposed proto-tonality and the other of ME proto-tonality, are equivalent and even identical (compare Table 8.1 with Proposition 8.14), in evaluating relative explanatory power such assumptions may conveniently be ignored. We thus obtain the following "reduced" definitions, 8.15 for proposed proto-tonality, and 8.16 for ME proto-tonality. With regard to Conditions 8.15 E–F and 8.16 D–E, review Theorem 8.12.

Definition 8.15.   Proposed Proto-tonality (reduced)

A. Primary intervals.
B. Efficiency.
C. Coherence.
D. Diatonic tone systems.
E. Functional klangs.
F. Efficient voice leading.

Definition 8.16.   ME Proto-tonality (reduced)

A. a-tone ET.

B. Composite maximally even sets $\overset{(a,\ b;\ i,\ j)}{CME}$.

C. $b = \lfloor a/2 \rfloor + 1$.

D. Generic maximally even sets $\overset{(b,\ m;\ k)}{GME}$.

E. $b = 2m \pm 1$.

"generalization claim" appears to be unfounded, most notably for the reason that by Tymoczko's theory "nearly even" chords need not connect efficiently to *all* their transpositions (for example, the usual mod-12 "diatonic set" does *not* connect efficiently to its tritone transposition). Another recent work, where, under the assumption of 12-tone ET, "smooth voice leading" and "near evenness" play a central role, is Cohn (2012); see especially pp. 33–37.

Comparing Definitions 8.15 and 8.16 one immediately sees that the effective number of assumptions needed to obtain the result $(a, b; c, d; e) = (12, 7; 7, 4; 2)$ is six in the case of proposed proto-tonality and only five in the case of ME proto-tonality. Thus, ME proto-tonality is slightly more powerful than proposed proto-tonality descriptively. How do the theories compare, however, in terms of *explanatory* power? To find out we shall consider the extent to which assumptions may be reduced to high-level principles.

Consider the proposed theory. Conditions 8.15 B and D are fully accounted for by high-level principles (see Table 8.1). Thus, the theory may effectively be reduced further to only four assumptions, namely A, C, E, and F.

Let us turn now to ME proto-tonality. To what extent may Definition 8.16 be trimmed down by similarly appealing to high-level principles? For the sake of argument let us assume that a Principle of Maximal Evenness exists. That is to say, given x slots equally spaced around the circumference of some circle together with y tokens to be distributed among these slots, it is indeed natural, as Clough and Douthett claim (1991, p. 96), to distribute the tokens "as evenly as possible."

Note first that the x slots themselves are assumed *a priori* to be equally distributed; thus, Condition 8.16A, a-tone equal temperament, is irreducible.[10] Moreover, given free choice, to attain evenness, indeed *maximal* evenness, one would of course select integers x and y such that y divides x. If y does not divide x and in particular if x and y are coprime, one would expect a theory that posits a *principle* of maximal evenness to provide a very good rationale for the self-defeating choice. Since rationales for assuming $b = \lfloor a/2 \rfloor + 1$, implying $\gcd(a, b) = 1$, or $b = 2m \pm 1$, implying $\gcd(b, m) = 1$, do not seem to exist, the putative ME *principle* cannot cover Conditions 8.16 B and D; one cannot, in other words, simultaneously posit *a principle* of maximal evenness and assume coprime integers. Thus, despite our efforts, Definition 8.16 cannot be reduced to fewer than five assumptions. In terms of explanatory adequacy, in other words, proposed proto-tonality, with only four assumption, is slightly more powerful than ME proto-tonality.

To break the near tie one might ask the following important question. Given a conceivable pair of *tonal* theories based one on proposed proto-tonality and the other on ME proto-tonality, how would *such* theories fare in terms of explanatory power?

Part II of the present study is precisely a tonal theory based on the proto-tonal Part I. The theory makes *renewed* use of assumptions 8.15 A and C; that is, it harvests results from these assumptions beyond those attained in Part I. See Sect. 9.2 for a theory of chromaticism based on the usual primary intervals, and Sect. 10.4 for a theory of context-free chromatic communication based on the usual coherence algorithm. Moreover, renewed use of assumption E is made in Agmon's (1995) theory of harmonic functionality.

---

[10] See Clough and Douthett (1991, p. 94), Definition 1.1.

In the final analysis then, the proposed theory emerges as having significantly greater explanatory power than the theory of ME proto-tonality. In fact, only one assumption of proposed proto-tonality, namely efficient voice leading, is left unaccounted for.[11] This compares with no fewer than five "orphan" assumptions of ME proto-tonality, two of which involve the idea of maximal evenness itself.

References

Agmon, E. (1991). Linear transformations between cyclically generated chords. *Musikometrika, 3*, 15–40.

Agmon, E. (1995). Functional harmony revisited: A prototype-theoretic approach. *Music Theory Spectrum, 17*(2), 196–214.

Callender, C., Quinn, I., & Tymoczko, D. (2008a). Generalized voice-leading spaces. *Science, 320*, 346–348. doi:10.1126/science.1153021.

Callender, C., Quinn, I., & Tymoczko, D. (2008b). Supporting online material for Callender et al. 2008a. http://www.sciencemag.org/cgi/content/full/320/5874/346/DC1. Accessed 10 Jan 2012.

Clough, J., & Douthett, J. (1991). Maximally even sets. *Journal of Music Theory, 35*(1–2), 93–173.

Cohn, R. (2012). *Audacious euphony*. New York: Oxford University Press.

Kunst, J. (1973). Music in Java: Its history, its theory, and its technique (2 vols., E. L. Heins, Ed.). The Hague: Nijhoff.

Rahn, J. (1978). Javanese Pélog tunings reconsidered. *Yearbook of the International Folk Music Council, 10*, 69–82.

Rasch, R. (2002). Tuning and temperament. In T. Christensen (Ed.), *The Cambridge history of Western music theory* (pp. 193–222). Cambridge: Cambridge University Press.

Riemann, H. (1875). Die objective Existenz der Untertöne in der Schallwelle. *Allgemeine Deutsche Musikzeitung, 5*.

Shackford, C. (1961). Some aspects of perception I. *Journal of Music Theory, 5*(2), 162–202.

Shackford, C. (1962a). Some aspects of perception II. *Journal of Music Theory, 6*(1), 66–90.

Shackford, C. (1962b). Some aspects of perception III (addenda). *Journal of Music Theory, 6*(2), 295–303.

Tymoczko, D. (2006a). The geometry of musical chords. *Science, 313*, 72–74. doi:10.1126/science.1126287.

Tymoczko, D. (2006b). Supporting online material for Tymoczko 2006a. http://www.sciencemag.org/cgi/content/full/313/5783/72/DC1. Accessed 10 Jan 2012.

Tymoczko, D. (2011). *A geometry of music: Harmony and counterpoint in the extended common practice*. Oxford: Oxford University Press.

Vos, J. (1986). Purity ratings of tempered fifths and major thirds. *Music Perception, 3*(3), 221–258.

Ward, D. (1970). Musical perception. In J. Tobias (Ed.), *Foundations of modern auditory theory* (pp. 407–447). New York: Academic Press.

---

[11] Although the present study falls short of taking this step, efficient voice leading may be accounted for in terms of a hypothetical principle of "least work." See the discussion following Definition 7.33. There is of course a long and respectable theoretical tradition in support of voice-leading efficiency.

Part II
The Languages of Western Tonality

Chapter 9
Tonal Preliminaries

Abstract The usual diatonic system is "dyadic," for it privileges two intervals, the perfect octave and fifth; the usual harmonic system is "triadic," for it privileges, in addition, the major and minor thirds (Sect. 9.1). The dyadic and triadic privileged intervals support, respectively, a dyadic/triadic notion of "consonance." Every consonance other than the perfect prime has a unique "root," such that, if the root is also the lower note, the consonance is "stable." Section 9.2 studies the non-diatonic subset of the "cluster" (the set of all notes that may be received relative to the diatonic core, reduced to their register-zero representatives). It is shown that the subset consists of two length-five segments of the line of fifths, extending the seven-element core at either end to form a line-of-fifths segment totaling 17 elements exactly.

On the basis of Theorem 8.3 henceforth we shall write $3S_\varphi^\kappa$ for a usual harmonic system $HS_\varphi^\kappa = (DTS_\varphi^\kappa,\ GKS,\ CP)$, to which we shall refer as "triadic" (hence the "3" in "$3S_\varphi^\kappa$"), and $2S_\varphi^\kappa$ for a usual diatonic system DTS_φ^κ with core $CORE^\kappa$ and cluster $CLUST$, to which we shall refer as "dyadic" (hence the "2"). In general we write nS_φ^κ, $n = 2,\ 3$, and refer to the system as "n-adic." Note that for every triadic tone system $3S_\varphi^\kappa = HS_\varphi^\kappa$ there exists a dyadic system $2S_\varphi^\kappa = DTS_\varphi^\kappa$ satisfying $2S_\varphi^\kappa \in 3S_\varphi^\kappa$. The significance of the terms "dyadic" and "triadic" should become clear soon enough.

9.1 Dyadic and Triadic Consonance and Stability

The following proposition restates an important proto-tonal result. The origins of this result may be traced back to the distinction between a non-empty and an empty harmonic system, Definition 7.25.

E. Agmon, *The Languages of Western Tonality*, Computational Music Science, 147
DOI 10.1007/978-3-642-39587-1_9, © Springer-Verlag Berlin Heidelberg 2013

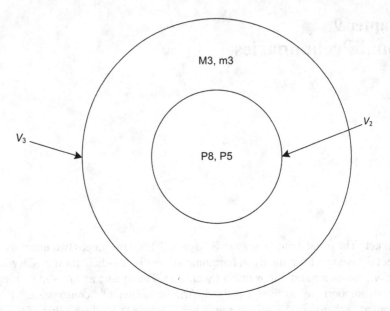

Fig. 9.1 The dyadic set of systemically privileged intervals as a proper subset of the triadic set

*Proposition 9.1. Let nS_φ^κ be an n-adic tone system.

Then there exists a set V_n of systemically privileged note intervals relative to nS_φ^κ
such that

$$V_2 = \{P8, \ P5\} \subset V_3 = V_2 \cup \{m3, \ M3\}.$$

The systemically privileged dyadic intervals V_2 are the perfect octave and fifth, intervals that have been generalized as the cognitive octave (a, b) and the quintic element (c, d). The systemically privileged triadic intervals V_3 include, in addition, the "tertial" minor and major third, intervals, whose "generic" component has been generalized as the klang generator e; see Fig. 9.1.

The existence of systemically privileged intervals V_n leads to the following important definition.

Definition 9.2. Dyadic/Triadic Consonance (Dissonance)

Let $(q, \ r)$ be a member of the n-adic set V_n of systemically privileged intervals. Let $P = ((s, \ t), \ (s', \ t')) \in N \times N$ be an ordered pair of notes, and set $(u, v) = (s', \ t') - (s, \ t)$.

A. We shall refer to P as *an n-adic consonance* if $(u, \ v) \equiv \pm(q, \ r)$.
B. If P is not n-adically consonant we shall refer to P as *n-adically dissonant*.

Tenney's (1988) "consonance/dissonance-concepts" 2 and 3, identified historically with the periods of ca. 900–1300 and ca. 1300–1700 AD, respectively, correspond to the dyadic/triadic distinction. The dyadic classification of consonance, however, dates back at least to Boethius (early sixth century)[1]; the triadic classification persisted at least through the beginning of the twentieth. Moreover, though anticipated in treatises dating from as early as the thirteenth century, the triadic "consonance concept" seems not to have fully usurped the dyadic concept until late in the fourteenth century or early in the fifteenth. See Gut (1976) for a convenient summary of consonance/dissonance classifications from the ninth through the sixteenth centuries.

By Definition 3.29 privileged pitch intervals are measured *up* from the fundamental; by Definition 8.2 correspondences are assumed between privileged note intervals and privileged pitch intervals, for example, between a "quintic element" and log 1.5. We therefore have the following definition.

Definition 9.3. Root (of a consonance)

Let $P = ((s, \ t), \ (s', \ t'))$ be an n-adic consonance. Set $(u, \ v) = (s', \ t') - (s, \ t)$ and let $(q, \ r)$ be a member of the n-adic set V_n of systemically privileged intervals.

We shall refer to $(s, \ t)$ (respectively, $(s', \ t')$) as *the root of P* if one of the following two conditions, A or B, holds.

A. $(u, \ v) = l(12, \ 7)$ for some strictly positive (negative) l.
B. $(u, \ v) \equiv (q, \ r) \neq (12, \ 7)$ (respectively, $(u, \ v) \equiv -(q, \ r) \neq -(12, \ 7)$).

The existence of roots seems to have been first pointed out by Hindemith (1937, p. 68). "Numerous experiments have convinced me that the feeling that one tone of an interval has more importance than the other is just as innate as the ability to judge intervals exactly—everyone hears the lower tone of a fifth as the principal tone; the ear cannot be persuaded to attribute primary importance to the upper tone."

Consider the two consonances (a) and (b) depicted in Fig. 9.2. Regardless of direction of measurement (from low to high or from high to low), in (a) the root is the lower note, while in (b) it is the upper. But how, indeed, should these consonances be measured, from low to high or from high to low? Note that the two options yield different results. For example, if (a) is measured from high to low it is octave equivalent to an ascending *perfect fourth*.

On the one hand, measuring a consonance *from* the root seems natural, such that (a), for example, is an ascending fifth. On the other hand, it also seems natural to measure a consonance from *its lower note* (cf. the figured-bass convention) such that (b), for example, is an ascending fourth. Be that as it may, we shall refer to a consonance the root of which is also the lower note as *stable*. Unlike a stable consonance such as the perfect octave or fifth, in an unstable consonance, for example the perfect fourth, there is a conflict between the two measuring conventions. The instability of the perfect fourth may help explain its notorious

---

[1] The mid ninth-century treatise *Musica enchiriadis* states as follows (Erickson 1995, p. 13): "Just as letters, when they are randomly combined with each other, often will not make acceptable words or syllables, so too in music there are certain intervals which produce the symphonies. A symphony is a sweet combination of different pitches joined to one another. There are three simple or prime symphonies, out of which the remaining are made. Of the former, they call one *diatessaron*, another *diapente*, the third *diapason*."

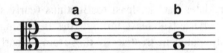

Fig. 9.2 Two rooted consonances. Regardless of direction of measurement, in (**a**) the root is the lower note, whereas in (**b**) it is the upper

resistance to fit comfortably within a clear-cut consonance/dissonance dichotomy. At least since the thirteenth century and practically through modern times, theorists have vacillated considerably concerning the status of the perfect fourth as consonant, dissonant, or both.[2]

The following definition extends the usage of "consonance" and "dissonance" to a set of more than two notes.

Definition 9.4. Consonant Set

Set $n = 2$, 3, and let S be a non-empty set of notes.

A. We shall refer to S as *n-adically consonant* if every $P \in S \times S$ is n-adically consonant.

B. If S is not n-adically consonant we shall refer to S as *n-adically dissonant*.

Note that in order for S to be consonant, *every* pair $P \in S \times S$ must be consonant; by contrast, it suffices for *one* pair P to be dissonant, for S to be dissonant.

Example 9.5. $S = \{(0, 0), (4, 2), (8, 4)\} = \{C, E, G\sharp\}$ is dyadically as well as triadically dissonant. In particular, $((0, 0), (8, 4)) = A5$ is dissonant. Note that *every* distinct pair of elements $P \in S \times S$, for example $((0, 0), (4, 2)) = M3$, is dissonant dyadically.

Definition 9.6. Root (of a consonant set)

Let S be an n-adically consonant set of at least two distinct notes.

We shall refer to $(\underline{s}, \underline{t}) \in S$ as *the root of S* and shall write $(\underline{s}, \underline{t}) = \sqrt{S}$, if for every $(s, t) \in S$, $(s, t) \neq (\underline{s}, \underline{t})$, $(\underline{s}, \underline{t})$ is the root of the n-adic consonance $((\underline{s}, \underline{t}), (s, t))$.

Example 9.7. Let $S = \{(0, 0), (4, 2), (7, 4), (12, 7)\} = \{C, E, G, C_1\}$ be a triadically consonant set. Then $C = \sqrt{S}$.

Note that in the case of consonant *chords*, a root in the sense of Definition 9.6 is generically the root of the klang that the chord expresses, in the sense of Definitions 7.19 and 7.4.[3]

---

[2] Writing on organum in the eleventh century, Guido d'Arezzo seems to have preferred a three-voice setting with the principle voice "sandwiched" between two organal voices, one situated a perfect fourth *below*, and the other, a perfect fifth *above* (Babb 1978, p. 77). This may well reflect the finding that the root of the perfect fifth is the lower note, whereas the root of the perfect fourth is the upper note.

[3] A chord, to be exact, is *a sequence* of notes. By ignoring order and repetition, a sequence is reduced to a set. Definitions 9.4 and 9.6 may be applied to chords as sequences reduced to sets.

9.2   The Chromatic Content of the Cluster

Definition 9.8. Accidental; Natural, Sharp, Flat

Let # be an integer.

We shall refer to the set AX of all intervals $(\#,\ 0)$ as *the set of accidentals*. In particular, we shall refer to the accidental $(0, 0)$ as *natural*, to $(1, 0)$ as *sharp*, and to $(-1, 0)$ as *flat*.

Note that the natural is the "perfect prime," the sharp is the "augmented prime," and the flat is the "diminished prime" (Chap. 4).

In connection with the following definition, review Definition 6.7. Recall that a dyadic tone system $2S_\varphi^\kappa$ is a member of every triadic system $3S_\varphi^\kappa$.

Definition 9.9. Chromatic/Non-chromatic Note

Let $2S_\varphi^\kappa = DTS_\varphi^\kappa$ be a dyadic tone system with core $CORE^\kappa$ and cluster $CLUST$. Let $AX = \{(\#,\ 0)\}$ be the set of accidentals and let $(s',\ t') \equiv (s,\ t) \in CLUST$.

If $(s',\ t') \equiv (w,\ x) + (\#,\ 0)$ for some $((w,\ x),\ (\#,\ 0)) \in CORE^\kappa \times AX, \# \neq 0$, we shall write

$$(s',\ t') = \mathrm{ALT}((w,\ x),\ \#)$$

and shall refer to $(s',\ t')$ as *chromatic* or *chromatically altered* (relative to $CORE^\kappa$). Otherwise, we shall refer to $(s',\ t')$ as *non-chromatic*.

*Proposition 9.10. Let $(s',\ t') \equiv (s,\ t) \in CLUST$.

A. If $(s',\ t')$ is non-chromatic there exists a unique core element (w, x) such that $(s',\ t') \equiv (w,\ x)$.

B. If $(s',\ t')$ is chromatic there exists a unique core element (w, x) and a unique accidental $(\#, 0)$ such that $(s',\ t') = \mathrm{ALT}((w,\ x),\ \#)$.

Example 9.11. Consider a dyadic tone system $2S_\varphi^{-1}, CORE^{-1} = \{C,\ D,\ \ldots,\ B\}$. Then

$$G\# = (8, 4) = \mathrm{ALT}((7, 4), 1);$$
$$A\flat = (8, 5) = \mathrm{ALT}((9, 5), -1).$$

Example   9.12. Consider   a   dyadic   tone   system $2S_\varphi^{-6}, CORE^{-6} = \{C, D\flat, E\flat, F, G\flat, A\flat, B\flat\}$. Then

$$A = (9, 5) = \mathrm{ALT}((8, 5), 1);$$
$$B\flat\flat = (9, 6) = \mathrm{ALT}((10, 6), -1).$$

The relation ALT is *core-relative*. Thus, the representation of a chromatic element $(s',\ t')$ as an "altered" core element in the sense of Definition 9.9 may differ from how

(s', t') is represented via conventional notation as an "altered" white note C, D,..., B. For example, relative to $CORE^{-6}$ the *chromatic* note A *natural* is represented as a chromatically altered *non-chromatic* A *flat* (Example 9.12).

Chromatic alteration (relative to the natural core) was known already in the Middle Ages. The "ladders" (a) and (b) of Fig. 1.3, from the ninth-century treatise *Scolica enchiriadis*, may be interpreted as representing $(-9, -5) \equiv (3, 2) = E\flat$ as a chromatically lowered $(-8, -5) \equiv (4, 2) = E$. Other paired ladders similarly represent $(-6, -4) \equiv (6, 3) = F\sharp$ as a chromatically raised $(-7, -4) \equiv (5, 3) = F$.

Writing in the second half of the thirteenth century, John of Garland states that "false music is when they make a semitone out of a whole tone and vice versa. Every whole tone is divisible into two semitones, and as a consequence, the sign designating the semitone can be applied to all whole tones."[4] Dahlhaus (1990, p. 178) asserts that "the diatonic-chromatic systems presented in the treatises of the thirteenth to the fifteenth centuries vary between having 12, 14, or 17 degrees." In particular (*ibid.*, p. 181),

> the 17-tone system with the chromatic degrees b♭, e♭, a♭, d♭, g♭, f♯, c♯, g♯, d♯, and a♯, which could be hypothetically inferred from the example in the *Ars contrapunctus secundum Philippum de Vitriaco* [see Fig. 9.3] was explicitly presented by Prosdocimo de' Beldomandi in his *Libellus monochordi* of 1413. Prosdocimo constructs it by the double division of all the whole tones in the diatonic scale: "And in this way, over the entire monochord, you will be able to have two semitones between any two consecutive letters of the musical hand sounding a whole tone" [Et isto modo per totum monochordum habere poteris bina semitonia inter quaslibet duas litteras immediatas in manu musicali tonum resonantes].[5]

In connection with the following proposition recall that we write Q_j for the note $(s, t) \equiv (0, 0) + j(c, d)$, $0 \le s \le a - 1$. Recall also that Q_j^i refers to the i-element segment of the line of fifths starting with Q_j (Definition 5.19).

*Proposition 9.13. Let $2S_\varphi^\kappa$ be a dyadic tone system and let (s_m, t) be a chromatic (non-chromatic) cluster element satisfying $s_m \equiv 7m \pmod{12}$, $0 \le m - \kappa \le 11$. Then $7 \le m - \kappa \le 11$ $(0 \le m - \kappa \le 6)$.

Example 9.14. Consider a dyadic tone system $2S_\varphi^{-1}$, $CORE^{-1} = \{$C, D, ..., B$\}$, and let $(s_m, t) \in CLUST$, $s_m \equiv 7m \pmod{12}$, $0 \le m + 1 \le 11$.
If (s_m, t) is chromatic then $6 \le m \le 10$. Equivalently, $s_m = 6, 1, 8, 3, 10$.

Before we state and prove an important theorem it should be useful to consult Table 9.1; review Definition 6.2.

Conventionally notated chromatic cluster elements (s_m, t) are arranged in five columns $m = 6, 7, ..., 10$ such that $s_m \equiv 7m \pmod{12}$, and seven rows such that core elements $Q_n = (w_n, x_n)$, $-1 \le n \le 5$, satisfy $(s_m, t) - Q_n$ is octave

---

[4] "Musica falsa est, quando de tono faciunt semitonium, et e converso. Omnis tonus divisibilis est in duo semitonia et per consequens signa semitonia designantia in omnibus tonis possunt applicari." Latin text (after Coussemaker, 1864–1876, Vol. 1, p. 166, from *Introductio secundum Johannem de Garlandia*) and corresponding English translation from Dahlhaus (1990, p. 173).

[5] Dahlhaus provides a reference to Coussemaker (1864–1876), Vol. 3, p. 257. On p. 179 Dahlhaus cites Riemann's interpretation of Fig. 9.3 "as representing a 14-tone system with b♭, e♭, a♭, f♯, c♯, g♯, and d♯. See Riemann 1974, footnote on p. 237.

CSIII:26

Fig. 9.3 From *Ars contrapunctus secundum Philippum de Vitriaco* (de Vitry, 1864–1876)

Table 9.1 Chromatic cluster elements relative to the natural core (left-hand column), displayed in terms of Definition 6.2

	$s_6 = 6$	$s_7 = 1$	$s_8 = 8$	$s_9 = 3$	$s_{10} = 10$
$Q_{-1} = F$	G♭	D♭	A♭	E♭	B♭
$Q_0 = C$	–	D♭	A♭	E♭	B♭
$Q_1 = G$	F♯	–	A♭	E♭	B♭
$Q_2 = D$	F♯	C♯	–	E♭	B♭
$Q_3 = A$	F♯	C♯	G♯	–	B♭
$Q_4 = E$	F♯	C♯	G♯	D♯	–
$Q_5 = B$	F♯	C♯	G♯	D♯	A♯

equivalent to a primary interval, unless $s_m - w_n \equiv 6 \bmod 12$ (empty cells). The table thus represents all chromatic cluster elements satisfying Definition 6.2, given the natural core as reference.

Note that for every s_m there exist exactly two enharmonically related chromatic notes (s_m, t), namely $\mathrm{ALT}(Q_{m-5}, -1)$ and $\mathrm{ALT}(Q_{m-7}, 1)$. For example, for $s_8 = 8$ we have $A\flat = (8, 5) = \mathrm{ALT}(Q_3, -1) = \mathrm{ALT}(A, \flat)$ and $G\sharp = (8, 4) = \mathrm{ALT}(Q_1, 1) = \mathrm{ALT}(G, \sharp)$.

Theorem 9.15. Let $2S_\varphi^\kappa$ be a dyadic tone system and let (s_m, t) be a chromatic cluster element satisfying $s_m \equiv 7m \pmod{12}$, $0 \le m - \kappa \le 11$.

Then there exist core elements $(w, x) = Q_{m-5}$ and $(w', x') = Q_{m-7}$ such that one of the following two conditions, A or B, holds.

A. $(s_m, t) \equiv Q_{m-12} = \mathrm{ALT}((w, x), -1)$, $(s_m, t) \in Q_{\kappa-5}^5$.

B. $(s_m, t) \equiv Q_m = \mathrm{ALT}((w', x'), 1)$, $(s_m, t) \in Q_{\kappa+7}^5$.

To prove the theorem we shall first prove two lemmas. Recall that the core is a set of diatonic notes (Definition 6.21).

Lemma 9.16. Let $2S_\varphi^\kappa$ be a dyadic tone system and let $(s_m, \ t)$ be a chromatic cluster element satisfying $s_m \equiv 7m$ (mod 12), $0 \leq m - \kappa \leq 11$.

Then there exists a diatonic note Q_ε, $\varepsilon = m - 6$, such that $s_m \equiv 7(\varepsilon + 6)$ (mod 12).

Proof. Using Proposition 9.13, for every chromatic $(s_m, \ t)$, $7 \leq m - \kappa \leq 11$, there exists a diatonic Q_ε, $1 \leq \varepsilon - \kappa \leq 5$, such that $\varepsilon = m - 6$. Since $s_m \equiv 7m$ (mod 12), we have $s_m \equiv 7(\varepsilon + 6)$ (mod 12). Q.E.D.

Lemma 9.17. Let $2S_\varphi^\kappa$ be a dyadic tone system. Let Q_n be diatonic, $0 \leq n - \kappa \leq 6$, and let $(s_m, \ t)$ be chromatic, $s_m \equiv 7m$ (mod 12), $7 \leq m - \kappa \leq 11$. Let Q_ε be diatonic, $\varepsilon = m - 6$, $\varepsilon \neq n$.

Then one of the following two conditions, A or B, holds.

A. $n < \varepsilon$, and $(s_m, \ t) \equiv Q_\varepsilon + (6, \ 4)$.
B. $n > \varepsilon$, and $(s_m, \ t) \equiv Q_\varepsilon + (6, \ 3)$.

Proof. By Definition 6.5, if $n \neq \varepsilon$ we have

$$(s_m, \ t) \equiv Q_n + (y, \ z)_k \equiv Q_{n+k}$$

for some usual primary interval $(y, \ z)_k$, implying that $s_m \equiv 7(n + k)$ (mod 12). By Lemma 9.16 $s_m \equiv 7(\varepsilon + 6)$ (mod 12), and therefore $n + k \equiv \varepsilon + 6$ (mod 12), or equivalently,

$$k = (\varepsilon - n) + (6 + 12l)$$

for some integer l.

Since $0 \leq n - \kappa \leq 6$, $1 \leq \varepsilon - \kappa \leq 5$, we have $|\varepsilon - n| \leq 5$. Suppose that $l \neq -1, \ 0$. Then $|k| \geq 13$, contradicting Theorem 5.8, by which $|k| \leq 5$. Thus

$$(s_m, \ t) \equiv Q_{n+k} = Q_{\varepsilon \pm 6} \equiv Q_\varepsilon \pm (6, \ 3).$$

Suppose that $n < \varepsilon$ ($n > \varepsilon$) and suppose by contradiction that $(s_m, \ t) \equiv Q_\varepsilon + (6, \ 3)$ ($Q_\varepsilon + (6, \ 4)$). This is impossible, since $k = (\varepsilon - n) + 6$ (($\varepsilon - n) - 6$) implies that $|k| \geq 7$, again contradicting Theorem 5.8. Q.E.D.

Proof of the theorem. Let Q_ε be diatonic, $\varepsilon = m - 6$, $\varepsilon \neq n$. By Lemma 9.17 either $(s_m, \ t) \equiv Q_\varepsilon + (6, \ 4)$ or $(s_m, \ t) \equiv Q_\varepsilon + (6, \ 3)$. Thus $(s_m, \ t) \equiv Q_{(m-6) \pm 6}$, that is, $(s_m, \ t) \equiv Q_{m-12}$ or $(s_m, \ t) \equiv Q_m$.

Set

$$Q_n = (w, \ x),$$
$$Q_{n'} = (w', \ x'), \quad \text{such that}$$
$$Q_{m-12} = \text{ALT}\big((w, \ x), \ \#\big),$$
$$Q_m = \text{ALT}\big((w', \ x'), \ \#'\big).$$

By Definition 9.9 we have $Q_{m-12} \equiv (w, \ x) + (\#, \ 0)$, $Q_m \equiv (w', \ x') + (\#', \ 0)$. It follows that

$$m - 12 - n \equiv m - n' \equiv 0 \pmod{7}. \tag{9.1}$$

Since $\kappa \leq n \leq 6 + \kappa$, $7 + \kappa \leq m \leq 11 + \kappa$, we have $m - 11 \leq n \leq m - 1$. To satisfy Equation 9.1 we therefore have $n = m - 5$, $n' = m - 7$. Q.E.D.

References

Babb, W. (Trans.) (1978). *Hucbald, Guido, and John on music: Three medieval treatises*. New Haven: Yale University Press.

Coussemaker, C. (Ed.) (1864–1876). *Scriptorum de musica medii aevi novam seriem* (4 Vols.). Paris: Durand. 1963. Reprint, Hildesheim: Olms.

Dahlhaus, C. (1990). *Studies on the origin of harmonic tonality* (R. Gjerdingen, Trans.). Princeton: Princeton University Press.

de Vitry, P. (1864–1876). *Ars contrapunctus secundum Philippum de Vitriaco*. In C. Coussemaker (Ed.), *Scriptorum de musica medii aevi novam seriem* (III, 23–27). Paris: Durand. 1963. Reprint, Hildesheim: Olms. Electronic ed. in *Thesaurus Musicarum Latinarum*, G. Di Bacco (Director). http://www.chmtl.indiana.edu. Accessed 10 Jan 2012.

Erickson, R. (Trans.). (1995). *Musica enchiriadis and Scolica enchiriadis*. New Haven: Yale University Press.

Gut, S. (1976). La notion de consonance chez les théoriciens du Moyen Age. *Acta Musicologica, 48*(1), 20–44.

Hindemith, P. (1937). *The craft of musical composition: Book I* (A. Mendel, Trans. & Rev. 1945). New York: Associated Music Publishers.

Riemann, H. (1974). *History of music theory: Polyphonic theory to the sixteenth century* (R. Haggh, Trans. & Ed.). New York: Da Capo.

Tenney, J. (1988). *A history of 'consonance' and 'dissonance'*. New York: Excelsior Press.

Chapter 10
Modal Communication

Abstract A "mode" (Sect. 10.1) consists of a core-like, seven-element segment of the line of fifths; a *consonant* subset of the core termed the "nucleus" (assumed to contain a maximal number of elements); and a message-like sequence of notes termed the "score." The root of the nucleus is termed "final." In a "dyadic mode" the nucleus is *dyadically* consonant, and is therefore an open fifth; in a "triadic mode" the nucleus is *triadically* consonant, and is therefore a major or minor triad. A "key" (respectively, "semi-key") is a mode, the nucleus of which (a privileged proper subset thereof) forms a minimal number of dissonances relative to the non-nucleus core elements. It is shown that a semi-key is not "Lydian"; moreover, a triadic key *is* "Ionian" or "Aeolian." Section 10.2 is a theory of modal communication. The theory is "context dependent" since, in effect, contextual cues that allow the final of the "transmitted mode" to be mapped into the final of the "received mode," are assumed to exist. Section 10.3 studies the "scale-degree" function by which cluster elements are represented in terms of their intervallic relation to the final. A distinction is drawn between "first-order" and "second-order" *chromatic* degrees, where a first-order degree is a primary interval or the augmented fourth. A mode is "robust" if the elements of its score, represented as degrees, are diatonic or first-order chromatic (Sect. 10.4). It is shown that robust modal communication satisfies not only the Communication Principle, but via a coherence-like algorithm, the Economical Principle as well. Finally, Sect. 10.5 introduces the notions of "congruent" and "standard" modes. Standard modes display no more than five flats or six sharps in their "accidental index" (known as the "key signature" in the case of keys).

10.1 Modes, Semi-keys, and Keys

Henceforth it should be convenient to refer to a chord expressing an m-ad (that is, an m-element usual klang) as *an m-ad* (even though the chord may consist of more than m elements); review Definition 7.19.

E. Agmon, *The Languages of Western Tonality*, Computational Music Science,
DOI 10.1007/978-3-642-39587-1_10, © Springer-Verlag Berlin Heidelberg 2013

Recall from Sect. 9.1 that "consonance" is "n-adic," that is, either dyadic or triadic. Review in particular Definitions 9.4 and 9.6, and note that we write $\sqrt{S}$ for the root of an n-adically consonant set S. Recall also that we write Q_j^i for the i-element segment of the line of fifths starting with $Q_j \equiv (0,\ 0) + j(7, 4)$.

Definition 10.1. Nucleus

Let S_α be the set of notes that constitutes the seven-element segment Q_α^7 of the line of fifths. Set $n = 2, 3$, and let $nNU \subset S_\alpha$ be an n-adically consonant set, $\sqrt{nNU} = Q_{\alpha+\mu}$ for some integer μ.

We shall refer to nNU as *an n-adic nucleus* (relative to S_α) if it contains a maximal number of elements.

Example 10.2. Let nNU be a subset of $S_{-1} = \{F, C, \ldots, B\}$. Suppose that μ varies over $0, 1, \ldots, 5$.

If the following condition, A or B, is satisfied (depending on n), then nNU is an n-adic nucleus relative to S_{-1}, $\sqrt{nNU} = F,\ C,\ \ldots,\ E$, respectively.

A. $2NU = \{F,\ C\},\ \{C,\ G\},\ \ldots,\ \{E,\ B\}$, respectively.
B. $3NU = \{F,\ A,\ C\},\ \{C,\ E,\ G\},\ \ldots,\ \{E,\ G,\ B\}$, respectively.

The example illustrates the following proposition.

*Proposition 10.3. Let S_α be the set of notes that constitutes the seven-element segment Q_α^7 of the line of fifths. Set $n = 2,\ 3$, and let $nNU \subset S_\alpha$ be an n-adically consonant set. Set

$$(w, x) = \sqrt{nNU} = Q_{\alpha+\mu},$$
$$(\overline{w}, \overline{x}) = Q_{\alpha+\mu+1} \equiv (w, x) + (7, 4).$$

Then nNU is an n-adic nucleus relative to S_α if, and only if, $0 \le \mu \le 5$, such that one of the following two conditions, A or B, holds.

A. $n = 2$ and $nNU = \{(w, x),\ (\overline{w}, \overline{x})\}$.
B. $n = 3$ and $nNU = \{(w, x),\ (w, x),\ (\overline{w}, \overline{x})\}$, where $x \equiv x + 2 \pmod 7$.

In other words, a dyadic nucleus is a perfect-fifth dyad and a triadic nucleus is a major or minor triad, that is, $(w, x) - (w, x) \equiv (4, 2),\ (3, 2)$.

We are now ready for the following pair of definitions.

Definition 10.4. Dyadic/Triadic Mode; Score; Final, Cofinal

Let nNU be an n-adic nucleus relative to S_α, and set $(w, x) = \sqrt{nNU} = Q_{\alpha+\mu}$, $(\overline{w}, \overline{x}) = Q_{\alpha+\mu+1} \equiv (w, x) + (7, 4)$. Let *SCORE* be a non-empty sequence over a repository R of notes.

We shall refer to *SCORE* as *a score* and to $nM_\alpha^\mu = (S_\alpha,\ nNU,\ SCORE)$ as *an n-adic mode with final (w, x) and cofinal $(\overline{w}, \overline{x})$*, if the following condition A is satisfied.

A. R is the set of all notes $(s', t') \equiv (s, t) \in Q_{\alpha-5}^{17}$.

Definition 10.5. Diatonic/Chromatic Score Element; Accidental Index

Let $nM_\alpha^\mu = (S_\alpha, nNU, SCORE)$ be an n-adic mode. Let $S_{\alpha-5}^{17}$ be the set of notes that constitutes the 17-element segment $Q_{\alpha-5}^{17}$ of the line of fifths.

A. We shall refer to a score element $(s', t') \equiv (s, t) \in S_\alpha$ as *diatonic*.
B. We shall refer to a score element $(s', t') \equiv (s, t) \in S_{\alpha-5}^{17} \setminus S_\alpha$ as *chromatic*.
C. We shall refer to $\alpha + 1$ as the mode's *accidental index*.

Example 10.6. Let $nM_{-1}^\mu = (S_{-1}, nNU, SCORE)$ be an n-adic mode, for some μ.

Then a score element is octave equivalent to one of the following 17 members of the line-of-fifths segment Q_{-6}^7, and is diatonic or chromatic as indicated:

chromatic	diatonic	chromatic
G♭, D♭, A♭, E♭, B♭,	F, C, G, D, A, E, B,	F♯, C♯, G♯, D♯, A♯

Moreover, depending on μ, the final (w, x) is F, C, G, D, A, or E, and, depending on n, is the root of a dyadic or triadic nucleus. For example, if $\mu = 1$ then $(w, x) = C$ and is the root of the dyadic nucleus {C, G} or the triadic nucleus {C, E, G}. Finally, the accidental index of nM_{-1}^μ is zero.

Since $7(7, 4) \equiv (1, 0)$ and $S_{-1} = \{F, C, \ldots, B\}$ is the natural core (the "white-note" collection), it is not difficult to see that the accidental index $\alpha + 1$ represents the number of sharps (if positive) or flats (if negative) with which S_α is conventionally notated (cf. "key signature").

The reader may have noted that S_α is a core-like construct and $SCORE$ is a message-like construct; moreover, the repository R (see Condition 10.4A) is a cluster-like construct (Definition 6.7; Theorem 9.15). These relations are of course intentional and shall be duly engaged in Sect. 10.2.

Note that a triple α, μ, n does *not* specify a unique mode $nM_\alpha^\mu = (S_\alpha, nNU, SCORE)$. Indeed, given S_α and nNU, there is an *uncountable* infinity of scores $SCORE$ such that $nM_\alpha^\mu = (S_\alpha, nNU, SCORE)$ is a mode.[1]

Definition 10.7. Mode Class

Fix an n-adic nucleus nNU relative to S_α. Let R be the set of all notes $(s', t') \equiv (s, t) \in Q_{\alpha-5}^{17}$.

We shall refer to the set nMC_α^μ of all modes $nM_\alpha^\mu = (S_\alpha, nNU, SCORE)$, where $SCORE$ is a non-empty sequence over R, as *an n-adic mode class*.

A mode class may be thought of as the set of all "melodies" that may be conceived relative to a given mode.

---

[1] The infinity of scores is uncountable because an infinite repository R of notes is assumed (see Definition 10.4). In practice R is finite (due to the finite number of registers), and thus the infinity of scores over R is countable.

Definition 10.8. Tribal Class

Set $\mu = Mu = 0$, $1, \ldots$, $5 = $ Lyd, Ion, Mixolyd, Dor, Aeol, Phryg, respectively.

We shall refer to the set nTC^μ of all n-adic mode classes nMC^μ_α such that α runs over all integers and μ is fixed, as *the n-adic Mu-ian tribal class*.

There are exactly six tribal classes (dyadic or triadic), namely Lydian, Ionian, Mixolydian, Dorian, Aeolian, and Phrygian. If nM^μ_α is an n-adic mode such that $nM^\mu_\alpha \in nMC^\mu_\alpha \in nTC^\mu$, we shall say that nM^μ_α *reduces to*, or *is reducible to*, *Mu-ian*. For example, for every α a mode nM^0_α is reducible to Lydian. Somewhat less formally, we shall simply refer to nM^0_α as "Lydian."

The nucleus of a mode is by definition consonant. However, nucleus elements may form dissonant intervals relative to *non*-nucleus members of S_α. In what follows we consider the implications of such dissonances. We begin by defining certain privileged, proper subsets of the nucleus.

Definition 10.9. Sub-nucleus

Let $nM^\mu_\alpha = (S_\alpha,\ nNU,\ SCORE)$ be an n-adic mode with final $(\underline{w},\ \underline{x})$ and cofinal $(\overline{w}, \overline{x})$.

We shall refer to a proper subset $nSUB$ of nNU as the *sub-nucleus* if one of the following two conditions, A or B, is satisfied.

A. $2SUB = \{(\underline{w}, \underline{x})\}$.

B. $3SUB = \{(\underline{w}, \underline{x}),\ (\overline{w}, \overline{x})\}$.

In other words, the sub-nucleus is a proper subset of the nucleus that consists of the final (if the mode is dyadic) or the final *and* cofinal (if the mode is triadic).

An idea closely related to Condition B of the following definition may be found in an unpublished manuscript of Godfrey Winham dated by Roger Maren 1968–1969; see Definitions 5–6 in Blasius (1997, p. 35); see also Fuller (1975).

Definition 10.10. Key; Semi-key

Let $nM^\mu_\alpha = (S_\alpha, nNU, SCORE)$ be an n-adic mode and let $nSUB$ be its sub-nucleus. Set $S_\alpha \backslash nNU = (nNU)^c$ (that is, $(nNU)^c$ is the complement of nNU relative to S_α).

A. We shall refer to nM^μ_α as *an n-adic semi-key* if $nSUB \times (nNU)^c$ contains a minimal number of dissonances.

B. We shall refer to nM^μ_α as *an n-adic key* if $nNU \times (nNU)^c$ contains a minimal number of dissonances.

The nuclei of keys (whether dyadic or triadic) are *contextually* the least dissonant; keys, therefore, are the most "stable" types of modes.

Consulting Table 10.1 and Fig. 10.1 should be helpful in connection with the following theorem; review Definitions 10.7 and 10.8.

Table 10.1 Modes, semi-keys, and keys (dyadic or triadic), and the tribal classes to which they reduce

	Dyadic	Triadic
Modes	Lydian, Ionian, Mixolydian, Dorian, Aeolian, Phrygian	Lydian, Ionian, Mixolydian, Dorian, Aeolian, Phrygian
Semi-keys	Ionian, Mixolydian, Dorian, Aeolian, Phrygian	Ionian, Mixolydian, Dorian, Aeolian
Keys	Ionian, Mixolydian, Dorian, Aeolian	Ionian, Aeolian

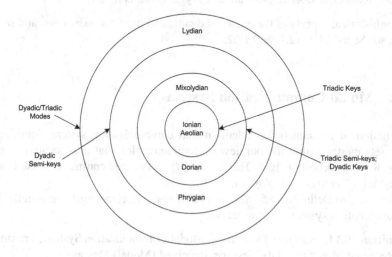

Fig. 10.1 Modes, semi-keys, and keys (dyadic or triadic), and the tribal classes to which they reduce

Theorem 10.11. Let $nM_\alpha^\mu = (S_\alpha, nNU, SCORE)$ be an n-adic mode and let $nSUB$ be its sub-nucleus. Set $S_\alpha \setminus nNU = (nNU)^c$.

A. If nM_α^μ is a dyadic (triadic) semi-key then nM_α^μ is not Lydian (Lydian or Phrygian).

B. If nM_α^μ is a dyadic (triadic) key then nM_α^μ is not Lydian or Phrygian (Lydian, Mixolydian, Dorian, or Phrygian).

In other words, a dyadic *key* is Ionian, Mixolydian, Dorian, or Aeolian; *a triadic key is Ionian or Aeolian.*

Proof. Set $U = nNU$, $nSUB$, $nU = U \times (nNU)^c$. Let $((s, t), (s', t')) \in nU$, and set $(s', t') - (s, t) = (u, v)$. Then nU is minimally dissonant if, and only if, $u \not\equiv 6$ (mod 12).

Since $u \equiv 6$ implies that (1) $\mu = 0$ if $U = \{(\underline{w}, \underline{x})\}$; (2) $\mu = 0$, 5 if $U = \{(\underline{w}, \underline{x}), (\overline{w}, \overline{x})\}$; and (3) $\mu = 0, 2, 3, 5$ if $U = 3NU$, the theorem follows. Q.E.D.

Definition 10.12. Major/Minor Mode

Let $3M_\alpha^\mu = (S_\alpha, 3NU, SCORE)$ be a triadic mode.

We shall refer to the mode as *major* or *minor* if $3NU$ is a major or minor triad, respectively.

*Proposition 10.13. Let $3M_\alpha^\mu$ be a triadic mode.

Then one of the following two conditions, A or B, holds.

A. $3M_\alpha^\mu$ reduces to Lydian, Ionian, or Mixolydian, and is major.
B. $3M_\alpha^\mu$ reduces to Dorian, Aeolian, or Phrygian, and is minor.

For historical aspects of the theory of dyadic and triadic modes, keys, and semi-keys, see Sects. 11.1, 12.1, and 12.2.

10.2 Modal Communication Systems

The notion of a (context-dependent) modal communication system, introduced next, sets modes within the purview of communication that is so central to this study. Review Definition 10.4. The "ν" in nM_κ^ν and related constructs is the Greek letter *Nu* ("κ" is the Greek *Kappa*).

Review also Definition 6.5 (note-reception system). Henceforth we assume that a note-reception system is not reflexive.[2]

Definition 10.14. (Context-Dependent) Modal Communication System; Transmitted/Received Mode; (Modal) Message, Received (Modal) Message

Let $NRS_\varphi^\kappa = (FTS_\varphi, CORE^\kappa, MSG/R)$ be a usual note-reception system with message MSG. Let $nM_\alpha^\mu = (S_\alpha, nNU, SCORE)$ and $nM_\kappa^\nu = (S_\kappa, nNU', SCORE')$ be two *n*-adic modes with finals $(\underline{w}, \underline{x})$ and $(\underline{w}', \underline{x}')$, respectively, $\underline{w} = \varphi$. Assume that $SCORE = MSG$, $SCORE' = MSG/R$.

We shall refer to nM_α^μ as the *transmitted mode*, to nM_κ^ν as the *received mode*; to $SCORE$ and $SCORE'$ as the *(modal) message* and the *received (modal) message*, respectively; and to $(nM_\alpha^\mu, nM_\kappa^\nu, NRS_\varphi^\kappa)$ as *a modal communication system*. We shall refer to a modal communication system as *context-dependent* if one of the following two conditions, A or B, is satisfied.

A. NRS_φ^κ is absolute and $\underline{w}' = \underline{w}$.
B. NRS_φ^κ is relative and $\underline{w}' = 0$.

Unless otherwise noted, we shall assume henceforth that a modal communication system is context-dependent.

---

[2] Reflexive modal communication of course exists yet is an uninteresting form of communication. The structurally interesting aspects of musical self-communication have been explored in Sect. 6.4.

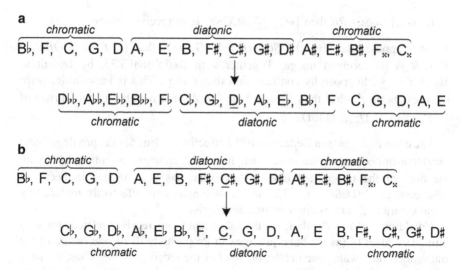

Fig. 10.2 An absolute (**a**) and a relative (**b**) modal communication system with the same transmitted, C$\sharp$ Aeolian mode. The received modes are Mixolydian with finals D$\flat$ and C, respectively

Before addressing the sense in which modal communication systems are "context-dependent," an example (10.15) that explicates Definition 10.14 should be useful; also, a proposition (10.16) that follows almost immediately from the definition brings to light an important property of such systems, namely "final preservation."

Example 10.15. As explained next, Fig. 10.2 depicts (a) an absolute modal communication system $(nM_3^4,\ nM_{-7}^2,\ NRS_1^{-7})$ and (b) a relative modal communication system $(nM_3^4,\ nM_{-2}^2,\ NRS_1^{-2})$.

Since $3 - 5 = -2$, in (a) as well as (b) every element of the message is octave equivalent to a member of the 17-element segment Q_{-2}^{17} of the line of fifths (see Cond. 10.4A). Every element of the *received* message is octave equivalent to (a) a member of Q_{-12}^{17} (since $-7 - 5 = -12$) and (b) a member of Q_{-7}^{17} (since $-2 - 5 = -7$). The figure clarifies that in both cases we have a transmitted Aeolian mode with final C$\sharp$. In both cases the mode is received Mixolydian. However, the received final is D$\flat$ in the absolute case (a) and C in the relative case (b). In particular, the short arrow clarifies that the final of the transmitted mode, if included in the message, is received as the final of the received mode.

Example 10.15 illustrates the following proposition.

Proposition 10.16. (Final Preservation)

Let $(nM_\alpha^\mu,\ nM_\kappa^\nu,\ NRS_\varphi^\kappa)$ be a modal communication system, where nM_α^μ and nM_κ^ν are modes with finals $(\underline{w}, \underline{x})$ and $(\underline{w}', \underline{x}')$ and scores *SCORE* and *SCORE'*, respectively, and NRS_φ^κ is a usual note-reception system with message *MSG* and received message *MSG/R*.

If $(\underline{w}, \underline{x}) \in SCORE$ then $(\underline{w}', \underline{x}') \in SCORE'$ is its received image.

Proof. Suppose that $(\underline{w}, \underline{x}) \in SCORE = MSG$, and that $(s', t') \in SCORE' = MSG/R$ is its received image. Together with Definition 3.35, by Definition 10.14 $s' = \underline{w}'$. Suppose by contradiction that $t' \neq \underline{x}'$. This is impossible, since there exists no t' other than $\underline{x}'$ such that $(\underline{w}', t')$ is a member of the cluster of NRS_φ^κ, namely $Q_{\kappa-5}^{17}$. Q.E.D.

The condition $\underline{w} = \varphi$ in Definition 10.14 effectively identifies the privileged note $(\underline{s}, \underline{t})$ transmitted as the pitch φ (see Definition 5.22, updating Definition 3.42), with the final of the transmitted mode. Thus, what has been termed in Sect. 3.4 "*Phi*-centricity" (Definition 3.35 and discussion) is now effectively replaced by "final-centricity," a transmitter-related assumption.

Conditions 10.14 A and B, on the other hand, are receiver-related, for they ultimately identify (as we have just seen in Proposition 10.16) the *image* of the transmitted final with, specifically, *the final* of the received mode. Thus, we have effectively replaced the problematic, receiver-related counterpart to *Phi*-centricity, namely *Phi*-image centricity, with an equally problematic counterpart to final-centricity, namely "final-image centricity."

When *Phi*-image centricity was posited in Sect. 3.4 we pledged to eventually set well-motivated conditions that render it superfluous. We have a way to go yet before reaching that stage (Sect. 14.2). Nonetheless, it seems reasonable to assume, at least tentatively, that receivers are able to judge the image of the final as privileged on the basis of "contextual" cues embodied in messages, for example, the temporal placement of the final (or octave equivalent) at their beginning and/or end. As Hucbald of Saint-Amand wrote sometime between 870 and 900 AD, "therefore they are called 'finals,' because anything that is sung finds its ending (*finem*) in [one of] them."[3] Note that within the framework of the present study such contextual considerations can have no more than informal status. Nonetheless, the term "*context-dependent* modal communication system" captures the sense in which modal communication, in general, depends on such contextual cues.

Note that final-image centricity does *not* guarantee that the received mode is reducible to the same tribal class as the transmitted one (for example, the transmitted mode may be Aeolian, the received mode Mixolydian, as in Example 10.15). Equivalently, the diatonic/chromatic partitioning of the message is not necessarily preserved.[4]

Modal communication systems assume a transmitter and receiver that are modally biased. To what extent do such systems satisfy the Communication Principle? A partial answer is provided by the following proposition, which follows easily

---

[3] Trans. from Cohen (2002, p. 322).

[4] See Fig. 10.2, where the diatonic (chromatic) notes of the received mode are not aligned with the diatonic (chromatic) notes of the transmitted mode. Consider a transmitted "D-Dorian" where (chromatic) B♭ is a frequent message element. The mode may easily be received as Aeolian.

from Definition 3.35. (The proposition, in fact, was already tacitly applied in proving Proposition 10.16.)

*Proposition 10.17. Let $(nM_\alpha^\mu, nM_\kappa^\nu, NRS_\varphi^\kappa)$ be a modal communication system, where nM_α^μ and nM_κ^ν are modes with scores *SCORE* and *SCORE'* respectively. Let $(s, t) \in SCORE$ be a message element, $(s', t') \in SCORE'$ its received image. Let $(\underline{w}, \underline{x})$ be the final of the transmitted mode.

Then one of the following two conditions, A or B, holds.

A. NRS_φ^κ is absolute and $s' = s$.
B. NRS_φ^κ is relative and $s' = s - \underline{w}$.

Before stating and proving a theorem addressing the relation between t and t', it should be useful to consult Fig. 10.3.

The figure depicts a modal communication system $(nM_3^4, \ nM_{-2}^2, \ NRS_1^{-2})$ (cf. Example 10.15 and Fig. 10.2b). The arrows depict possible mappings of (selected) message elements into their received images as per Definition 6.2. The five short arrows connect elements both of which are diatonic, and amount to a bijection from one set of five diatonic notes to the other. The longer arrows connect pairs one of which is chromatic. In such cases a message element (for example, E) may map into one of two received images (E♭ and D♯ in the figure); conversely, two distinct message elements (for example, B♭ and A♯) may have the same image (A in the figure).

Theorem 10.18. Let $(nM_\alpha^\mu, nM_\kappa^\nu, NRS_\varphi^\kappa)$ be a modal communication system, where nM_α^μ and nM_κ^ν are modes with finals $(\underline{w}, \underline{x})$ and $(\underline{w}', \underline{x}')$, respectively. Set $r = \underline{x}' - \underline{x}$, and let $(s, \ t)$ be a message element, (s', t') its received image.
Then $t' - t = r$, or $t' - t = r \pm 1$.

To prove the theorem we shall first prove two lemmas.

Lemma 10.19. Let $(nM_\alpha^\mu, nM_\kappa^\nu, NRS_\varphi^\kappa)$ be a modal communication system, where nM_α^μ and nM_κ^ν are modes with finals $(\underline{w}, \underline{x})$ and $(\underline{w}', \underline{x}')$, respectively. Set $r = \underline{x}' - \underline{x}$, and let $(s, \ t)$ be a message element, $(s', \ t')$ its received image.
If $(s, \ t)$ and $(s', \ t')$ are both diatonic then $t' - t = r$.

Proof. Set $(s, t) - (\underline{w}, \underline{x}) = (u, v) \equiv i(7, 4), (s', t') - (\underline{w}', \underline{x}') = (u', v') \equiv i'(7, 4)$. Since $(\underline{w}, \underline{x}) = Q_{\alpha+\mu}, (\underline{w}', \underline{x}') = Q_{\kappa+\nu}, 0 \le \mu, \ \nu \le 5$, if (s, t) and (s', t') are both diatonic we have $-5 \le i, \ i' \le 6$, implying that

$$(u', v') - (u, v) \equiv j(7, 4), |j| \le 11. \tag{10.1}$$

Suppose by contradiction that $t' - t = \underline{x}' - \underline{x} + \varepsilon, \varepsilon \ne 0$. By Proposition 10.17 $s' - s = \underline{w}' - \underline{w}$, and therefore

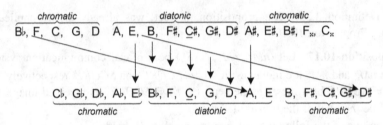

Fig. 10.3 Possible mappings of selected message elements into their received images in a modal communication system

$$(s', t') - (\underline{w}', \underline{x}') = ((s, t) - (\underline{w}, \underline{x})) + (0, \varepsilon),$$

that is,

$$(u', v') - (u, v) = (0, \varepsilon) \equiv j(7, 4), \quad |j| \geq 12.$$

Thus Equation 10.1 is contradicted. Q.E.D.

In connection with the following important lemma it should be useful to consult Fig. 10.3 once again. Consider the relation between the message elements B♭ and A♯, and the received A. The arrow A♯→A is parallel to the short, diatonic arrows, whereas the arrow B♭→A is not. Consider also the relation between the received elements E♭ and D♯ and the transmitted E, noting similarly the directions of the arrows.

Lemma 10.20. Let $(nM_\alpha^\mu, \ nM_\kappa^\nu, \ NRS_\varphi^\kappa)$ be a modal communication system, where nM_α^μ and nM_κ^ν are modes with finals $(\underline{w}, \ \underline{x}) = Q_{\alpha+\mu}$ and $(\underline{w}', \ \underline{x}') = Q_{\kappa+\nu}$ respectively. Set

$$Q_{\alpha-5}^{17} = U_\alpha, \quad Q_{\alpha-5}^{17} \backslash Q_\alpha^7 = C_\alpha;$$
$$Q_{\kappa-5}^{17} = U_\kappa, \quad Q_{\kappa-5}^{17} \backslash Q_\kappa^7 = C_\kappa,$$

and assume that one of the following two conditions, A or B, holds, for some j.

A. $Q_{\alpha+\mu+j} \in C_\alpha; Q_{\kappa+\nu+j} \notin U_\kappa.$

B. $Q_{\kappa+\nu+j} \in C_\kappa; Q_{\alpha+\mu+j} \notin U_\alpha.$

Then the following condition C or D respectively holds for some $j' \in \{j^+, j^-\}$, $j^\pm = j \pm 12.$

C. $Q_{\alpha+\mu+j} \in C_\alpha; Q_{\kappa+\nu+j} \in U_\kappa.$

D. $Q_{\kappa+\nu+j} \in C_\kappa; Q_{\alpha+\mu+j} \in U_\alpha.$

Proof. Suppose that Condition A holds. $Q_{\alpha+\mu+j} \in C_\alpha$ implies that one of the following two conditions 10.2 or 10.3 holds.

$$-5 \leq \mu + j \leq -1. \tag{10.2}$$
$$7 \leq \mu + j \leq 11. \tag{10.3}$$

$Q_{\kappa+\nu+j} \notin U_\kappa$ implies that one of the following two conditions, 10.4 or 10.5, holds.

$$\nu + j \leq -6. \tag{10.4}$$
$$\nu + j \geq 12. \tag{10.5}$$

Suppose that Condition 10.2 holds. Since $0 \leq \mu$, $\nu \leq 5$, 10.5 cannot hold. Moreover, we have $j \geq -10$ and therefore $\nu + j \geq -10$. Since $-5 \leq \mu + j \leq -1$ it follows that $j^+ = j + 12$ satisfies $7 \leq \mu + j^+ \leq 11$, and therefore $Q_{\alpha+\mu+j^+} \in C_\alpha$. Moreover, $2 \leq \nu + j^+ \leq 6$, and therefore $Q_{\kappa+\nu+j^+} \in U_\kappa$. One may similarly show that if Condition 10.3 holds, $Q_{\alpha+\mu+j^-} \in C_\alpha$ and $Q_{\kappa+\nu+j^-} \in U_\kappa$. Thus Condition A implies Condition C. Similarly, Condition B implies Condition D. Q.E.D.

Proof of the theorem. Suppose that $(s, t) \in SCORE$ is chromatic, and set for some j

$$(s, t) \equiv (\underline{w}, \underline{x}) + j(7, 4) \equiv Q_{\alpha+\mu+j}.$$

If $Q_{\kappa+\nu+j} \in U_k = Q_{k-5}^{17}$ then (s, t) and $(s', t') \equiv Q_{\kappa+\nu+j} \equiv (\underline{w}', \underline{x}') + j(7, 4)$ are a message element and its received image such that $t' - t = r$. Set $j' \in \{j^+, j^-\}$, $j^\pm = j \pm 12$, and suppose that $Q_{\kappa+\nu+j} \notin U_\kappa$. Then by Lemma 10.20 (s, t) and $(s', t') \equiv Q_{\kappa+\nu+j'} \equiv (\underline{w}', \underline{x}') + j'(7, 4)$ are a message element and its received image satisfying $t' - t = r - 1$ if $j' = j^+$ or $t' - t = r + 1$ if $j' = j^-$. By Lemma 10.19, if (s, t) and (s', t') are both diatonic then $t' - t = r$. Q.E.D.

10.3 Scale Degrees

Scale degrees are probably most familiar in their triadic guise, the objects do, re, mi/me, etc. of the "tonic Sol-Fa method" codified and disseminated by John Curwen in the nineteenth century. However, the idea of representing notes in terms of their relation to the final dates back to the "octave species" of medieval modal theory (see for example Cohen 2002, pp. 331–338). Indeed, the idea is (arguably) implicit in Pseudo-Odo's statement (early eleventh century), "a tone or mode is a rule that judges every melody according to its final."[5]

Our interest in scale degrees is more than historical, however. As we have seen in Sect. 10.2, modal communication systems fall short of satisfying the Communication Principle, for a received message falls short of being a transposed image of the transmitted one (Theorem 10.18). Scale degrees, and, particularly, a distinction between two types of *chromatic* degrees to be introduced shortly (Definition 10.25), shall prove useful in constructing modes of a special type to which we shall refer as "robust." As we shall see (Sect. 10.4), communication systems that employ robust modes satisfy the Communication Principle, and indeed, the Economical Principle as well.

Definition 10.21. Diatonic/Chromatic Scale Degree; Degree Cluster

Let $nM_\alpha^\mu = (S_\alpha, nNU, SCORE)$ be an n-adic mode with final $(\underline{w}, \underline{x})$, and let R be the set of all notes $(s', t') \equiv (s, t) \in Q_{\alpha-5}^{17}$. Let $\circ$ be a function from R into NVL.

A. We shall refer to $\circ(s', t') = (u, v)$ as *a diatonic (chromatic) degree* or *scale degree* if $(u, v) \equiv (s', t') - (\underline{w}, \underline{x})$, where $0 \leq u \leq 11$, and (s', t') is diatonic (chromatic).
B. We shall refer to the set $\circ CLUST^\mu$ of all degrees as *the Mu-ian degree cluster.*[6]
C. We shall refer to the set $\circ CLUST^\mu/d$ ($\circ CLUST^\mu/c$) of all diatonic (chromatic) degrees as *the Mu-ian diatonic (chromatic) degree cluster.*

The scale-degree function maps cluster-like elements (s', t') into ascending note intervals "specifically" no larger than eleven and octave equivalent to the interval (u, v) *from the final* $(\underline{w}, \underline{x})$ to (s', t'). The scale-degree function is a special case of Lewin's (1987, p. 31) LABEL function.

As proven next, the *Mu*-ian degree cluster and its diatonic and chromatic subsets are indeed dependent only on μ. Henceforth we shall write IQ_j^i for a segment of the *intervallic* line of fifths, a construct analogous to the line of fifths but consisting of note intervals rather than notes.

---

[5] "Tonus vel modus est regula, quae de omni cantu in fine diiudicat." Trans. in Atkinson (2009), p. 214.
[6] That is, Lydian if $\mu = 0$, Ionian if $\mu = 1$, etc.; review Definition 10.8.

a

$\overbrace{(6,4),(1,1),(8,5),(3,2),(10,6)}^{\text{chromatic}}\overbrace{(5,3),(0,0),(7,4),(2,1),(9,5),(4,2),(11,6)}^{\text{diatonic}}\overbrace{(6,3),(1,0),(8,4),(3,1),(10,5)}^{\text{chromatic}}$

b

$\overbrace{(9,6),(4,3),(11,7),(6,4),(1,1)}^{\text{chromatic}}\overbrace{(8,5),(3,2),(10,6),(5,3),(0,0),(7,4),(2,1)}^{\text{diatonic}}\overbrace{(9,5),(4,2),(11,6),(6,3),(1,0)}^{\text{chromatic}}$

Fig. 10.4 The *Mu*-ian degree cluster. (a) $\mu = 1$ (Ionian); (b) $\mu = 4$ (Aeolian)

Proposition 10.22. Let $nM_a^\mu = (S_a,\ nNU,\ SCORE)$ be an n-adic mode with final $(\underline{w},\ \underline{x})$. Let $°CLUST^\mu$ be the *Mu*-ian degree cluster, and let $°CLUST^\mu/d$ and $°CLUST^\mu/c$ be its diatonic and chromatic subsets, respectively.

Then the following three conditions, A, B, and C, hold.

A. $°CLUST^\mu = IQ^{17}_{-\mu-5}$.

B. $°CLUST^\mu/d = IQ^7_{-\mu}$.

C. $°CLUST^\mu/c = IQ^5_{-\mu-5} \cup IQ^5_{-\mu+7}$.

Proof. By Definition 10.5 $(s',\ t')$ is diatonic if $(s',\ t') \equiv (s,\ t) \in S$, and is chromatic if $(s',\ t') \equiv (s,\ t) \in Q^5_{a-5}$, Q^5_{a+7}. Since $(\underline{w}, \underline{x}) = Q_{a+\mu}$, together with Definition 10.21 the proposition follows. Q.E.D.

Example 10.23. Let $°CLUST^\mu$ be the *Mu*-ian degree cluster, $\mu = 1,\ 4$.

Then $°CLUST^\mu$ is the line-of-fifths segment $IQ^{17}_{-\mu-5}$ of Fig. 10.4 (a) and (b), respectively. The central segment $IQ^7_{-\mu}$ in each case is $°CLUST^\mu/d$. The two chromatic segments $IQ^5_{-\mu-5}$ and $IQ^5_{-\mu+7}$ flanking $°CLUST^\mu/d$ on either side are together $°CLUST^\mu/c$.

The following proposition states that, under certain conditions, one may determine from u whether a degree (u, v) is diatonic or chromatic.

*Proposition 10.24. Let $(u, v) \in °CLUST^\mu$ be a degree.

Then $u = 0,\ 7$ implies that $(u,\ v)$ is diatonic such that $v = 0,\ 4$. Moreover,

A. If $\mu \neq 0,\ 5$ then $u = 2,\ 5$ implies that (u, v) is diatonic such that $v = 1,\ 3$, and $u = 1,\ 6$ implies that (u, v) is chromatic.

B. If $\mu = 1$ $(\mu = 4)$ then $u = 4,\ 9,\ 11$ implies that (u, v) is diatonic (chromatic), and $u = 3,\ 8,\ 10$ implies that (u, v) is chromatic (diatonic), such that, in the diatonic cases, $v = 2,\ 5,\ 6$.

The following definition is crucial for subsequent developments.

Definition 10.25. First-Order/Second-Order Chromatic Degree

Let $(u,\ v) \in °CLUST^\mu/c$ be a chromatic degree.

If $(u,\ v) \in RVL \cup \{(6, 3)\}$ we shall refer to (u, v) as *first order*; otherwise, we shall refer to (u, v) as *second order*.

Example 10.26. Let $°CLUST^\mu/c$ be the *Mu*-ian chromatic degree cluster, $\mu = 1$ ($\mu = 4$).

Then A and B below (respectively, C and D below), are all the first and second-order chromatic degrees, respectively. The semi-colon indicates a discontinuity in terms of the line of fifths.

A. $(1, 1), (8, 5), (3, 2), (10, 6); (6, 3)$.
B. $(6, 4); (1, 0), (8, 4), (3, 1), (10, 5)$.
C. $(1, 1); (9, 5), (4, 2), (11, 6), (6, 3)$.
D. $(9, 6), (4, 3), (11, 7), (6, 4); (1, 0)$.

Refer back to Table 9.1. Suppose that the table represents chromatic score-elements in an *n*-adic mode with final C (respectively, A) reducible to Ionian (respectively, Aeolian). Then the first-order chromatic degrees are all the score-elements, represented as scale degrees, *displayed horizontally relative to the mode's final and cofinal* C and G (respectively, A and E): D♭, A♭, E♭, B♭, and F♯ (respectively, F♯, C♯, G♯, D♯, and B♭).[7] All the remaining score elements, represented as scale degrees, are second-order chromatic. As we shall see in Sect. 10.4, there exists an economical algorithm by which received pitches may be processed as diatonic or first-order chromatic degrees.

It is easily seen that the set of all chromatic degrees may be partitioned into five "enharmonic" pairs $((u, v), (u, v'))$, where (u, v) is first order, and (u, v') is second order; refer again to Example 10.26.

The following proposition states that under certain conditions one may determine from v whether (u, v) is a first- or second-order chromatic degree.

*Proposition 10.27. Let $(u, v) \in °CLUST^\mu/c$ be a chromatic degree.

Then $v = 0, 4$ implies that (u, v) is second order. Moreover, if $\mu = 1$ ($\mu = 4$) then $v = 2, 3, 6$ ($v = 1, 2, 5$) implies that (u, v) is first order such that $u = 3, 6, 10$ ($u = 1, 4, 9$).

In connection with the following theorem it should be useful to consult Examples 10.23 and 10.26.

Theorem 10.28. Let $°CLUST^\mu$ be the *Mu*-ian degree cluster, and let $D \subset °CLUST^\mu$ be a set of degrees.

Then the following three conditions, A, B, and C, are all equivalent.

A. $D = IQ_{-5}^{12} = RVL \cup \{(6, 3)\}$.
B. D is the set of all diatonic and first-order chromatic degrees.
C. D is the intersection $°CLUST^0 \cap °CLUST^1 \cap \ldots \cap °CLUST^5$.

To prove the theorem we shall first prove the following lemma.

---

[7] Review Definition 6.2.

Lemma 10.29. Let $°CLUST^u/c$ be the Mu-ian chromatic degree cluster, and let $D' \subset °CLUST^u/c$ be a set of chromatic degrees. Set $IQ_j^0 = \varnothing$ for every j.

Then the following two conditions, A and B, are equivalent.

A. $D' = IQ_{-(5+\mu)}^\mu \cup IQ_7^{5-\mu}$.

B. D' is the set of all second-order chromatic degrees.

Proof. By Proposition 10.22 $°CLUST^u/c = IQ_{-\mu-5}^5 \cup IQ_{-\mu+7}^5$. By Definition 10.25 $(u, v) \in °CLUST^u/c$ is first order if $(u, v) \in RVL \cup \{(6, 3)\} = IQ_{-5}^{12}$, and is second order otherwise. Together with $0 \le \mu \le 5$, the lemma follows. Q.E.D.

Proof of the theorem. By Proposition 10.22 $°CLUST^u/d = IQ_{-\mu}^7$ and by Definition 10.25 $(u, v) \in °CLUST^u/c$ is first order if $(u, v) \in RVL \cup \{(6, 3)\} = IQ_{-5}^{12}$. Together with $0 \le \mu \le 5$, the equivalence of Conditions A and B follows. Together with Lemma 10.29, the theorem follows. Q.E.D.

Following Heinrich Schenker, a useful "caret notation" for scale degrees is introduced in a series of definitions next. The notation renders explicit the status of a degree as diatonic or chromatic, as well as the status of a *chromatic* degree as first or second order. See Propositions 10.24 and 10.27.

Definition 10.30. (Caret notation for diatonic degrees)
Let (u, v) be a diatonic degree.

If $v = 0$, 4 we shall write $(u, v) = \widehat{v+1} = \hat{1}$, $\hat{5}$, respectively.
If $v = 1$, 2, 3, 5, 6 we shall write

A. $(u, v) = \widehat{v+1}^{\,-} = \hat{2}^-, \hat{3}^-, \hat{4}^-, \hat{6}^-, \hat{7}^-$ if $u = 1, 3, 5, 8, 10$, respectively.
B. $(u, v) = \widehat{v+1}^{\,+} = \hat{2}^+, \hat{3}^+, \hat{4}^+, \hat{6}^+, \hat{7}^+$ if $u = 2, 4, 6, 9, 11$, respectively.

Example 10.31. Relative to F Dorian we have:

$$°(F) = (0, 0) = \hat{1};$$
$$°(G) = (2, 1) = \hat{2}^+;$$
$$°(A\flat) = (3, 2) = \hat{3}^-;$$
$$°(B\flat) = (5, 3) = \hat{4}^-;$$
$$°(C_1) = (7, 4) = \hat{5};$$
$$°(D_1) = (9, 5) = \hat{6}^+;$$
$$°(\flat(E_1)) = (10, 6) = \hat{7}^-.$$

Table 10.2 Diatonic and first-order chromatic degrees relative to tribal class

Lydian	Ionian	Mixolydian	Dorian	Aeolian	Phrygian
$\flat\hat{2}$	$\flat\hat{2}$	$\flat\hat{2}$	$\flat\hat{2}$	$\flat\hat{2}$	$\hat{2}^{-}$
$\flat\hat{6}$	$\flat\hat{6}$	$\flat\hat{6}$	$\flat\hat{6}$	$\hat{6}^{-}$	$\hat{6}^{-}$
$\flat\hat{3}$	$\flat\hat{3}$	$\flat\hat{3}$	$\hat{3}^{-}$	$\hat{3}^{-}$	$\hat{3}^{-}$
$\flat\hat{7}$	$\flat\hat{7}$	$\hat{7}^{-}$	$\hat{7}^{-}$	$\hat{7}^{-}$	$\hat{7}^{-}$
$\flat\hat{4}$	$\hat{4}^{-}$	$\hat{4}^{-}$	$\hat{4}^{-}$	$\hat{4}^{-}$	$\hat{4}^{-}$
$\hat{1}$	$\hat{1}$	$\hat{1}$	$\hat{1}$	$\hat{1}$	$\hat{1}$
$\hat{5}$	$\hat{5}$	$\hat{5}$	$\hat{5}$	$\hat{5}$	$\hat{5}$
$\hat{2}^{+}$	$\hat{2}^{+}$	$\hat{2}^{+}$	$\hat{2}^{+}$	$\hat{2}^{+}$	$\sharp\hat{2}$
$\hat{6}^{+}$	$\hat{6}^{+}$	$\hat{6}^{+}$	$\hat{6}^{+}$	$\sharp\hat{6}$	$\sharp\hat{6}$
$\hat{3}^{+}$	$\hat{3}^{+}$	$\hat{3}^{+}$	$\sharp\hat{3}$	$\sharp\hat{3}$	$\sharp\hat{3}$
$\hat{7}^{+}$	$\hat{7}^{+}$	$\sharp\hat{7}$	$\sharp\hat{7}$	$\sharp\hat{7}$	$\sharp\hat{7}$
$\hat{4}^{+}$	$\sharp\hat{4}$	$\sharp\hat{4}$	$\sharp\hat{4}$	$\sharp\hat{4}$	$\sharp\hat{4}$

Definition 10.32. (Caret notation for first-order chromatic degrees)

Let (u, v) be a first-order chromatic degree. Set $v = 1,\ 2,\ 3,\ 5,\ 6$.

A. If $u = 1,\ 3,\ 5,\ 8,\ 10$ we shall write $(u, v) = \flat\widehat{(v+1)} = \flat\hat{2}, \flat\hat{3}, \flat\hat{4}, \flat\hat{6}, \flat\hat{7}$, respectively.

B. If $u = 2,\ 4,\ 6,\ 9,\ 11$ we shall write $(u, v) = \sharp\widehat{(v+1)} = \sharp\hat{2}, \sharp\hat{3}, \sharp\hat{4}, \sharp\hat{6}, \sharp\hat{7}$, respectively.

Definition 10.33. (Caret notation for second-order chromatic degrees)

Let $(u,\ v)$ be a second-order chromatic degree. Set (A) $v = 7,\ 4$ (respectively, $v = 0,\ 4$); (B) $v = 2,\ 3,\ 6$; (C) $v = 1,\ 2,\ 5$.

A. If $u = 11,\ 6$ (respectively, $u = 1,\ 8$) we shall write $(u, v) = \flat\widehat{(v+1)} = \flat\hat{1}, \flat\hat{5}$
$((u, v) = \sharp\widehat{(v+1)} = \sharp\hat{1}, \sharp\hat{5})$.

B. If $u = 2,\ 4,\ 9$ we shall write $(u, v) = \flat\widehat{(v+1)}^{*} = \flat\hat{3}^{*}, \flat\hat{4}^{*}, \flat\hat{7}^{*}$, respectively.

C. If $u = 3,\ 5,\ 10$ we shall write $(u, v) = \sharp\widehat{(v+1)}^{*} = \sharp\hat{2}^{*}, \sharp\hat{3}^{*}, \sharp\hat{6}^{*}$, respectively.

Note the asterisks in B and C. $\flat\hat{3}^{*} = (2, 2)$, for example, is a second-order chromatic degree (cf. Phrygian), as distinct from $\flat\hat{3} = (3, 2)$, a first-order chromatic degree.

Using the notational conventions of Definitions 10.30 and 10.32, the quintically organized Table 10.2 displays all diatonic and *first*-order chromatic degrees $(u,\ v)$ relative to μ, that is, relative to the tribal class (Definition 10.8). Note that sets of degrees relative to two different tribal classes (i.e., two different columns in the table) differ only in terms of the status of degrees other than $\hat{1}$ and $\hat{5}$ as diatonic or chromatic. For example, the Phrygian $\hat{2}^{-}$ is the same degree, namely $(1, 1)$, as the non-Phrygian $\flat\hat{2}$. Relative to Phrygian, however, $\hat{2}^{-}$ is diatonic, whereas the non-Phrygian $\flat\hat{2}$ is chromatic. Similarly, the Lydian $\hat{4}^{+}$ is the same degree, namely $(6, 3)$, as the non-Lydian $\sharp\hat{4}$, and so forth.

Finally, from Propositions 10.24 and 10.27 one may simplify the caret notation for scale degrees in certain contexts.

If modes reducible to Lydian and Phrygian are excluded (cf. keys), there is no need to distinguish between the diatonic/chromatic degrees $\hat{4}^-/\flat\hat{4}$ and $\hat{2}^+/\#\hat{2}$, nor between the first-order/second-order chromatic degrees $\#\hat{2}/\#\hat{2}^*, \flat\hat{3}/\flat\hat{3}^*, \#\hat{3}/\#\hat{3}^*$, and $\flat\hat{4}/\flat\hat{4}^*$. Therefore, if Lydian and Phrygian are excluded the modifiers $\pm$ and $*$ may conveniently be omitted for these degrees (in particular, $\flat\hat{3}$ and $\#\hat{3}$ are first-order chromatic, $\#\hat{2}$ and $\flat\hat{4}$ are second-order chromatic). Moreover, if all modes other than Ionian and Aeolian are excluded (cf. *triadic* keys), there is little danger of ambiguity in omitting these modifiers altogether, since usually it is contextually clear whether Ionian (major) or Aeolian (minor) is under discussion. Thus, if only Ionian and Aeolian are under discussion we shall often use the following simplified notation for diatonic and first-order/second-order chromatic degrees, respectively for Ionian and Aeolian:

$$\hat{1}, \flat\hat{2}/\#\hat{1}, \hat{2}, \flat\hat{3}/\#\hat{2}, \hat{3}, \hat{4}, \#\hat{4}/\flat\hat{5}, \hat{5}, \flat\hat{6}/\#\hat{5}, \hat{6}, \flat\hat{7}/\#\hat{6}, \hat{7};$$

$$\hat{1}, \flat\hat{2}/\#\hat{1}, \hat{2}, \hat{3}, \#\hat{3}/\flat\hat{4}, \hat{4}, \#\hat{4}/\flat\hat{5}, \hat{5}, \hat{6}, \#\hat{6}/\flat\hat{7}, \hat{7}, \#\hat{7}/\flat\hat{1}.$$

10.4   Robust and Semi-robust Communication Systems

By Theorem 10.18, the mapping of a transmitted mode with final $(\underline{w}, \underline{x})$ into a received mode with final $(\underline{w}', \underline{x}')$ fails to satisfy the Communication Principle because the interval $(s', t') - (s, t)$ from a message element (s, t) to its received image (s', t') may satisfy $t' - t = \underline{x}' - \underline{x}$ as well as $t' - t = (\underline{x}' - \underline{x}) \pm 1$ (thus the received message is not a transposed image of the transmitted one). As we shall see in the present section, if the transmitted and received modes are "robust" this deficiency may be remedied, such that the Economical Principle is satisfied as well.

Definition 10.34.   Robust Mode

Let $nM_\alpha^\mu = (S_\alpha, \; nNU, \; SCORE)$ be an n-adic mode, where $(s, t) \in SCORE$ is a score element.

We shall refer to nM_α^μ as *robust* if $°(s, t)$ is not second-order chromatic.

Example 10.35.   Consider an n-adic mode nM_α^1 reducible to Ionian, where (u, v) is a chromatic degree.

If $(u, v) = \flat\hat{2}, \flat\hat{3}, \#\hat{4}, \flat\hat{6}, \flat\hat{7}$, then the mode is robust.

Consider an n-adic mode nM_α^0 reducible to Lydian, where (u, v) is a chromatic degree.

If $(u, v) = \flat\hat{2}, \flat\hat{3}, \flat\hat{4}, \flat\hat{6}, \flat\hat{7}$, then the mode is robust.

Recall that the Lydian $\flat\hat{4} = (5, 3)$ is the same as the Ionian $\hat{4}^+$, except for being chromatic rather than diatonic (cf. Table 10.2). Conversely, the Ionian $\#\hat{4} = (6, 3)$ is the same as the Lydian $\hat{4}^+$.

Theorem 10.36 establishes that all the following are equivalent: (1) a modal communication system where the transmitted and received modes are both robust; (2) a modal communication system that satisfies the Economical Principle via a coherence-like algorithm; (3) a modal communication system that satisfies the Communication Principle.

*Theorem 10.36. Let $(nM_\alpha^\mu,\ nM_\kappa^\nu,\ NRS_\varphi^\kappa)$ be a modal communication system, where nM_α^μ and nM_κ^ν are modes with finals $(\underline{w}, \underline{x})$ and $(\underline{w}', \underline{x}')$ and scores $SCORE$ and $SCORE'$, respectively. Let $(s,\ t) \in SCORE$ be a message element, where $(s',\ t') \in SCORE'$ is its received image. Set $r = \underline{x}' - \underline{x}$.

Then the following two conditions, A and B, are equivalent. Moreover, if nM_α^μ is robust then the following three conditions, A, B, and C, are all equivalent.

A. nM_κ^ν is robust.
B. $t' - \underline{x}' = \left[\frac{7}{12} \cdot (s' - \underline{w}')\right] = \left[\frac{7}{12} \cdot (s' - \underline{w}' - 7)\right] + 4.$
C. $t' - t = r.$

The theorem follows from the following two lemmas.

Lemma 10.37. The following two conditions, A and B, are equivalent.

A. $\{(u, v)\}$ satisfies $u = 0,\ 1,\ \ldots,\ 11, v = \left[\frac{7}{12} \cdot u\right] = \left[\frac{7}{12} \cdot (u - 7)\right] + 4.$
B. $\{(u, v)\} = IQ_{-5}^{12}$, the set of all diatonic and first-order chromatic degrees.

Proof. It can easily be checked that Condition A entails Condition B. Suppose that Condition B holds.

If $u \neq 1,\ 6$, using Definition 5.14 (Coherent Tone System) we have

$$v =$$

$$\left[\frac{7}{12} \cdot u\right] = \left[\frac{7}{12} \cdot u - 4\right] + 4 =$$

$$\left[\frac{7}{12} \cdot u - \left(4 + \frac{1}{12}\right)\right] + 4 = \left[\frac{7}{12} \cdot u - \frac{49}{12}\right] + 4 =$$

$$\left[\frac{7}{12} \cdot (u - 7)\right] + 4.$$

If $u = 6$ we have

$$\left[\frac{7}{12} \cdot u\right] = 3 = \left[\frac{7}{12} \cdot (u - 7)\right] + 4,$$

and if $u = 1$ we have

$$\left[\frac{7}{12} \cdot (u - 7)\right] + 4 = 1 = \left[\frac{7}{12} \cdot u\right].$$

Q.E.D.

Lemma 10.38. Let $(nM_\alpha^\mu,\ nM_\kappa^\nu,\ NRS_\varphi^\kappa)$ be a modal communication system, where nM_α^μ and nM_κ^ν are modes with finals $(\underline{w}, \underline{x})$ and $(\underline{w}', \underline{x}')$ and scores $SCORE$ and $SCORE'$, respectively. Let $(s, t) \in SCORE$ be a message element, where $(s', t') \in SCORE'$ is its received image. Set $r = \underline{x}' - \underline{x}$.

Then the following two conditions, A and B, are equivalent.

A. nM_α^μ and nM_κ^ν are both robust.
B. $t' - t = r$.

Proof. Set $(s, t) \equiv (\underline{w}, \underline{x}) + IQ_j$, $(s', t') \equiv (\underline{w}', \underline{x}') + IQ_{j'}$, for some j, j' By Definition 10.21 $IQ_j = {}^\circ(s, t)$, $IQ_{j'} = {}^\circ(s', t')$. By Proposition 10.17 $s' - s = \underline{w}' - \underline{w}$, and thus $j \equiv j'$ (mod 12).

If nM_α^μ and nM_κ^ν are both robust by Theorem 10.28 $- 5 \le j$, $j' \le 6$, implying that $j' = j$. Thus $t' - t = \underline{x}' - \underline{x} = r$. Conversely, if $t' - t = \underline{x}' - \underline{x} = r$ then $j \equiv j'$ (mod 7). Thus $j \equiv j'$ (mod 84), implying that $j = j'$. Since this result is independent of μ and ν, by Theorem 10.28 $- 5 \le j$, $j' \le 6$, implying that nM_α^μ and nM_κ^ν are both robust. Q.E.D.

Definition 10.39. (Semi-)robust Communication System
Let $(nM_\alpha^\mu,\ nM_\kappa^\nu,\ NRS_\varphi^\kappa)$ be a context-dependent modal communication system.

A. We shall refer to the system as *semi-robust* if nM_κ^ν is robust.
B. We shall refer to a semi-robust modal communication system as *robust* if nM_α^μ is robust.

Example 10.40. Figure 10.5 depicts mappings of message elements into their received images in (a) a robust and (b) a semi-robust relative communication system $(nM_3^4,\ nM_{-2}^2,\ NRS_1^{-2})$. Compare with Fig. 10.3.

Semi-robust communication systems may be thought of as generating, for every message element, a *default* received image that is either diatonic or first-order chromatic, *economically using the coherence-like algorithm 10.36B*. This implies

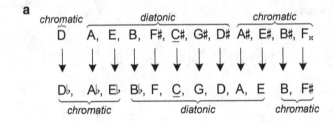

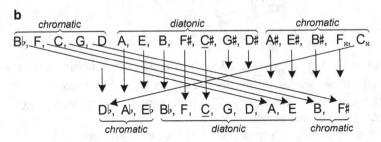

Fig. 10.5 Mappings of message elements into their received images in (**a**) a robust and (**b**) a semi-robust relative communication system

that contextual cues are needed for the receiver to override the default in the case of a transmitted *second*-order chromatic degree. See also Sect. 12.3, as well as Chap. 15. Robust communication systems satisfy the Communication Principle in the sense that the received message is a transposition of the transmitted one.

Two points already made in connection with (context-dependent) modal communication systems in general should be emphasized (see the discussion following Proposition 10.16). First, we have yet to offer a "context-free" theory of final-image centricity. Second, as Example 10.40 clearly demonstrates, a (semi-)robust communication system, still, does not preserve the transmitted tribal class (in the example, Aeolian is mapped into Mixolydian). Equivalently, except for the final and cofinal diatonic message elements may be mapped into chromatic received ones, and vice versa (for example, in the example chromatic A♯ is mapped into diatonic A, while diatonic E is mapped into chromatic E♭). These issues are all resolved in the context-free theory of *tonic*-image centricity offered in Chap. 14.

An interesting comparison may be made at this juncture between dyadic and triadic tonality. The nucleus of a dyadic mode, represented as a set of degrees, is $\left\{\hat{1}, \hat{5}\right\}$ regardless of the tribal class into which the mode may be reduced. By contrast, there exists a bijection between the two distinct nuclei, namely $\left\{\hat{1}, \hat{3}^{+}, \hat{5}\right\}$ and $\left\{\hat{1}, \hat{3}^{-}, \hat{5}\right\}$, and the two distinct tribal classes, namely Ionian and Aeolian, into which triadic *keys* may be reduced. Suppose contextual cues exist by which the received image of the "tonic triad" (not just the final) acquires privileged status (for example, the tonic triad is the first element of the "harmonic message"). Then the tribal class, namely major or minor, is preserved, and with it, the diatonic/chromatic partitioning of the message.[8]

10.5 Congruent and Standard Modes

We conclude this chapter with two definitions that shall prove useful subsequently.

Definition 10.41. Congruent Modes
Let $nM_\alpha^\mu = (S_\alpha,\ nNU,\ SCORE)$ and $nM_\beta^\mu = (S_\beta,\ nNU,\ SCORE')$ be two n-adic Mu-ian modes with finals $(\underline{w}, \underline{x})$ and $(\underline{w}', \underline{x}')$, respectively. Assume that $SCORE$ and $SCORE'$ are sequences of equal length.
We shall refer to nM_α^μ and nM_β^μ as *congruent* if the exchange $X : SCORE \to SCORE'$ satisfies $X(s, t) - (s, t) = (\underline{w}', \underline{x}') - (\underline{w}, \underline{x})$.

Example 10.42. The triadic keys $3M_{-1}^1$ ("C major") and $3M_{-6}^1$ ("D♭ major") such that $SCORE$ and $SCORE'$ are as in Fig. 10.6, are congruent.

If the transmitted and received modes of a modal communication system are congruent, then the Communication Principle is satisfied; moreover, the tribal class is preserved, and with it, the diatonic/chromatic partitioning of the message.

Definition 10.43. Standard Mode
Let $nM_\alpha^\mu = (S_\alpha,\ nNU,\ SCORE)$ be an n-adic mode.
We shall refer to the mode as *standard* if $(w, x) \in S_\alpha$ satisfies $0 \le x \le 6$.

By the following proposition a mode is standard if and only if its accidental index (Definition 10.5) consists of no more than five flats or six sharps.

Proposition 10.44. Let $nM_\alpha^\mu = (S_\alpha,\ nNU,\ SCORE)$ be an n-adic mode.
Then nM_α^μ is standard if, and only if, $-6 \le \alpha \le 5$.
Proof. Set $(w_i,\ x_i) = i(7,\ 4) \oplus l_i(12,\ 7)$ for some l_i, $(w_i,\ x_i) \in S_\alpha$, $i = \alpha$, $\alpha + 1, \ldots,\ \alpha + 6$.
We have $0 \le w_i \le 11$, and therefore $l_i = -\left\lfloor \frac{7i}{12} \right\rfloor$. Since $x_i = 4i + 7l_i$ satisfies $0 \le x_i \le 6$ if, and only if,

---

[8] In dyadic tonality, the problem of tribal-class preservation may be addressed by means of an understanding that chromatic message elements are "statistically" less prevalent than their diatonic counterparts (for example, in "C Ionian" B♭ is less prevalent than B). Challenging "superficial scholars" who ". . . contend that the entire system is in nowise changed because of altering one or another of the semitones," even if the alteration persists through ". . .an entire song," Glarean (Glarean 1965, p. 113) implicitly alludes to such a tacit, "statistical" understanding, for he concedes that an *occasional* alteration does not, indeed, change the mode. See also Sects. 11.1 and 12.1.

Fig. 10.6 The scores of two congruent triadic keys, C and D♭ major

$$-\left\lfloor \frac{4i}{7} \right\rfloor = l_{ij} = -\left\lfloor \frac{7i}{12} \right\rfloor,$$

it follows that nM_α^μ is standard if, and only if, $-6 \le i \le 11$. Thus $-6 \le \alpha \le 5$. Q.E.D.

In the following three chapters we address dyadic and triadic modes from a variety of perspectives that do not concern communication specifically. Following this relatively informal detour, we return in Chap. 14 to the Communication Principle and finally offer a context-free theory of final-image centricity, indeed, *tonic*-image centricity. We do so by constructing special types of triadic keys to which we refer as "tonalities."

References

Atkinson, C. (2009). *The critical nexus: Tone-system, mode, and notation in early medieval music.* Oxford: Oxford University Press.
Blasius, L. (1997). *The music theory of Godfrey Winham.* Princeton: Department of Music, Princeton University Press.
Cohen, D. (2002). Notes, scales, and modes in the earlier middle ages. In T. Christensen (Ed.), *The Cambridge history of Western music theory* (pp. 307–363). Cambridge: Cambridge University Press.
Fuller, R. (1975). A structuralist approach to the diatonic scale. *Journal of Music Theory, 19*(2), 182–210.
Glarean, H. (1965). *Dodecachordon* (C. Miller, Trans.). American Institute of Musicology: Rome.
Lewin, D. (1987). *Generalized musical intervals and transformations.* New Haven: Yale University Press. 2007. Reprint, Oxford: Oxford University Press

Chapter 11
Topics in Dyadic and Triadic Theory

Abstract In Sect. 11.1 the relation between Glarean's "dodecachordal" theory and Lippius's triadic modal theory on the one hand, and the theory of dyadic and triadic modes and semi-keys, on the other, is discussed. Section 11.2 addresses, in the triadic context, issues of consonance and stability. Section 11.3 studies two important relationships between triadic keys, the "relative" and the "parallel." Finally, Sect. 11.4 addresses the relationship between the theory of *robust* triadic keys and Schenker's notion of "mixture."

11.1 Glarean, Lippius, and Modal Theory

Although modal theory dates from the late ninth or early tenth century, for many centuries the existence of two dyadic tribal classes (Definition 10.8), namely Ionian and Aeolian, was not recognized. With admirable courage, Glarean (1547) challenges the Medieval, church-sanctioned "octenary" doctrine, which he finds suspect theoretically as well as empirically. He offers instead the following, "dodecachordal" modal theory:

> The musical modes are nothing but the consonant species of the octave itself, and the very ones (*species*) which are joined together from the various species of [consonant] fifths and fourths, as we have said above concerning intervals.[1]

The "octave" to which Glarean refers is a "diatonic collection," that is, a set S_α corresponding to a seven-element segment Q_α^7 of the line of fifths. In keeping with an age-old tradition, Glarean is probably thinking in terms of either $S_{-1} = \{$F, C,

---

[1] Book I, Chapter 11: "Modi musici nihil aliud sunt quam ipsius Diapason consonantiae species, quae et ipsae ex variis diapente ac diatessaron speciebus conflantur, ut supra de intervallis diximus." Trans. from Houghton (1967, p. 293). See also Lester (1989, p. 4).

E. Agmon, *The Languages of Western Tonality*, Computational Music Science, DOI 10.1007/978-3-642-39587-1_11, © Springer-Verlag Berlin Heidelberg 2013

..., B}, so-called *cantus durus*, or $S_{-2} = \{B\flat, F, ..., E\}$, so-called *cantus mollis*. "Species of the octave" are the seven cyclic permutations of the scalar ordering of the collection (see Proposition 6.31), that is, (F, G, ..., E), (G, A, ..., F), ..., (E, F, ..., D), assuming *cantus durus*. Finally, "species of the octave... joined together from the various species of [consonant] fifths and fourths" is the set of all permutations such that the interval from the first element in the permutation to the fifth element is consonant, namely a perfect fifth. In other words, the permutation (B, C, ..., A) is excluded.

Note that the emphasis on the first and fifth elements in a permutation is suggestive of a dyadic nucleus (Definition 10.1).[2] The traditional "authentic" vs. "plagal" distinction, which Glarean addresses in the paragraph that follows the definition just quoted, also implies the existence of a dyadic nucleus. "Authentic" and "plagal" may be viewed as two types of scores (Definition 10.4). In an "authentic" score there exists a score element $(\underline{s}, \underline{t})$ octave equivalent to the final, such that every score element (s, t) satisfies $\underline{s} \leq s \leq \underline{s} + 12$; similarly, in a "plagal" score there exists a score element $(\overline{s}, \overline{t})$ equivalent to *the cofinal* such that every score element (s, t) satisfies $\overline{s} \leq s \leq \overline{s} + 12$.[3] Thus, although more restricted in terms of the assumed "background system" and message, Glarean's dodecachordal definition of "mode" may be viewed as equivalent to Definition 10.4, under the dyadic condition.

In a well-known passage, Glarean (1965, pp. 129–131) points to a "problem" with Lydian and Phrygian, in a manner suggestive of dyadic semi-keys and keys, or of triadic semi-keys (Definition 10.10; see Table 10.1 and Fig. 10.1, as well as Theorem 10.11 and its proof).

> Modes are also changed from one into another but not with equal success. For in some cases the change is scarcely clear even to a perceptive ear, indeed, often with great pleasure to the listener, a fact which we have frequently declared is very common today in changing from the Lydian to the Ionian.... But in other cases the changing seems rough, and scarcely ever without a grave offense to the ears, as changing from the Dorian to the Phrygian....
>
> ...It is also evident that the Lydian and Hypolydian modes have a common fifth, namely, the third species [of fifth]; the Phrygian and Hypophrygian have a common fifth, the second species, each of which includes the tritone [relative to the final and cofinal, respectively, EA], a hard interval, and somewhat unsuitable to the diatonic system.... And thus if one changes the Ionian and Hypoionian into the Dorian and Hypodorian, the fifth is changed but is still without a tritone; for this reason, the ears are not offended, but rather one will be pleased by the changing of the modes....

---

[2] Hucbald's notion of *socialitas*, "the recurrence of modal quality in notes a perfect fifth or fourth apart" (Cohen 2002, p. 322), is already suggestive of a dyadic, final-cofinal modal nucleus, as are the "block" diagrams of *Scolica enchiriadis*, that span a perfect fifth (see Fig. 1.2).

[3] This is a rather literal rendering of the traditional distinction, as formulated in relation to dyadic monophony. In attempting to apply the distinction to triadic polyphony it was necessary to conceive the score as a set of monophonic "sub-scores," each corresponding to a "part" of the polyphonic texture. The authentic/plagal distinction was codified in monophonic terms already in the late ninth or early tenth century in the so-called "new exposition" of *Alia musica*. The analysis of modes in terms of species of fifths and fourths dates back to the so-called "Reichenau School" of the eleventh century.

But contrariwise, if one wishes to go from the Dorian or the Hypodorian to the Phrygian or Hypophrygian, he then enters into modes whose fifth contains a tritone, a sharp interval, as we said, so that it seems as if another kind of song has been created. Thus the hearing, affected by the newness of the sound, perceives the unsuitable change and is stunned, as it were. Anyone who has ears accustomed to the modes will find these things inherent in their very nature.[4]

Dyadic keys or triadic semi-keys may help explain Glarean's (1547, *passim*) cryptic references to only three modes, on *ut*, *re*, and *mi*. For example, when introducing his twelve modes he states that "[many learned men of this day] are acquainted with only eight modes, and others also proclaim that three, *ut, re, mi*, are sufficient, just as ordinary players use them."[5] If $\alpha = -1, -2$ (that is, the accidental index is zero or minus one, "*cantus durus*" or "*cantus mollis*"), and $(\underline{w}, \underline{x}) = (0, 0), (2, 1) = ut, re$ (that is, the final is either C or D), then an "*ut*-mode" is reducible to either Ionian or Mixolydian, and a "*re*-mode" to either Dorian or Aeolian (a *cantus durus* "*mi*-mode" is of course reducible to Phrygian). However, if Glarean conceives a "*mi*-mode" as "plagal" Aeolian, his "*ut, re, mi*" modes are in fact keys (if dyadic) or semi-keys (if triadic): Lydian *and Phrygian* are excluded.[6] Review Table 10.1 and Fig. 10.1; see also Sect. 12.2.

The triadic conception of mode, though hinted at by Zarlino in 1558, was first stated explicitly by Lippius. Compare the following statement from Lippius (1612), fol. I1r-I1v, with Proposition 10.13.

Legitimate [primary mode] is either *naturalior* (which has the *naturalior* triad), or *mollior* (which has the *mollior* triad). Both species of legitimate modes are themselves trinities, the one—Ionian, Lydian, and Mixolydian; the other—Dorian, Phrygian, and Aeolian. And thus there are six simple primary legitimate modes. Counting their plagals... there are twelve modes.[7]

Interestingly, Lippius (*ibid.*) notes that "Ionian with its secondary, Hypoionian, having the triad c-e-g (bo, di, lo), is the most natural and primary of all in today's music (many past and present writers do not agree with this)."[8]

---

[4] See also Lester (1989), pp. 5–6.

[5] 1965, p. 103. See Judd (1992, p. 437), and Powers (1992, p. 21).

[6] Zarlino (1558, Book IV, p. 30) notes that many compositions that appear to be in mode 3 (Phrygian) are in fact in mode 10 (Hypoaeolian). See Wiering (1998, pp. 88–89). Glarean himself makes a similar statement (1965, p. 258): "Yet because the Hypoaeolian has the same octave as this mode [Phrygian], one finds examples of the Phrygian which differ from the Hypoaeolian only in the ending." See also Judd (1992).

[7] "Legitimus est alius Naturalior qui tenet Triadem Harmonicam Naturaliorem: alius Mollior, qui Triadem Molliorem obtinet. Uterque Trinus est juxta Species Triadum: ille Jonicus, Lydius, et Mixolydius: hic Dorius, Phrygius et AEolius: ut ita sex sint Simplices Modi Primarii Legitimi et duodecim, cum suis [hupotropois], Hypoionico, Hypolydio, Hypomixolydio, Hypodorio, Hypophrygio, et Hypoaeolio sortiti appellationem à Gentibus quibus cuique suus placebant." Trans. from Lester (1989), p. 43.

[8] "Omnium Naturalissimus et Primus in hodiernâ Musicâ (contrà quàm plerique Veteres et Recentiores autumant) est Jonicus cum suo Secundario Hypoionico habens Triadem Harmonicam propriam. c. e. g. bo, di, lo." Trans. from Lester (1989), p. 43.

11.2 Aspects of Triadic Consonance and Stability

In connection with the following definition, review Definition 9.2.

Definition 11.1. Perfect/Imperfect Triadic Consonance
   Let $P = ((s, t), (s', t'))$ be a triadic consonance, and set $(u, v) = (s', t') - (s, t)$.

A. We shall refer to P as *perfect* if $(u, v) \equiv (0, 0), \ \pm(7, 4)$.
B. We shall refer to P as *imperfect* if $(u, v) \equiv \pm(3, 2), \ \pm(4, 2)$.

   The hierarchy of "perfect" vs. "imperfect" triadic consonances reflects the finding that the dyadically privileged intervals, P8 and P5, are a subset of the triadic set, P8, P5, M3, and m3; cf. Fig. 9.1.
   Recall that a consonance the root of which is also the lower tone is stable. In view of the perfect/imperfect triadic hierarchy, in a triadic context we shall refer to the fifth as *strongly stable* and to the fourth as *strongly unstable*; we shall refer to thirds as *weakly stable* and to sixths as *weakly unstable*.

Example 11.2. Consider the three "C major" triads of Fig. 11.1 relative to a figured-bass convention by which intervals are measured *from* the lowest note, and only from that note. Then every triad corresponds to exactly two intervals, excluding the perfect prime. Reduced modulo the perfect octave, in (a) the two intervals are a strongly stable perfect fifth and a weakly stable major third. As a result, the "root-position" triad, in addition to being consonant, is stable. In (b), on the other hand, we have a weakly stable minor third and a weakly unstable minor sixth; the consonant, "first-inversion" triad is therefore neither stable nor unstable. Finally, in (c) we have a strongly unstable perfect fourth and a weakly unstable major sixth; the "second-inversion" triad, therefore, though consonant, is unstable.

   A second-inversion major/minor triad need not always sound unstable. Suppose that, for "contextual" reasons, the figured-bass convention is momentarily suspended such that the bass relinquishes its referential status in favor of a triad's root. Then second-inversion triads may sound stable. The six-four chords, to which Aldwell and Schachter (2003, pp. 320–322) refer as "consonant," seem to satisfy this condition.
   Finally, Definition 9.2 guarantees that a triadic consonance is a "sensory consonance" (Terhardt 1976, 1984). However, the reverse relation does not hold. Sensory consonance (or "euphony") does *not* guarantee "consonance" in the sense of Definition 9.2. Indeed, a sensory consonance, including the psychoacoustical octave, may be dissonant. Review Fig. 2.1 and discussion; see also Example 9.5.

*Proposition 11.3. Let $P = ((s, t), (s', t'))$ be a pair of notes and set $(s', t') - (s, t) = (u, v) \equiv i(7, 4)$.

A. P is a perfect consonance if, and only if, $|i| = 0, 1$.
B. P is an imperfect consonance if, and only if, $|i| = 3, 4$.
C. P is a dissonance if, and only if, $|i| = 2$ or $|i| \geq 5$.

Fig. 11.1 The three figured-bass positions of a major triad

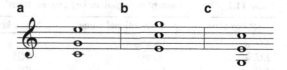

11.3 Relative and Parallel Triadic Keys

Since a triadic *key* is reducible only to Ionian or Aeolian and is major or minor, respectively (see Table 10.1, Fig. 10.1, and Proposition 10.13), henceforth it should suffice to refer to triadic keys as "major" or "minor." Moreover, it should suffice to write $+K_{\alpha^+}$ and $-K_{\alpha^-}$ for major and minor keys $3M_\alpha^1$ and $3M_\beta^4$, respectively, $\alpha^+ = \alpha$, $\alpha^- = \beta$, such that the combined notation $\pm(K_\alpha)$ stands for *either* $+K_{\alpha^+}$ *or* $-K_{\alpha^-}$.

Conventionally it is customary to refer to a major/minor key not by $Q_{\alpha^\pm}$ (i.e., the first element of the core under quintic order) but equivalently by the major/minor final Q_{α^++1} or Q_{α^-+4}. For example, $+K_{-4}$ is "E♭ major" since E♭ $= Q_{-3}$; similarly, $-K_4$ is "G♯ minor" since G♯ $= Q_8$, etc.[9]

Following common usage we shall refer henceforth to the final of a key as *tonic*, and to its nucleus as the *tonic triad*. Also, we shall refer to the accidental index of a key as *key signature* or just *signature*.

Definition 11.4. Relative Major/Minor Keys

Let $+K_{\alpha^+}$ and $-K_{\alpha^-}$ be a pair of keys, one major and the other minor, with tonics $Q_{t^\pm}$, respectively, $t^+ = \alpha^+ + 1$, $t^- = \alpha^- + 4$.

We shall refer to the pair as *relative* if $\alpha^+ = \alpha^-$ or equivalently, $t^- = t^+ + 3$.

Example 11.5. $+K_{-8} =$ C♭ major and $-K_{-8} =$ A♭ minor are a relative pair of major/minor keys.

$+K_4 =$ B major and $-K_4 =$ G♯ minor are a *standard* relative pair, that is, a pair of relative major/minor keys that satisfy $-6 \leq \alpha^\pm \leq 5$ (the key signature consists of no more than five flats or six sharps; see Definition 10.43 and Proposition 10.44).

Table 11.1 lists the 24 *standard* major/minor key *classes* $\pm(KC_\alpha)$ vertically by key signature from small (five flats) to large (six sharps).[10] Relative pairs are aligned horizontally.

We now turn to another important major/minor key-relationship.

---

[9] This is unlike the practice by which one refers to a (dyadic) mode only by *Mu*, that is, by the tribal class, Lydian, Ionian, etc., to which it may be reduced (see Definition 10.8). Recall, however, that a dyadic mode is traditionally assumed to satisfy $\alpha = -1$, -2 (*cantus durus, cantus mollis*), so that a given *Mu* specifies at most two distinct finals.

[10] A key class is a mode class in the sense of Definition 10.7. Note that the number of standard major/minor *keys* is indefinitely large (because a key consists of *a score*, in addition to a core and nucleus), unlike the 24 standard major/minor key classes. The number of key *classes* reduces to 24 only under the assumption of standard representation (that is, the key signature consists of no more than five flats or six sharps).

Table 11.1 The 24 standard major/minor key classes. Relative pairs are aligned horizontally

Major key class.	Conventional name	Minor key class	Conventional name
$+KC_{-6}$	D♭ major	$-KC_{-6}$	B♭ minor
$+KC_{-5}$	A♭ major	$-KC_{-5}$	F minor
$+KC_{-4}$	E♭ major	$-KC_{-4}$	C minor
$+KC_{-3}$	B♭ major	$-KC_{-3}$	G minor
$+KC_{-2}$	F major	$-KC_{-2}$	D minor
$+KC_{-1}$	C major	$-KC_{-1}$	A minor
$+KC_0$	G major	$-KC_0$	E minor
$+KC_1$	D major	$-KC_1$	B minor
$+KC_2$	A major	$-KC_2$	F♯ minor
$+KC_3$	E major	$-KC_3$	C♯ minor
$+KC_4$	B major	$-KC_4$	G♯ minor
$+KC_5$	F♯ major	$-KC_5$	D♯ minor

Definition 11.6. Parallel Major/Minor Keys

Let $+K_{\alpha^+}$ and $-K_{\alpha^-}$ be a pair of keys, one major and the other minor, with tonics $Q_{t^\pm}$, respectively, $t^+ = \alpha^+ + 1$, $t^- = \alpha^- + 4$.

We shall refer to the pair as *parallel* if $t^+ = t^-$ or equivalently, $\alpha^- = \alpha^+ - 3$.

Example 11.7. $+K_{-8} = $ C♭ major and $-K_{-11} = $ C♭ minor are a parallel pair of major/minor keys.

$+K_4 = $ B major and $-K_1 = $ B minor are a *standard* parallel pair.

Note that unlike relative keys, given a standard key, a parallel key that is also standard does not necessarily exist.

*Proposition 11.8. Let $+K_{\alpha^+}$ and $-K_{\alpha^-}$ be a parallel pair of keys with tonics $Q_{t^\pm}$, respectively, $t^+ = \alpha^+ + 1$, $t^- = \alpha^- + 4$.

Then both keys are standard if, and only if, $-2 \leq t^+ \leq 6$.

In Fig. 11.2 the tonics of all standard major/minor keys (in upper/lower-case letters, respectively) are ordered horizontally by fifths. Illustrating Proposition 11.8, parallel pairs are vertically aligned (for example, B♭ major and B♭ minor).

11.4 Robust Triadic Keys and Schenker's "Mixture"

By Definition 10.34 a mode is "robust" if a score element, represented as a scale degree (u, v), is not second-order chromatic. For example, a major triadic key is robust if[11]

---

[11] Concerning the caret notation for scale degrees, review Sect. 10.3.

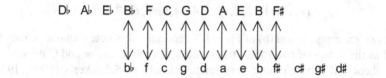

Fig. 11.2 Standard parallel major/minor keys

Fig. 11.3 Two Beethoven excerpts as robust keys. (**a**) Piano Sonata in C major, Op. 53 ("Waldstein"), I, mm. 1–13; (**b**) Piano Sonata in C minor, Op. 27/1, II, 1–16

$$(u, v) = \hat{1}, \flat\hat{2}, \hat{2}, \flat\hat{3}, \hat{3}, \hat{4}, \#\hat{4}, \hat{5}, \flat\hat{6}, \hat{6}, \flat\hat{7}, \hat{7}.$$

The two excerpts (a) and (b) of Fig. 11.3, represented as note sequences, may be viewed as the scores of two robust triadic keys, namely C major and C minor.[12]

The theory of robust triadic keys relates closely to Schenker's (1906, 1935) influential idea of major/minor "mixture" (*Mischung*), that is, "using tones from the parallel minor in a major key or the reverse" (Aldwell and Schachter 2003, p. 401). Indeed, chords in major that include $\flat\hat{3}, \flat\hat{6},$ or $\flat\hat{7},$ such as $\text{I}\flat$, VI, IV$\flat$, or V^7/IV, or chords in minor that include $\#\hat{3}, \#\hat{6},$ or $\#\hat{7},$ such as I$\#$, IV$\#$, or V$\#$, are among the most prevalent chromatic chords.[13] And yet, so are chords that include $\flat\hat{2}$ or $\#\hat{4}$ such as $\flat$II, V^7/V, and the so-called augmented-sixth chords, all of which cannot be explained in terms of major/minor mixture.

Interestingly, Rothstein notes that

> at one point early in the book (§§39–40), Schenker [1906] hypothetically includes all the modes on a single tonic under the rubric of mixture, so that F$\#$ (from C Lydian) is included within the direct orbit of a C tonic. He quickly banishes the church modes, however, retaining only the "Phrygian" second degree. (2003, footnote on p. 221)

In other words, Schenker's (1906) mixture-derived degrees were at some point conceived as a set of five, specifically, the first-order chromatic degrees.[14] See also Sects. 12.3 and 13.3.

Proposition 11.9. Let $+K_{\alpha^+}$ and $-K_{\alpha^-}$ be a pair of robust relative keys with scores $SCORE^+$ and $SCORE^-$, respectively. Let $(s, t)^\pm \in SCORE^\pm$ be a score element, and set $°(s, t)^\pm = (u, v)^\pm = IQ_{i^\pm}$.

Then $s^+ \equiv s^-$ (mod 12) if, and only if, one of the following two conditions, A or B, holds.

A. $i^- = i^+ - 3$, where $-2 \le i^+ \le 6$.
B. $i^- = i^+ + 9$, where $-5 \le i^+ \le -3$.

Proof. Using Definition 10.21,

$$Q_{\alpha^+ + 1} + IQ_{i^+} \equiv (s, t)^+,$$
$$Q_{\alpha^- + 4} + IQ_{i^-} \equiv (s, t)^-.$$

Since the keys are relative we have $\alpha^+ = \alpha^-$. Suppose that $s^+ \equiv s^-$ (mod 12). Then $i^+ - i^- \equiv 3$ (mod 12). Since $-5 \le i^\pm \le 6$ (Theorem 10.28), Condition

---

[12] In (a) one must exclude from consideration the non-harmonic grace-note C$\#$ in m. 4. Concerning the representation of scores as "scores" (that is, note sequences), see Sect. 7.1.

[13] "Roman numerals" may be viewed as the chordal analogues to scale degrees. In general the notational device shall be employed informally, following mainstream harmonic theory. See, however, Definition 14.18, "Harmonic Degree."

[14] Rothstein (2003) notes that by Schenker's (1906) terminology mixture is not a "chromatic" phenomenon.

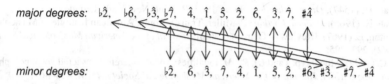

major degrees: ♭2̂,   ♭6̂,   ♭3̂, ♭7̂,   4̂,   1̂,   5̂,   2̂,   6̂,   3̂,   7̂,   #4̂

minor degrees: ♭2̂,   6̂,   3̂,   7̂,   4̂,   1̂,   5̂,   2̂,   #6̂, #3̂,   #7̂, #4̂

Fig. 11.4 Score elements of two robust relative keys are enharmonically related if, and only if, their scale-degree representations are vertically aligned or diagonally connected

Fig. 11.5 Chopin, Scherzo, Op. 31. (**a**) Mm. 1–9; (**b**) mm. 49–58

A or B follows. Suppose that Condition A or B holds. Then $i^+ - i^- \equiv 3 \pmod{12}$, implying that $s^+ \equiv s^- \pmod{12}$. Q.E.D.

Figure 11.4 illustrates the proposition. For a pair of robust relative keys the relation $s^+ \equiv s^- \pmod{12}$ holds, where $(s, t)^\pm$ is a score element, if, and only if, $°(s, t)^\pm$ is a pair of vertically aligned or diagonally connected degrees.

The two excerpts of Fig. 11.5, from Chopin's Scherzo, Op. 31, may be viewed as the scores of a relative pair of robust keys, namely B♭ minor in (a) and D♭ major in (b). Note, for example, that a pair of score elements $(s, t)^-$ in (a) and $(s, t)^+$ in (b) satisfy $s^- \equiv 9 \equiv s^+ \pmod{12}$, if, and only if, $°(s, t)^- = \#7̂$, $°(s, t)^+ = ♭6̂$ (see the asterisks).

References

Aldwell, E., & Schachter, C. (2003). *Harmony and voice leading* (3rd ed.). Belmont: Wadsworth Group.

Cohen, D. (2002). Notes, scales, and modes in the earlier middle ages. In T. Christensen (Ed.), *The Cambridge history of Western music theory* (pp. 307–363). Cambridge: Cambridge University Press.

Glarean, H. (1547). *Dodecachordon*. Basel. 1967. Reprint, New York: Broude.

Glarean, H. (1965). *Dodecachordon* (C. Miller, Trans.). Rome: American Institute of Musicology.

Houghton, E. (1967). [Review of Glarean (1965)]. *Journal of the American Musicological Society,* *20*(2), 292–295.

Judd, C. (1992). Modal types and *Ut, Re, Mi* tonalities: Tonal coherence in sacred vocal polyphony from about 1500. *Journal of the American Musicological Society, 45*(3), 428–467.

Lester, J. (1989). *Between modes and keys: German theory 1592–1802*. Stuyvesant: Pendragon.

Lippius, J. (1612). *Synopsis musicae novae*. Strasbourg.

Powers, H. (1992). Is mode real? Pietro Aron, the octenary system, and polyphony. *Basler Jahrbuch, 16,* 9–53.

Rothstein, W. (2003). A reply to Brian Hyer. *Journal of Music Theory, 47*(1), 215–222.

Schenker, H. (1906). *Harmonielehre*. Stuttgart: Cotta.

Schenker, H. (1935). *Der freie Satz* (Rev. 1956). Vienna: Universal.

Terhardt, E. (1976). Ein psychoakustisch begründetes Konzept der Musikalischen Konsonanz. *Acustica, 36,* 121–137.

Terhardt, E. (1984). The concept of musical consonance: A link between music and psychoacoustics. *Music Perception, 1,* 276–295.

Wiering, F. (1998). Internal and external views of the modes. In C. Judd (Ed.), *Tonal structures in early music* (pp. 87–107). New York: Garland.

Zarlino, G. (1558). *Le istitutioni harmoniche*. Venice. 1965. Reprint, New York: Broude.

Chapter 12
Modes, Semi-keys, and Keys: A Reality Check

Abstract Section 12.1 analyzes Harold Powers's provocative claim that "mode is not real." It is shown that this claim is conceivably true only under the medieval, "octenary" doctrine. Section 12.2 is a critique of Gregory Barnett's related claim that the seventeenth-century "church keys" "are not modes." It is shown that to the contrary, the church keys are precisely triadic semi-keys. Finally, Sect. 12.3 revisits empirical data, originally put forward by Krumhansl and Kessler which support the existence of a nucleus-core-cluster hierarchy from a receiver-related perspective, all in the context of triadic keys. Transmitter-related data, which support the existence of a distinction between first- and second-order chromatic degrees, is presented. This latter finding undermines the notion (suggested by Krumhansl and others), that listeners form an internal representation of tonality on the basis of note distribution.

12.1 The Octenary Doctrine and the "Reality of Mode"

In 1992 Harold Powers stunned the musicological world by pronouncing that mode is a fictitious construct: "... the answer to the rhetorical question in my title—'is mode real?'—is 'no': at least, 'no' in the sense in which the term 'mode' is customarily used in connection with Renaissance polyphony" (p. 12).

It is all too easy to explain away Powers's pronouncement as the expression of deep frustration. After all, was it not Pietro Aron who stated already in 1525 that an explanation of the modes in polyphony "... was abandoned by the celebrated musicians... not through ignorance but merely because it proved otherwise troublesome and exacting at the time"?[1] Quoting Aron, Judd begins her 2002 essay on Renaissance modal theory by making a number of suggestions as to why "the word

---

[1] Trans. from Strunk (1998, p. 417).

E. Agmon, *The Languages of Western Tonality*, Computational Music Science, DOI 10.1007/978-3-642-39587-1_12, © Springer-Verlag Berlin Heidelberg 2013

'mode' is one of the most richly textured and problematic terms of Renaissance discourse about music" (p. 364). Subsequently she states:

> Issues such as these prompted Harold Powers, one of the most prominent scholars of the history of mode, to pose the question "Is Mode Real?" Powers's provocative title was not simply a rhetorical gesture but rather the culmination of a scholarly career which consistently hammered away at modern notions of "modality" as an inherent property of music of the Renaissance, analogous to, yet distinct from, common-practice "tonality." (p. 365)

But Powers, author of the landmark article "Mode" in *The New Grove Dictionary of Music and Musicians* (1980), is not someone easily frustrated or intimidated by difficulties or problems. Most of the 1992 article relates, in fact, more to its subtitle, "Pietro Aron, the Octenary System, and Polyphony," than to its title (pp. 21–43). Powers (1992, p. 23) sets himself the exceedingly difficult task of showing that Aron's method of modal assignment, baffling as it seems, at times, from a modern perspective, nonetheless obeys a quirky logic all of its own:

> ... the interesting questions are not what assignments Aron made for which pieces, or even whether his theory makes sense in our terms, for in many respects it does not. What is interesting is whether it makes sense in his terms, which it does, and brilliantly, sometimes with what a couple of centuries later would be called Jesuitical casuistry.

With breathtaking virtuosity Powers solves not only the "easy cases," as he puts it, but most of the hard ones as well, that is, "...Aron's [modal] assignments [that] have proven rather puzzling" (*ibid.*, p. 31).

Powers, in short, was not "prompted" to question the reality of mode by the concept's supposedly inherently problematic nature, as Judd and others (for example, Rivera 1993, p. 73), would have it. Indeed, Powers couldn't care less if "modality" gives *us* modern scholars a hard time. For "mode," he believes,

> ... is all bound up in sixteenth-century musical culture, not only as a living doctrine of the music of the church and a heritage from the Middle Ages but also as a musical construct being experimented with by members of the culture, from both humanistic and traditional points of view; it is thoroughly "emic" and requires study on its own terms, as well as in relation to any music with which it may be connected. (1981, p. 439)

Powers, in other words, is more than happy to embrace "mode" as an "emic," culturally bound construct, Jesuitical casuistry and all. As an "etic," rationally defensible concept, however, "mode," for Powers, is *really* unreal.

Powers's pronouncement that mode is not real may fruitfully be studied in terms of four claims, listed below. Essential to these claims is the notion of "tonal type," which refers to a notational feature of Renaissance printed music. A tonal type (henceforth, TT) is a triple (Σ, Φ, C)—*Sigma* for *Signature*, *Phi* for *Final*, and *C* for *Clef*—where $\Sigma = \emptyset, \flat$ is the notated signature (usually either an empty signature or a signature of one flat); Φ is the notated root of the final triad (usually C, D, F, G, or A, as well as E if $\Sigma = \emptyset$ or B$\flat$ if $\Sigma = \flat$); and $C = $ HI, LO is the notated clef combination (usually, either high clefs, the so-called *chiavette*, or the low, so-called "normal" clefs). Powers's four claims, then, are the following:

1. As a theoretical construct, "mode" is not really real.
2. As ink marks on paper, TTs are as "real" as one may possibly wish.

3. TTs in Renaissance culture "represent" modes. In other words, there exists a relation from TTs to modes.
4. The relation from TTs to modes is *not* a function; in particular, a given TT may represent more than one mode.

As we shall see, one may safely accept Claim 2 as true. One may also accept Claim 3 as true, noting that despite the anti-theoretical Claim 1, the claim is theory-dependent. Claim 4 is true, however, only under the so-called "octenary" theoretic scheme. Under the alternative, dodecachordal scheme, tonal types *are* modes, and therefore, if tonal types are real (Claim 2), then so are dodecachordal modes. Since Powers fails to support his octenary bias with argument (in fact, he can hardly contain his hostile sentiments towards Glarean, the most notable proponent of dodecachordal theory), his claim that mode is not real, if true, applies only to octenary modes. This result, however, is far from surprising, given the serious flaws of octenary theory, both logically and empirically, pointed out by Glarean and others.

We shall now consider each of the four claims in turn.

Claim 1: "Mode" Is a Theoretical Fabrication

Powers makes little effort to conceal his deep-seated distrust of theorists and theories. Referring to "theorists from other musical cultures" he goes so far as to conclude the 1992 article by stating that "... the ingenuity with which they worked out their hypothetical models and theoretical fabrications [*sic*] is right up there with the fancies and elaborations of the tonal and atonal theorizing with which we are more familiar. Plus ça change..." Indeed, although for Powers (1992, p. 18) "... Aron and Glarean are of major import as theorists of polyphonic modality," he is quick to remind us that "... they were [mere?] theorists; we must treat them with proper respect, as distinguished colleagues from another musical age, not as mere informants."

Happily for the purposes of the present discussion, there is no need to address Powers's anti-theoretic rhetoric.

Claim 2: Tonal Types Are Real

Strikingly different is Powers's attitude towards the theory of tonal types as applied to the study of Renaissance music. "Hermelink classified Palestrina's compositions *objectively* according to their various combinations of system, cleffing, and final" he states with approval (1981, p. 439), "and only then did he *subjectively* analyze and illustrate each type with respect to its musical properties" (emphasis added).

For Powers, in other words, not only is the act of classifying Renaissance compositions by TTs qualitatively distinct from the act of analyzing their musical properties, the former act is clearly of superior value.

Powers's objective/subjective dichotomy is highly misleading, however, for it draws attention away from the crucial question of communication. A listener, after all, has no choice but to "subjectively" analyze the musical properties of a performed composition, for in general its "objective" notation is not available for scrutiny. This is quite apart from the question of whether notation can always be trusted (as Powers assumes), as a faithful representation of a composition's musical properties.

Despite these reservations, we may safely accept the claim, that TTs are real, as true.

Claim 3: TTs in Renaissance Culture "Represent" Modes

Powers (1992, p. 14) notes that "... from the second quarter of the 16th century onwards, composers themselves came more and more to make conscious use of tonal types in an orderly way, to represent the members of modal systems for symbolic or didactic purposes. ..." In other words, even though modes are dubious constructs, in Renaissance culture TTs may be said to "represent" them. For example, the tonal type (♭, F, HI) (that is, one-flat signature, F final, high clefs) represents mode 5 (Lydian). As Powers (1981, p. 439) stresses, "... a tonal type may be intended to *represent* a mode in a categorical scheme; that is not to say, though, that the tonal type in question *is* that mode."

Let us tentatively accept Powers's distinction between "representing" a mode and being one. The question remains: what are those entities, namely modes, that TTs are said to represent?

Powers would have preferred, of course, not to be hard-pressed for an answer. However, although "in the second half of the century, cyclic sets of works began to appear that explicitly are claimed to have been composed according to modes" (1981, p. 435), the *exact* relation of TTs to modes in such cycles is often open to interpretation. For example, Cipriano de Rore's first book of five-voice madrigals (1542) is "unmistakably intended as modal" (1981, p. 443). But although Powers finds an orderly relation from TTs to modes in madrigals 1–17, he concedes that "the last three madrigals stand outside the cyclic plan." In other words, independently of a given madrigal's "objective" position within the cycle, Powers is somehow able to determine, "subjectively" as it were, whether or not it makes sense to claim that its TT "represents" this mode or another. As he notes, "... the assignment of a piece to a mode should not be blatantly incompatible with *theoretical descriptions of the mode*. That is, one could not suppose that the tonal type ♭-g_2-G [i.e., (♭, G, HI)] could ever represent mode 6, or that tonal type ♮-c_1-G [(∅, G, LO)] could ever represent mode 5, and so on" (emphasis added). Against his will, Powers finds himself dependent on the "theoretical fabrications" of his "distinguished colleagues from another musical age."

Given that this is the case, it is legitimate to ask: What exactly *does* the theoretical description of mode consist of? Surely, it consists of the notions "background system of notes" (to which Powers 1992, p. 15, refers as the "Guidonian diatonic"), "final," and "ambitus." In other words, a given modal assignment may be judged "blatantly incompatible with theoretical descriptions of the mode" if Σ, Φ, and C fail to correspond ("blatantly," at least) to the theoretically defined background system, final, and ambitus, respectively.

The assumption that such correspondences necessarily exist, though convenient, is of course simplistic. This is because, once again, "background system," "final," and "ambitus" *must be communicated*; it does not suffice for them to exist as ink on paper. Thus, for example, $\Sigma = \varnothing$ does not guarantee that so-called *cantus durus* is the background system of notes, for it is possible that each and every B is individually lowered by a flat sign. Similarly, $\Phi = G$ does not guarantee that G is the "real" final,[2] and $C = \text{HI}$ does not guarantee a higher register (of the highest voice) relative to $C = \text{LO}$.

Nonetheless, for the sake of argument we may certainly accept the claim that there exists a relation from TTs to modes, such that the notated signature, final, and clefs correspond, respectively, to the theoretical notions of background system, final, and ambitus.

Claim 4: The Relation from TTs to Modes Is Not a Function

Note that TTs may readily be construed as equivalent, under certain restrictions, to (triadic) modes (Definition 10.4). As we have seen, the signature Σ corresponds to the background system; the root Φ of the final triad corresponds to the final; and the cleffing C corresponds to the ambitus. Similarly, a mode is uniquely specified by a seven-element "core" orderable by fifths starting with Q_α (for some α), a final $\left(\underline{w},\ \underline{x}\right) = Q_{\alpha+\mu}$, for some μ, $0 \leq \mu \leq 5$; and a score. Therefore, if $\alpha = -1,\ -2$ (equivalently, the signature is either empty or contains one flat), $\left(\underline{w},\ \underline{x}\right) = \text{C}, \text{D}, \text{F}$, G, or A, as well as B♭ if $\alpha = -2$ or E if $\alpha = -1$, and there are somehow two main types of scores, namely HI ("authentic") and LO ("plagal"), we have that Σ is equivalent to the core, Φ to the final, and C to the score.[3]

---

[2] As Powers himself notes (1992, footnote on p. 28), "Marchetto had written that it would be senseless to call a piece that had the species of mode 3 throughout and then simply tacked on a D sol re at the end, mode 1 rather than mode 3...."

[3] The relation of C (cleffing) to the ambitus—in comparison to the relation of Σ (signature) to the core and of Φ to the final—is rather inconsistent. For example, on p. 451 Powers (1981) states that "the fact that the registral contrast is the reverse of the norm—the plagal representative in the

By Claim 3 there exists a relation in Renaissance culture from TTs into modes. By Claim 4, however, this relation is *not* a function: "... there are one-to-many correspondences going both ways: most of the modal categories can be represented by more than one tonal type, and occasionally a single tonal type can be found representing more than one modal category" (1981, p. 451). It is clear that for Powers it is the *second* type of one-to-many correspondence, "a single tonal type ... representing more than one modal category," that is crucial to his claim that mode is not real. Immediately after making his provocative claim in the 1992 article (see the opening paragraph of this section) he adds: "A 16th-century piece is not in a 'mode' that is part of a 'modal system' in a way analogous to the way an 18th-century piece is necessarily in a 'tonality' that is part of the 'tonal system'." And how exactly *is* "modality," for Powers, distinct from "tonality"? The following paragraph makes clear.

> If we could interview three theorists of the late 19th century, of no matter what ontological or epistemological bias—let us say, Hugo Riemann, F. A. Gevaert, and Ebenezer Prout— and ask each to name the tonality of Beethoven's Pastoral Symphony or Tempest Sonata, their answers would agree: F Major and d minor, respectively. Or if we were to show each a diatonic movement or piece, of the period 1750–1850, with no key signature and a final root-position Major triad having pitch-class C in the bass, they would agree that those rudimentary and purely objective features—diatonic content, no key signature, final C-Major triad—minimally marked "the tonality" of the item as "C Major." But let us imagine some item of 16th-century vocal polyphony with the same rudimentary objective markers—that is, diatonic content, no key signature, and a concluding root-position C-Major triad—and let me add even one further restriction: the piece is set in the so-called "chiavette" (clefs g_2, c_2, c_3, F_3). Now if we could ask three theoretically sophisticated musicians of the late 16th century to name the mode of that piece, we might get three different answers altogether. Orlando di Lasso's student Leonhard Lechner would call such a piece mode 6, Hypolydian if you prefer. Pietro Aron's disciple Aiguino would call such a piece mode 7, that is a variety of Mixolydian with an "extraordinary" final on c'. And for Heinrich Glarean's follower Alexander Utendal, the last piece in his "Seven penitential psalms .. plus five themes .. from the prophets .. accommodated .. to the twelve modes of the Dodecachordon," with the same minimal markers, was Hypoionian, that is mode 12. (1992, pp. 10–11)

Now Powers's conception of "tonality," as well as the analogy that he draws between "tonality" and "modality," is seriously flawed. In the first case, similarly to what we saw in connection with Claim 3, disregarding the question of communication he identifies tonality with such *notational* features as signature and final triad. In the second case, he assumes that locutions such as (say) "F major" and "Lydian" are analogous, where in fact they are not: "F major" specifies not only the tribal class to which the mode may be reduced, namely "major" (Ionian), but also the final, namely "F."[4] Be that as it may, it is clear that for Powers "modality," unlike

---

modal pair with the same final lies higher than the authentic, not lower—is of no consequence. Lasso's intentions are perfectly clear from the ordering alone." Correspondingly, the distinction between "authentic" and "plagal" modal messages can hardly be made rigorous.

[4] See also Sect. 11.3, footnote 9 in particular.

"tonality," is not real, precisely because, unlike "tonality," a function from its "minimal markers" (the tonal types), to its "categories" (the modes), does not exist.

Here, then, is the crucial question. Why is it that Powers does not find a function from TTs to modes? The answer is as simple as it is startling. *Powers refuses to accept that the number of modal categories is exactly twelve.* Consider the tonal type ($\varnothing$, C, HI) that he uses as an example in his imaginary sixteenth-century interview. Under a dodecachordal scheme this TT may (reasonably) be said to represent exactly one category, namely Hypoionian. This is true of all similar cases of "a single tonal type ... representing more than one modal category"; in particular, ($\flat$, F, HI) represents Ionian, not Ionian *or* Lydian.

Note well that we are *not* claiming that the dodecachordal modality of this or that polyphonic composition is never, "subjectively" as it were, open to interpretation. Rather, a dodecachordal mode is uniquely specified by *an agreed-upon* set of "background system," "final," and "ambitus" (a set that may or may not correspond, in a given case, to Powers's "minimal markers," though for present purposes we assume that it does). At issue, once again, is an essential distinction between "mode" and "modal *communication*." Modal communication is not only context dependent, but, like all forms of communication, comes with no guarantee of success. It is therefore perfectly possible that the same *transmitted* mode be received differently by different receivers.[5]

Our analysis has led to the conclusion that *by Powers's own criterion*, dodecachordal modality is analogous to tonality, and must count as "real." Indeed, under the dodecachordal scheme Powers's distinction between "being" a mode and "representing" one is either vacuous or else reduces to the distinction between an authentic/plagal mode and the authentic/plagal tribal *class* to which it may be reduced (see Definition 10.8). In other words, under the constraints noted above (a signature that is either empty or contains one flat, and so forth) the function from TTs to modes is a bijection; for all practical purposes, therefore, TTs *are* modes. However, if "mode" is understood as an authentic/plagal tribal *class*, authentic/plagal Lydian, Ionian, and so forth, the function from TTs to modes is not one-to-one, such that TTs, indeed, may be said to "represent" modes. For example, both ($\varnothing$, D, HI) and ($\flat$, G, LO) "represent," that is, are reducible to, Hypodorian.[6]

One might have expected Powers to at least *acknowledge* the connection between his octenary bias and his provocative claim that mode is not real. Yet quite to the contrary, towards the end of the 1992 article he makes every possible effort to downplay the significance of the octenary/dodecachordal distinction, even to the point of trying to convince his readers that "the significant difference between

---

[5] Consider Lodovico Zacconi, who assigns Palestrina's madrigal "Vestiva i colli," with "minimal markers" ($\varnothing$, A, HI) to mode 2 (Hypodorian), even though, as Powers does not fail to point out (1974, p. 34), his "...twelve modes include the degree A as an Aeolian *finalis*." Yet it is perfectly possible that, due to the madrigal's *Prima parte* ending on D, as well as some local emphases on D (see, for example, the beginning of the first phrase), for Zacconi the final of this madrigal was D, not A.

[6] See Powers (1981), p. 440.

Aron's and Glarean's theories about modality is not the difference between eight modes and twelve modes ..." (p. 43). Moreover, rather than arguing rationally in favor of octenary modality, early on in the same article Powers launches against his intellectual adversaries, particularly Heinrich Glarean, what regretfully can only be described as a thinly disguised yet cleverly orchestrated *ad hominem* attack.

The attack begins on p. 17 by dubbing Zarlino a plagiarist, a move that draws attention away from the finding that Glarean's theory was remarkably quick to find supporters on the continent (cf. Lester 1989, p. 7: "only eleven years after the publication of the *Dodecachordon*, Zarlino accepts the twelve modes with neither question nor acknowledgement"). On the following page Powers acknowledges that "by the last quarter of the 16th century composers were cognizant of two basic modal theories, each with two or more varieties." However, "the great masters," de Rore, Lasso, and Palestrina, "represented" in their works the octenary system. Only "various lesser musicians," among whom Powers counts Claude Le Jeune, "from time to time composed works demonstrating their interest in one or another of the current twelve-mode systems."

The attack reaches its climax on pp. 21–22, where Powers compares Glarean to Aron. Although the characterization of Glarean as "a Catholic humanist" (p. 21) may not strike one as derogatory at first, in retrospect one realizes that its main purpose is to underscore the finding that Glarean was not a professional musician. Aron, after all, "was a cantor and magister of characteristically medieval scholastic bent" (p. 22). (Glarean is thus subtly cast together with the "lesser musicians" of the sixteenth century who favored the dodecachordal system.)[7] Be that as it may, Aron, for Powers, is by far the greater intellectual hero. "Rather than synthesize a theory and then hunt up, or cook up [*sic*], illustrations for it" Powers states, "he undertook to apply an already existing theory in toto to any and all written polyphony as found in the repertory of his time."

This statement is way out of line on at least three counts. First, "to apply an already existing theory" is apparently a case of plagiarism only if the theory is dodecachordal; to be the *originator* of a theory, on the other hand, is to "synthesize" (that is, fabricate) one, at least if the theory, once again, is dodecachordal. Second, selecting appropriate illustrations for one's dodecachordal theory is a despicable "hunt." By contrast, applying the octenary theory to a large repertoire is an admirable feat, no matter that one must resort to "Jesuitical casuistry" in the process. Finally, as Powers knows all too well, other than the rejected "Hyperaeolian" (the "authentic" B-mode) the only modes for which Glarean was forced to "cook up" *polyphonic* examples are the *true* Hypolydian or Lydian (as distinct from transposed Hypoionian or Ionian). Though Powers may choose to be tolerant of and even amused by Lanfranco's "literally specious device" by

---

[7] Even though Glarean was not a professional musician, his musical intuition is remarkably keen, and his ability to express it verbally is impressive. See, for example, the passage from *Dodecachordon*, quoted in Sect. 11.1, where Glarean describes the aurally disturbing tritone of Lydian and Phrygian (Book II, Chapter 11).

which F-G-A-B-c is supposed to retain its identity as the third species of fifth even if B is replaced by B♭ (1992, p. 16), he should certainly know better than to ridicule Glarean (or anyone else, for that matter) for refusing to accept such a "sleight-of-[Guidonian]-hand."[8]

Anyone reading *Dodecachordon* can hardly fail to be moved by Glarean's Prefatory Letter to Cardinal Otto Truchsess von Waldburg, which opens with the tale of a subversive Greek musician, Timotheus of Miletus (Glarean 1965, p. 37):

> Most Reverend Father: In book 14 Athenaeus relates that according to Artemon, Timotheus of Miletus, a very famous authority on music, was censured by the Lacedaemonians as being the corruptor of ancient and austere music because he used a system which had more strings than did the *magadis*. Divus Severinus [Boethius] also declares in the preface of *De Musica* that Timotheus was expelled from Laconia because he added one string to the usual number of strings, and made music more effeminate. And he recounts in Greek the decree pertaining to Timotheus, in which the following is contained: "Therefore the Spartans were inflamed with anger against Timotheus of Miletus because he, by imparting a multiple kind of music, was detrimental to the minds of the youths whom he had received for teaching, and interfered with the sobriety of virtuous conduct." Following Greek writers, Boethius says this about Timotheus.
>
> If this is so, and it has been transmitted by trustworthy writers, what am I to think is going to happen to me, who would add four modes to the eight modes of musical song which for so many centuries now have been celebrated among all, and who would make a *dodecachordon* from an *octochordon*; who would reproach all former times for ignorance, as it were, and censure them for negligence; nay more, who would even recall the two modes rejected by all former men, cast off, relegated to exile and dead as it were, and now, God willing (as the expression goes), who would accord them a homecoming and bring them back to life; who am indeed a person deserving to be driven out, expelled, and thrust out, not only from Laconia, but from the whole world in which rational men live. Unless I shall have cleared myself of these harsh charges, these grave accusations, and shall have shown the reader that the matter is different from that for which I may be reproached, what remains but that I yield in defeat and pay the penalty for my audacity?

As Fuller (1996, p. 193) notes in reference to this passage,

> So dangerous does a hostile religious reaction appear to Glarean that he not only preempts attack by imagining his own trial and graceful submission to sentencing should his eloquence fail to produce a successful defense, but also closes his "preface" with a humble submission of *Dodecachordon* to the College of Cardinals "for examination by the moderators of all church law." They will, he trusts, find that he has treated his subject in a manner "mindful of Christian piety and the dignity of the Church."

---

[8] Powers (1998, footnote on p. 339) repeats the charge that "dodecachordal theorists," for whom "...of course an F-tonality with B-flat would have to be regarded as a transposition of the corresponding 'Ionian' C-mode," "... were faced with the problem of finding (or inventing) representative musical instances for their 'true' Lydian and Hypolydian, the F-modes with B-natural," as if to pretend that the fourth species of fifth is the third species is no problem at all. As we have seen in Sect. 11.1, Glarean in fact offers a very convincing explanation for what he describes as "changing from the Lydian to the Ionian." Glarean's explanation is the basis for our own Definition 10.10 (key, semi-key). By Theorem 10.11, which follows from the definition, a semi-key is not reducible to Lydian. See also Sect. 12.2.

In the final analysis, however, it is not Glarean who should be standing there, defending his case, so to speak, in front of the Supreme Court for Music-Theoretical Disputes. In Hucbald's late ninth- or early tenth-century formulation of the octenary modal system A, B, and C are simply "passed over" as potential finals in favor of D, E, F, and G.[9] Politics aside, therefore, it is Hucbald and his followers, not Glarean, who must defend *their* blatantly *ad hoc* rejection of no fewer than three finals. For, as Glarean most aptly puts it, ". . . it is also worthy of censure that he [Gaffurius], with the common lot, places four final keys on seven octave-modes, having rejected three when only one, the ♮ should deserve to be rejected" (Glarean 1965, p. 102).[10]

In one of the most extreme cases in the history of Western music of theory lagging behind practice, the recognition of six modal finals (rather than just four) comes some seven centuries too late. By that time, Western music has undergone some dramatic changes. Although Glarean's modal theory is essentially dyadic, as recognized explicitly in the early seventeenth century by Johannes Lippius (and already suggested by Zarlino in 1558), the modal system of Renaissance polyphony was for all practical purposes triadic.

12.2   The Seventeenth-Century "Church Keys" as Triadic Semi-keys

Table 12.1 reproduces Table 10.1. The table shows that the tribal classes, to which dyadic (respectively, triadic) semi-keys may be reduced, fall short of including Lydian (respectively, Lydian and Phrygian). I propose that the so-called "church keys" of seventeenth-century music are triadic semi-keys (Definition 10.10).[11]

---

[9] "Quatuor a primis tribus . . . ," literally, "the four [notes] after the first three." In Babb's (1978, p. 38) translation: "passing over the first three notes, the next four, namely the lichanos hypaton [D], the hypate meson [E], the parhypate meson [F], and the lichanos meson [G] are used in constructing the four modes or tropes."

[10] "Sed illud quoque reprehensione dignum, quod cum uulgo quatuor finaleis ponit claueis in septem diapason modulis, reiectis tribus, cum una dumtaxat ♮ reijcienda esset." Citing Gerbert's *Scriptores* (I, p. 41), Miller states in his Introduction to Glarean 1965 that "as early as the 9th century, . . . Aurelian reports that there were some singers who thought certain antiphons could not be adopted to the existing modal formulas, and thereupon Charlemagne ordered that four more modes should be added" (p. 19). Powers (1992, pp. 21–22) notes that Glarean's "construction of twelve modes" was "influenced" and "in a sense justified" by "a dodecachordal construction of the monk and abbott William of Hirsau, as well as by the references to modes beyond the Gregorian eight (*toni medii*) by Berno of Reichenau. Glarean had read both these 11th-century authors in a manuscript to which he had access in the years 1530–1536, where he also was able to read Boethius and other authors." Fuller (1996, footnote on p. 199) notes that Johannes Gallicus [Legrense] ". . . accepts a, b♮, and c as legitimate (not irregular) finals," although "there is no evidence that Glarean was acquainted with Gallicus's treatise or ideas. . . ."

[11] The term "church keys" originates with Lester (1978), later reworked, together with Lester (1977), into Lester (1989). Lester explains (1989, pp. 78–79) that the term accords with seventeenth-century usage (in particular, Adriano Banchieri's *tuoni ecclesiastico*). Referring to

Table 12.1 Modes, semi-keys, and keys (dyadic or triadic), and the tribal classes to which they reduce

	Dyadic	Triadic
Modes	Lydian, Ionian, Mixolydian, Dorian, Aeolian, Phrygian	Lydian, Ionian, Mixolydian, Dorian, Aeolian, Phrygian
Semi-keys	Ionian, Mixolydian, Dorian, Aeolian, Phrygian	Ionian, Mixolydian, Dorian, Aeolian
Keys	Ionian, Mixolydian, Dorian, Aeolian	Ionian, Aeolian

One may immediately object. If the church keys are indeed triadic semi-keys, then how is it that seventeenth-century theorists do not seem to have described them as such? Moreover, why is it that *contemporary* scholars go so far as to insist that "church keys are not modes" (Barnett 1998, p. 249), and therefore, contrary to common belief, a historical transition from "modality" to "tonality" (that is, from the modes through the church keys to the keys) not only did not occur in practice (Barnett 2002, p. 408), but could not have occurred, in principle?[12]

Concerning the first objection, one might note that it is not only simplistic, but contrary to the spirit of rational, critical inquiry, to assume that theories that are temporally (or geographically) proximate to a given practice are *necessarily* the most reliable theories of that practice.[13] In general, and in music in particular, theory seems to lag behind practice. In the previous section it was argued at length that modal theory is precisely a case in point, and in fact represents one of the most extreme such cases in the history of Western music (in practice Ionian and Aeolian existed for centuries prior to their theoretical recognition by Glarean).[14]

Atcherson (1973), who uses the term "pitch-key mode," Lester (1989, footnote on p. 78) notes that the church keys are not "a 'strictly seventeenth-century phenomenon,' for they are used from the late sixteenth century well into the eighteenth century, and are even cited in Koch's *Musikalisches Lexikon* of 1802 (article *Kirchentöne*, pp. 833–834)."

[12] Cf. Powers (1992, pp. 11–12): "... modality and tonality may be different kinds of phenomenon, and therefore not related through any of the simple evolutionary sequences to which we are today accustomed, such as: 'the modal system was displaced by the tonal system'; or, 'modality evolved into tonality'; or, 'the ancestors of our Major and minor scales were the Ionian and Aeolian modes'." Aspects of Powers's provocative essay have been discussed at length in the previous section.

[13] Cf. Christensen (1993, p. 25): "I consider it a fallacy of proximity to measure the value of a given theory in direct proportion to its chronological contiguity with the musical repertory to which it is applied." This is not to say, of course, that one should not pay close attention to such "chronologically contiguous" theories, treating them with the utmost respect.

[14] In Sect. 8.2 it was suggested that (categorical) 12-tone equal temperament represents an equally extreme case of theory lagging behind practice. There was a *technical* reason for the late arrival of ET theory, namely, the non-existence prior to the seventeenth century of essential mathematical tools, in particular, logarithmic calculation. As noted in the previous section, in the case of modal theory the sanctioning of the octenary system by the church was a powerful obstacle to exposing its empirical as well as logical flaws.

Suppose that the church keys are indeed triadic semi-keys, and consider the obstacles facing a seventeenth-century theorist in conceptualizing them as such.

First, even though dodecachordal theory was at least half a century old, the traditional, church-sanctioned octenary system continued to exert its force. As a result, a seventeenth-century theorist did not even have the comfort of knowing for sure that there are *six* tribal classes to begin with, not just four.[15] Moreover, even though a triadic conception of mode was articulated very clearly early in the century by Johannes Lippius, the dyadic/triadic dichotomy as such was not clearly recognized. Since triadic semi-keys reduce to only four tribal classes, whereas dyadic semi-keys reduce to five (see Table 12.1), we have a perfect recipe for confusion.

"The teaching of the *Tuoni*, or *Modi*" writes Giovanni Maria Bononcini in 1673, "is very difficult material because of the diversity of opinions as to both their number and their name." Angelo Berardi follows suite in 1689, noting that "one should not wonder that these modes have been called different things, have been considered in different ways, and have been reversed from low to high and vice versa." Maurizio Cazzati, in a 1663 mode-related polemic with his colleague Giulio Cesare Arresti sums up the matter as follows:

> Many authors have written on the modes, and in particular Zarlino... expressly says that there are twelve of them. Zagoni [Zacconi]... also affirms that there are twelve. Pietro Pontio... says that there are only eight. Angleria... holds the same opinion, ... *and he says that many have written about the formation and recognition of the modes, but one confusingly different from another; and for this reason many cannot perceive in what mode a composition may be, [even] when seeing it, much less when only hearing it.* (Cazzati's emphasis)[16]

And yet, consider Bononcini, whose 1673 treatise *Musico prattico*, together with two treatises by Berardi, "contain the most extensive writings on pitch organization" (Barnett 1998, p. 251). Bononcini begins the chapter entitled "Which of the above-named modes are ordinarily used by composers" (p. 137) by stating that "seven modes are ordinarily used by composers."[17] Using dodecachordal nomenclature Bononcini identifies these modes as 11 and 12 (authentic and plagal Ionian), 8 (plagal Mixolydian), 1 and 2 (authentic and plagal Dorian), and 9 and 10 (authentic and plagal Aeolian)[18]; compare with Table 12.1. Indeed, as Barnett (1998, p. 255)

---

[15] Tribal classes are defined in 10.8. Recall that two modes reducible to the same tribal class and sharing the same final (say, two "Dorian modes" with final D) may nonetheless be distinct, since they may have different scores (Definition 10.4). Therefore, the theory proposed in this study makes it perfectly possible to distinguish an "authentic" mode from a "plagal" one (review Sect. 11.1). However, since a definition of "authentic" vs. "plagal" that reflects actual (polyphonic) practice does not seem to exist, for present purposes it should suffice to distinguish modes reducible to the same tribal class by their finals, ignoring the existence of scores.

[16] All three authors are quoted and translated in Barnett (1998), pp. 250–251. As noted in the previous section, well over a century earlier Pietro Aron voiced similar sentiments.

[17] Barnett (1998), footnote on p. 255.

[18] Barnett (1998), Table 3 (p. 256).

shows, Bononcini organizes his Op. 6 *Sonate da chiesa* (Venice, 1672) precisely in terms of these four tribal types.

Thus, against all odds, for at least one important seventeenth-century theorist the church keys are exactly the triadic semi-keys. What, however, does contemporary scholarship have to say on this matter?

We might begin by noting that ever since Atcherson (1973, p. 228) suggested that major and minor did not "descend" from Ionian and Aeolian (see Lester 1989, pp. 94–95), it became fashionable in musicological circles to challenge this common-sense belief. Harold Powers, possibly the greatest authority on mode of our time, headed this movement (see footnote 12). As we have seen in the previous section, owing to his octenary bias Powers was forced to deny not only the existence of a connection between "modality" and "tonality," but also the very viability of "mode" as a theoretical concept.

Gregory Barnett, in "Modal Theory, Church Keys, and the Sonata at the End of the Seventeenth Century," a work (1998) already cited a number of times in the course of this section, sadly follows Powers's lead. For Barnett, "although known as *tuoni* among seventeenth-century theorists, *church keys are not modes*: they originated in a specific musical practice, not in theory as did the twelve modes; they are eight in number, not twelve; and they do not conform to the rules of polyphonic modality, such as the proper use of a particular species of perfect fourth and fifth in each mode" (p. 249, emphasis added).

One may easily dismiss Barnett's second and third arguments. The church keys, though reducible to a proper *subset* of the six triadic tribal classes, are no less "modal" for that. Moreover, it is impossible for the church keys to "conform to the [octenary!] rules of polyphonic modality." In fact, the octenary modes themselves do not conform to these rules. For example, the 4th species of fifth combined with the 3rd species of fourth is "improperly" referred to as "Lydian" (mode 5).

We remain with Barnett's first argument, namely, that church keys are not modes because "they originated in a specific musical practice, not in theory as did the twelve modes." As he immediately explains, ". . . the church keys arose as tonalities meant for the polyphonic setting of the psalm tones, which became more and more prevalent throughout the seventeenth century in Catholic offices, particularly in lavish Vespers settings."

An argument of this type of course confounds the question of *essence* with that of *origin*: Oranges, after all, are oranges, whether from Jaffa or Valencia. Barnett must show, therefore, that the essence of church keys *reflects* their (supposed) origin, in order to support his claim that they are not modes.

In the latter part of his article Barnett attempts to do exactly that. "To further establish the origins of seventeenth-century tonalities in the psalm tones" he writes on p. 266, ". . . we can make specific determinations of a composition's affinity with one or another psalm tone on the basis of cadential points and other compositional details. Tonalities relating to two of the eight psalm tones, the fourth and the eighth, afford particularly good illustrations in this regard." Barnett then proceeds to show that seventeenth-century "G-tonality" sonatas emphasize the fourth scale degree. Moreover, "Phrygian E-tonality" sonatas also emphasize the fourth scale degree, making them often sound to "modern" ears "A-Aeolian."

However, these phenomena have a straightforward explanation independent of psalm tones. Mixolydian "G-tonalities" tend naturally to gravitate towards C; and the ambiguity of "E-Phrygian vs. A-Aeolian" of "Phrygian E-tonalities" may well reflect the precarious status of Phrygian as a *dyadic* semi-key but not a triadic one (review Table 12.1).[19] In short, despite numerous repetitions of the claim that church keys are not modes due to their psalm-tone origin,[20] Barnett fails to establish any viable logical connection between the (supposed) origin of the church keys in psalm tones and their non-modal nature.[21]

One must consider another facet of Barnett's argument that church keys are not modes because "they originated in a specific musical practice, not in theory as did the twelve modes," one that does not concern the psalm tones so much as it does a more general distinction between "practice" and "theory." The question of theory versus practice surfaces several times in Barnett's study, quite apart from the psalm tones, in connection with the modality or non-modality of the church keys. Unfortunately, Barnett (as we shall see) defines "practice" in terms of "theory," thus making it impossible to draw a logical conclusion from the distinction.

Recall that Bononcini describes the church keys in dodecachordal modal terms that correspond to triadic semi-keys. Bononcini, however, apparently represents a minority in this regard. Barnett cites a number of other seventeenth-century theorists who describe the church keys in octenary terms. In addition, he cites a number of *composers* of collections of instrumental music the order of "tonalities" of which adheres, or seems to adhere in part (unlike Bononcini's Op. 6), to an octenary scheme (pp. 258–260, esp. Tables 5 and 6). From these findings Barnett concludes as follows (p. 260): "... Bononcini's twelve-mode theorizing simply does not fit *the practice* of his time." And further: "Given *the practice* of the latter half of the seventeenth century, then, we should recognize the essential validity of Bononcini's observation that only seven modes were in use in his time, but we must also take issue with his explanation of them in terms of traditional modal theory" (emphases added).

---

[19] In other words, unlike the extinct Lydian, a Phrygian semi-key may have existed in the seventeenth century due to remnants of dyadic modal conception and perception.

[20] For example, "... none of the tonalities in Tables 5 and 6 are modal, transposed or otherwise. Instead, they originate in ecclesiastical psalmody." "... This system of tonalities—often described as modes by the theorists...—consists of the church keys that originated in the accompaniment of psalms on the organ" (p. 260). "Bononcini's set of seven finals and key signatures originates in these psalm tone tonalities, not in the modes" (p. 261). "This core set derives, not from the modes, but from tonalities originating in the eight psalm tones used in the Catholic offices" (Abstract, p. 281). See also footnote 21.

[21] In footnote 34 (p. 277) Barnett dismisses Peter Allsop's (1992) modal-based account of precisely such "G-tonality" and "E-tonality" compositional characteristics as he accounts for in psalm-tone terms. However, Barnett fails to support his dismissal with argument. Indeed, he claims to have demonstrated that "... psalm tone characteristics, *not modal features*, shaped these tonalities" (emphasis added), where in fact the emphasized clause is merely asserted, never demonstrated.

These statements miss the mark on two crucial points. First, even assuming that Bononcini indeed voiced a minority opinion within the seventeenth-century church-key scene, this by itself is no ground for marginalizing his views.[22] Science is a matter of critical inquiry, not public opinion. The history of science is replete with examples of minority views that became over time mainstream knowledge. Second, the reference to *practice* in these statements is highly misleading. Unless one defines "practice" in terms of "theory" and in so doing renders the distinction, as already noted, useless, it is not *the practice* of his time into which "Bononcini's twelve-mode theorizing simply does not fit," but rather *the theory* of his time. With possibly one or two exceptions, *in practice* the octenary-minded composers that Barnett cites use exactly the same mode classes (or, to avoid the term, "tonalities") that Bononcini cites as "ordinarily used by composers"; they simply refer to some of them by different names.[23]

Barnett commits an even graver offence against Bononcini (and the scientific spirit) than marginalizing his ideas merely on the ground that (apparently) they did not conform to the majority opinion of the time. In his Table 8a Barnett takes the liberty of "re-conceptualizing" Bononcini's seven "ordinarily used" modes (and their transpositions) in octenary terms, ostensibly in order to obtain ". . . a composite set of tonalities that may be tested against a representative selection from the late seicento sonata repertory" (p. 262). Twisting the meaning of "theory" and "practice" to serve his needs while at the same time contradicting an earlier statement that "Bononcini's theory is consistent with his practice" (p. 256), Barnett states that the table "uncouples his [Bononcini's] practice from his theory." The blatantly octenary-biased maneuver includes, among other misrepresentations, ". . . substituting a D-tonality with two sharps for his [Bononcini's] D-tonality with one flat" (conceived as Aeolian, or mode 9), a misrepresentation in support of which Barnett cites ". . . the precedent set by Arresti and others who use a D-tonality with one or two sharps to represent the seventh *tuono*,"[24] as well as demoting the D-Aeolian itself to the status of *tonus peregrinus* (pp. 262–265).

In view of such findings one may seriously believe that Barnett is referring to no other but himself, when stating on p. 276 that "studies that assume some vague form of modality to be in effect during this period and that do not ground their findings in the treatises of the period misunderstand both modal theory and its relation to musical practice." But of course, a lengthy footnote attached to this statement reveals otherwise. With no argument of any substance, but with much insinuation, Barnett proceeds to dismiss one by one valuable ideas put forth by such scholars as Robert

---

[22] One is reminded of Powers's (1992, p. 18) similar move by which composers of the late sixteenth century who favored the dodecachordal system (for example, Le Jeune) are marginalized. See the previous section.

[23] The two possible exceptions involve an apparent use of Lydian by Antonii (see Table 6 on p. 259). Barnett, however, may have neglected to mention that the signatures in question are "incomplete."

[24] Barnett continues: "The D-tonality with two sharps also appears far more frequently in the sonata literature, whereas that with one flat occurs only infrequently in practice."

Wienpahl, John Suess, and, as already mentioned, Peter Allsop (see footnote 21).[25] In particular, for no other reason than ostensibly having "... no basis in the theory chronologically or geographically closest to the repertory under consideration" Barnett rejects Owens's (1998, p. 186) very sensible plea for a "neo-modal" approach, "... a modern hybrid that reduces Glarean's twelve modes to five transposable scale-types: Dorian, Phrygian, Mixolydian, Aeolian, and Ionian."[26]

The concept of mode engendered in the past much controversy and confusion; if studied rationally there is absolutely no reason that it should continue to do so today.

12.3   On the Reality of Triadic Keys

> In our endeavor to understand reality we are somewhat like a man trying to understand the mechanism of a closed watch. He sees the face and the moving hands, even hears its ticking, but he has no way of opening the case. If he is ingenious he may form some picture of a mechanism which could be responsible for all the things he observes, but he may never be quite sure his picture is the only one which could explain his observations.
> —Albert Einstein and Leopold Infeld, *The Evolution of Physics* (1938), p. 31

At both ends of the communicative process, that is, the composer's end where a "message" is conceived, and the listener's end where the message is received from the transmitted signal, the evidence for the existence of keys is persuasive.

Consider, for example, the notational device known as "key signature." Though not fully standardized until the second half of the eighteenth century, key signatures have been used by composers of triadic-tonal music to specify the "core," that is, the seven-element line-of-fifths segment essential to every mode. The key signature also implies the existence of a nucleus (a major or minor triad). Though not *uniquely* specified by the key signature, the implied nucleus is one of two triadic subsets of the core that define a pair of "relative" keys.

Indeed, the hierarchy by which the nucleus of a given key is a subset of its core, which in turn is a subset of its cluster (the latter being the 17-element segment of the line of fifths representing all diatonic and chromatic notes associated with the key), leads to at least two testable predictions, one concerning listeners, and the other, composers. Listeners of triadic music, one might predict, perceive keys in terms of a nested hierarchy of notes as depicted in Fig. 12.1. In particular, the tonic triad is

---

[25] Barnett dismisses Suess's ideas on purely terminological grounds, insinuating that "the mention of specific Greek-named modes" does not promote a "clear understanding of the modal practice."

[26] Owens cites Reese (1954, p. 186) in this regard. "In any event, it is plain that in polyphony only five modes mattered for practical purposes. Glareanus himself emphasizes that the Lydian pair, as modified into Ionian and Hypoionian, has almost completely supplanted the unmodified pair. Moreover, the distinction between an authentic mode and its plagal is, in polyphony, an academic one. ... This leaves, as the really fundamental modes of Late Renaissance polyphony, the Dorian, Phrygian, Mixolydian, Aeolian, and Ionian."

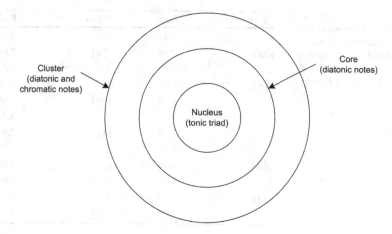

Fig. 12.1 The nested hierarchy Nucleus-Core-Cluster

differentiated from non-tonic diatonic notes, while diatonic notes in general are differentiated from chromatic notes. With regard to composers, one might similarly predict that there exists a correlation between compositional emphasis (for example, by repetition) and the category to which a note in a given key belongs. In particular, members of the tonic triad are more emphasized than non-members, while diatonic notes in general are more emphasized than chromatic notes.

Deutsch and Feroe's (1981) idea, that "pitch sequences" in tonal music are represented in terms of nested "alphabets," is related to the first, listener-oriented prediction. Suggesting the existence of levels of representation corresponding to the cluster and core, they write as follows (p. 509): "One may think of the twelve-tone chromatic scale as the parent alphabet from which families of alphabets are derived. The alphabets most commonly employed in tonal music are the major and minor diatonic scales...." Subsequently they suggest a level of representation corresponding to the nucleus as well: "Another common alphabet employed in tonal music is the arpeggiation of a triad." Lerdahl's (2001, p. 47) "basic space" is "a rendering of Deutsch and Feroe's idea of hierarchically organized alphabets." The space consists of five levels: "Level a is octave (or root) space, level b is fifth space, level c is triadic space, level d is diatonic space, and level e is chromatic space."[27]

As Lerdahl notes (*ibid.*, p. 48), "the basic space itself is obvious—we are all aware of octaves, triads, and diatonic and chromatic scales...." And yet, the famous "probe tone" experiments of Krumhansl and Kessler (1982), where experienced musicians were given a key-suggesting musical context (a major or minor triad, or a conventional cadential progression), and were then asked to rate how well an

---

[27] Lerdahl's levels b and a are easily theorized, respectively, as the final-cofinal subset of the nucleus, and further, the final all by itself. We assume that Lerdahl's basic space is naturally "tonic oriented."

Table 12.2 The "probe-tone ratings" of Krumhansl and Kessler (Redrawn from Krumhansl (1990), Table 2.1 on p. 30, by permission of Oxford University Press)

Major degree	Rating	Minor degree	Rating
$\hat{1}$	6.35	$\hat{1}$	6.33
$\flat\hat{2}/\sharp\hat{1}$	2.23	$\flat\hat{2}/\sharp\hat{1}$	2.68
$\hat{2}$	3.48	$\hat{2}$	3.52
$\flat\hat{3}/\sharp\hat{2}$	2.33	$\hat{3}$	5.38
$\hat{3}$	4.38	$\sharp\hat{3}/\flat\hat{4}$	2.60
$\hat{4}$	4.09	$\hat{4}$	3.53
$\sharp\hat{4}/\flat\hat{5}$	2.52	$\sharp\hat{4}/\flat\hat{5}$	2.54
$\hat{5}$	5.19	$\hat{5}$	4.75
$\flat\hat{6}/\sharp\hat{5}$	2.39	$\hat{6}$	3.98
$\hat{6}$	3.66	$\sharp\hat{6}/\flat\hat{7}$	2.69
$\flat\hat{7}/\sharp\hat{6}$	2.29	$\hat{7}$	3.34
$\hat{7}$	2.88	$\sharp\hat{7}/\flat\hat{1}$	3.17

equal-tempered pitch "fit with" the context in a musical sense (see Krumhansl 1990, pp. 25–31), were apparently needed to convince many researchers that triadic listeners indeed distinguish chromatic from diatonic elements, and non-tonic diatonic elements from elements of the tonic triad. The ratings, from Krumhansl (1990, p. 30), are given in Table 12.2.[28] Figures 12.2 and 12.3 display the information graphically for major and minor, respectively. In panel (a) of each figure the bars represent percentages of the total rating; in panel (b) slices represent the categories of Fig. 12.1.

There are seven diatonic degrees and five chromatic ones, not differentiating first- from second-order chromatic degrees. Therefore, by the null hypothesis of equal distribution the diatonic degrees should have accumulated 58.33% of the total rating, and the chromatic degrees, 41.67%. As may be seen, however, in major the actual percentages are 71.86% and 28.14%, respectively, and in minor, 69.26% and 30.73%. Similarly, there are three tonic degrees and four non-tonic diatonic. Again, by the null hypothesis the tonic degrees should have accumulated 42.86% of the total *diatonic* rating, and the non-tonic diatonic, 57.14%. However, the actual percentages in major are 53.02% and 46.98%, respectively, and in minor, 53.4% and 46.6%.

Krumhansl and Kessler (1982, p. 343) analyze the data as follows:

In both key profiles the tonic, C, received higher ratings than all the other tones: $t(9) = 16.84$ for major, and $t(9) = 13.42$ for minor, $p < .001$ for both. In addition, all nontonic scale tones (using the harmonic form for minor) had higher average ratings than did nondiatonic tones: $t(9) = 6.05$ and 9.23, $p < .001$, for major and minor, respectively. Within the set of diatonic tones, the components of the tonic chord, C, E, and G in major and C, E♭ (D♯) [sic], and G in minor, were judged as fitting more closely with the major and minor elements than

---

[28] Krumhansl displays the ratings, for minor as well as major, in terms of the notes C, C♯/D♭, D, D♯/E♭, E, F, F♯/G♭, G, G♯/A♭, A, A♯/B♭, and B. In Table 12.2 these labels are replaced with the appropriate scale degrees for major and minor, on the assumption that a chromatic degree is first *or* second order. Thus, for example, Krumhansl's "E" becomes $\hat{3}$ in major and $\sharp\hat{3}/\flat\hat{4}$ in minor.

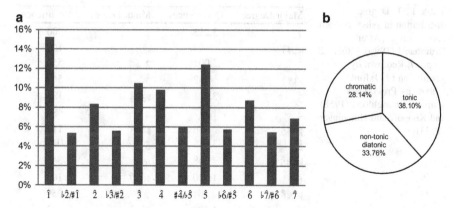

Fig. 12.2 Percentages of probe-tone rating, major. (**a**) Separately for each degree; (**b**) grouped by category. Data from Table 12.2

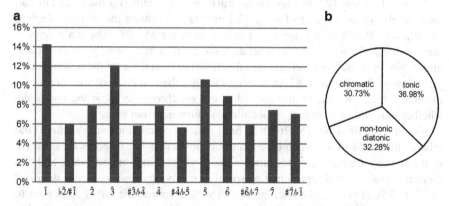

Fig. 12.3 Percentages of probe-tone rating, minor. (**a**) Separately for each degree; (**b**) grouped by category. Data from Table 12.2

were the other diatonic tones: $t(9) = 16.28$ and 9.77, $p < .001$, for major and minor, respectively. Thus, the ratings in this study strongly confirmed the hierarchy obtained by Krumhansl and Shepard (1979).

We now turn to the second, composer-oriented prediction.

On the basis of studies by Youngblood (1958) and Knopoff and Hutchinson (1983), Krumhansl (1990, p. 67) presents a table showing the distribution of scale degrees as notated in the vocal parts of selected compositions by Hasse, Mozart, Schubert, Schumann, Mendelssohn, and Richard Strauss (see Table 12.3). Note that no distinction is made between first- and second-order chromatic degrees.[29]

---

[29] As Krumhansl notes (*ibid.*), "in both studies, all pitches were reduced to a single octave and transposed to a common key; these transpositions were always determined from the written key signature, taking no account of transitions or modulations. In the second study [Knopoff and

	Major Degree	Occurrences	Minor Degree	Occurrences
Table 12.3 Degree distribution in selected triadic compositions [After Krumhansl (1990), Table 3.3 on p. 67. Redrawn by permission of Oxford University Press. Data sources: Youngblood (1958) and Knopoff and Hutchinson (1983)]	$\hat{1}$	3,213	$\hat{1}$	906
	$\flat\hat{2}/\#\hat{1}$	194	$\flat\hat{2}/\#\hat{1}$	103
	$\hat{2}$	3,001	$\hat{2}$	550
	$\flat\hat{3}/\#\hat{2}$	352	$\hat{3}$	564
	$\hat{3}$	3,111	$\#\hat{3}/\flat\hat{4}$	124
	$\hat{4}$	1,947	$\hat{4}$	430
	$\#\hat{4}/\flat\hat{5}$	556	$\#\hat{4}/\flat\hat{5}$	117
	$\hat{5}$	3,615	$\hat{5}$	1,042
	$\flat\hat{6}/\#\hat{5}$	348	$\hat{6}$	343
	$\hat{6}$	1,840	$\#\hat{6}/\flat\hat{7}$	100
	$\flat\hat{7}/\#\hat{6}$	361	$\hat{7}$	259
	$\hat{7}$	1,504	$\#\hat{7}/\flat\hat{1}$	272
	Total	20,042	Total	4,810

Figures 12.4 and 12.5 display the information graphically, for major and minor, respectively, in the manner of Figs. 12.2 and 12.3. In major the diatonic degrees account for 90.96% of all degrees, and in minor, for 85.22%. The tonic degrees account for 54.52% and 64.8% of all *diatonic* degrees, respectively for major and minor. Not only are these percentages much higher than those of the null hypothesis, namely 58.33% and 42.86%, respectively, their statistical significance is extremely high. In fact, in all cases (diatonic vs. chromatic, tonic vs. non-tonic, whether in major or in minor), probability is indistinct from zero.[30]

Krumhansl (1990, pp. 75–76), who finds a strong correlation between these (and related) findings and her probe-tone ratings, believes that "... listeners are sensitive to the relative frequencies and durations with which tones are sounded, and this gives rise to an internal representation specifying varying degrees of tonal stability" (*ibid.*, p. 76). However, the distributions as well as ratings are rather analogous to the exterior of Einstein's metaphorical watch (see this section's motto), the mechanism of which (like the internal representation of tonality) is inaccessible to direct observation.

Consider an enharmonic pair of chromatic degrees such as $\flat\hat{6}/\#\hat{5}$. If Krumhansl is correct, that "... the relative frequencies and durations with which *tones are sounded...* gives rise to an internal representation specifying varying degrees of tonal stability" (emphasis added), then the distribution of (say) $\flat\hat{6}$ vs. $\#\hat{5}$ in tonal compositions should be roughly 50/50. This is because the *sounds* associated with

---

Hutchinson], explicit changes in key signature were taken into account. (The first study [Youngblood] does not specify what is done in the case of a change of key signature, if relevant.) The published tables show the total number of times that each tone of the chromatic scale was sounded in the vocal lines of the pieces; the durations of the tones are not taken into account in the analysis." Again, Krumhansl's labels have been replaced, as in Table 12.2 (see footnote 28).

[30] Note, however, that $\hat{5}$ is more prevalent than $\hat{1}$, that $\hat{2}$ is only slightly less prevalent than $\hat{3}$, and that, in minor, $\#\hat{7}/\flat\hat{1}$ is more prevalent than $\hat{7}$.

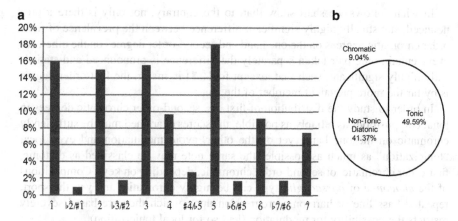

Fig. 12.4 Percentages of degree occurrence, major. (**a**) Separately for each degree; (**b**) grouped by category. Data from Table 12.3

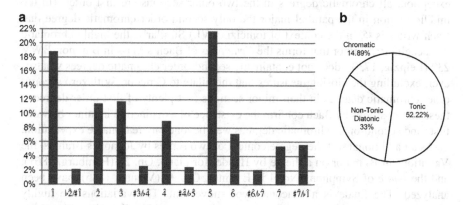

Fig. 12.5 Percentages of degree occurrence, minor. (**a**) Separately for each degree; (**b**) grouped by category. Data from Table 12.3

such degrees are indistinguishable from those of notes that are octave equivalent. Why should composers bother, therefore, to make a distributional distinction in such cases?[31]

---

[31] Even apart from chromaticism, the notion that degree distribution gives rise to the internal representation of tonality seems dubious. Note, for example, that even though $\hat{5}$ can be more prevalent than $\hat{1}$, as in the distribution data presented (see Figs. 12.4 and 12.5), the tonic remains the most privileged tonal element. Huron (2006, p. 150) has recently voiced strong support for the notion, originally advanced by Krumhansl, that "... one of the primary factors influencing tonality perception is the simple frequency of occurrences of different tones." Citing the 2003 PhD dissertation of Bret Aarden, he notes that "... in the case of scale-degree distributions, Aarden found that listeners' expectations are pretty well on the mark." However, in Aarden's major/minor analyses of the "distribution of scale tones," impressive as they are in terms of sheer sample size, "all pitches are enharmonic." See Huron (2006), Figs. 9.1 and 9.2 on pp. 148–149.

In what follows we shall show that, to the contrary, not only is there a pronounced, statistically highly significant difference between the prevalence of first-
order chromatic degrees on the one hand and second-order degrees on the other, for
every enharmonic pair taken separately the difference is pronounced and statistically highly significant, such that, except for ♭$\hat{2}$/♯$\hat{1}$ in major, the first-order degree
is by far the more prevalent member of the pair.

In order to study the distribution of first- vs. second-order chromatic degrees in
tonal compositions as reliably as possible, the scores examined must be sufficiently
chromatic on the one hand, yet on the other, avoid modulation and even local
"tonicization" as much as possible (the same note may be classified as diatonic,
first-order chromatic, or second-order chromatic, depending on key). Compositions
of the *chaconne* or *passacaglia* type can be highly chromatic; and yet, the short,
repeated bass line or harmonic progression upon which they are based severely
restricts the possibility for modulation (less so for local tonicization).

A glance at the score of J. S. Bach's monumental Chaconne from the D-minor
Partita for violin solo, BWV 1004 (Köthen, ca. 1720), will reveal that with no
exception, all chromatic degrees in the two outer sections are first order. (In the
middle section in the parallel major the only second-order chromatic degree that
Bach writes is ♯$\hat{5}$, in the context of tonicizing VI.) Similarly, the highly chromatic
passacaglia in E minor that forms the *Crucifixus* of Bach's Mass in B minor, BWV
232 (Leipzig, 1733), does not contain any second-order chromatic degrees whatsoever, excluding the closing measures that modulate to G major. With zero second-
order chromatic degrees in their minor sections (yet plenty of first-order degrees),
these compositions by Bach confirm the existence of a distinction in minor between
first- and second-order chromatic degrees well beyond any reasonable expectation.

As an additional test the degree content of two scores by Johannes Brahms, the
Variations in B♭ major on a theme by Handel for piano, Op. 24 (Hamburg, 1861),
and the *finale* of Symphony No. 4 in E minor, Op. 98 (Vienna, 1885), have been
analyzed. The finale is a chaconne-type movement. The variations are highly
chromatic, and yet, Handel's eight-measure theme is strictly diatonic, with neither
modulations nor tonicizations. Unlike the Youngblood (1958) and Knopoff and
Hutchinson (1983) studies cited earlier, first- and second-order chromatic degrees
were differentiated.

Before turning to the results, a few procedural notes are in order.

Each score was partitioned into short segments, namely, notated measures in
Op. 98 and notated *half* measures in Op. 24.[32] Within each segment, a "1" or a "0"
was used to indicate whether a given degree is represented at least once
(in whatever register), or not at all. In other words, within a given segment
repetitions were ignored. For each of the 17 diatonic and chromatic degrees the
number of occurrences was then identified with the total number of 1s the degree

---

[32] Somewhat inconsistently, section repeats in Op. 24 indicated by formal repeat signs have been
ignored, but not the occasional *varied* repeats that Brahms composes. See for example Vars.
8 and 9.

has accumulated over all segments. (The grand total of degrees thus counted was 2,427 in Op. 24 and 1,239 in Op. 98.)

In both cases, sections in the parallel key, indicated by a change of key signature, have been excluded from consideration.[33] In addition, the highly chromatic coda of Op. 98 has been excluded, starting with m. 251. In Op. 24, the concluding fugue has been similarly excluded, as well as Var. 21, which is clearly in the *relative* key.

Brahms's notation was the decisive criterion in classifying chromatic degrees as first or second order. Nonetheless, judgment had to be exercised in certain cases. For example, in Op. 98 *the strings and non-transposing woodwinds* were considered decisive, in rare cases where a conflict of notation among the various instrumental groups was found. Somewhat more problematic are mm. 85−86 of Op. 24 (Var. 9). Despite Brahms's "sharp" notation, suggesting the prolongation of "$\sharp$V," these measures were read "in flats," that is, as prolonging $\flat$VI.[34]

Figures 12.6 and 12.7 are similar in format to Figs. 12.4 and 12.5, except that in (a) first- and second-order chromatic degrees are differentiated. In (a) one also finds a negligible percentage of non-diatonic notes that do not correspond to either first- or second-order chromatic degrees ("other"). Such cases invariably arise from modulatory processes.

Consider the percentages in (b), where first- and second-order chromatic degrees are *not* differentiated. Against the null hypothesis of 58.33%, diatonic degrees account for 83.4 % of all degrees in Op. 24 and for 76.51% in Op. 98 (probability in both cases is indistinct from zero). Against the null hypothesis of 42.86%, tonic degrees account for 49.8% of all *diatonic* degrees in Op. 24 (highly significant at $p < 2 \cdot 10^{-10}$), and for 48.84% in Op. 98 (highly significant at $p < 0.00012$).

Finally, consider Fig. 12.8, where the distribution of first- and second-order chromatic degrees relative to the total number of *chromatic* degrees, is analyzed. By the null hypothesis the five first-order chromatic degrees should have accounted for 50% of the total count, and similarly for the five second-order degrees. However, not only do we find that the first-order chromatic degrees account for no less than 73.23% in Op. 24 and 91.35% (!) in Op. 98, for every enharmonically related pair *except* $\flat\hat{2}/\sharp\hat{1}$ in major the first-order degrees are by far the majority. (The reverse relation holds in the case of $\flat\hat{2}/\sharp\hat{1}$ in major.) These relations are all statistically highly significant, at $p<0.01$.

---

[33] Mm. 105−128 in Op. 98, Vars. 5, 6, and 13 in Op. 24.

[34] Mm. 85−88 (with upbeat) represent one of few cases in Op. 24 where Brahms writes a varied repeat (see footnote 32). However, this particular case is quite unlike any other, since it does not involve just "surface" changes as registration, part distribution, etc. In mm. 85−86 Brahms "repeats" mm. 81−82 *a half-step higher*. The sharp notation may be Brahms's humorous way of referring to his rather free "repetition," since ignoring accidentals the notes are the same. Be that as it may, taking these measures at face value has a marginal effect on the statistics. For example, the percentages for tonic, non-tonic diatonic, and chromatic degrees (cf. Fig. 12.6b) are 41.38%, 41.83%, and 16.8%, respectively. The percentages for first- and second-order chromatic degrees (cf. Fig. 12.8a) are 70.7% and 29.3%, respectively.

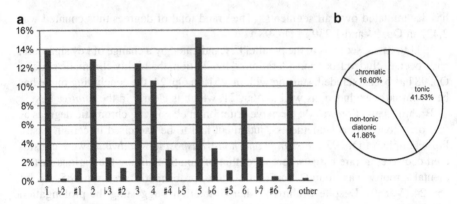

Fig. 12.6 Percentages of degree occurrence in Brahms, Op. 24 (B♭ major). (**a**) Separately for each degree; (**b**) grouped by category

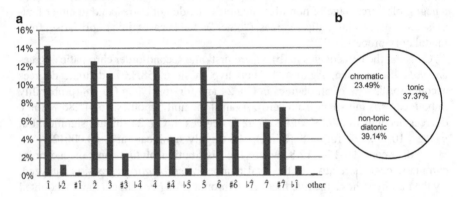

Fig. 12.7 Percentages of degree occurrence in Brahms, Op. 98, IV (E minor). (**a**) Separately for each degree; (**b**) grouped by category

One may wonder why the result, first-order chromatic degrees are more prevalent than second-order degrees, is more pronounced in minor, such that, in one case in major, namely ♭$\hat{2}$/♯$\hat{1}$, it is the *second*-order degree that is more prevalent. Figure 12.9 suggests an answer. The figure presents all non-tonic major and minor diatonic triads in C major and C minor, preceded by their so-called "applied dominants." As may be seen, in minor every resulting chromatic degree is first order; in major, by contrast, some of the applied chords contain second-order degrees (black note heads). In particular, V/II contains ♯$\hat{1}$, V/III contains ♯$\hat{2}$, and V/VI contains ♯$\hat{5}$.

In summary, the distinction between the cluster, core, and nucleus of keys is supported by empirical evidence relating to both composers and listeners.

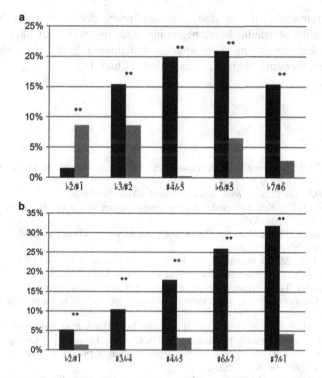

Fig. 12.8 First- vs. second-order chromatic degrees in Brahms, Op. 24 (**a**), and Op. 98, IV (**b**). ** = highly significant at $p < 0.01$

Fig. 12.9 "Applied dominants" to all non-tonic major and minor diatonic triads in C major (**a**) and C minor (**b**). *Black note heads* indicate second-order chromatic degrees

Moreover, the distinction between first- and second-order *chromatic* degrees is supported by empirical evidence relating to composers. Researchers who believe that the chromatic distinction is nonetheless arbitrary must show that unlike composers, listeners do not distinguish between enharmonic pairs of first- and second-order chromatic degrees.[35]

---

[35] Note that a "probe-tone"-type experiment is not feasible in this case, since enharmonically equivalent degrees are indistinguishable by pitch.

For the remainder of this study we shall probe deeper into the "common-practice" reality of triadic keys, beginning with the notion of "key distance" (Chap. 13) and concluding with what is sometimes referred to in the music-psychological literature as "tonality induction" (Chap. 15).

References

Aarden, B. (2003). *Dynamic melodic expectancy*. PhD diss., School of Music, Ohio State University.

Allsop, P. (1992). *The Italian "trio" sonata*. Oxford: Clarendon Press.

Atcherson, W. (1973). Key and mode in seventeenth-century music theory books. *Journal of Music Theory, 17*, 204–233.

Babb, W. (Trans.). (1978). *Hucbald, Guido, and John on music: Three medieval treatises*. New Haven: Yale University Press.

Barnett, G. (1998). Modal theory, church keys, and the sonata at the end of the seventeenth century. *Journal of the American Musicological Society, 51*(2), 245–281.

Barnett, G. (2002). Tonal organization in seventeenth-century music theory. In T. Christensen (Ed.), *The Cambridge history of Western music theory* (pp. 407–455). Cambridge: Cambridge University Press.

Christensen, T. (1993). Music theory and its histories. In C. Hatch & D. Bernstein (Eds.), *Music theory and the exploration of the past* (pp. 9–39). Chicago: University of Chicago Press.

Deutsch, D., & Feroe, J. (1981). The internal representation of pitch sequences in tonal music. *Psychological Review, 88*(6), 503–522.

Einstein, A., & Infeld, L. (1938). *The evolution of physics*. New York: Simon and Schuster.

Fuller, S. (1996). Defending the *Dodecachordon*: Ideological currents in Glarean's modal theory. *Journal of the American Musicological Society, 49*, 191–224.

Glarean, H. (1965). *Dodecachordon* (C. Miller, Trans.). Rome: American Institute of Musicology.

Huron, D. (2006). *Sweet Anticipation: Music and the Psychology of Expectation*. Cambridge: MIT Press.

Judd, C. (2002). Renaissance modal theory: Theoretical, compositional, and editorial perspectives. In T. Christensen (Ed.), *The Cambridge history of Western music theory* (pp. 364–406). Cambridge: Cambridge University Press.

Knopoff, L., & Hutchinson, W. (1983). Entropy as a measure of style: The influence of sample length. *Journal of Music Theory, 27*, 75–97.

Krumhansl, C. (1990). *Cognitive foundations of musical pitch*. New York: Oxford University Press.

Krumhansl, C., & Kessler, E. (1982). Tracing the dynamic changes in perceived tonal organization in a spatial representation of musical keys. *Psychological Review, 89*(4), 334–368.

Krumhansl, C., & Shepard, R. (1979). Quantification of the hierarchy of tonal functions within a diatonic context. *Journal of Experimental Psychology: Human Perception and Performance, 5*(4), 579–594.

Lerdahl, F. (2001). *Tonal pitch space*. Oxford: Oxford University Press.

Lester, J. (1977). Major-minor concepts and modal theory in Germany, 1592–1680. *Journal of the American Musicological Society, 30*, 208–253.

Lester, J. (1978). The recognition of major and minor keys in German theory: 1680–1730. *Journal of Music Theory, 22*, 65–103.

Lester, J. (1989). *Between modes and keys: German theory 1592–1802*. Stuyvesant: Pendragon.

Owens, J. (1998). Concepts of pitch in English music theory, c. 1560–1640. In C. Judd (Ed.), *Tonal structures in early music* (pp. 183–246). New York: Garland.

Powers, H. (1974). The modality of 'Vestiva i colli.' In R. Marshall (Ed.), *Studies in Renaissance and Baroque music in honor of Arthur Mendel* (pp. 31–46). Kassel: Bärenreiter.

Powers, H. (1980). *Mode. The new Grove dictionary of music and musicians*. London: Macmillan.

Powers, H. (1981). Tonal types and modal categories in Renaissance polyphony. *Journal of the American Musicological Society, 34*(3), 428–470.

Powers, H. (1992). Is mode real? Pietro Aron, the octenary system, and polyphony. *Basler Jahrbuch, 16*, 9–53.

Powers, H. (1998). From psalmody to tonality. In C. Judd (Ed.), *Tonal structures in early music* (pp. 275–340). New York: Garland.

Reese, G. (1954). *Music in the Renaissance*. New York: Norton.

Rivera, B. (1993). Finding the *soggetto* in Willaert's free imitative counterpoint: A step in modal analysis. In C. Hatch & D. Bernstein (Eds.), *Music theory and the exploration of the past* (pp. 73–102). Chicago: University of Chicago Press.

Strunk, O. (Ed.). (1998). *Source readings in music history* (Rev. ed., L. Treitler, Ed.). New York: Norton.

Youngblood, J. (1958). Style as information. *Journal of Music Theory, 2*, 24–35.

Chapter 13
A Neo-Riepelian Key-Distance Theory

Abstract In Sect. 13.1 the (implied) key-distance theories of Heinichen, Kellner, and Weber are contrasted with the (incomplete) theory of Riepel. For Riepel, the parallel key, the tonic of which is chromatic relative to the home key, is more distant from the home key than a key (for example, the relative) the tonic of which is diatonic. Section 13.2 examines the prevalent belief that Weber's theory has been empirically validated by Krumhansl and her associates. Finally, Sect. 13.3 posits a "neo-Riepelian" theory of key distance. Unlike other theories, by neo-Riepelian theory a distance between two keys does not necessarily exist; as a result, except for diatonic key relations, key distances in general do not conform to what is known in algebra as "metric space."

Tonal compositions often "modulate," that is, are a composite of more than one key. By the prevalent view any two keys are related; indeed, there exists *a metric* on all keys such that *a distance* between two keys is always defined.

In the present chapter a radically different view is offered. There exist keys that are inherently unrelated; moreover, the algebraic notion of *a metric space* applies only to "closely related keys," that is, keys the tonic of which, as Aldwell and Schachter state (2003, p. 449), "functions as a diatonic chord" (relative to the "home key"). A metric space is a set together with a real-valued "distance" function satisfying the following three properties:

A. The distance from A to B equals 0 if, and only if, A = B.
B. The distance from A to B equals the distance from B to A (symmetry).
C. The distance from A to C is no larger than the sum of the distances from A to B and from B to C (triangle inequality).

It should be useful to begin this chapter with a brief historical survey. As we shall see, the proposed theory of key distance has historical roots in the eighteenth century.

E. Agmon, *The Languages of Western Tonality*, Computational Music Science,   217
DOI 10.1007/978-3-642-39587-1_13, © Springer-Verlag Berlin Heidelberg 2013

13.1   Key-Distance Theories of the Eighteenth and Nineteenth Centuries

Considered as a polygon-type graph on which distance is defined as the smallest number of consecutive edges connecting two vertices (Fig. 13.1b), Heinichen's "musical circle" (1711, p. 261), of which a later version (Heinichen 1728) is reproduced as Fig. 13.1a, constitutes a metric space in the algebraic sense.[1]

The key metric implied by Heinichen's circle, however, seems intuitively unsatisfying. There are far too many "degrees" of key-relatedness, namely thirteen. The shortest distance (or smallest degree) is of course zero (for example, C major to C major); the longest distance, however, is no less than twelve (for example, C to F♯ major). Between these two extremes C major to either D or A minor is an example of a first-degree relationship; C major to either G or F major is a second-degree relationship, and so forth. As has often been observed, it does not seem intuitively satisfying that D and A minor are closer to C major than are F and G major.[2]

Kellner's 1732 scheme represents a substantial improvement over Heinichen's (Fig. 13.2a). In Fig. 13.2b the scheme is interpreted in term of two circular graphs, one for major and the other for minor, such that *relative* pairs of keys, one from each circle, are connected. The set of first-degree relationships that results seems more convincing than Heinichen's; moreover, the overall number of degrees of key-relatedness is reduced to seven.

Figure 13.3 reproduces Gottfried Weber's (1830–1832, Vol. 2, p. 86) *Tabelle der Tonartenverwandtschaften*, one of the first attempts to construct a key metric where, in addition to both major or minor keys related by a fifth, the set of first-degree relationships includes not only relative keys, but also parallel ones.[3] As Bernstein (2002, p. 784) explains,

> Weber classified keys according to their *Verwandtschaftgrade* or degrees of relationship with the tonic: first-degree relationships occur between adjacent keys on the horizontal and

---

[1] Every connected graph on which a similar distance is defined is a metric space. Heinichen (1728, p. 837) announces the chapter devoted to his "musical circle" with a caption that refers to the "relationship... of all keys" (*Verwandtschaft... aller Modorum Musicorum*). Lester (1989, pp. 108–109) notes that the musical circle "...is presented [by Heinichen] not as a revolutionary method of establishing a new tonal system, but as a practical convenience to aid in modulation from one key to another.... Heinichen allows modulations not only from one key to another in order in either direction, but also by using alternate keys (for instance, C major to F major). Skipping keys in this manner works for a single modulation, but, as Heinichen notes, is hardly possible for continued use." In Fig. 13.1b and subsequent diagrams upper- and lower-case letters represent major and minor triads/keys, respectively.

[2] Undoubtedly referring to Heinichen's circle, Mattheson (1735) offers an "Improved Musical Circle, which leads around through all keys better than the ones previously invented" (see Werts 1985, p. 97). However, Mattheson's circle does not contribute to reducing the overall number of degrees of key-relatedness, and its first- and second-degree relationships do not seem intuitively more satisfying than those offered by Heinichen.

[3] The *Arbre Généalogique de l'harmonie* (ca. 1767) of François-Guillaume Vial anticipates Weber's table. See Lester (1992), pp. 229–230.

Fig. 13.1 (a) Heinichen's (1728) "musical circle." (b) Heinichen's circle as a connected graph

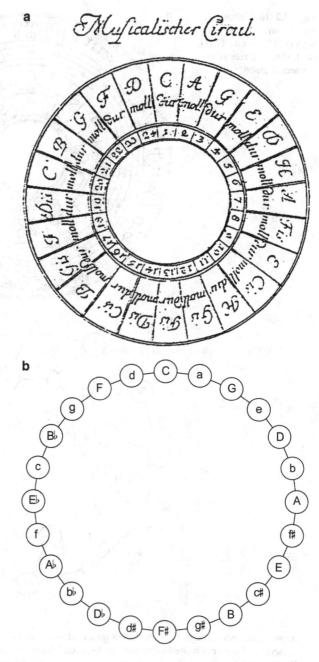

vertical axes of Weber's chart. For example, G major, F major, A minor, and C minor are related to C major in the first degree. Keys immediately adjacent to those related to the tonic in the first degree stand in a second-degree relationship to the tonic. Thus, D major, G minor, E♭ major, A major, F minor, D minor, E minor, and B♭ major are all related to C

Fig. 13.2 (a) Kellner's
circular arrangement of
keys (1737; 1st ed., 1732).
(b) Kellner's circle as a
connected graph

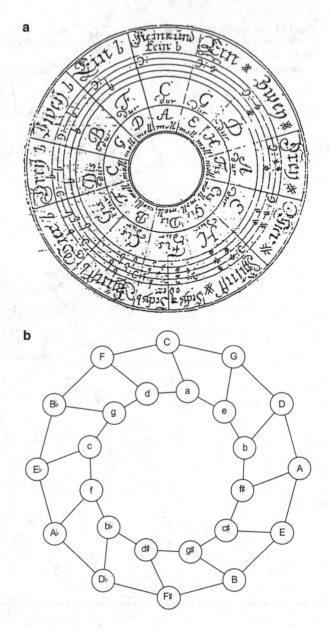

major in the second degree. Third-degree relationships occur between the tonic and keys
adjacent to those keys related to the tonic in the second degree. B minor, E major, F♯ minor,
B♭ minor, A♭ major, and E♭ minor all stand in a third-degree relationship to C major.

The relation of Weber's implicitly toroidal grid to Kellner's circle is rendered
explicit in Fig. 13.4, which is identical to Fig. 13.2b except for the added curved

Fig. 13.3 Weber's "table
of key relationships"

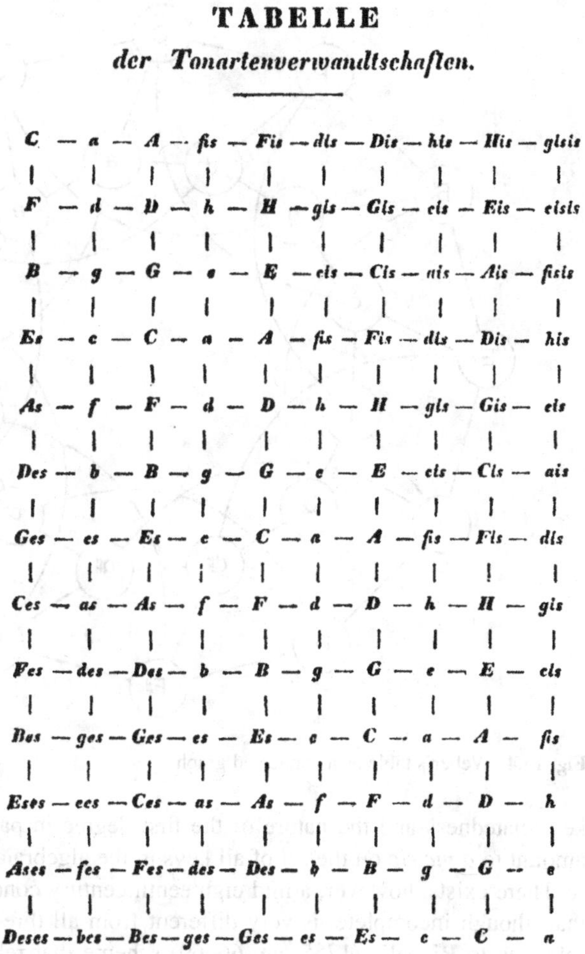

TABELLE
der Tonartenverwandtschaften.

```
C  —  a  —  A  —  fis  —  Fis  — dis  —  Dis  —  his  —  His  —  gisis
|     |     |     |     |      |      |      |      |      |
F  —  d  —  D  —  h  —  H  — gis —  Gis  —  eis  —  Eis  —  eisis
|     |     |     |     |      |      |      |      |      |
B  —  g  —  G  —  e  —  E  — eis —  Cis  —  ais  —  Ais  —  fisis
|     |     |     |     |      |      |      |      |      |
Es  —  c  —  C  —  a  —  A  —  fis  —  Fis  —  dis  —  Dis  —  his
|     |     |     |     |      |      |      |      |      |
As  —  f  —  F  —  d  —  D  —  h  —  H  — gis —  Gis  —  eis
|     |     |     |     |      |      |      |      |      |
Des  —  b  —  B  —  g  —  G  —  e  —  E  — eis —  Cis  —  ais
|     |     |     |     |      |      |      |      |      |
Ges  —  es  —  Es  —  c  —  C  —  a  —  A  —  fis  —  Fis  —  dis
|     |     |     |     |      |      |      |      |      |
Ces  —  as  —  As  —  f  —  F  —  d  —  D  —  h  —  H  —  gis
|     |     |     |     |      |      |      |      |      |
Fes  —  des  — Des  —  b  —  B  —  g  —  G  —  e  —  E  —  eis
|     |     |     |     |      |      |      |      |      |
Bes  —  ges  —  Ges  —  es  —  Es  —  c  —  C  —  a  —  A  —  fis
|     |     |     |     |      |      |      |      |      |
Eses  —  ees  — Ces  —  as  —  As  —  f  —  F  —  d  —  D  —  h
|     |     |     |     |      |      |      |      |      |
Ases  — fes  —  Fes  — des  —  Des  —  b  —  B  —  g  —  G  —  e
|     |     |     |     |      |      |      |      |      |
Deses  — bes  — Bes  — ges  — Ges  —  es  —  Es  —  c  —  C  —  a
```

edges connecting parallel keys.[4] Weber's torus reduces the number of degrees of
key-relatedness from Kellner's seven down to a reasonable four. Completing
Bernstein's list, the following keys are related to C major by the fourth degree:
C♯ major, C♯ minor, F♯ major, G♯ minor, and B major.

To summarize, we have seen three theories of key relationship from the eighteenth and nineteenth centuries, Heinichen's, Kellner's, and Weber's. Though
different from each other in terms of the overall number of degrees of

---

[4] Concerning the toroidal implications of Weber's grid, see Westergaard (1996), p. 15. It should be
useful to refer henceforth to Weber's table as "Weber's torus," even though Fig. 13.4 does not
render its toroidal structure explicit.

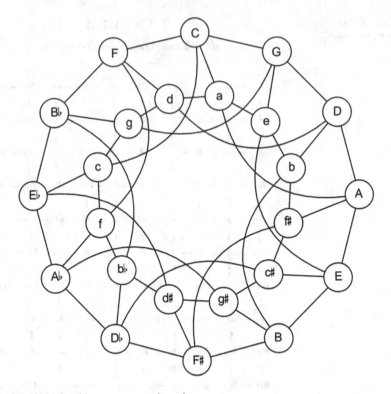

Fig. 13.4 Weber's table as a connected graph

key-relatedness and the nature of the first degree in particular, all three theories amount to *a metric* on the set of all keys in the algebraic sense.[5]

There exists, however, a mid eighteenth-century conception of key-relatedness that, though incomplete, is very different from all three theories just cited. I am referring to Riepel's (1755, pp. 66–69) scheme that relates six keys to C major, namely the major keys G and F, and the minor keys A, E, D, and C. The relation of five of the six keys to C is set in metaphorical terms that are drawn from the socio-economic structure of the eighteenth-century rural farm: C major is the master (*Meyer*), G major is the chief servant (*Oberknecht*), A minor is the chief maid (*Obermagd*), and so forth. C minor, however, is an exception. Riepel appeals to a very different *topos* when he dubs the key "black Margaret" (*schwarze Gredel*).[6]

---

[5] Bernstein's (2002, p. 784) assessment that "Weber's tonal grid exhaustively measures all key relationships according to their proximity to any tonic key, and thus supplants the more limited conceptual mapping of key relations afforded by the eighteenth-century music circle..." is misleading. The eighteenth-century musical circle, we have seen, implies an equally exhaustive (though different) key metric.

[6] According to Ratner (1980, p. 50), *schwarze Gredel* is "a local nickname for a Swedish queen whose swarthy complexion made her look like a man." See, however, Wheelock (1993), footnote on p. 203.

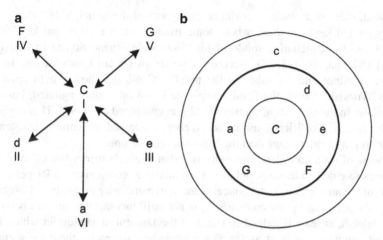

Fig. 13.5 Ratner's "solar" arrangement of keys. (**a**) From Ratner (1980). (**b**) An alternative representation that includes C minor

Much has been made of Riepel's "tonal hierarchy" vis-à-vis the social as well as gender-related biases in which it is couched (for example, Hyer 2002; Wheelock 1993). However, its significance as an alternative to theories such as Kellner's and Weber's has been practically ignored. For example, Riepel is mentioned by neither Krumhansl (2005) in her "brief introduction and history" to "the geometry of musical structure," nor by Lerdahl (2001, pp. 42–47) in his survey of "previous approaches" to the "concept of pitch space." A notable exception is Ratner (1980, pp. 48–51), who describes the eighteenth-century "key system" as either "solar" or "polar." Ratner depicts the solar conception, which he identifies with Riepel, with a diagram reproduced here as Fig. 13.5a. An alternative representation that includes the *schwarze Gredel* that Ratner omits is given in Fig. 13.5b.

Although Riepel's "solar" scheme is incomplete, it represents a conception of key-relatedness that is strikingly different from Kellner's as well as Weber's. For Riepel the keys most closely related to C major are those the tonic of which is a subset of the C-major diatonic collection, that is, *non-chromatic, consonant degrees of C major*. By contrast, a key like C minor, the tonic of which is chromatic relative to C major, is necessarily more distant. (The keys most closely related to C major by Kellner's scheme are a proper subset of Riepel's; the diatonic/chromatic distinction is irrelevant for Weber, for whom the parallel key is related to the home key in the first degree.)

As Lester notes,

Theorists as early as Zarlino explained that regular cadential points occur on the notes of the perfect chord built on the modal final—on 1, 3, and 5. By the early eighteenth century, theorists recognized that although the dominant is a common goal of key changes, the mediant, at least in major keys, does not often play that role. They found various ways of explaining that the closely related keys are those whose tonic triads exist in the original key. In a major key, close changes are to 2, 3, 4, 5, and 6, while in a minor key, the goals are 3, 4, 5, 6, and 7. (1992, p. 215)

Indeed, there is no lack of evidence in support of the principle by which "the closely related keys are those whose tonic triads exist in the original key."[7] For example, in the concluding rondo of his "Waldstein" Piano Sonata in C major, Op. 53 (Vienna, 1803–1804), Beethoven writes two main episodes, one in the relative A minor and the other in the parallel C minor. Though both episodes have a "Turkish" flavor, the C-minor episode is not only more agitated, but also occurs later in the movement (mm. 175–220, as compared to 71–98). This suggests that Beethoven, like Riepel and unlike Weber, conceived the chromatic, parallel relationship as more distant than the diatonic, relative one.

In view of such considerations, why is it that Weber's theory has enjoyed and continues to enjoy so much popularity, particularly in comparison to Riepel's?

Part of the answer, no doubt, concerns the systematic, elegant quality of Weber's theory. Riepel's theory, by comparison, is not only incomplete, but seems some-what childish, at least if judged in terms of the fanciful metaphors in which it is couched. However, at least as far as the contemporary music-theoretic scene is concerned another factor seems to have weighed heavily in favor of Weber's theory, namely music psychology. I am referring, of course, to Krumhansl and Kessler's (1982) often-cited study (see also Krumhansl 1990a), a study that has been widely interpreted as an empirical validation of Weber's theory.

Before presenting a "neo-Riepelian" theory of key distance, therefore, it should be useful to consider the relationship between the psychological findings of Krumhansl and her associates and Weber's torus.

13.2   The Krumhansl/Kessler Torus and Its Relation to Weber's

Krumhansl and Kessler (1982) summarize their findings as follows:

> After reliable rating profiles were obtained for major and minor keys, which serve as distinctive markers of the instantiated key [cf. Table 12.2 and Figs. 12.2, 12.3], the profiles were shifted and intercorrelated. This provided a measure of distances between any pair of keys (major or minor) based on the similarity of the tonal hierarchy in the two keys.... The multidimensional scaling technique, which transforms a set of measured inter-object proximities into a spatial configuration of points so as to best account for the proximity data, was applied to the matrix of correlations. That analysis produced a very regular configuration of points in four dimensions that accounted almost perfectly for the correlations computed between the rating profiles. *The 24 major and minor keys were situated on the surface of a torus so as to directly reflect the circle of fifths relations as well as the parallel and relative relations between major and minor keys.* (p. 362, emphasis added)

It should be noted at the outset that at least prior to her association with the so-called "neo-Riemannian" movement (see, for example, Krumhansl 1998),

---

[7] See also Aldwell and Schachter (2003), p. 448 ff.

Krumhansl is rather balanced in advertising the significance of her results. In particular, Krumhansl and Kessler (1982, pp. 351–362) qualify the psychological validity of their torus in the context of *actual* modulating sequences of chords. "We suggest, then," they summarize the section on "the developing and changing sense of key," "that trajectories of the sort presented here, which trace the key sense as it develops and changes over time, may more fully capture the perceptual phenomena of shifting tonal regions *than simple schemes that classify pairs of keys in terms of their relative distances*" (p. 362, emphasis added). In reference to Werts's (1985) toroidal model of key relationships as well as Thompson's (1986) study of perceived key change in Bach chorales, Krumhansl (1990a) even goes so far as to concede that "these considerations suggest that the assumption of symmetrical distances made by the multidimensional scaling analysis is incorrect, as noted also by Krumhansl and Kessler (1982), *but no completely satisfactory account of asymmetries in key relations based on the probe tone data has yet been devised*" (p. 49, emphasis added). Indeed, Krumhansl never measures the sense of key distance directly. Instead, she manipulates other types of data *on the assumption* that the result of such manipulation correlates closely with the desired sense.

Despite these reservations, many were quick to capitalize on Krumhansl's findings. In a section entitled "Experimental Support," Lerdahl (1988, p. 339) notes that "Krumhansl and Kessler (1982) have established a regional space almost identical to Figure 17." The reference is to Weber's torus, to which Lerdahl refers, in view of Schoenberg's (1954) similar if not identical "chart of regions," as the "Weber/Schoenberg regional space." Referring to the same representation Saslaw (1991, p. 125) follows suit, stating that "the work of psychologists Carol Krumhansl and Edward Kessler bears out this representation by means of psychological testing." More recently, in a study entitled "The Cortical Topography of Tonal Structures Underlying Western Music," Janata *et al.* (2002, p. 2167) state in reference to Krumhansl and Kessler's study that ". . . there is a direct correspondence between music-theoretic and cognitive descriptions of the harmonic organization of tonal music." In what follows such claims shall be placed under close scrutiny.[8]

Figure 13.6a is the Krumhansl/Kessler torus as drawn in Krumhansl 1990a. It is clear that the objects on which distance is defined are classes of *enharmonic* keys.[9] In other words, Krumhansl and Kessler implicitly assume that, for example, "C" represents not only C major, but also B♯ major, D♭♭ major, and so forth.[10]

---

[8] Note that the claims challenged here are positivistic: *Krumhansl's results prove Weber's theory.* Cohn's (2007, pp. 110–111) critique of Lerdahl (2001), though bearing some noteworthy points of contact with the argument that follows, is "negativistic": the theory of "tonal pitch space" is *inconsistent with*, and therefore *falsified by*, (some of) Krumhansl's data.

[9] More precisely, classes of enharmonic key *classes* in the sense of Definition 10.7. However, for present purposes we may assume that keys have no scores (Definition 10.4), such that "key class" reduces to "key."

[10] Such an assumption is implicit in circular key metrics in general, including Heinichen's and Kellner's. Note in Fig. 13.6 that in order to close the circles of fifths and major thirds, Krumhansl

Fig. 13.6 The Krumhansl/
Kessler torus. (**a**) From
Krumhansl (1990a).
(**b**) From Krumhansl and
Kessler (1982). Copyright
© 1982 American
Psychological Association.
Reproduced with
permission

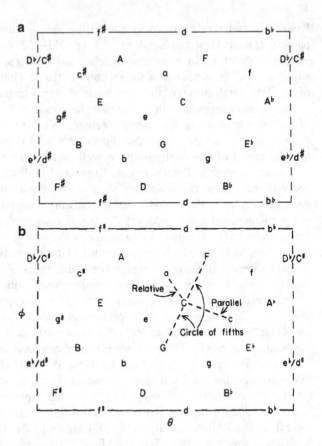

Krumhansl and Kessler (1982, p. 345) note "a striking similarity" between their
representation and Schoenberg's chart of regions. Given that Krumhansl and
Kessler study the same set of objects as does Schoenberg (namely classes of
enharmonic keys), and given that they manipulate data relating to these objects
on the basis of the following two assumptions, this is not as surprising as they
suggest.

- Key distance is symmetrical. This follows from the finding that correlation is by
  definition a symmetrical relation, and the "measure of distances between any
  pair of keys" is a correlation of their respective profiles. As noted before,
  Krumhansl (1990a) concedes that this assumption may be incorrect.
- Key distance satisfies the triangle inequality. As Krumhansl (1990a, p. 41)
  discloses concerning the multidimensional scaling program that was used, "...
  the distances between points (usually computed as Euclidean distance) are
  assumed to have metric properties such as the triangle inequality...."

---

and Kessler write D♭/C♯ and e♭/d♯. This move implies that every "key" in their representation is in
fact an equivalence class of enharmonic keys.

In other words, the Krumhansl/Kessler torus, like Weber's, is *a priori* a metric on classes of enharmonic major/minor keys.

This, however, is also where the similarity between the two constructs ends. Unlike Weber's torus, where distance is measured discretely as the smallest number of edges connecting two vertices, distance on the Krumhansl/Kessler torus is measured *continuously*. As Krumhansl and Kessler (1982, p. 345) note, "... precise quantitative comparisons between interkey distances can be made from the torus representation." Thus, although the Krumhansl/Kessler torus, like Weber's, is a metric space, the two constructs engage fundamentally different concepts of distance and therefore cannot really be compared.

Note that continuous and discrete distances are equally "precise," the former as real numbers, the latter as integers. Therefore, when Krumhansl and Kessler (*ibid.*) claim that continuity in this context is an "advantage" they undoubtedly mean that continuous measurement is more "data driven" and therefore more "psychologically real" than discrete measurement, which is theory driven.[11] Indeed, this interpretation of their remark is borne out by Krumhansl's (1990b, pp. 310–311) discussion of another of her multidimensional scaling solutions, namely, the 1979 conical representation of "intertone distance." Responding to Butler's (1989) critique of what he refers to as "the tonal hierarchy theory," Krumhansl states:

> This conical representation is not a theoretical model, but instead a summary of psychological data. It derives from an experiment (Krumhansl 1979) in which all possible pairs of chromatic key tones in an octave range were presented following major key and major triad contexts. Listeners were instructed to rate how similar the first tone is to the second, and the resulting matrix of rating judgments was analyzed by using multidimensional scaling. ...
>
> None of these characteristics, including the conical shape itself, was determined from theoretical considerations; the spatial configuration was unconstrained except by the similarity judgments themselves. ...

Now empirical data in general and psychological data in particular tend to be continuous. This does not mean, however, that the realities that the data (presumably) reflect are necessarily continuous themselves. So long as Krumhansl is content to interpret her spatial configurations in strictly continuous rather than discrete terms, the relevance of the concept of "theory" to the kind of activity she describes may indeed be minimal (though, as we have seen, theoretical assumptions do constrain the manner in which she manipulates data). Unfortunately however, Krumhansl wants to have it both ways.

Recall the emphasized clause from the Krumhansl and Kessler passage cited initially: "The 24 major and minor keys were situated on the surface of a torus *so as to directly reflect the circle of fifths relations as well as the parallel and relative relations between major and minor keys.*" This claim, which Krumhansl and

---

[11] Apparently because Schoenberg highlights the first-degree relations to C major or C minor on his chart, Krumhansl and Kessler also state (*ibid.*) that "the [Krumhansl/Kessler] torus has the advantage [over Schoenberg's chart of regions] of simultaneously depicting all interkey relations, not just those immediately surrounding a single major or minor key" (i.e., C major or C minor). Clearly, however, like Weber's chart, Schoenberg's has no fixed center of reference.

Kessler illustrate with a figure reproduced above as 13.6b, is seriously misleading, for it suggests that the four relations cited are "first-degree relations" in Weber's, *discrete* sense.

Table 13.1 reproduces Krumhansl's (1990a) Table 2.4, listing the correlations that were fed into the multidimensional scaling computer program. As may be seen, only F and G major have identical values relative to C major, namely 0.591. The value of A minor is higher, namely 0.651, and that of C minor is lower, namely 0.511. Therefore, short of introducing additional, *ad hoc* assumptions, the data simply do *not* support the grouping of F and G major, C and A minor, as a set of keys worthy of special attention in terms of their relation to C major. Indeed, any such grouping flies in the face of E minor, with a value, 0.536, *higher* than that of C minor.[12] Krumhansl does not seem able to accept the consequences of her "data-driven" concept of distance. If distance is measured continuously rather than discretely, *then* "degree of relatedness" *is continuous as well.* "Precision," in other words, is not necessarily an "advantage"; it can be a serious drawback as well.

Nowhere is Krumhansl's refusal to accept the implications of continuity more painfully evident than in her 1990a discussion of another toroidal solution, one where key distances are derived from "harmonic hierarchies" rather than key profiles (pp. 182–187). The representation, reproduced here as Fig. 13.7, may *look* very similar to Fig. 13.6a. However, since "precision" is an overriding concern, the two representations are in fact distinct: compare Table 13.2, listing the correlation values from which Fig. 13.7 was derived, with Table 13.1. In particular, if F and G major, C, *E*, and A minor, are closest to C major by key-profile correlation (not necessarily in this order), then F and G major, C, *F*, G, and A minor, are closest to C major by harmonic-hierarchy correlation. (This depends, of course, on how "closest" is defined. Strictly speaking, only A minor is closest to C major by key-profile correlation, and only C minor is closest to C major by harmonic-hierarchy correlation, excluding, of course, the identity relation.) Nonetheless, Krumhansl (1990a, p. 186) misleadingly states that "it is striking that the results obtained in the present analysis for the harmonic hierarchies *are virtually identical* to those obtained earlier for the tonal hierarchies. Both kinds of hierarchies *generate essentially the same conception* of the degree to which differ-ent abstract tonal centers are related to one another. The degree of relatedness, moreover, *is highly consistent with music-theoretical descriptions.*"[13]

---

[12] In their discussion on pp. 345–346 Krumhansl and Kessler note some of these fine distinctions. For example, they note "the closer distance between C major and A minor than between C major and C minor." However, although they note that "C major and E minor are closer than are C major and D minor," they conveniently fail to mention that E minor is closer to C major than is C minor.

[13] Emphasis added. Krumhansl goes on to claim that "the convergence between the two maps of key distance derived from the tonal and harmonic hierarchies is of considerable interest for a number of reasons" (p. 187), listing no fewer than three.

	C Major	C Minor
C major	1.000	0.511
C♯/D♭ major	−0.500	−0.158
D major	0.040	−0.402
D♯/E♭ major	−0.105	0.651
E major	−0.185	−0.508
F major	0.591	0.241
F♯/G♭ major	−0.683	−0.369
G major	0.591	0.215
G♯/A♭ major	−0.185	0.536
A major	−0.105	−0.654
A♯/B♭ major	0.040	0.237
B major	−0.500	−0.298
C minor	0.511	1.000
C♯/D♭ minor	−0.298	−0.394
D minor	0.237	−0.160
D♯/E♭ minor	−0.654	0.055
E minor	0.536	−0.003
F minor	0.215	0.339
F♯/G♭ minor	−0.369	−0.673
G minor	0.241	0.339
G♯/A♭ minor	−0.508	−0.003
A minor	0.651	0.055
A♯/B♭ minor	−0.402	−0.160
B minor	−0.158	−0.394

Table 13.1 The correlations between keys from which the Krumhansl/Kessler torus was derived (From Krumhansl (1990a), Table 2.4 on p. 38. By permission of Oxford University Press)

Fig. 13.7 Key distance derived from "harmonic hierarchies." From Krumhansl (1990a), Fig. 7.4 on p. 187. By permission of Oxford University Press

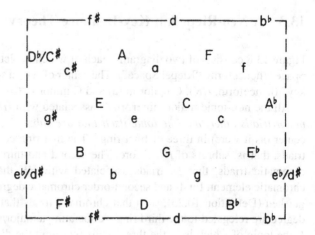

In summary, Krumhansl's work does *not* "bear out" Weber's torus by means of psychological testing, as Saslaw and others believe. As Krumhansl herself insists, her work is a summary of psychological data. As is generally the case in the empirical sciences when attempting to extrapolate from data to theory, it is impossible to extrapolate from Krumhansl's data to Weber's theory.

	C Major	C Minor
Table 13.2 The data from which Fig. 13.7 was derived (From Krumhansl (1990a), Table 7.10 on p. 183. By permission of Oxford University Press)		
C major	1.000	0.738
C♯/D♭ major	−0.301	−0.224
D major	−0.141	−0.320
D♯/E♭ major	−0.013	0.405
E major	−0.139	−0.256
F major	0.297	0.194
F♯/G♭ major	−0.407	−0.281
G major	0.297	0.175
G♯/A♭ major	−0.139	0.123
A major	−0.013	−0.286
A♯/B♭ major	−0.141	0.031
B major	−0.301	−0.298
C minor	0.738	1.000
C♯/D♭ minor	−0.298	−0.373
D minor	0.031	−0.189
D♯/E♭ minor	−0.286	0.072
E minor	0.123	−0.096
F minor	0.175	0.245
F♯/G♭ minor	−0.281	−0.321
G minor	0.194	0.245
G♯/A♭ minor	−0.256	−0.096
A minor	0.405	0.072
A♯/B♭ minor	−0.320	−0.189
B minor	−0.224	−0.373

13.3 A Neo-Riepelian Key-Distance Theory

Figure 13.8 consists of two diagrams, each of which depicts a "Neo-Riepelian Key Space" (henceforth, "Riepel Space"). The center of such a space represents a "home key" (henceforth, *HK*), C major in (a) and C minor in (b).

All the non-tonic major/minor triads associated with *HK*, that is, *all the major/ minor triads other than the tonic itself that are subsets of HK's cluster*, orbit the center (as it were) in three distinct rings. The first ring consists of all the *diatonic* triads, that is, subsets of *HK*'s core. The second and third rings consist of all the chromatic triads, that is, triads associated with *HK* that contain at least one chromatic element. First- and second-order chromatic degrees, however, are distinguished (Definition 10.25), such that chromatic triads that contain a second-order degree are relegated to the third ring. Associating a major/minor triad T with a key K the tonic of which is T, the three orbits represent the distance of $K \neq HK$ from *HK*. Thus, $K \neq HK$ can be distant from *HK* by one, two, or three degrees, depending on whether K inhabits the first, second, or third ring. The distance of *HK* from itself is of course zero.

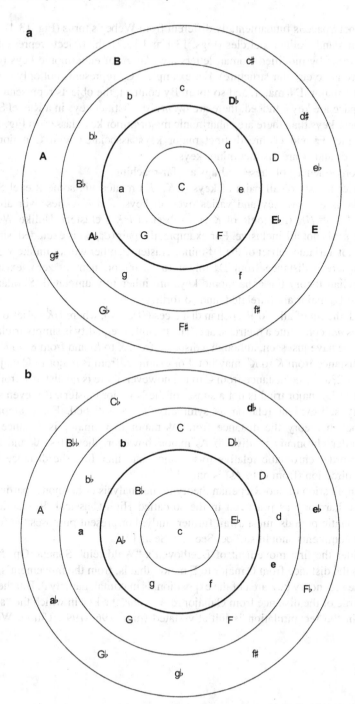

Fig. 13.8 Two Riepel Spaces. (**a**) The C-major space. (**b**) The C-minor space

A Riepel Space is fundamentally different from Weber's torus (Fig. 13.4). As in Heinichen's and Kellner's circles (Figs. 13.1 and 13.2), the objects represented in Weber's torus by modified Roman letters are *classes* of enharmonic keys (otherwise, there is no circular structure). For example, "C" represents not only C major but also B♯ major, D♭♭ major, and so forth. By contrast, the objects represented in a Riepel Space are keys. Indeed, there are *twenty-six* distinct keys in a Riepel Space, that is, more keys than there are enharmonic major/minor key classes. In Fig. 13.8a, for example, F♯ and G♭ are distinct major keys associated with C major, and similarly, d♯ and e♭ are distinct minor keys.

The consequences of these findings are far-reaching.

Consider the set of all pairs of keys (*HK*, *K*) related via some Riepel Space, where *HK* is a home key and varies over all keys, and *K* varies over all keys associated with *HK* (the tonic of *K* is a subset of *HK*'s cluster). Unlike Weber's torus, the set is not all-inclusive. For example, the pair (d♯, e♭) is excluded, since E♭ minor is not a triadic subset of the D♯-minor cluster. In other words, unlike Weber's theory, where a distance from D♯ minor to E♭ minor, namely zero, exists, by neo-Riepelian theory the enharmonic keys are inherently unrelated. Similarly, B major and D♭ major are unrelated, and so forth.

Indeed, the set of all neo-Riepelian distances (*HK*, *K*), where *HK* varies over all keys, does *not* constitute a metric space. The triangle inequality is simply irrelevant, since, as we have just seen, although a distance from *K* to *K'* and from *K'* to *K''* may exist, a distance from *K* to *K''* may not. For example, from B major to C major the distance is 2, as is the distance from C to D♭; however, there is *no* distance from B to D♭ major (a D♭-major triad is not a subset of the B-major cluster). But even such a seemingly self-evident relation as symmetry is not satisfied. For example, by neo-Riepelian theory the distance from A♭ major to C major is 3, since E♮ is second-order chromatic relative to A♭ major; however, the notes A♭ and E♭ are both *first*-order chromatic relative to C major, and therefore the distance in the opposite direction (from C to A♭) is only 2.[14]

The application of neo-Riepelian theory to the analysis of harmony, particularly chromatic harmony as practiced in the so-called High-Classical, Romantic, and Post-Romantic periods, must await further study. For present purposes the following brief comments should suffice. See also Sect. 15.2.

Consider the first movement of Beethoven's "Waldstein" Sonata, Op. 53. By Fig. 13.8 the distance from C major to E major, that is, from the movement's home key to the secondary key-area of the exposition, is maximal, namely 3. But then, the same is true of the distance from C major *to A major*, the key in which the "second theme" in the recapitulation is initially stated (mm. 196–199). Unlike Weber's

---

[14] In Fig. 13.8 keys *K* in bold typeface indicate that the distance from *K* to *HK* is different from the distance from *HK* to *K*.

Fig. 13.9 Schubert, String Quintet in C major, D. 956, II, mm. 91–94

torus, where A major is closer to C major than is E major, by neo-Riepelian theory the two keys are equidistant from C major.[15]

By contrast, the closing measures of the slow movement of Schubert's Quintet in C major, D. 956 (Vienna, ca. 1828), seem to defy the strictures of neo-Riepelian theory (Fig. 13.9). Aldwell and Schachter (2003, pp. 545–546) analyze the striking F-*minor* triad of m. 92 (asterisked in the figure) as "♭II♭" in E major (the home key). Since the F-minor triad is tonicized, their analysis suggests contrary to neo-Riepelian theory that a relation between the keys of E major and F minor exists. Indeed, the analysis suggests that *contrary to the notion of a diatonic system* (Definition 6.21) the note A♭ can be a received element relative to the E-major core.

Aldwell and Schachter explain the unusual chromatic chord as a case of "double mixture," that is, "applying secondary mixture to a triad achieved through simple mixture" (*ibid.*, p. 541); they define "secondary mixture" as "altering the quality of a triad without using scale degrees from the parallel mode."[16] The F-minor triad, then, is a transformation by secondary mixture of an F-*major* triad (♭II), itself the result of "simple" mixture applied to an F-*sharp* minor triad (II). In particular, the note A♭, by which the quality of the triad is altered from major to minor, is *not* a (diatonic) degree in E minor (the parallel of E major).

---

[15] The key-scheme of the Waldstein Sonata is anticipated by Beethoven in the G-major Piano Sonata, Op. 31 No. 1, where B major in the exposition (m. 66 ff.) is answered in the recapitulation by E major (mm. 218–225). The apparent symmetry by which III♯ and VI♯ are equidistant from the tonic is also confirmed by Brahms's Symphony No. 3 in F major, Op. 90, where in the first movement A major in the exposition (m. 36 ff.) is answered in the recapitulation by D major (mm. 149–153). See also Beethoven's "Pastoral" Symphony, Op. 68, where a move from B♭ major to D major in the development of the first movement (mm. 151–190) is answered by a move from G major to E major (mm. 197–236).

[16] As Rothstein (2003, p. 217) notes, the concepts of "secondary" and "double" mixture, and even the term "double mixture," originate with Schenker (1906).

Fig. 13.10 The diatonic
subspace of a Riepel Space
forms a metric space

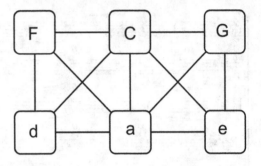

What, however, is the relation of secondary mixture to (simple) mixture? None, if one accepts Aldwell and Schachter's definition at face value (the quality of a triad is altered *without* using scale degrees from the parallel mode). Yet assuming that their usage of "secondary" is not unrelated to its usage in "secondary dominant" (a construct to which Aldwell and Schachter refer rather as "applied dominant"), the term would seem to imply that just as a secondary dominant is "simple" *from the perspective of a key other than the home key*, so is secondary mixture. In other words, there exists a key (one or more) other than the home key in relation to which secondary mixture may be viewed as simple mixture. A moment's reflection will reveal that a diatonic F-major triad may be transformed via (simple) mixture into F minor in exactly four different keys (counting $\hat{2} \rightarrow \flat\hat{2}$ as a case of mixture): B♭ major, F major, C major, and G minor.

Unless, then, "secondary mixture" is an *ad hoc* construct that bears no relation to simple mixture, Schubert's F-minor triad, as a case of secondary mixture, must be viewed as V♭ in B♭, I♭ in F, IV♭ in C, or VII♭ in g. Two of these four possibilities, namely I♭ in F and IV♭ in C, seem to yield a satisfying analysis of the passage. In particular, the progression *leading into* F minor is suggestive of V-I♭ in F major, whereas the progression *departing from* F minor is suggestive of IV♭-I in C major.

Consider finally Fig. 13.10. The figure shows that the strictly diatonic subspace of a Riepel Space (the C-major space of Fig. 13.8a in the present case) constitutes a metric space. Not only does a distance between every pair of keys in the subspace exist, the set of all distances, as may easily be verified, satisfy the conditions of symmetry and the triangle inequality. For example, the distance from F major to E minor is 2, because the E minor triad contains a first-order chromatic degree, namely B♮, relative to F major; the distance in the opposite direction is also 2, because the F major triad contains a first-order chromatic degree, namely F♮, relative to E minor.

The dark border surrounding the first, diatonic ring in each of the two Riepel Spaces depicted in Fig. 13.8 is like a warning sign: "Leave the Diatonic Realm at Your Own Risk!" Do not assume, in any case, that chromatic key relationships will abide by the same, predictable rules that diatonic key relationships have conveniently taught us to expect.

References

Aldwell, E., & Schachter, C. (2003). *Harmony and voice leading* (3rd ed.). Belmont: Wadsworth Group.

Bernstein, D. (2002). Nineteenth-century harmonic theory: The Austro-German legacy. In T. Christensen (Ed.), *The Cambridge history of Western music theory* (pp. 778–811). Cambridge: Cambridge University Press.

Butler, D. (1989). Describing the perception of tonality in music: A critique of the tonal hierarchy theory and a proposal for a theory of intervallic rivalry. *Music Perception, 9*, 219–242.

Cohn, R. (2007). [Review of Lerdahl 2001]. *Music Theory Spectrum, 29*(1), 101–114.

Heinichen, J. (1711). *Neu erfundene und gründliche Anweisung.* Hamburg: Schiller.

Heinichen, J. (1728). *Der Generalbass in der Komposition.* Dresden: Heinichen. 1994. Reprint, Hildesheim: Olms.

Hyer, B. (2002). Tonality. In T. Christensen (Ed.), *The Cambridge history of Western music theory* (pp. 726–752). Cambridge: Cambridge University Press.

Janata, P., Birk, J., Van Horn, J., Leman, M., Tillmann, B., & Bharucha, J. (2002). The cortical topography of tonal structures underlying Western music. *Science, 298*, 2167–2170.

Kellner, D. (1732). *Treulicher Unterricht im General-Bass.* Hamburg: Kissner. 1737. 2nd ed., Hamburg: Herold. 1979. Reprint of 2nd ed., Hildesheim: Olms.

Krumhansl, C. (1979). The psychological representation of musical pitch in a tonal context. *Cognitive Psychology, 11*, 346–374.

Krumhansl, C. (1990a). *Cognitive foundations of musical pitch.* New York: Oxford University Press.

Krumhansl, C. (1990b). Tonal hierarchies and rare intervals in music cognition. *Music Perception, 7*(3), 309–324.

Krumhansl, C. (1998). Perceived triad distance: Evidence supporting the psychological reality of neo-Riemannian transformations. *Journal of Music Theory, 42*(2), 265–281.

Krumhansl, C. (2005). The geometry of musical structure: A brief introduction and history. *ACM Computers in Entertainment, 3*(4), 1–14.

Krumhansl, C., & Kessler, E. (1982). Tracing the dynamic changes in perceived tonal organization in a spatial representation of musical keys. *Psychological Review, 89*(4), 334–368.

Lerdahl, F. (1988). Tonal pitch space. *Music Perception, 5*(3), 315–349.

Lerdahl, F. (2001). *Tonal pitch space.* Oxford: Oxford University Press.

Lester, J. (1989). *Between modes and keys: German theory 1592–1802.* Stuyvesant: Pendragon.

Lester, J. (1992). *Compositional theory in the eighteenth century.* Cambridge: Harvard University Press.

Mattheson, J. (1735). *Kleine General-Bass Schule.* Hamburg: Kissner.

Ratner, L. (1980). *Classic music: Expression, form, style.* New York: Schirmer.

Riepel, J. (1755). *Grundregeln zur Tonordnung insgemein* (Vol. II of *Anfangsgründe zur musikalischen Setzkunst*). Frankfurt: Wagner. 1996. Reprint, Vienna: Böhlau.

Rothstein, W. (2003). A reply to Brian Hyer. *Journal of Music Theory, 47*(1), 215–222.

Saslaw, J. (1991). Gottfried Weber's cognitive theory of harmonic progression. *Studies in Music from the University of Western Ontario, 13*, 121–144.

Schenker, H. (1906). *Harmonielehre.* Stuttgart: Cotta.

Schoenberg, A. (1954). *Structural functions of harmony* (H. Searle, Ed., Rev. 1969). New York: Norton.

Thompson, W. (1986). *Judgments of key change in Bach chorale excerpts: An investigation of the sensitivity to keys, chords, and voicing.* PhD diss., Queen's University, Kingston.

Weber, G. (1830–1832). *Versuch einer geordneten Theorie der Tonsetzkunst* (3rd Rev. Ed.). Mainz: Schott.

Werts, D. (1985). The musical circle of Johannes Mattheson. *Theoria, 1*, 97–131.

Westergaard, P. (1996). Geometries of sounds in time. *Music Theory Spectrum, 18*(1), 1–21.

Wheelock, G. (1993). *Schwartze Gredel* and the engendered minor mode in Mozart's operas. In R. Solie (Ed.), *Musicology and difference: Gender and sexuality in music scholarship* (pp. 201–222). Berkeley: University of California Press.

Chapter 14
Tonal Communication

Abstract A heptad (Sect. 14.1) is a set of seven diatonic and first-order chromatic degrees conceived as a subset of a modal cluster (represented as a set of degrees). A heptad satisfies two properties. In a "generic" sense, it contains exactly one representative of each degree; moreover, the third degree of a *triadic* heptad *is diatonic*. Relative to a given mode, there exist exactly 32 dyadic heptads, and 16 triadic heptads. In particular, there are 16 Ionian (major) and 16 Aeolian (minor) triadic heptads. Two heptads are "type equivalent" if, in a specific sense, one can be represented as a cyclic permutation of the other. A "tonal" heptad (Sect. 14.2) is a member of a pair of triadic heptads, one major and the other minor, such that, among other properties, the heptads are *not* type equivalent. It is shown that a tonal heptad is either "natural major" or harmonic minor. Moreover, a modal communication system that employs "tonalities," that is, keys, the scores of which are representable as tonal heptads, is a *context-free* system in the sense that no contextual cues are needed for the receiver to judge the image of the transmitted final as privileged.

Robust modal communication satisfies the Communication Principle but at the price of a "contextual" assumption we have termed in Sect. 10.2 "final-image centricity." By final-image centricity the receiver is able to judge as privileged the image of the transmitted final. The assumption is "contextual" in the sense that it relies on cues that (one may assume informally) are present in messages, for example, the placement of the final (or octave equivalent) at a temporally privileged position in the transmitted message such as its beginning and/or end. It is high time that we offer a context-free theory of modal communication. Given that our focus has shifted since Chap. 10 to triadic keys the finals of which are known as "tonics," the context-free theory is in fact a theory of *tonal* communication. As we shall see, tonal communication is not only context free, but is tribal-class preserving (that is, major/minor preserving), a property equivalent to the preservation of the diatonic/chromatic partitioning of the message.

E. Agmon, *The Languages of Western Tonality*, Computational Music Science,
DOI 10.1007/978-3-642-39587-1_14, © Springer-Verlag Berlin Heidelberg 2013

We begin this last phase of our journey with heptads, which are special subsets of the set of diatonic and first-order chromatic degrees.

14.1 Dyadic and Triadic Heptads

Definition 14.1. Heptad

Set $0 \leq \mu \leq 5$, $n = 2, 3$, and let nH^{μ} be a seven-element subset of the (interval-lic) line-of-fifths segment $IQ^{12}_{-5} = ((1, 1), (8, 5), \ldots, (6, 3)) = (\text{m2}, \text{m6}, \ldots, \text{A4})$.

We shall refer to nH^{μ} as *an n-adic Mu-ian heptad* if the following two conditions, A and B, are satisfied.

A. For every $v = 0, 1, \ldots, 6$ there exists exactly one u such that $(u, v) \in nH^{\mu}$.
B. If $n = 3$ and $\mu = 0, 1, 2$ ($\mu = 3, 4, 5$) then $(4, 2) \in nH^{\mu}$ $((3, 2) \in nH^{\mu})$.

We shall think of a *Mu*-ian heptad as a set of diatonic and first-order chromatic degrees representing a subset of the *Mu*-ian degree cluster (Definition 10.21) and shall refer to the heptad as Lydian, Ionian, ..., Phrygian, depending on *Mu* (Definition 10.8). We shall refer to a member of the heptad as *diatonic* or *chromatic* depending on *Mu*, as per Table 10.2.

In other words, an *n*-adic *Mu*-ian heptad is a set of seven diatonic and first-order chromatic degrees conceived as a subset of the *Mu*-ian degree cluster *and partitioned into "diatonic" vs. "chromatic" elements depending on Mu*. A heptad satisfies two properties. In a generic sense, a heptad contains exactly one representative of each degree[1]; moreover, the third degree of a *triadic* heptad *is diatonic*.

Example 14.2. Let nH^{μ} be a dyadic, Ionian or Aeolian heptad.
Then nH^{μ} is a set of exactly seven degrees A or B, respectively.

A. $\hat{1}, \flat\hat{2}$ *or* $\hat{2}, \flat\hat{3}$ *or* $\hat{3}, \hat{4}$ *or* $\sharp\hat{4}, \hat{5}, \flat\hat{6}$ *or* $\hat{6}, \flat\hat{7}$ *or* $\hat{7}$.
B. $\hat{1}, \flat\hat{2}$ *or* $\hat{2}, \hat{3}$ *or* $\sharp\hat{3}, \hat{4}$ *or* $\sharp\hat{4}, \hat{5}, \hat{6}$ *or* $\sharp\hat{6}, \hat{7}$ *or* $\sharp\hat{7}$.

Let nH^{μ} be a *triadic*, Ionian or Aeolian heptad.
Then nH^{μ} is a set of exactly seven degrees C or D, respectively.

C. $\hat{1}, \flat\hat{2}$ *or* $\hat{2}, \hat{3}, \hat{4}$ *or* $\sharp\hat{4}, \hat{5}, \flat\hat{6}$ *or* $\hat{6}, \flat\hat{7}$ *or* $\hat{7}$.
D. $\hat{1}, \flat\hat{2}$ *or* $\hat{2}, \hat{3}, \hat{4}$ *or* $\sharp\hat{4}, \hat{5}, \hat{6}$ *or* $\sharp\hat{6}, \hat{7}$ *or* $\sharp\hat{7}$.

Since a dyadic heptad results from exactly five independent binary choices (in the Ionian case $\flat\hat{2}/\hat{2}$, $\flat\hat{3}/\hat{3}$, $\hat{4}/\sharp\hat{4}$, $\flat\hat{6}/\hat{6}$, and $\flat\hat{7}/\hat{7}$), whereas the number of choices in the case of a triadic heptad is only four, $\flat\hat{2}/\hat{2}$, $\hat{4}/\sharp\hat{4}$, $\flat\hat{6}/\hat{6}$, and $\flat\hat{7}/\hat{7}$, we have the following proposition.

---

[1] Julian Hook's (2011) "spelled heptachords" are similarly "letter distinct." A heptad, however, is not a spelled heptachord.

Proposition 14.3. Fix $\mu = 0, 1, \ldots, 5$, and let $\{nH^\mu\}$ be the set of all dyadic (triadic) *Mu*-ian heptads.

Then the set contains exactly $2^5 = 32$ $(2^4 = 16)$ elements.

In Table 14.1 subsequently in this section the 32 dyadic Ionian heptads are displayed, and in Table 14.2—the 16 Ionian·(major) and 16 Aeolian (minor) *triadic* heptads. First, however, we shall study some properties by which heptads may usefully be characterized.

Definition 14.4. Depth (of a heptad)

Let nH^μ be an n-adic *Mu*-ian heptad. Let i and j satisfy i is minimal and j is maximal such that $IQ_i, IQ_j \in nH^\mu$, and set $\delta = (j - i) - 6$.

We shall refer to δ as *the depth of nH^μ*.

In other words, the depth of a heptad is the distance in fifths between the two most "extreme" members of the heptad (in terms of the line of fifths), such that the distance of six fifths (i.e., the heptad represents *a connected* segment of the line of fifths) is set to zero.

Example 14.5. The depth of the dyadic Ionian heptad $2H^1 = \{\hat{1}, \hat{2}, \flat\hat{3}, \hat{4}, \hat{5}, \flat\hat{6}, \hat{7}\}$ is 3, since $\flat\hat{6} = (8, 5) = IQ_{-4}$ where $i = -4$ is minimal, and $\hat{7} = (11, 6) = IQ_5$ where $j = 5$ is maximal; moreover, $(j - i) -6 = (5 + 4) - 6 = 3$.

Since $IQ_7 = (1, 0)$ and since heptads, by definition, cannot consist of both a diatonic degree (u, v) and a chromatic degree $(u \pm 1, v)$, a heptad of depth 1 does not exist. Therefore, if nH^μ is a heptad of depth δ, then $\delta \in \{0, 2, 3, 4, 5\}$.

The depth of a heptad and its "degree-interval set" (Definition 14.7, ahead) are related. We begin with "degree interval."

Definition 14.6. Degree Interval

Let H be a heptad. Let $((u, v), (u', v')) \in H \times H$, and set $(q, r) \equiv (u', v') - (u, v)$, $0 \le q \le 11$.

We shall refer to (q, r) as *the degree interval from (u, v) to (u', v')*.

Definition 14.7. Degree-Interval Set

Let H be a heptad.

We shall refer to the set D of all degree intervals (q, r) from (u, v) to (u', v'), where $((u, v), (u', v')) \in H \times H$, as *the degree-interval set relative to H*.

*Proposition 14.8. Let H be a heptad of depth δ, and let D_δ be the degree-interval set relative to H. Then $D_0 = \{d5, m2, \ldots, A4\}$, such that

$$D_2 \setminus D_0 = \{d4, A5\},$$
$$D_3 \setminus D_2 = \{A2, d7\},$$
$$D_4 \setminus D_3 = \{d3, A6\},$$
$$D_5 \setminus D_4 = \{A3, d6\}.$$

Definition 14.9. Saturation (of a heptad)

We shall refer to the number of chromatic degrees that are members of a heptad H as its *saturation*.

It is easily seen that the maximal saturation in the case of a dyadic (triadic) heptad is five (four).

Finally, in order to define subsequently a sense by which two heptads may usefully be said to be equivalent we shall represent heptads in a manner reminiscent of the medieval, "tetrachordal" representation of modes.

Definition 14.10. Signature (of a heptad)

Let $H = \{(u_0, 0), (u_1, 1), \ldots, (u_6, 6)\}$ be a heptad.

We shall refer to the ordered set $\Sigma(H) = (u_1 - u_0, u_2 - u_1, \ldots, u_6 - u_5, 12 - u_6)$ as *the signature of H*.

Example 14.11. Consider the dyadic Ionian heptad $H = 2H^1 = \{\hat{1}, \hat{2}, \flat\hat{3}, \hat{4}, \hat{5}, \flat\hat{6}, \hat{7}\}$. Then $\Sigma(H) = (2, 1, 2, 2, 1, 3, 1)$.

Note the special conditions under which the following proposition is true.

*Proposition 14.12. Let H and H' be two triadic heptads, each either Ionian or Aeolian.

Then $\Sigma(H) = \Sigma(H')$ if, and only if, $H = H'$.

We are now ready for the following definition.

Definition 14.13. Heptad Type Equivalence; Heptad Type Class

Let $H = nH^\mu$ and $H' = nH^\nu$ be two n-adic heptads, one *Mu*-ian and the other *Nu*-ian, with signatures $\Sigma(H)$ and $\Sigma(H')$, respectively.

A. We shall say that H and H' are *type equivalent* if $\Sigma(H')$ is a cyclic permutation of $\Sigma(H)$.

B. We shall refer to the set of all heptads H' that are type equivalent to H as *a type class*.

Example 14.14. The dyadic Ionian heptad $H = 2H^1 = \{\hat{1}, \hat{2}, \flat\hat{3}, \hat{4}, \hat{5}, \hat{6}, \flat\hat{7}\}$ and the dyadic Aeolian heptad $H' = 2H^4 = \{\hat{1}, \hat{2}, \sharp\hat{3}, \sharp\hat{4}, \hat{5}, \sharp\hat{6}, \sharp\hat{7}\}$ are type equivalent. We have $\Sigma(H) = (2, 1, 2, 2, 2, 1, 2)$, $\Sigma(H') = (2, 2, 2, 1, 2, 2, 1)$, a cyclic permutation of $\Sigma(H)$.

An equivalent definition of type equivalence is given in the following proposition.

*Proposition 14.15. Let H and H' be two heptads.

Then the heptads are type equivalent if, and only if, there exists an ordering $(u_1, v_1), (u_2, v_2), \ldots, (u_7, v_7)$ on H and an ordering $(u'_1, v'_1), (u'_2, v'_2), \ldots, (u'_7, v'_7)$ on H' such that for some (q, r), $(u'_i, v'_i) \equiv (u_i, v_i) \oplus (q, r)$, $i = 1, 2, \ldots, 7$.

Figure 14.1 illustrates the proposition, using the two heptads of Example 14.14. Arrows represent transposition by major sixth.

Finally, in Table 14.1 the 32 dyadic Ionian heptads are listed by depth, saturation, and type class (dark borders). As may be seen, the heptads fall into exactly 16 type classes, such that no more than six heptads are members of the same class.

Fig. 14.1 Two type-equivalent dyadic heptads. *Arrows* represent transposition by major sixth

$$\hat{1},\ \hat{2},\ \flat\hat{3},\ \hat{4},\ \hat{5},\ \hat{6},\ \flat\hat{7}$$

$$\downarrow\quad\downarrow\quad\downarrow\quad\downarrow\quad\downarrow\quad\downarrow\quad\downarrow$$

$$\#\hat{6},\#\hat{7},\ \hat{1},\ \hat{2},\#\hat{3},\ \#\hat{4},\ \hat{5}$$

Table 14.1 The 32 dyadic Ionian heptads. Dark borders indicate type equivalence

depth	saturation	dyadic Ionian heptad
0	0	$\{\hat{1}, \hat{2}, \hat{3}, \hat{4}, \hat{5}, \hat{6}, \hat{7}\}$
	1	$\{\hat{1}, \hat{2}, \hat{3}, \#\hat{4}, \hat{5}, \hat{6}, \hat{7}\}$
	1	$\{\hat{1}, \hat{2}, \hat{3}, \hat{4}, \hat{5}, \hat{6}, \flat\hat{7}\}$
	2	$\{\hat{1}, \hat{2}, \flat\hat{3}, \hat{4}, \hat{5}, \hat{6}, \flat\hat{7}\}$
	3	$\{\hat{1}, \hat{2}, \flat\hat{3}, \hat{4}, \hat{5}, \flat\hat{6}, \flat\hat{7}\}$
	4	$\{\hat{1}, \flat\hat{2}, \flat\hat{3}, \hat{4}, \hat{5}, \flat\hat{6}, \flat\hat{7}\}$
2	1	$\{\hat{1}, \hat{2}, \flat\hat{3}, \hat{4}, \hat{5}, \hat{6}, \hat{7}\}$
	2	$\{\hat{1}, \hat{2}, \hat{3}, \#\hat{4}, \hat{5}, \hat{6}, \flat\hat{7}\}$
	2	$\{\hat{1}, \hat{2}, \hat{3}, \hat{4}, \hat{5}, \flat\hat{6}, \flat\hat{7}\}$
	3	$\{\hat{1}, \flat\hat{2}, \flat\hat{3}, \hat{4}, \hat{5}, \hat{6}, \flat\hat{7}\}$
3	1	$\{\hat{1}, \hat{2}, \hat{3}, \hat{4}, \hat{5}, \flat\hat{6}, \hat{7}\}$
	2	$\{\hat{1}, \flat\hat{2}, \hat{3}, \hat{4}, \hat{5}, \hat{6}, \flat\hat{7}\}$
	2	$\{\hat{1}, \hat{2}, \flat\hat{3}, \#\hat{4}, \hat{5}, \hat{6}, \hat{7}\}$
	2	$\{\hat{1}, \hat{2}, \flat\hat{3}, \hat{4}, \hat{5}, \flat\hat{6}, \hat{7}\}$
	3	$\{\hat{1}, \flat\hat{2}, \hat{3}, \hat{4}, \hat{5}, \flat\hat{6}, \flat\hat{7}\}$
	3	$\{\hat{1}, \hat{2}, \flat\hat{3}, \#\hat{4}, \hat{5}, \hat{6}, \flat\hat{7}\}$
4	1	$\{\hat{1}, \flat\hat{2}, \hat{3}, \hat{4}, \hat{5}, \hat{6}, \hat{7}\}$
	2	$\{\hat{1}, \hat{2}, \hat{3}, \#\hat{4}, \hat{5}, \flat\hat{6}, \hat{7}\}$
	2	$\{\hat{1}, \flat\hat{2}, \hat{3}, \hat{4}, \hat{5}, \flat\hat{6}, \hat{7}\}$
	2	$\{\hat{1}, \hat{2}, \flat\hat{3}, \#\hat{4}, \hat{5}, \flat\hat{6}, \hat{7}\}$
	3	$\{\hat{1}, \hat{2}, \hat{3}, \#\hat{4}, \hat{5}, \flat\hat{6}, \flat\hat{7}\}$
	3	$\{\hat{1}, \flat\hat{2}, \flat\hat{3}, \hat{4}, \hat{5}, \hat{6}, \hat{7}\}$
	3	$\{\hat{1}, \flat\hat{2}, \flat\hat{3}, \hat{4}, \hat{5}, \flat\hat{6}, \hat{7}\}$
	4	$\{\hat{1}, \hat{2}, \flat\hat{3}, \#\hat{4}, \hat{5}, \flat\hat{6}, \flat\hat{7}\}$
5	2	$\{\hat{1}, \flat\hat{2}, \hat{3}, \#\hat{4}, \hat{5}, \hat{6}, \hat{7}\}$
	3	$\{\hat{1}, \flat\hat{2}, \hat{3}, \#\hat{4}, \hat{5}, \flat\hat{6}, \hat{7}\}$
	3	$\{\hat{1}, \flat\hat{2}, \hat{3}, \#\hat{4}, \hat{5}, \hat{6}, \flat\hat{7}\}$
	3	$\{\hat{1}, \flat\hat{2}, \flat\hat{3}, \#\hat{4}, \hat{5}, \hat{6}, \hat{7}\}$
	4	$\{\hat{1}, \flat\hat{2}, \hat{3}, \#\hat{4}, \hat{5}, \flat\hat{6}, \flat\hat{7}\}$
	4	$\{\hat{1}, \flat\hat{2}, \flat\hat{3}, \#\hat{4}, \hat{5}, \flat\hat{6}, \hat{7}\}$
	4	$\{\hat{1}, \flat\hat{2}, \flat\hat{3}, \#\hat{4}, \hat{5}, \hat{6}, \flat\hat{7}\}$
	5	$\{\hat{1}, \flat\hat{2}, \flat\hat{3}, \#\hat{4}, \hat{5}, \flat\hat{6}, \flat\hat{7}\}$

Interestingly, the dyadic Ionian heptads correspond exactly to the north-Indian *thaats* as described in Jairazbhoy (1971, p. 46). Indeed, the correspondence between north-Indian musical theory and the theory of dyadic Ionian heptads is remarkable. Consider the following excerpts from Jairazbhoy:

> In North Indian musical theory seven notes (*svar*) are recognized..., Sa, Re (or Ri), Ga, Ma, Pa, Dha and Ni.... The Indian nomenclature is comparable to that of Western tonic-solfa: there is no absolute or fixed pitch attached to the notes, and the ground-note (the note which serves as the point of reference of the scale) is called Sa, irrespective of its pitch....
> Of these seven notes, Sa and Pa (I and V) are 'immovable notes' (*acal svar*)—they have no flat or sharp positions and Pa is always a perfect fifth above the Sa. The remaining five notes are 'movable notes' (*cal svar*). These each have two possible positions, a semitone apart. One of these is called *śuddh* (pure) which is comparable to the 'natural' of the West. In the *śuddh* scale, *Bilāval*, composed of Sa, Pa and the five movable notes in their *śuddh* position, the distribution of tones and semitones corresponds to that in the Western major scale. [*Footnote*: In its present-day application the *śuddh* concept does not entail the idea of parent scale from which other scales are derived, but serves only as a standard for comparison.]
> When the movable notes are not in the *śuddh* position, they are called *vikṛit*—altered. In the case of Re, Ga, Dha and Ni (II, III, VI and VII) they are a semitone lower than their *śuddh* counterparts and are called *komal*—soft, tender. The altered Ma (IV), however, is a semitone above the *śuddh* position, and is called *tīvr*—strong, intense. (1971, pp. 32–33)

Henceforth we shall focus on major and minor *triadic* heptads $3H^1$ (Ionian) and $3H^4$ (Aeolian) to which we shall refer simply as "major" and "minor," respectively. Also, to simplify notation we shall write

$$3H^1 = +H, \quad 3H^4 = -H.$$

Figure 14.2 quotes three structure-defining passages from Liszt's monumental B-minor Sonata (Weimar 1853): the opening *Lento assai* (mm. 1–7), the closing measures of "the slow movement" just before the fugal reprise (mm. 453–459), and the closing *Lento assai* (mm. 750–760). Each passage contains two "descending-octave patterns," the second of which is a varied repetition of the first. Note that Patterns 5 and 6 are completed by the piece's very last note.

Every pattern except 4, represented as a set of degrees *relative to the framing octave as tonic*, is a (triadic) heptad. In particular, relative to G and F♯, respectively, Patterns 1 and 3 represent the minor heptad $\{\hat{1}, \flat\hat{2}, \hat{3}, \hat{4}, \hat{5}, \hat{6}, \hat{7}\}$ of depth 0 and saturation 1; relative to G as tonic Pattern 2 represents the minor heptad $\{\hat{1}, \hat{2}, \hat{3}, \sharp\hat{4}, \hat{5}, \hat{6}, \sharp\hat{7}\}$ of depth 4 and saturation 2; and relative to B Patterns 5 and 6 represent the *major* heptad $\{\hat{1}, \flat\hat{2}, \hat{3}, \hat{4}, \hat{5}, \flat\hat{6}, \flat\hat{7}\}$ of depth 3 and saturation 3. Pattern 4 is an exception due to the G double-sharp, a *second*-order chromatic note relative to F♯. However, relative to A♯ as tonic the pattern represents the minor heptad $\{\hat{1}, \flat\hat{2}, \hat{3}, \hat{4}, \hat{5}, \hat{6}, \sharp\hat{7}\}$ of depth 4 and saturation 2. Interestingly, by such an interpretation the pattern anticipates, enharmonically, the B♭-minor fugal reprise that follows.

Rimsky-Korsakov (1930, 6) was apparently the first to refer not only to the minor heptad $\{\hat{1}, \hat{2}, \hat{3}, \hat{4}, \hat{5}, \hat{6}, \sharp\hat{7}\}$ as "harmonic" but also to the major heptad

Fig. 14.2 Liszt, Piano Sonata in B minor, mm. 1–7, 453–459, and 750–760

major degrees: ♭$\hat{2}$, ♭$\hat{6}$, ♭$\hat{3}$, ♭$\hat{7}$, $\hat{4}$, $\hat{1}$, $\hat{5}$, $\hat{2}$, $\hat{6}$, $\hat{3}$, $\hat{7}$, ♯$\hat{4}$

$\updownarrow$ $\updownarrow$ $\updownarrow$ $\updownarrow$ $\updownarrow$ $\updownarrow$ $\updownarrow$ $\updownarrow$ $\updownarrow$ $\updownarrow$ $\updownarrow$

minor degrees: ♯$\hat{4}$, ♯$\hat{7}$, ♯$\hat{3}$, ♯$\hat{6}$, $\hat{2}$, $\hat{5}$, $\hat{1}$, $\hat{4}$, $\hat{7}$, $\hat{3}$, $\hat{6}$, ♭$\hat{2}$

Fig. 14.3 Aligned pairs of major/minor degrees are line-of-fifths inverses

$\{\hat{1}, \hat{2}, \hat{3}, \hat{4}, \hat{5}, ♭\hat{6}, \hat{7}\}$, thus expressing terminologically an interesting relationship that holds between the two.

*Proposition 14.16. Let $\{\pm H\}$ be the 16 major/minor heptads.

Then there exists a bijection R from $\{+H\}$ onto $\{-H\}$ such that there exists a bijection R′ from $+H$ onto R($+H$) satisfying the following condition A.

A. For every $IQ_{i^+} \in +H$, R′(IQ_{i^+}) = IQ_{i^-} implies that $i^+ + i^- = 1$.

In lieu of a proof, consider Fig. 14.3.

Two sets of diatonic and first-order chromatic degrees $IQ_{i^\pm}$, major and minor, are displayed such that the major set is a left-to-right segment of the line of fifths whereas the minor set directly below is a right-to-left segment (equivalently, a left-to-right segment of the line of fourths). As a result, if IQ_{i^+} and IQ_{i^-} are aligned vertically, then $i^+ + i^- = 1$. Reading a major heptad ^+H from the top row of the figure, a corresponding minor heptad ^-H may be read from the bottom row as the set of aligned elements (and vice versa). For example, the harmonic-minor heptad $\{\sharp\hat{7}, \hat{2}, \hat{5}, \hat{1}, \hat{4}, \hat{3}, \hat{6}\}$ is aligned with the harmonic-major heptad $\{\flat\hat{6}, \hat{4}, \hat{1}, \hat{5}, \hat{2}, \hat{3}, \hat{7}\}$. Such exchanges of a major (minor) heptad with a minor (major) heptad exist, because, as may be seen in the figure, the bijection R' from the major to the minor degrees preserves the diatonic $\hat{3}$, while exchanging $\hat{1}$ with $\hat{5}$ and vice versa, and similarly for the diatonic pairs $\{\hat{2}, \hat{4}\}$ and $\{\hat{6}, \hat{7}\}$, as well as the chromatic pair $\{\flat\hat{2}, \sharp\hat{4}\}$. Moreover, $\flat\hat{6}$ is exchanged with $\sharp\hat{7}$, whereas $\flat\hat{7}$ is exchanged with $\sharp\hat{6}$.

We shall refer to a major/minor pair of heptads $\{+H, -H\}$ as *Rimskyian* if $R(+H) = -H$. It is easily seen that the two members of a Rimskyian pair $\{+H, -H\}$ are of equal depth and saturation.

Example 14.17. Refer back to Fig. 11.5. Excluding a G♮ or F♭ in (b) the two scores, represented respectively as sets of degrees relative to B♭ and D♭, constitute a Rimskyian pair, namely harmonic minor/major. Note that since the keys B♭ minor and D♭ major are relative, we have

$$R'(\flat\hat{6}) = R'(^\circ B\flat\flat) = {}^\circ A = \sharp\hat{7},$$

where B♭♭ and A are enharmonic (cf. Proposition 11.9).

In Table 14.2 the 16 major heptads and 16 minor heptads are listed vertically by depth and saturation, similarly to Table 14.1. Also similarly to Table 14.1, dark borders indicate type equivalence. Type-equivalent heptads of depth 3, however, are indicated also by white vs. grey shading. Thus, unlike heptads of depth 0, 2, or 4, no major/minor type-equivalent heptads of depth 3 are Rimskyian pairs (aligned horizontally in the table).

Some triadic heptads are identified parenthetically by name. Though most names are more or less standard (for example, "acoustic major"), some are neologisms ("natural major," "pseudo-Phrygian," "acoustic minor"). Note that the pseudo-modal heptads *are chromatic*. For example, unlike the Phrygian *mode*, where $\hat{2} = (1, 1) = \hat{2}^-$ is diatonic (cf. Table 10.2), relative to pseudo-Phrygian $\flat\hat{2} = (1, 1)$ is chromatic.

14.2 Scales and Tonalities

Definition 14.18. Harmonic Degree
Let H be a major/minor heptad. Set $HD = \{(u_0, v_0), (u_1, v_1), (u_2, v_2)\}$, $HD \subset H$, such that $v_1 \equiv v_0 + 2$, $v_2 \equiv v_0 + 4 \pmod 7$.

We shall refer to HD as *a harmonic degree* (relative to H). We shall write $HD = I^H, II^H, \ldots, VII^H$ if $v_0 = 0, 1, \ldots, 6$, respectively. We shall refer to the harmonic degrees $I^H, II^H, \ldots, VII^H$ as *tonic, supertonic, mediant, subdominant, dominant, submediant,* and *subtonic*, respectively, all relative to H.

Table 14.2 The 32 major and minor heptads. Dark borders (and white/grey shading for depth-3 heptads) indicate type equivalence. Horizontally aligned heptads are Rimskyian pairs

depth	saturation	major heptads	minor heptads
0	0	$\{\hat{1},\hat{2},\hat{3},\hat{4},\hat{5},\hat{6},\hat{7}\}$ ("natural major")	$\{\hat{1},\hat{2},\hat{3},\hat{4},\hat{5},\hat{6},\hat{7}\}$ (natural minor)
0	1	$\{\hat{1},\hat{2},\hat{3},\sharp\hat{4},\hat{5},\hat{6},\hat{7}\}$ (pseudo-Lydian)	$\{\hat{1},\flat\hat{2},\hat{3},\hat{4},\hat{5},\hat{6},\hat{7}\}$ (pseudo-Phrygian)
0	1	$\{\hat{1},\hat{2},\hat{3},\hat{4},\hat{5},\hat{6},\flat\hat{7}\}$ (pseudo-Mixolydian)	$\{\hat{1},\hat{2},\hat{3},\hat{4},\hat{5},\sharp\hat{6},\hat{7}\}$ (pseudo-Dorian)
2	2	$\{\hat{1},\hat{2},\hat{3},\sharp\hat{4},\hat{5},\hat{6},\flat\hat{7}\}$ (acoustic major)	$\{\hat{1},\flat\hat{2},\hat{3},\hat{4},\hat{5},\sharp\hat{6},\hat{7}\}$ ("acoustic minor")
2	2	$\{\hat{1},\hat{2},\hat{3},\hat{4},\hat{5},\flat\hat{6},\flat\hat{7}\}$ (melodic major)	$\{\hat{1},\hat{2},\hat{3},\hat{4},\hat{5},\sharp\hat{6},\sharp\hat{7}\}$ (melodic minor)
3	1	$\{\hat{1},\hat{2},\hat{3},\hat{4},\hat{5},\flat\hat{6},\hat{7}\}$ (harmonic major)	$\{\hat{1},\hat{2},\hat{3},\hat{4},\hat{5},\hat{6},\sharp\hat{7}\}$ (harmonic minor)
3	2	$\{\hat{1},\flat\hat{2},\hat{3},\hat{4},\hat{5},\hat{6},\flat\hat{7}\}$	$\{\hat{1},\hat{2},\hat{3},\sharp\hat{4},\hat{5},\sharp\hat{6},\hat{7}\}$
3	3	$\{\hat{1},\flat\hat{2},\hat{3},\hat{4},\hat{5},\flat\hat{6},\flat\hat{7}\}$ (Ahava Raba)	$\{\hat{1},\hat{2},\hat{3},\sharp\hat{4},\hat{5},\sharp\hat{6},\sharp\hat{7}\}$
4	1	$\{\hat{1},\flat\hat{2},\hat{3},\hat{4},\hat{5},\hat{6},\hat{7}\}$	$\{\hat{1},\hat{2},\hat{3},\sharp\hat{4},\hat{5},\hat{6},\hat{7}\}$
4	2	$\{\hat{1},\hat{2},\hat{3},\sharp\hat{4},\hat{5},\flat\hat{6},\hat{7}\}$	$\{\hat{1},\flat\hat{2},\hat{3},\hat{4},\hat{5},\hat{6},\sharp\hat{7}\}$
4	2	$\{\hat{1},\flat\hat{2},\hat{3},\hat{4},\hat{5},\flat\hat{6},\hat{7}\}$	$\{\hat{1},\hat{2},\hat{3},\sharp\hat{4},\hat{5},\hat{6},\sharp\hat{7}\}$
4	3	$\{\hat{1},\hat{2},\hat{3},\sharp\hat{4},\hat{5},\flat\hat{6},\flat\hat{7}\}$	$\{\hat{1},\flat\hat{2},\hat{3},\hat{4},\hat{5},\sharp\hat{6},\sharp\hat{7}\}$
5	2	$\{\hat{1},\flat\hat{2},\hat{3},\sharp\hat{4},\hat{5},\hat{6},\hat{7}\}$	$\{\hat{1},\flat\hat{2},\hat{3},\sharp\hat{4},\hat{5},\hat{6},\hat{7}\}$
5	3	$\{\hat{1},\flat\hat{2},\hat{3},\sharp\hat{4},\hat{5},\flat\hat{6},\hat{7}\}$	$\{\hat{1},\flat\hat{2},\hat{3},\sharp\hat{4},\hat{5},\hat{6},\sharp\hat{7}\}$
5	3	$\{\hat{1},\flat\hat{2},\hat{3},\sharp\hat{4},\hat{5},\hat{6},\flat\hat{7}\}$	$\{\hat{1},\flat\hat{2},\hat{3},\sharp\hat{4},\hat{5},\sharp\hat{6},\hat{7}\}$
5	4	$\{\hat{1},\flat\hat{2},\hat{3},\sharp\hat{4},\hat{5},\flat\hat{6},\flat\hat{7}\}$	$\{\hat{1},\flat\hat{2},\hat{3},\sharp\hat{4},\hat{5},\sharp\hat{6},\sharp\hat{7}\}$

Example 14.19. Let H be the major heptad $\{\hat{1},\flat\hat{2},\hat{3},\hat{4},\hat{5},\hat{6},\hat{7}\}$ of depth 4 and saturation 1.

Then, respectively, $I^H, II^H, \ldots, VII^H =$

$$\{\hat{1},\hat{3},\hat{5}\}, \{\flat\hat{2},\hat{4},\hat{6}\}, \{\hat{3},\hat{5},\hat{7}\}, \{\hat{4},\hat{6},\hat{1}\}, \{\hat{5},\hat{7},\flat\hat{2}\}, \{\hat{6},\hat{1},\hat{3}\}, \{\hat{7},\flat\hat{2},\hat{4}\}.$$

Let H be the harmonic minor heptad $\{\hat{1},\hat{2},\hat{3},\hat{4},\hat{5},\hat{6},\sharp\hat{7}\}$.

Then, respectively, $I^H, II^H, \ldots, VII^H =$

$$\{\hat{1}, \hat{3}, \hat{5}\}, \{\hat{2}, \hat{4}, \hat{6}\}, \{\hat{3}, \hat{5}, \sharp\hat{7}\}, \{\hat{4}, \hat{6}, \hat{1}\}, \{\hat{5}, \sharp\hat{7}, \hat{2}\}, \{\hat{6}, \hat{1}, \hat{3}\}, \{\sharp\hat{7}, \hat{2}, \hat{4}\}.$$

Note that the "quality" of a harmonic degree (see Definition 14.20 ahead) is inherited from the given heptad. Indeed, the quality of a harmonic degree is not restricted to, say, "major," "minor," "augmented," and "diminished." For example, if $H = \{\hat{1}, \flat\hat{2}, \hat{3}, \hat{4}, \hat{5}, \hat{6}, \hat{7}\}$ (major) we have $V^H = \{\hat{5}, \hat{7}, \flat\hat{2}\}$, $VII^H = \{\hat{7}, \flat\hat{2}, \hat{4}\}$, as in the example above.

It should be useful to have a formal definition for the quality of a harmonic degree.

Definition 14.20. Quality of a Harmonic Degree; Standard Quality; Major/Minor Quality

Let $HD = \{(u_0, v_0), (u_1, v_1), (u_2, v_2)\}$ be a harmonic degree, $v_1 \equiv v_0 + 2$, $v_2 \equiv v_0 + 4$ (mod 7). Set $u_1 \equiv u_0 + q_1$, $u_2 \equiv u_0 + q_2$ (mod 12), $0 \leq q_1, q_2 \leq 11$.

A. We shall refer to the set $\{q_1, q_2\}$ as *the quality of HD*.
B. If $q_2 = 7$ such that $q_1 = 3, 4$ we shall say that the quality of *HD is standard*.
C. If the quality of *HD* is standard such that $q_1 = 4$ ($q_1 = 3$) we shall say that the quality of *HD is major (minor)*.

Note that for every heptad H the quality of the *tonic* harmonic degree relative to H is standard, and specifically, is major if H is major and minor if H is minor.

Definition 14.21. Tendency Degree (Melodic)

Let H be a major/minor heptad. Set $(\underline{u}, \underline{v}) \in \{(0, 0), (7, 4)\} = \{\hat{1}, \hat{5}\}$.

A. We shall refer to $(u, v) \in H$ as *a (melodic) tendency degree* if $(u, v) \equiv (\underline{u}, \underline{v}) \oplus \pm(1, 1)$.
B. We shall refer to a tendency degree $(u, v) \equiv (\underline{u}, \underline{v}) \oplus \pm(1, 1)$ as *primary (secondary)* if $(\underline{u}, \underline{v}) = \hat{1}$ $((\underline{u}, \underline{v}) = \hat{5})$.

By Definition 14.21 the primary melodic tendency degrees are $\hat{7}$ (diatonic, major), $\sharp\hat{7}$ (chromatic, minor), and $\flat\hat{2}$ (chromatic, major and minor). The secondary tendency degrees are $\flat\hat{6}$ (chromatic, major), $\hat{6}$ (diatonic, minor), and $\sharp\hat{4}$ (chromatic, major and minor).

We are now ready for the following definition. Review Definitions 14.4, 14.9, and 14.13.

Definition 14.22. Tonal Heptads

Let $T = \{+H, -H\}$ be a pair of heptads, one major and the other minor, with saturation σ^+ and σ^-, respectively. Assume that the quality of the dominant harmonic degree of both heptads is standard (that is, either major or minor).

We shall refer to T and its members as *tonal* if the following three conditions, A, B, and C, are satisfied.

A. $+H$ and $-H$ are not type equivalent.

B. The sum $\sigma^+ + \sigma^-$ is minimal.

C. The dominant harmonic degree contains a primary melodic tendency degree.

A study of Table 14.2 will confirm the following proposition.

*Proposition 14.23. Let $\{+H,-H\}$ be a pair of heptads, one major and the other minor.

Then $\pm H$ is tonal if, and only if, $+H = \{\hat{1}, \hat{2}, \hat{3}, \hat{4}, \hat{5}, \hat{6}, \hat{7}\}$ ("natural major") and $-H = \{\hat{1}, \hat{2}, \hat{3}, \hat{4}, \hat{5}, \hat{6}, \sharp\hat{7}\}$ (harmonic minor). The quality of the dominant harmonic degree, in either case, is major.

By Proposition 14.23 a tonal heptad is natural major if major, and harmonic minor if minor. Why, however, should we be interested in tonal heptads? What, in other words, is the significance of Definition 14.22?

Our interest in pairs of heptads, one major and the other minor, reflects the duality by which triadic keys are either Ionian and major or Aeolian and minor (Theorem 10.11). Our interest in *the dominant* harmonic degree (rather than, say, the subdominant), and similarly, in primary melodic tendency degrees, reflects the finding that following $\hat{1}$ the most privileged degree is $\hat{5}$ (not, say, $\hat{4}$). Moreover, we are interested in a dominant the quality of which is standard, because a representation of such a dominant as a set (or sequence) of notes shares with the tonic harmonic degree the property of consonance (the dominant harmonic degree is a "co-nucleus," so to speak).

We shall now show that Conditions A and B of Definition 14.22, by which the heptads of a tonal pair are not type equivalent and the sum of their saturations is minimal, respectively express the Communication and Economical Principles. First, however, we must establish a connection between heptads *and keys*.

In the following definition we write $^\circ SCORE$ for the representation of the score of a major/minor key as a set of degrees. Recall from Sect. 11.3 that we write $+K_{\alpha^+}$ for a major key $3M_\alpha^1$ and $-K_{\alpha^-}$ for a minor key $3M_\beta^4$, $\alpha^+ = \alpha$, $\alpha^- = \beta$. The combined notation $\pm(K_\alpha)$ stands for *either* $+K_{\alpha^+}$ *or* $-K_{\alpha^-}$.

Definition 14.24. Major/Minor Scale; Complete Scale; Major/Minor Tonality

Let $\pm(K_\alpha)$ be a major/minor key with score $SCORE^\pm$, respectively, and let $\pm H$ be a major/minor heptad.

A. We shall refer to $\pm(K_\alpha)$ as *a major/minor scale* (relative to $\pm H$) if $^\circ SCORE^\pm \subset \pm H$, respectively.

B. We shall refer to a scale $\pm(K_\alpha)$ as *complete* if $^\circ SCORE^\pm = \pm H$.

C. We shall refer to a scale $\pm(K_\alpha)$ relative to a major/minor tonal heptad as *a major/minor tonality*.

In other words, we refer to a major (minor) key as a major (minor) *scale* if there exists a major (minor) heptad such that every score element, represented as a degree, is a member of the heptad. If *every* degree of the heptad is represented in the score at least once, the scale is complete; finally, if the heptad is *tonal* the scale is a *tonality*.[2] Note that unless a scale is complete, its score need not represent every degree of the related heptad.

Example 14.25. Refer back to the six "descending-octave patterns" of Liszt's B-minor Sonata (Fig. 14.2). With the exception of Pattern 4 every pattern is (the score of) a complete scale the tonic of which is represented by the framing octave. Pattern 4 may be seen as a complete minor scale with tonic A♯, thus anticipating the B♭-minor fugue that follows. None of the scales is a tonality.

We may now make sense of our assumption that tonal heptads are not type equivalent (Cond. 14.22A); review Definitions 10.14 and 10.41.

Proposition 14.26. Fix a pair $\{+H, -H\}$ of heptads, one major and the other minor, and let (K, K', NRS_φ) be a modal communication system, *not context dependent*, such that K is a complete scale relative to H and K' is a complete scale relative to H', $H, H' \in \{+H, -H\}$.

If $+H$ and $-H$ are not type equivalent then K' is congruent to K.

Proof. Since K and K' are complete H and H' are type equivalent. Therefore, since $+H$ and $-H$ are not type equivalent, $H' = H = \pm H$, implying that K' is congruent to K. Q.E.D.

Note that the result K' is congruent to K is achieved *without* making use of so-called "final-image centricity" (see the discussion following Proposition 10.16), the problematic assumption that the image of the transmitted final is privileged also for the receiver. In other words, if receiver and transmitter alike *fix a pair* $\{+H, -H\}$ of non-type-equivalent heptads, one major and the other minor, modal communication is "context free" in the sense that final-image centricity is a superfluous assumption. Moreover, since K and K' are congruent the major/minor tribal-class is preserved; equivalently, the diatonic/chromatic partitioning of the message is preserved.

We have just seen that Condition 14.22A, $+H$ and $-H$ are not type equivalent, expresses the Communication Principle. It is not difficult to see that Condition 14.22B, the sum $\sigma^+ + \sigma^-$ of saturations is minimal, expresses the Economical Principle. For the larger the saturation of $+H$ or $-H$ the more difficult it is for the receiver to reference these heptads to the *natural* major or minor heptads, respectively. Consider, for example, the mental effort involved in referencing a major heptad such as $\hat{1}, \flat\hat{2}, \hat{3}, \sharp\hat{4}, \hat{5}, \flat\hat{6}, \flat\hat{7}$, to $\hat{1}, \hat{2}, \hat{3}, \hat{4}, \hat{5}, \hat{6}, \hat{7}$.

Finally, we have the following definition. Review Definitions 10.14 and 14.24.

---

[2] We distinguish *tonality* (a scale relative to a tonal heptad) from *Tonality* ("tonal language," in the broad sense, cf. *Tonalität*). We do not, however, consistently use capitalization to distinguish the latter sense of the word from the former.

Definition 14.27. Tonal Communication System

We shall refer to the non-context-dependent modal communication system (K, K', NRS_φ), where K and K' are two tonalities, possibly incomplete, as *a tonal communication system*.

Note that we do not assume that the two tonalities K and K' are necessarily relative to the same tonal heptad. In other words, although the receiver expects a tonal message, whether the message is major ("natural major") or minor (harmonic minor), is not known in advance.

What happens if the receiver's expectation that the message be "tonal," in the sense of Definition 14.27, is not sustainable? This is the topic of the next and final chapter.

References

Jairazbhoy, N. (1971). *The Rāgs of north Indian music: Their structure and evolution.* Middletown: Wesleyan University Press.

Hook, J. (2011). Spelled heptachords. In C. Agon et al. (Eds.), *Mathematics and computation in music: Third international conference, MCM 2011* (pp. 84–97). Berlin: Springer.

Rimsky-Korsakov, N. (1930). *Practical manual of harmony* (J. Achron, Trans.). New York: Carl Fischer.

Chapter 15
The Tonal Game

Abstract The Tonal Game (Sect. 15.1) is a fallback strategy by which a transmitted score is processed as a major or minor key. The strategy consists of three main defaults, the order of which is motivated by the Economical Principle: a *tonality* (first major, then minor)—the only context-free default; a *robust* key; and finally, a *key*. Chopin's Mazurka, Op. 24/2, offers highly instructive examples of the Tonal Game at work, including a contextually motivated overruling of the very first default, a major tonality. Finally, Sect. 15.2 studies a possible connection between the extraordinary tonal richness of Chopin's Mazurka and the emergence early in the nineteenth century of "Tonality" as a notion of both synchronic and diachronic content, most notably in the work of François-Joseph Fétis.

15.1 The Tonal Game

The Tonal Game is a strategy by which receivers process a transmitted score as a major or minor key. The Tonal Game is a fallback strategy. In other words, the signal (a sequence of categorically equal-tempered pitches) is processed in terms of a series of progressively weaker assumptions, such that, if the strongest assumption fails, the next in line takes its place, and so forth, until the strongest assumption compatible with the signal is reached. The set of nested circles of Fig. 15.1 depicts the series of assumptions—or *defaults*—that constitute the Tonal Game. By the first default (the innermost circle) the signal is processed as a tonality, and specifically, *a major* one. However, if this assumption proves unsustainable a minor tonality is assumed instead. If the signal may be processed as neither a major nor a minor tonality the receiver will consider in turn two additional possibilities, first a *robust* key and finally a key.

Consider in turn robust keys vs. keys, tonalities vs. robust keys, and major vs. minor tonalities.

In the first case, to process a signal in terms of some robust key is more economical since no contextual input is necessary to distinguish between

E. Agmon, *The Languages of Western Tonality*, Computational Music Science, 251
DOI 10.1007/978-3-642-39587-1_15, © Springer-Verlag Berlin Heidelberg 2013

Fig. 15.1 The three main
default levels of the
Tonal Game

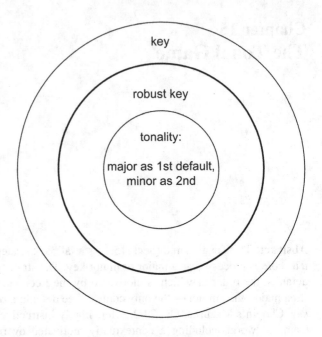

enharmonic pairs of chromatic degrees (for example, ♭$\hat{6}$/♯$\hat{5}$). Similarly in the second
case (tonalities vs. robust keys), to process a signal in terms of some tonality is more
economical since no contextual input is necessary to judge as privileged the image
of the transmitted tonic. Finally, in the third case (major vs. minor tonalities) to
process a signal in terms of some major tonality is more economical since major
tonalities are non-chromatic, and therefore, as pointed out in Sect. 14.2, are less
demanding in terms of cognitive resources. In other words, the Tonal Game is
motivated by the Economical Principle.

The Tonal Game compares interestingly with Weber's (1830–1832) "Principle
of Simplicity" (Saslaw's 1991 term). "How and by what means," writes Weber,
"and according to which laws is the ear moved to feel this or that harmony as tonic?
Or, in other words, how is it attuned to this or that key, or reattuned from one to
another?. . . The principles applying here are rather simple, in that they rest on the
assumption of the greatest possible simplicity, namely on the supreme principle:
The ear understands each combination of tones in the simplest, most natural, most
obvious manner possible" (Vol. 2, p. 109; trans. from Saslaw 1991, p. 122).[1]

---

[1] See Bent (1994), pp. 157–183, and Moreno (2004), pp. 128–159. In a similar vein, though not
specifically in connection with key-judgment, Riemann (1914/15) refers to a ". . . *Principle of the
Greatest Possible Economy for the Musical Imagination* [that] moves directly toward the rejection
of more complicated structures, where other possible meanings suggest themselves that weigh less
heavily on the powers of interpretation. . . ." (Wason and Marvin 1992, p. 88, original emphasis).
Weber's "Principle of Simplicity" and Riemann's "Principle of the Greatest Possible Economy for
the Musical Imagination" may both be seen as versions of the Economical Principle. Saslaw (1991,
footnote on p. 139) notes "a striking parallel" between Weber's principle and one of the principles
of gestalt theory.

Interestingly, a transmitted tonality need not be complete in order for the receiver to form, context free, an image congruent to it (cf. Proposition 14.26). Indeed, there exist "minimal cue-cells," defined next, that do not even contain $\hat{1}$ (Proposition 15.4, ahead). Review Definition 14.27, and recall that we write $°SCORE$ for the representation of a score as a set of degrees.

Definition 15.1. Cue-Cell; Minimal Cue-Cell

Let QC^+ (QC^-) be a non-empty subset of the natural-major (harmonic-minor) heptad, and let $(K,\ K',\ NRS_\varphi)$ be a tonal communication system, where K is a major/minor tonality with score $SCORE^\pm$ such that $QC^\pm = °SCORE^\pm$, respectively.

A. We shall refer to QC^+ (QC^-) as *a cue-cell for major (minor)* if, subject to the assumption that K' is not minor unless major is first ruled out, K' is congruent to K.

B. We shall refer to a cue-cell $QC^\pm$ as *minimal* if it contains a minimal number of elements.

Example 15.2. $\{\hat{2},\hat{4},\hat{7}\}$ is a cue-cell for major, and indeed, a minimal one.

Consider a tonal communication system $(K,\ K',\ NRS_\varphi)$ such that K is F major with score G, B♭, E Then, assuming by default that K' is major, K' is congruent to K. Indeed, if the receiver has absolute pitch and assumes that K' is standard (that is, its signature contains no more than five flats or six sharps), then $K' = K$.

$\{\hat{2},\hat{5},\hat{6},\sharp\hat{7}\}$ is a cue-cell for minor, and indeed, a minimal one.

Consider a tonal communication system $(K,\ K',\ NRS_\varphi)$ such that K is B♭ minor with score (C, F, G♭, A). The default assumption that K' is major is not sustainable in this case. Thus K' is minor and is congruent to K. Indeed, if the receiver has absolute pitch and assumes that K' is standard, then $K' = K$.

Counterexample 15.3. $\{\hat{4},\hat{7}\}$ is *not* a cue-cell for major.

Consider a tonal communication system $(K,\ K',\ NRS_\varphi)$ such that K is F major with score (B♭, E). Then, assuming by default that K' is major, K' is not necessarily congruent to K. For example, for a receiver with absolute pitch K' may be B major with score (A♯, E).

$\{\hat{1},\hat{3},\hat{5},\sharp\hat{7}\}$ is *not* a cue-cell for minor.

Consider a tonal communication system $(K,\ K',\ NRS_\varphi)$ such that K is B♭ minor with score (B♭, D♭, F, A). The default assumption that K' is major is not sustainable in this case. Thus K' is minor. However, K' is not necessarily congruent to K. For example, for a receiver with absolute pitch K' may be D minor with score (B♭, C♯, F, A).

*Proposition 15.4. Let $QC^\pm$ be a set of diatonic and first-order chromatic degrees.

Then $QC^\pm$ is a minimal cue-cell for major/minor if, and only if, one of the following two conditions, A or B, is satisfied.

A. $QC^+ = \{\hat{1}, \hat{4}, \hat{7}\}, \{\hat{2}, \hat{4}, \hat{7}\}, \{\hat{3}, \hat{4}, \hat{7}\}, \{\hat{4}, \hat{5}, \hat{7}\}, \{\hat{4}, \hat{6}, \hat{7}\}.$

B. $QC^- = \{\hat{1}, \hat{2}, \hat{3}, \sharp\hat{7}\}, \{\hat{1}, \hat{3}, \hat{4}, \sharp\hat{7}\}, \{\hat{1}, \hat{3}, \hat{6}, \sharp\hat{7}\}, \{\hat{1}, \hat{5}, \hat{6}, \sharp\hat{7}\}, \{\hat{2}, \hat{3}, \hat{5}, \sharp\hat{7}\}, \{\hat{2}, \hat{5}, \hat{6}, \sharp\hat{7}\},$
    $\{\hat{3}, \hat{4}, \hat{5}, \sharp\hat{7}\}, \{\hat{4}, \hat{5}, \hat{6}, \sharp\hat{7}\}.$

Note that the primary tendency degree $\hat{7}$ (major) or $\sharp\hat{7}$ (minor) is a member of every (minimal) cue-cell.

Proposition 15.4 captures an important aspect of what is sometimes referred to in the music-psychological literature as "tonality induction." "A few tones of a tune are usually enough for the average listener to establish a scale and determine whether succeeding tones belong to the scale," writes Vos (2000, p. 403). Brown and Butler (1981, p. 48), who coined the term "tonal cue-cell," note in particular that "...three-tone subsets [of every "diatonic" pitch-set] can be tonic-determinate if those subsets include the tones of the tritone, plus any other member of the set. Such subsets are univalent and should provide an unambiguous indication of tonal center..."[2] The idea is arguably implicit already in Fétis's (2008, pp. 38–39) statement concerning the so-called "dominant seventh." "When it is heard," writes Fétis, "there is no further doubt as to the key; the entire secret of tonality is revealed by the relationship of the fourth degree with the dominant, and by the attractive relationship of this fourth degree with the leading tone."[3] Gjerdingen's (1988) "$\hat{1} - \hat{7}\ldots\hat{4} - \hat{3}$ schema" and Kirkendale's (1979, p. 91) "pathotype" schema $\hat{5}-\hat{6}-\sharp\hat{7}-\hat{1}$ may also be regarded as cue-cells (the latter for minor). It should be stressed, however, that cue-cells are "tonic-inductive" only under the assumptions of the Tonal Game. That is to say, *tonalities* are assumed rather than merely (robust) keys; moreover, a minor tonality is not assumed unless a major tonality is first ruled out.[4]

The Tonal Game accounts for "... the inherent tendency of minor to move to III" (Aldwell and Schachter 2003, p. 229), a tendency that has no symmetrical counterpart in major (namely, to move to VI). In particular, the Tonal Game predicts that a minor tonality will give way to its relative major as soon as $\sharp\hat{7}$ (chromatic) gives way to $\hat{7}$ (diatonic). As Aldwell and Schachter note (2003, p. 228), "... the minor mode can tonicize III without any chromatic alteration." (Tonicizing VI in major, by comparison, requires a *second*-order chromatic degree, namely $\sharp\hat{5}$.) "Indeed" they note in a footnote on p. 229, "beginning students sometimes find it hard to prevent their exercises in minor from slipping into the relative major whether they want them to or not."

If a signal cannot be processed as the score of some tonality (for example, a signal consisting of the categorically equal-tempered pitches 0, 1, and 2) by the

---

[2] Brown and Butler's (1981) notion of a tonal cue-cell is indebted to Browne (1981).

[3] "Lorsque celui-ci se fait entendre, il n'y a plus de doute sur le ton; tout le secret de la tonalité est révélé par le rapport du quatrième degré avec la dominante, et par le rapport attractif de ce quatrième degré avec la note sensible." (Fétis 1853, p. 38)

[4] Note again that cue-cells are "context-free tonic-inducers." In particular, they do not engage the expectation that scores *contain* the tonic, let alone begin with it.

Fig. 15.2 Chopin, Mazurka, Op. 24/2, mm. 1–4

Tonal Game the receiver will assume a key instead (if possible, robust). In such a case the receiver must rely on contextual (for example, temporal) cues in order to judge the image of a transmitted tonic as privileged.[5]

Consider the opening four measures of Chopin's C-major Mazurka, Op. 24, No. 2 (Paris, ca. 1834–1835; Fig. 15.2). The signal associated with these measures does not *contradict* the receiver's default assumption of a major tonality; and yet, represented as a set of degrees the transmitted score is not a cue-cell for major, and therefore may be processed in terms of more than one standard major key, namely C or G (assuming a receiver with absolute pitch). Nonetheless, there seems to be a clear preference for C.

To be sure, the passage *begins* with a C-major triad, thus offering a strong temporal cue in favor of C major. And yet, the passage is otherwise rather neutral in terms of emphasizing either one of the two alternating chords, C and G. The "C-centric" quality of this passage seems rather to engage the notion implicit in "tonal heptad" (Definition 14.22), namely that I *and* V (not I and IV) are the two most privileged harmonic degrees.[6]

It should be useful to devote the remainder of this section to a detailed study of Chopin's Mazurka, for it offers highly instructive examples of the Tonal Game at work, including a contextually motivated overruling of the very first default, a major tonality. Figure 15.3 depicts the Mazurka's opening 90 measures (up to the reprise) from the point of view of a receiver with absolute pitch that applies the rules of the Tonal Game to the signal, usually eight measures at a time. Standard keys are assumed by default.[7]

---

[5] See also Brown (1988).

[6] See the discussion following Proposition 14.23. Although I-V in C is preferable to IV-I in G (as an interpreted signal), in the final analysis the Mazurka's introductory measures remain tonally ambiguous to some extent. Indeed, Chopin seems to address the introduction's latent ambiguity in the coda (mm. 105–120). Mm. 109–112, in particular, suggest both I-V in C (cf. mm. 1–4), and IV-I in G (cf. mm. 105–108).

[7] To save space, Chopin's varied repetitions of eight-measure units are replaced in Fig. 15.3 with exact repetitions, indicated by repeat signs (sections b and B1). Moreover, Chopin's *two*fold repetition of the four-measure group 73–76 (the second time with the left hand transposed an octave lower) is similarly abbreviated. In mm. 6 and 8 contextually implied tones are inserted parenthetically (cf. the parallel measures 10 and 12, respectively), applying the idea of "imaginary continuo" (see Sect. 7.1). Note that the four-measure coda of the A section (mm. 53–56) is placed next to the four-measure introduction, mm. 1–4, again to save space.

Fig. 15.3 Tonal analysis of Chopin, Mazurka Op. 24/2

The Tonal Game yields context-free the C-major and D♯-minor tonalities of the a2 and B2 sections, respectively. These tonalities respectively represent the Mazurka's home key and "point of furthest remove," to borrow Ratner's (1980, pp. 225–227) colorful term. By contrast, the D♭-major robust key of the B1 section is context dependent. D♭ seems a better choice than the A♭-major alternative (see mm. 62–64) since I-V is, again, a more natural "middleground" progression than IV-I (cf. the similar foreground dilemma posed by mm. 1–4).

Of particular interest is the b-section. Strong temporal cues support an F-major analysis, *despite the context-free C-major tonality dictated by the Tonal Game.* Note that Fig. 15.3 displays this section with a one-flat signature. The F major robust *key* is in fact a pseudo-Lydian scale.[8]

Probably in order to enhance the impact of the contrasting B-section Chopin deliberately avoids "black keys" in the A-section. As a result, the a1-section, taken literally, is (contextually) an A natural-minor scale. Nonetheless, it seems impossible *not* to posit an implied G♯ in m. 8 (and similarly in m. 12), where a seventh-chord most unusually lacks a qualifying third (see footnote 7). Since G♮s are similarly implied in mm. 6 and 10, it seems preferable to read this passage as an A-minor *robust key.*[9] C-major and A-minor *tonalities*, however, may be heard locally (mm. 5–6 and 7–8, respectively), assuming an implied G♯ in m. 8 (and ignoring the *melodic* Gs in m. 7).[10]

Chopin notates the B-section, which begins rather abruptly in D♭ major, with a five-flat signature throughout; in particular, the inverse signature change takes place only in m. 89, the A-minor reprise. In Fig. 15.3, by comparison, the empty signature returns already in m. 85, that is, four measures earlier than notated by Chopin. Moreover, a signature change to six *sharps* (for D♯ minor) takes place in m. 73.

Although E♭ minor may seem to make better sense than D♯ minor in view of the preceding excursion to D♭ major, D♯ minor makes better sense in view of the A-minor reprise that follows. In other words, the B2-section is in a sense in two congruent enharmonic keys at once. The notated *standard* key of D♯ minor thus represents in Fig. 15.3 the non-standard E♭ minor as well.

How can one account for the intuition that, even in retrospect, the B-section seems to begin *abruptly* in D♭ major, whereas the transition from the D♯-minor point-of-furthest-remove to the A-minor reprise seems smooth?

Schachter (1999, p. 137) believes that "the boundaries of keys are often indistinct." Nothing, indeed, seems to prevent one from hearing the beginning of the B-section, chromatically, still in C major: ♭VI[7]-♭II. By the Tonal Game, however, this is not quite the case. Since ♭$\hat{5}$ (G♭) is *second*-order chromatic, the "C major"

---

[8] Cf. Table 14.2. Chopin, who retains the empty signature throughout the A-section, nonetheless writes the B₂ of m. 27 with a *cautionary* natural (similarly in m. 35). Thus, the existence of B♭—"in the background" so to speak—is implied.

[9] The avoidance of G♮ in the a1-section, at least harmonically, is amply compensated for in the a2-section that immediately follows.

[10] Cf. the similarly local A♭ major tonality, mm. 62–64.

relative to which the chromatic progression is hypothetically heard is necessarily a key, not a robust key, let alone a tonality. By comparison, to hear the B1-section in D♭ major is to hear a robust key, and with mm. 63–64 excluded, a tonality. A robust key, let alone a tonality, supersedes a key (Fig. 15.1).[11]

The situation in B2 is very different. A D♯-minor *tonality* is established in m. 73, and is maintained through m. 87 (the D♯ minor of m. 88 is at best a robust key). Thus, unlike the C-major key, which is no match for a D♭-major tonality or robust key in B1, *as a tonality* the D♯ minor of the B2-section prevails even as A minor begins to emerge as a tonal center in m. 85.[12] Note that even though D♯ and A minor overlap for three full measures, the boundaries of each, as tonality and robust key, respectively, are distinct.

15.2   Chopin's Mazurka, Op. 24, No. 2, and Fétis's "Tonal Perfection"

The analysis of the A and B sections of Chopin's Mazurka, Op. 24/2, presented in Fig. 15.3, is in fact a composite of eight or nine separate analyses, each representing a segment of the piece, usually eight measures long.[13] Is it possible to form a more unified view of the piece based on these analyses?

Figure 15.4 represents such an attempt. The tonics of the various keys posited in Fig. 15.3, all of which are related to C major, are plotted on the C-major Riepel Space (cf. Fig. 13.8). In particular, starting at the C-major center and ending with A minor, number-labeled arrows trace the Mazurka's "modulatory path" up to the reprise. For example, the Mazurka's first two modulatory moves, from C major to A minor and back, are represented by the double-headed arrow labeled "1–2." One notes immediately that in the A-section distances from the C-major center are no larger than 1. The B-section starts with a distance-2 "leap" from C to D♭ major, subsequently reaching the E♭/D♯ minor Point of Furthest Remove, the distance of which from the C-major center is indeed maximal, namely 3.

Parenthetical numbers in bold represent *relative* key-distances (again according to neo-Riepelian theory), that is, distances relative *to the origin of a given modulation*, rather than the home key, C major. Thus, moves 1–4, all in the A-section, are all of distance 1, while move 5 from the end of the A-section (C major) to the beginning of the B-section (D♭ major) is of distance 2. The D♭→e♭ move that follows

---

[11] M. 57 may be heard momentarily as a "German" augmented-sixth chord, in which case the C-major key is robust (♯$\hat{4}$, unlike ♭$\hat{5}$, is first-order chromatic). However, the resolution to D♭ in m. 58 rules out such a hearing in retrospect.

[12] In real time one is hardly aware that an A-minor arrival is imminent until m. 88. However, given the four-measure groups and the emphasis on the "half-diminished sonority," in retrospect one realizes that, if A minor is present in m. 88, it must have been present already in m. 85.

[13] Except for the "retransition" to the A-minor reprise the segments are all non-overlapping.

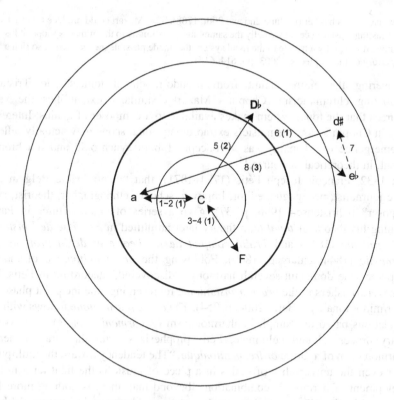

Fig. 15.4 The modulatory path in Chopin's Mazurka, Op. 24/2, plotted on the C-major Riepel Space. *Parenthetical numbers* in *bold* represent *relative* key distances, to the extent that they exist

(number 6) is again of distance 1 (relative to D♭ major). Only the final move 8, from the D♯-minor Point of Furthest Remove to the A-minor reprise, is of distance 3.

Note the "silent" move e♭→d♯ (number 7) represented by a dashed arrow. There is no (relative) distance attached to this move, since by neo-Riepelian theory none exists. To borrow Lewin's (1984, 347) language, e♭→d♯ represents a "flaw," a "splice," a "hidden seam," a "topographical... feature of the spaces in which the music moves." Although the set of all eight relative distances fails to comply with the axioms of a metric space (for example, the distance C→D♭ does not equal the distance D♭→C, not to mention that a distance e♭→d♯ simply does not exist), this is not the case with the first four distances, involving the closely-related keys C, a, and F, all in the diatonic A-section.

Edward Aldwell and Carl Schachter conclude their classic text *Harmony and Voice Leading* by comparing their very first example, Mozart's C-major Piano Sonata K. 545, with their very last, also by Mozart: the Piano Trio in E major, K. 542. "In their use of the tonal language" the authors write,

> ... the two excerpts could hardly be more divergent, with the simplest diatonic relationships on the one hand and the most daring chromaticism on the other. Yet, these passages are not only from works of the same composer, but from works completed within a

few days of each other (on June 2nd and 26th, 1788). That Mozart could produce two such contrasting masterpieces at virtually the same time is testimony to the immense scope of his genius. It is equally a tribute to the tonal system that made possible the creation of so rich a repertory of masterpieces. (2003, pp. 614–615)

Covering the entire gamut from pseudo-modal diatonicism to Tristan-anticipating chromaticism, Chopin's Mazurka similarly exemplifies the vast resources that the tonal system makes available to a composer of genius. Interestingly, in Chopin's case the music's extraordinary tonal scope may actually reflect the emergence of "Tonality" as a concept of both synchronic and diachronic content, in theoretical discourse.[14]

In 1832, François-Joseph Fétis (1784–1871), that "indefatigable Belgian ... music journalist, pedagogue, editor, librarian, scholar, ethnographer, theorist, and composer" (Christensen 1996, p. 37), gave a series of eight lectures in Paris outlining his theory of *tonalité*, a theory later amplified in *Esquisse de l'histoire de l'harmonie* (1840) and *Traité complet de la théorie et de la pratique de l'harmonie* (1844; enlarged, 1849). Following the *ordre unitonique* of modal polyphony, the dominant-seventh harmony ("discovered," according to Fétis, by Monteverdi) ushers in the *ordre transtonique*, representing "the incipient phase of major/minor tonality" (Berry 2004, p. 254). The *ordre pluritonique* follows with its modulations based on "simple" enharmonicism (*enharmonie simple*). The evolutionary process should culminate, Fétis prophesizes, with the "transcendent" enharmonicism of a future *ordre omnitonique*. "The tendency toward the multiplicity or even the universality of tonics in a piece of music is the final term in the development of harmony's combinations; beyond that, there is nothing more for these combinations."[15] Fétis's lectures, "... delivered between 23 May and 17 July 1832, at No. 13 Rue-des-Capucines" (Berry 2004, footnote on p. 256), were reported "on subsequent Saturdays in *Revue musicale*, VIe année..., nos. 17–25 (26 May–21 July 1832), with the exception of no. 19 (9 June 1832)."

As Fétis proudly recalls,

... in one of the meetings of the course on the philosophy of music that I gave in Paris in 1832, I spoke of the future of harmony and of tonality, whose final stage ought to be the establishment of relationships among all the keys, major and minor, and as a consequence, the establishment of harmonic progressions heretofore unheard of—an artistic phenomenon to which I have given the name *ordre omnitonique*. Liszt was present at this lecture; he was struck by the novelty of my idea and, later on, he accepted it as a kind of incontrovertible truth. He then determined he would try to apply the idea to piano music. (Bloom 2006, pp. 435–436)

---

[14] I am indebted to William Rothstein for suggesting a Chopin-Liszt-Fétis connection in this context.

[15] "La tendance vers la multiplicité, ou même l'universalité des tons dans une pièce de musique, est le terme final du développement des combinaisons de l'harmonie; au-delà, il n'y a plus rien pour ces combinaisons" (Fétis 1853, p. 195). Trans. from Berry (2004), p. 255.

Indeed, Liszt is known to have composed a *Prélude Omnitonique*, the manuscript of which "... was exhibited in London in 1904 but. ..has since disappeared" (Walker 1970, p. 362).[16]

It is not known whether Chopin, who arrived in Paris just eight months prior, was also present among Fétis's audience. However, he undoubtedly made contact with the ideas of the Belgian savant, if not by actually attending his lectures then second-hand through his close friend and colleague Liszt. Alternatively, he may have read the reports published in the *Revue musicale*. After all, it was the very same Fétis who published in the very same venue a review of Chopin's February 26 *Salle Pleyel* debut, prophesizing (March 3, 1832) that "if M. Chopin's later works fulfill his early promise he will undoubtedly make himself a brilliant and deserved reputation" (Eigeldinger 1986, p. 290). Even prior to this important event, in a letter to his Warsaw teacher Joseph Elsner dated 14 December, 1831, Chopin refers rather respectfully to "... Fétis, whom I know and from whom one can actually learn a lot..." (Sydow 1962, p. 104).

"Tonal perfection," an idea articulated by Fétis in the final *Revue musicale* report of July 21st, may have made a particularly deep impression on the budding composer:

> One would be in error, however,... to believe that by the future necessity of frequently using the *ordre omnitonique*, one will make no more use of the other *ordres* of tonality. God forbid that it should be so! Each one of the *ordres* has its advantages, its qualities that we must necessarily be careful not to renounce, because that would be to impoverish the art on the one side while enriching it on the other. The mixture of the four *ordres*, each of them being employed appropriately, will be the final stage of tonal perfection; this perfection will be founded simultaneously on suitability and variety.[17]

Could it be that Op. 24/2 is Chopin's response to Fétis's challenge? We will probably never know for sure. Yet the musical evidence in support of such a conjecture is tantalizing.

Following the somewhat nebulous opening (mm. 1–4), the Mazurka's pseudo-modal sections a1 and b, which self-consciously avoid any explicit dominant seventh (see Fig. 15.3), are strikingly suggestive of Fétis's *ordre unitonique*.

Although Chopin strays into the *ordre transitonique* already in the A-section by ending the a2-section with a strong V^7-I cadence, only in the B-section does the V^7 chord truly come into its own. According to Fétis, what distinguishes Monteverdi

---

[16] For more on Liszt's (presumably) lost prelude, see Berry 2004, footnote on p. 257. See *ibid.*, p. 258, for additional evidence corroborating Liszt's presumed allegiance to Fétis's ideas.

[17] P. 198. "On serait cependant dans l'erreur, dit-il, si l'on croyait que par la nécessité future de l'emploi fréquent de l'ordre omnitonique, on ne fera plus usage des autres ordres de tonalités: à Dieu ne plaise qu'il en soit ainsi! Chacun de ces ordres a ses avantages, ses qualités auxquels il faut bien se garder de renoncer, car ce serait appauvrir l'art d'un côté pendent qu'on l'enrichirait de l'autre. Le mélange des quatre ordres, chacun d'eux étant employé à propos, sera le dernier terme de la perfection tonale; cette perfection sera fondée à la fois sur la convenance et la variété." Cited and translated in Berry 2004, pp. 256–257.

from his predecessors is the unprepared seventh of his dominants.[18] One can hardly envision a seventh more *un*prepared than the G♭ of m. 57, the beginning of the B-section; not only is this seventh approached by a dissonant leap of an augmented fourth in the upper voice, since black keys are altogether avoided in the A-section this G♭ is not even *obliquely* prepared. This is in marked contrast to the dominant seventh in the a2-section, whose seventh F is fully prepared as the third of the previous, D-minor chord. The dominant seventh and its close relative, the diminished seventh chord, become important agents of modulation in the B-section. Note the tonicization of A♭ major as the dominant of D♭ in mm. 63–64 and 71–72, and the repeated tonicizations of E♭ minor, starting in mm. 75–76.

Does Chopin follow Fétis beyond the first two "orders," the *unitonique* and the *transitonique*, into the realm of the *pluritonique* and *omnitonique* as well? I believe he does. The hallmark of the *ordre pluritonique* is modulation by enharmonic reinterpretation, involving in particular the enharmonically equivalent dominant seventh chord and the "German" augmented sixth, and the inversions of the diminished seventh chord. Consider again the dominant seventh on A♭ in m. 57. In the context of the previously established C-major key one tends to hear a German augmented sixth; only in retrospect does it become clear that the chord is in fact a dominant seventh.[19]

As Berry notes, Fétis described in his lectures

> ... three forms that the *omnitonique* might take. ... [T]he third category. ... was advanced enough in conception that Fétis had to fabricate his own examples, which demonstrated the resolution of the note D in sixteen different ways: beginning as the fifth of a dominant-seventh harmony in C, it then progressed to various keys through harmonic alterations and substitutions. (2004, p. 257)

Berry continues in a footnote:

> No notated examples accompany the published lecture report (nor any of the reports...); descriptions are verbal, though presumably examples were played and/or notated when Fétis gave the actual lectures. Nonetheless, examples of the third and most advanced mode of *omnitonique* must have been similar to those notated in the *Traité*, pp. 184–189.

Figure 15.5 gives one of these *Traité* examples (2008, p. 183). Following a triple downbeat delay a Tristan Chord in the second half of the first measure resolves in the second measure to a first-inversion A-minor tonic (the parallel fifths in the upper voices are probably an oversight). It is not inconceivable that this example influenced the remarkable retransition of Chopin's Mazurka (mm. 85–89), where a half-diminished II[7] in E♭ minor is interpreted as a Tristan chord in A minor.

---

[18] Fétis's theory of *tonalité* is indebted to Alexandre-Étienne Choron (1771–1834), who (apparently) coined the term *tonalité* in 1810. See Simms (1975).

[19] As Berry (2004, p. 256) notes, on May 12th 1832, just days before starting his lecture series, Fétis published a review of Gottfried Weber's *Versuch*. His *ordre pluritonique*, and particularly, the *omnitonique*, seem to resonate with Weber's *Mehrdeutigkeit* ("multiple meaning"). On Weber and multiple meaning, see Saslaw (1990–1991).

Fig. 15.5 A progression illustrating the *ordre omnitonique* from Fétis's *Traité*. Note the Tristan Chord in the first measure

Regardless, of whether or not Chopin consciously sought to fulfill Fétis's vision of "tonal perfection," in Op. 24/2 he certainly demonstrated not only the scope of his genius, but also the astonishing scope of the tonal system, which "... must rank among the great achievements of the human spirit" (Aldwell and Schachter 2003, p. 615). No musical system known to man seems to surpass the tonal system, not merely in terms of sheer complexity, but more significantly in terms of complexity *that is communicable*. It therefore seems safe to predict that the tonal system will never die away, at least so long as the communication-thirsty human spirit lives.

References

Aldwell, E., & Schachter, C. (2003). *Harmony and voice leading* (3rd ed.). Belmont: Wadsworth Group.

Bent, I. (Ed.). (1994). *Music analysis in the nineteenth century* (Vol. I). Cambridge: Cambridge University Press.

Berry, D. (2004). The meaning(s) of 'without': An exploration of Liszt's *Bagatelle ohne Tonart*. *19th-Century Music, 27*(3), 230–262.

Bloom, P. (2006). Fétis's review of the Transcendental Etudes. In H. Gibbs & D. Gooley (Eds.), *Franz Liszt and his world* (pp. 427–440). Princeton: Princeton University Press.

Brown, H. (1988). The interplay of set content and temporal context in a functional theory of tonality perception. *Music Perception, 5*(3), 219–250.

Brown, H., & Butler, D. (1981). Diatonic trichords as minimal tonal cue-cells. *In Theory Only, 5* (6–7), 39–55.

Browne, R. (1981). Tonal implications of the diatonic set. *In Theory Only, 5*(6–7), 3–21.

Christensen, T. (1996). Fétis and emerging tonal consciousness. In I. Bent (Ed.), *Music theory in the age of romanticism* (pp. 37–56). Cambridge: Cambridge University Press.

Eigeldinger, J.-J. (1986). *Chopin, pianist and teacher, as seen by his pupils* (N. Shohet, K. Osostowicz & R. Howat, Trans. & R. Howat, Ed.). Cambridge: Cambridge University Press.

Fétis, F.-J. (1853). *Traité complet de la théorie et de la pratique de l'harmonie* (5th ed.). Paris: Brandus. Electronic ed. in *Traités français sur la musique*, G. Di Bacco (Director). http://www.chmtl.indiana.edu/tfm. Accessed 10 Jan 2012.

Fétis, F.-J. (2008). *Complete treatise on the theory and practice of harmony* (P. Landey, Trans.). New York: Pendragon.

Gjerdingen, R. (1988). *A classic turn of phrase: Music and the psychology of convention*. Philadelphia: University of Pennsylvania Press.

Kirkendale, W. (1979). *Fugue and fugato in Rococo and Classical chamber music* (M. Bent, Trans. & Author). Durham: Duke University Press.

Lewin, D. (1984). Amfortas's prayer to Titurel and the role of D in *Parsifal*: The tonal spaces of the drama and the enharmonic C♭/B. *19th-Century Music, 7*(3), 336–349.

Moreno, J. (2004). *Musical representations, subjects, and objects*. Bloomington: Indiana University Press.

Ratner, L. (1980). *Classic music: Expression, form, style*. New York: Schirmer.

Riemann, H. (1914/15). Ideen zu einer 'Lehre von den Tonvorstellungen.' *Jahrbuch der Musikbibliothek Peters 21/22*, 1–26. Reprint 1965.

Saslaw, J. (1990–1991). Gottfried Weber and multiple meaning. *Theoria 5*, 74–103.

Saslaw, J. (1991). Gottfried Weber's cognitive theory of harmonic progression. *Studies in Music from the University of Western Ontario, 13*, 121–144.

Schachter, C. (1999). Analysis by key: Another look at modulation. In J. Straus (Ed.), *Unfoldings: Essays in Schenkerian theory and analysis* (pp. 134–160). New York: Oxford University Press. Reprinted from *Music Analysis 6*(3), 1987.

Simms, B. (1975). Choron, Fétis, and the theory of tonality. *Journal of Music Theory, 19*(1), 112–139.

Sydow, B. (Ed.). (1962). *Selected correspondence of Fryderyk Chopin* (A. Hedley, Trans.). London: Heinemann.

Vos, P. (2000). Tonality induction: Theoretical problems and dilemmas. *Music Perception, 17*(4), 403–416.

Walker, A. (1970). Liszt and the twentieth century. In A. Walker (Ed.), *Franz Liszt: The man and his music* (pp. 350–364). New York: Taplinger.

Wason, R., & Marvin, W. E. (1992). Riemann's *Ideen zu einer 'Lehre von den Tonvorstellungen'*: An annotated translation. *Journal of Music Theory, 36*(1), 69–117.

Weber, G. (1830–1832). *Versuch einer geordneten Theorie der Tonsetzkunst* (3rd Rev. ed.). Mainz: Schott.

Appendix A: Mathematical Preliminaries

Definition A1. Cartesian Product

Let X and Y be two non-empty sets.

The Cartesian product of X and Y, denoted $X \times Y$, is the set of all ordered pairs, a member of X followed by a member of Y. That is,

$$X \times Y = \{(x, y) \mid x \in X, \ y \in Y\}.$$

Example A2. Let $X = \{0, \ 1\}, Y = \{x, y, z\}$.

Then the Cartesian product $X \times Y$ of X and Y is

$$\{(0, x), \ (0, y), \ (0, z), \ (1, x), \ (1, y), \ (1, z)\}.$$

Definition A3. Relation

Let X and Y be two non-empty sets.

A subset of $X \times Y$ is *a relation from X to Y*; a subset of $X \times X$ is *a relation in X*.

Example A4. Let $X = \{0, \ 1\}, Y = \{x, y, z\}$.

Then

$$R = \{(0, x), \ (1, x), \ (1, y), \ (1, z)\},$$
$$R' = \varnothing,$$

are relations from X to Y. (R' is a relation because the empty set $\varnothing$ is a subset of every set.) Moreover,

$$R'' = \{(0, 0), \ (1, 0), \ (1, 1)\}$$

is a relation in X.

Definition A5. Function

Let X and Y be two non-empty sets.

E. Agmon, *The Languages of Western Tonality*, Computational Music Science, 265
DOI 10.1007/978-3-642-39587-1, © Springer-Verlag Berlin Heidelberg 2013

A *function* f *from X into Y* is a subset of $X \times Y$ (i.e., a relation from X to Y) with the following property. For *every* $x \in X$, there exists *exactly one* $y \in Y$, such that $(x, y) \in$ f.

The set X is called *the domain* of f. The set of all $y \in Y$ such that, for some $x \in X$, $(x, y) \in$ f, is called *the range of* f, and is denoted $\mathfrak{R}(f)$. For every $(x, y) \in$ f we call y *the value of* f *at x*, and write:

$$f(x) = y.$$

We sometimes write $f : X \to Y$ to denote the function f from X into Y. We also call $f : X \to Y$ *a mapping of X into Y*.

Example A6. Let $X = \{0, 1\}$, $Y = \{x, y, z\}$.
Then

$$f = \{(0, x), \ (1, x)\}$$

is a function from X into Y satisfying $f(0) = f(1) = x$, $\mathfrak{R}(f) = \{x\}$.

Example A7. Let $X = \{x, y, z\}$, $Y = \{0, 1\}$.
Then

$$g = \{(x, 0), \ (y, 0), \ (z, 1)\}$$

is a mapping of X into Y satisfying $g(x) = g(y) = 0$, $g(z) = 1$. Note that the range of g in this case, unlike the range of f in Example A6, is Y.

Definition A8. Surjection
Let $f : X \to Y$ be a function.
We shall refer to f as a function from X *onto* Y, or *a surjection*, if $\mathfrak{R}(f) = Y$.

Definition A9. Injection (One-to-One Function)
Let $f : X \to Y$ be a function.
We shall say that f *is a one-to-one function from X into Y*, or *an injection*, if $f(x) = f(x')$ implies that $x = x'$ for every x, $x' \in X$.

Example A10. Let $X = \{x, y, z\}$, $Y = \{0, 1, 2, 3\}$.
Then

$$h = \{(x, 2), \ (y, 3), \ (z, 1)\}$$

is a one-to-one mapping of X into Y, or an injection, since $h(x) \neq h(y) \neq h(z) \neq h(x)$.

Definition A11. Bijection
Let $f : X \to Y$ be a function.
If f is both a surjection and an injection we shall say that f *is a one-to-one function from X onto Y*, or *a bijection*.

Example A12. Let $X = \{x, y, z\}$, $Y = \{0, 1, 2\}$.
Then

$$i = \{(x, 2), \ (y, 0), \ (z, 1)\}$$

is a one-to-one function from X onto Y, or a bijection. We have both $i(x) \neq i(y) \neq i(z) \neq i(x)$ and $\mathfrak{R}(i) = \{i(x), i(y), i(z)\} = Y$.

Definition A13. Induced Function
Let X and Y be two non-empty sets, and let f be a function from X into Y. Let X' be a non-empty subset of X, and let f′ be a function from X' into Y.
We shall say that f′ *is induced by* f, if, for every $x' \in X'$, $f'(x') = f(x')$.
If f′ is induced by f, we shall refer to f′ as *the restriction of* f *to the set* X'.

Example A14. Let $h : X \to Y$ be as in Example A10, and let $X' = \{x, z\} \subset X = \{x, y, z\}$.
Then the function

$$h' = \{(x, 2), \ (z, 1)\}$$

is induced by h.

Definition A15. Semigroup
Let S be a non-empty set, and let $\oplus$ be an operation on S, that is, a mapping of $S \times S$ into S.
We shall refer to $S = \{S, \ \oplus\}$ as *a semigroup* if $\oplus$ is associative. That is, for every s, t, and u in S, $(s \oplus t) \oplus u = s \oplus (t \oplus u)$.

Definition A16. Group; Abelian Group
Let $S = \{S, \ \oplus\}$ be a semigroup.
We shall refer to S as *a group* if S has an identity element e, and every element s in S has an inverse $-s$. In other words, for every element s in S there exists:

A. An element e such that $s \oplus e = s = e \oplus s$.
B. An element $-s$ such that $s \oplus -s = e = -s \oplus s$.

If S is commutative, that is, $s \oplus t = t \oplus s$ for every s, t in S, we shall refer to S as "abelian."

Example A17. Let $\mathbb{R}$ be the set of real numbers and let $+$ be the usual operation of addition on the reals.
Then $\{\mathbb{R}, \ +\}$ is a group. The identity element of the group is 0, and the inverse of every element x in $\mathbb{R}$ is $-x$.
Let $\mathbb{R}^{\#} = \mathbb{R} \backslash \{0\}$ and let $\cdot$ be the usual operation of multiplication on the reals.
Then $\{\mathbb{R}^{\#}, \ \cdot\}$ is a group. The identity element of the group is 1, and the inverse of every element x in $\mathbb{R}^{\#}$ is $1/x$.

Definition A18. Homomorphism

Let $S = \{S, \oplus\}$ and $S' = \{S', \otimes\}$ be two semigroups, and let f be a mapping of S into S'.

We shall refer to f as a homomorphism of S into S' if

$$f(s \oplus t) = f(s) \otimes f(t)$$

for every s, $t \in S$.

Example A19. Let $S = \{\mathbb{R}, +\}$ be the group of all real numbers under addition, and let $S' = \{\mathbb{R}^+, \cdot\}$ be the group of all strictly positive real numbers under multiplication. Fix a strictly positive number B, and let $f(x) = B^x$ for every x in $\mathbb{R}$.

Then f is a homomorphism of S into S'. We have:

$$f(x + y) = B^{x+y} = B^x \cdot B^y = f(x) \cdot f(y)$$

for every x, $y \in \mathbb{R}$.

Appendix B: ℤ Modules and Their Homomorphisms

Definition B1. Ring

Let R be a non-empty set, and let $+$ and $\cdot$ be two operations on R.

We shall refer to $R = \{R, +, \cdot\}$ as *a ring* if $\{R, +\}$ is an abelian group, $\{R, \cdot\}$ is a semigroup, and the following two conditions, A and B, are satisfied for every α, β, and γ in R.

A. $\gamma \cdot (\alpha + \beta) = (\gamma \cdot \alpha) + (\gamma \cdot \beta)$.

B. $(\alpha + \beta) \cdot \gamma = (\alpha \cdot \gamma) + (\beta \cdot \gamma)$.

If the semigroup $\{R, \cdot\}$ has an identity element we shall refer to R as *a ring with identity*; if the operation $\cdot$ is commutative we shall refer to R as *a commutative ring*.

Example B2. Let $+$ and $\cdot$ be the usual operations of addition and multiplication on the reals.

Then $R = \{R, +, \cdot\}$ is a commutative ring with identity if

A. $R = \mathbb{Z}$ is the set of integers.
B. $R = \mathbb{Q}$ is the set of rational numbers.
C. $R = \mathbb{R}$ is the set of real numbers.

Definition B3. Module

Let $R = \{R, +, \cdot\}$ be a ring with identity 1, let $S = \{S, \oplus\}$ be an abelian group, and let $\bullet$ be a function from $R \times S$ into S. Write $\bullet(\alpha, s) = \alpha \bullet s$.

We shall refer to $S = \{R, S, \bullet\}$ as *a module over R* if $1 \bullet s = s$ for every $s \in S$, and the following three conditions, A, B, and C, are satisfied for every $\alpha, \beta \in R$, $s, t \in S$.

E. Agmon, *The Languages of Western Tonality*, Computational Music Science,
DOI 10.1007/978-3-642-39587-1, © Springer-Verlag Berlin Heidelberg 2013

A. $(\alpha + \beta) \bullet s = (\alpha \bullet s) \oplus (\beta \bullet s)$.

B. $\alpha \bullet (s \oplus t) = (\alpha \cdot s) \oplus (\alpha \bullet t)$.

C. $\alpha \bullet (\beta \bullet s) = (\alpha \cdot \beta) \bullet s$.

The following proposition, which may be checked easily against Definition B3, states that any abelian group may be viewed as a module over the *ring of integers* in a unique way.

Proposition B4. Let $\{R, +, \cdot\}$ be the ring of integers, let $\{S, \oplus\}$ be an abelian group with identity e, and let $\bullet$ be a function from $\mathbb{Z} \times S$ into S.

Then $S = \{R, S, \bullet\}$ is a module if, and only if, $0 \bullet s = e$, and the following two conditions, A and B, are satisfied for every natural n and every s in S.

$$\overset{n \quad times}{}$$

A. $n \bullet s = \overbrace{s \oplus \ \ldots \ \oplus s}^{n \ \ times}$.

B. $(-n) \bullet s = -(n \bullet s)$.

We shall refer henceforth to a module over the ring of integers as *a ℤ module.*

A homomorphism from group S into group S' is a mapping from S into S' that preserves the group "addition" (see Appendix A). If S and S' are two *modules* over the same ring R, a homomorphism from S into S' is a group homomorphism from S into S' that preserves the module "multiplication."

Definition B5. Module Homomorphism

Let $S = \{R, S, \bullet\}$ and $S' = \{R, S', *\}$ be a two modules, and let f be a mapping of S into S'.

We shall refer to f as *a module homomorphism of S into S'* if f is a group homomorphism of S into S' such that $f(\alpha \bullet s) = \alpha * f(s)$ for every $\alpha \in R, s \in S$.

If S and S' are two ℤ modules we have the following homomorphism theorem.

Theorem B6. Let $S = \{R, S, \bullet\}$ and $S' = \{R, S', *\}$ be two ℤ modules, let e be the identity element of the group $S = \{S, \oplus\}$, and let e' be the identity element of the group $S' = \{S', \otimes\}$. Let f be a group homomorphism of S into S'.

Then f is a module homomorphism of S into S'.

To prove the theorem we shall first state a lemma, the proof of which may be found in practically every basic text on abstract algebra.

Lemma B7. Let S and S' be two groups with identity elements e and e', respectively, and let f be a homomorphism of S into S'.

Then $f(e) = e'$.

Proof of the theorem. Easily from the group-homomorphism assumption, and since S and S' are both ℤ modules, for a natural n we have

$$\underbrace{}_{n \;\; times}$$

$$f(n \bullet s) = \overbrace{f(s \oplus \ldots \oplus s)}^{n \;\; times} = \overbrace{f(s) \otimes \ldots \otimes f(s)}^{n \;\; times} = n*f(s).$$

Using Lemma B7 we have

$$f(s \oplus -s) = f(e) = f(s) \otimes f(-s) = e',$$

and therefore $f(-s) = -f(s)$. Q.E.D.

Index

Page number **in bold** indicates a formal definition; page number *in italics* indicates a footnote location.

Printed in the United States
By Bookmasters